India Studies in Business and Economics

The Indian economy is considered to be one of the fastest growing economies of the world with India amongst the most important G-20 economies. Ever since the Indian economy made its presence felt on the global platform, the research community is now even more interested in studying and analyzing what India has to offer. This series aims to bring forth the latest studies and research about India from the areas of economics, business, and management science. The titles featured in this series will present rigorous empirical research, often accompanied by policy recommendations, evoke and evaluate various aspects of the economy and the business and management landscape in India, with a special focus on India's relationship with the world in terms of business and trade.

More information about this series at http://www.springer.com/series/11234

Neelam Rani · Surendra Singh Yadav
Pramod Kumar Jain

Mergers and Acquisitions

A Study of Financial Performance, Motives and Corporate Governance

Springer

Neelam Rani
Indian Institute of Management Shillong
Shillong, Megalaya
India

Pramod Kumar Jain
Department of Management Studies
Indian Institute of Technology Delhi
New Delhi
India

Surendra Singh Yadav
Department of Management Studies
Indian Institute of Technology Delhi
New Delhi
India

ISSN 2198-0012 ISSN 2198-0020 (electronic)
India Studies in Business and Economics
ISBN 978-981-10-2202-9 ISBN 978-981-10-2203-6 (eBook)
DOI 10.1007/978-981-10-2203-6

Library of Congress Control Number: 2016947377

Printed on acid-free paper

This Springer imprint is published by Springer Nature
The registered company is Springer Science+Business Media Singapore Pte Ltd.

Foreword

Mergers and Acquisitions (M&A), as mentioned by Rani, Yadav and Jain, are ways 'to gain access to new resources and new markets'. In a merger, two companies are combined and in an acquisition a company takes over another company. Both the processes assume that 'two separate companies together create more value compared to being on an individual stand'. In India, in post liberalization era, many companies have adopted M&A as a strategy to grow with the expectation of improving their competitiveness in the global market. In their current volume on Mergers and Acquisitions, Rani, Yadav and Jain, through rigorous research methodology, examine the experiences that the Indian companies have gone through in adopting M&A as a strategy for expansion and improving competitiveness. In particular, the study examines:

- Abnormal returns to the shareholders of acquiring firms, if any, on the announcement of M&A decisions of firms;
- Long-term financial performances of the firms adopting M&A strategy;
- Management views why Indian firms adopt M&A as a part of their corporate strategy; and
- Corporate Governance of firms and its short term and long term impacts on firms adopting M&A strategy.

The authors of the volume consider M&A to be very significant in corporate finance. In responding to the usual question whether or not M&A result in positive returns, the study shows evidence that the share holders get positive abnormal returns on the day the firms announce their M&A decisions. The share holders also get abnormally high returns over multiday period. The study suggests that M&A create wealth for the shareholders.

The empirical evidences show that the profitability of Indian firms in the post M&A period has been higher than that over the pre M&A period. The authors suggest that it has been the impact of M&A. Thus M&A is an appropriate way for expansions of firms in India. The authors could have examined the behavior of value addition per employee to assess to what extent firms' competitiveness has improved after M&A.

In assessing the management views on why Indian firms adopt M&A as a strategic tool for firms, the authors did a survey among the Finance Directors of firms which have gone for M&A. To achieve synergy is why primarily firms go for M&A. The next two reasons are to consolidate and to adopt a strategy for inorganic growth.

Corporate governance is a key to building trust of investors in the economy. The authors' view that corporate governance has an impact on M&A in firms. To assess corporate governance in a firm, they propose a corporate governance index. They have shown how this index would be used in assessing the impact of the corporate governance in firms on performance of M&A. The computation of corporate governance as suggested by the authors involves certain scoring methods. It is not clear how the picture would get affected if the scoring mechanism is changed.

An empirical study on measuring impact of mergers and acquisitions on financial performance, motives and impact of corporate governance on performance of acquiring firms is really desirable academic exercise. The authors have done a comprehensive study, probably a pioneering study, on the experience of firms who have gone for M&A as a strategic tool for growth and expansion. The authors have adopted a very rigorous approach for the study. The conclusions are based on precise statistical tools. The insights the authors bring out from the study are significant and would be of immense use to the policy makers and to the firms who would consider mergers and acquisitions as strategic tools. I am sure the study would inspire more research on M&A experience in India and bring more insight so that M&A becomes an effective strategic tool for Indian firms.

Dr. Neelam Rani, Prof. Surendra Singh Yadav and Prof. Pramod Kumar Jain deserve complements of all the researchers in corporate finance for leading this research effort. All those associated with the publication of this book also deserve appreciation.

Prof. Jahar Saha
Former Director
Indian Institute of Management Ahmedabad
India

Preface

Globalization and liberalization have led firms from emerging markets like India to gain access to new resources and new markets. Two of the strategies of this access are mergers and acquisitions as they increase revenues, reduce costs and make the firms globally competitive. Of late, mergers and acquisitions (M&A) have grown at a rapid pace, which calls for an in-depth research as to what drives firms towards these phenomena and how it affects them financially.

The present monograph presents a research work relating to the impact of mergers and acquisitions on the returns in short and long terms. For the purpose, well-established research techniques, namely, event study methodology and two experimental designs, viz., 'before-and-after design' and 'after-only design' have been used. Besides these techniques, two surveys have also been conducted for top-level Indian corporate managers of the organizations that adopted the strategy of M&A. The surveys aim to gauge the managerial views about the corporate governance practices and the motives of mergers and acquisitions respectively. The findings of the survey are corroborated with the secondary data analysis.

The notable finding of the research is that market starts reacting prior to the announcement. The moment the information is made public; investors start reacting and the stock price jumps high, providing positive abnormal returns to the investors. Cross-border as well as domestic acquisitions have created value for shareholders of the acquirer company on the announcement. The results indicate that value creation is higher for cross-border acquisitions vis-a-vis domestic acquisitions. The acquisitions financed with cash experience higher returns than the acquisitions financed with stock. The acquirers of unlisted target firms experience higher returns than the acquirers of listed target firms. The acquirers earn when target remains as a wholly owned subsidiary. In contrast, the shareholders of acquirer lose when the target firm is absorbed with the operations of the acquiring firm. The acquisitions of targets from non-US developed market outperform the return from the acquisition of US targets.

Survey findings reveal that the primary motive of mergers in India during 2003–2015 has been to take advantage of synergies. Operating economies, increased market share and financial economies (lower risk leading to lower cost of capital) have been indicated in order of importance as the desired synergies to be gained through corporate mergers and acquisitions in India.

M&As appear to have been financially beneficial for the acquiring companies. Practice of corporate governance has progressed in a big way in Indian companies as revealed by their mean score; mean corporate governance score has also improved over time. There are several companies which proactively took initiatives and introduced good governance norms and standards even before these became mandatory. Companies in service sector have better corporate governance score than others. There is a positive association between corporate governance score and shareholders' wealth due to announcements of mergers and acquisitions. Companies with better corporate governance create higher shareholders wealth in short term. Companies having higher corporate governance score show better financial performance on the basis of all measures of rate of return. Companies with higher corporate governance score show better valuations.

Based on the findings of the research study, the following recommendations have been made for the investors: (i) *Earlier he sells, more he gains in case he wants to earn abnormal short-term returns.* (ii) An investor can also earn substantial returns if the shares of the acquiring company are purchased two days prior to the announcement day and sold two days after the announcement day. (iii) The announcement of cross-border acquisitions provides much higher returns than that for domestic acquisitions. In addition, the cumulative abnormal returns in the case of cross-border acquisitions are relatively more lasting while they are temporary in the case of domestic acquisitions. (iv) The announcement of complete acquisitions of target firm as a wholly owned subsidiary provides much higher returns than that for partial/ majority control acquisitions. Besides, the cumulative abnormal returns in the case of complete acquisitions are relatively more lasting while they are temporary in the case of partial/majority control acquisitions. (v) The announcement of acquisitions financed with cash payment provides substantial returns. (vi) As far as agency costs are concerned, investments in companies with better corporate governance score are more profitable.

Based on the findings of the research study, the following recommendations have been made for the corporate managers and policy makers: (i) The study suggests that the Indian managers adopt mergers and acquisitions as effective strategy for corporate growth. It brings attention of the managers to consider cross-border as well as domestic acquisitions as an option to strengthen their competitiveness as the effects of these announcements appear to be a good indicator of longer term success. (ii) Managers should think of cash as a mode of payment to finance mergers. (iii) The management may acquire the target firm as a subsidiary and may absorb it with its own operations later on. (iv) The management should be aware of the need for efficient corporate governance structure and mechanism to control information asymmetry. (v) The findings that firm performance is significantly influenced by effective corporate governance could serve to justify regulatory measures towards enforcing healthy corporate governance regime and initiatives to encourage companies to adopt and adhere to these measures.

Shillong, India Neelam Rani
New Delhi, India Surendra Singh Yadav
New Delhi, India Pramod Kumar Jain

Acknowledgements

At the outset, we would like to thank the Almighty for His blessings to inspire us to undertake this academic endeavor. The work has been possible with the cooperation, help, encouragement, guidance and wishes of many people and we express our sincere thanks to all of them.

We are grateful to Prof. R.K. Shevgaonkar, Ex-Director, Indian Institute of Technology (IIT) Delhi, Prof. V. Ramgopal Rao, Director, IIT Delhi and Prof. Amitabha De, Director, Indian Institute of Management (IIM) Shillong for their kind support and cooperation. We express our sincere thanks to Prof. Kanika T. Bhal, Head, Department of Management Studies, IIT Delhi for her motivation to pursue this task. We are also thankful to all the colleagues in the Department of Management Studies, IIT Delhi, and in IIM Shillong for their encouragement and good wishes for this endeavor.

In addition, we are genuinely obliged to all the respondents of the survey, who took out time from their busy schedules to provide data for this work. Special thanks are due to Ms. Dhanya Jothimani, (Research Scholar, DMS) for her support from time to time.

We have a word of appreciation for the excellent support from Sagarika Ghosh and Nupoor Singh and their team members of Springer for the speedy and excellent publication of the book.

Professor Pramod Kumar Jain acknowledges his wife Uma for her patience, understanding, cooperation, and encouragement.

Dr. Neelam Rani takes this opportunity to express her deepest gratitude to most revered gurus and co-authors, Profs. Surendra Singh Yadav and Pramod Kumar Jain, for their valuable guidance, inspiration, motivation and untiring efforts in completion for the work.

Dr. Neelam Rani expresses her sincere gratitude to Dr. Paul Calluzzo, Assistant Parofessor, Smith School of Business, Ontario, Canada for his "Happy to help" approach. It was not possible to complete work without his help.

Last but not least, we are grateful to our family members for their continuous encouragement.

Neelam Rani
Surendra Singh Yadav
Pramod Kumar Jain

Contents

About the Authors

Neelam Rani is Assistant Professor at Indian Institute of Management Shillong, India. She obtained her Ph.D. from Indian Institute of Technology Delhi. She has been a Fulbright Visiting Scholar at Rutgers Business School, the State University of New Jersey, Newark. She is a recipient of various awards such as NSE prize for Best Thesis in Financial Economics, outstanding paper awards by Amity International Business School, Noida in 2013 and Indian Institute of Capital Markets, Mumbai in 2014. She has been awarded the 3E Innovative Young Researcher Award. She has 20 years of teaching and research experience in subjects related to management accounting, financial management, costing and engineering economics and industrial economics. She has contributed/presented more than 75 papers in journals and conferences.

Surendra Singh Yadav is Professor of Finance at the Department of Management Studies, Indian Institute of Technology (IIT Delhi), India. He was the Head of the Department of Management Studies for six years. He teaches corporate finance, international finance, international business, and security analysis and portfolio management. He has been Visiting Professor at the University of Paris, Paris School of Management, INSEEC Paris, and the University of Tampa, USA. He has published 12 books and contributed more than 230 papers to research journals and conferences. He has also contributed more than 30 papers to financial/economic newspapers. He is the editor-in-chief of the *Journal of Advances in Management Research* (JAMR) published by Emerald Publishing, UK.

Pramod Kumar Jain is Professor of Finance and the Modi Chair Professor at the Department of Management Studies, Indian Institute of Technology (IIT Delhi), India. He has been the Dalmia Chair Professor as well. Recently, he has been awarded with 'Best Faculty Award' at IIT Delhi. He has more than 40 years of teaching experience in subjects related to management accounting, financial management, financial analysis, cost analysis, and cost control. He has been a visiting faculty at the AIT Bangkok; University of Paris; Howe School of Technology

Management at Stevens Institute of Technology, New Jersey; and ICPE, Ljubljana. He has authored three well-known text books published by TMH and more than ten research monographs. He has contributed more than 150 research papers in journals of national and international repute.

Abbreviations

AAR	Average Abnormal Returns
BSE	Bombay Stock Exchange
CAAR	Cumulative Average Abnormal Returns
CAPM	Capital Asset Pricing Model
CATR	Current Assets Turnover Ratio
CSLA	Credit Securities Lyonnais Agency
EDIFAR	Electronic Data Information Filing and Retrieval system
FATR	Fixed Assets Turnover Ratio
M&A	Mergers and Acquisitions
NCR	National Capital Region
NPM	Net Profit Margin
NSE	National Stock Exchange
OCFR	Operating Cash Flow Ratio
OPM	Operating Profit Margin
ROCE	Return On Capital Employed
ROE	Return On Equity funds
SEBI	Securities and Exchange Board of India
SENSEX	Sensitivity Index
SOX (2002)	Sarbanes Oxley Legislation (2002)
TATR	Total Assets Turnover Ratio
UK	United Kingdom
USA/US	United States of America

List of Figures

List of Tables

Chapter 1
Mergers and Acquisitions: An Introduction

Abstract This chapter is aimed at providing brief outline of the research presented in this monograph. It has described the reasons underlying mergers and acquisitions (M&A), the theoretical perspectives, and motivations for adopting the strategy of mergers and acquisitions. Additionally, the chapter also describes the objectives, scope, need, significance of the study, research methodology (in brief), and the chapter plan of the research.

Keywords Hubris · Synergy · Behavioral hypothesis · Neo classical hypothesis · Managerialism hypothesis · Agency theory · Diversification · Corporate governance

1.1 Introduction

Mergers and acquisitions (M&A) are used as instruments of momentous growth and are increasingly getting accepted by Indian firms as critical option of business strategy to increase competitiveness. They are widely used in emerging industries such as information technology, pharmaceuticals, telecommunications, business process outsourcing as well as in traditional industries to gain strength, expand the customer base, reduce competition or enter into a new market or product segment. M&A may be undertaken as a flexible strategy to access the market through an established brand, *inter alia*, to get a market share, to eliminate competition, to reduce tax liabilities or to acquire competence or to set off accumulated losses of one entity against the profits of another entity.

The motives for acquirers (engaging in mergers and acquisitions) are well documented in the literature with the synergy motive associated with positive wealth effects for acquirers while zero or negative wealth effects are said to be driven by hubris as well as managerialism (Berkovitch and Narayanan 1993). Synergy results when the value of the combined firm is greater than the sum of the acquirer firm and target firm as individual firms and this can be achieved by combining firms in the same industry sector (operational synergy) , when firms have different financial resources (financial synergy) or different managerial

N. Rani et al., *Mergers and Acquisitions*, India Studies
in Business and Economics, DOI 10.1007/978-981-10-2203-6_1

resources (managerial synergy). Whether shareholders of acquiring company experience any effect on their wealth from mergers and acquisitions or not has been a matter of ongoing debate among academic researchers. Jensen (1986) stated that availability of free cash flow results in value-reducing mergers. Shleifer and Vishney (1989) contend that managers might make investments that increase managerial value to shareholders but do not improve shareholders' returns.

Agency problems exist when managers serve their own interests at the expense of their shareholders (Williamson 1984). Agency problems create need for effective corporate governance to align the interest of mangers and shareholders (Baysinger and Hoskisson 1990). Ever since Manne (1965) and Marris (1964) framed the phrase "the market for corporate control", the phenomenon of mergers and acquisitions has been closely associated with corporate governance. A great deal of theory and evidence support that takeovers address the governance problems. Mergers and acquisitions are well-suited events to conduct an empirical study of their impact on corporate governance and, in turn on valuation. In this context, the present study proposes to investigate the short-term as well long-term performance of mergers and acquisitions. The study also examines impact of corporate governance practices of the acquiring firms on their performance.

Acquisitions as growth strategy have received attention from developed as well as emerging economies. They have been extensively used by managers as an expansion strategy. Globalization and liberalization have led firms from emerging markets like India to become more aggressive and opt for mergers and acquisitions to fight the competitive battle. Recently, mergers and acquisitions have grown at a rapid pace, which calls for research to analyze what drives firms for this phenomenon and how it affects firms and markets (Andrade et al. 2001; Holmstrom and Kaplan 2001).

Researchers have put forward many hypotheses to explain the motives and reasons underlying M&A. Extant literature classifies M&A into two categories: Neoclassical and Behavioral theories (Mueller and Yurtoglu 2007).

Neoclassical economic theory assumes that corporate management acts to maximize wealth of shareholders; consequently, M&As are expected to increase shareholders' wealth. Neoclassical theories include synergy hypothesis and market for corporate control hypothesis. *Behavioral hypothesis* states that growth-maximizing managers use acquisitions for their own motives of empire building and prefer to undertake wealth-destroying acquisitions; in this case, shareholders of acquiring firm experience negative return due to agency problems. Behavioral hypotheses include managerial discretion hypothesis (Seth et al. 2000), hubris hypothesis (Roll 1986) and overvaluation hypothesis (Shleifer and Vishney 2003). These major hypotheses are summarized as follows:

Synergy hypothesis states that if mergers and acquisitions generate synergies, the acquiring firms experience positive returns on the announcement. The synergy hypothesis proposes that acquisitions take place when the value of the combined firm is greater than the sum of the values of the individual firms (Bradley et al. 1988; Seth 1990).

Market for corporate control hypothesis describes the mergers and acquisition as a way to replace managers who are not able to maximize the value of their firms due to incompetence or agency problems (Mueller and Yurtoglu 2007). According to this hypothesis, mergers, and acquisitions generate non-negative returns to the acquiring firm's shareholders.

The managerialism hypothesis suggests that managers embark on acquisitions to maximize their own utility at the expense of the shareholders of the firm. Managerialism arises when managers use acquisitions for their own motives of empire building and destroy their own shareholders' wealth in the process.

The hubris hypothesis suggests that the managers of the acquiring firm make mistakes in evaluating target firms, but undertake acquisitions presuming that their valuations are correct.

Overvaluation hypothesis states that hubris occurs when management in the acquiring firm makes a mistake in estimating the value of the target leading to overpayment and as a result a wealth transfer from acquiring to target shareholders.

Table 1.1 lists some of the most prominent theories about the motives and determinants of mergers and acquisitions.

Cross-border mergers and acquisitions have gained in popularity over the last few years.

Factors, such as technological development, globalization, increased economic integration and international trade, favorable regulation and policy changes, firm restructuring, target firm undervaluation, and the strong global financial market to finance mergers and acquisitions have possibly led to an unprecedented wave of cross-border mergers and acquisitions worldwide during the last few years (Kiymaz 2004). Gaughan (2014, p. 69) mentions that fifth merger wave has led to the emergence of a new breed of acquirer in 2000s called emerging market acquirers. Emerging market multinationals, embarking upon acquiring cross-border

Table 1.1 Theories on motives of M&A

Theory	Motivation
Synergy	Improves operating efficiency through economies of scale or scope Lowers cost of capital by smoothing cash flow
Diversification	Positions the firm in higher growth markets
Market power	Increases market share
Hubris (managerial pride)	Acquirers believe that their valuations of targets are more accurate than that done by markets
Agency problems and mismanagement	Replace managers who are not acting in the best interests of the owners
Managerialism	Increases the size of a company to increase the power and pay of managers
Tax considerations	Obtain unused net operating losses and tax credits, asset a write-ups

Source DePamphilis (2001, p. 18)

companies to take advantage of regional and global business opportunities is a phenomenon which is intensified during early nineties.

Cross-border M&As have been adopted as a strategic initiative by a large number of firms in multiple regions across the globe. While cross-border M&As have a number of factors in common with domestic M&As, they also have unique characteristics and important differences. The motivations of cross-border M&As are largely similar to those of domestic M&As. However, due to their international nature, there are some specific factors which govern cross-border transactions such as favorable changes in economic and regulatory environment in foreign countries, low foreign tax rates, exchange rates and client base abroad. In addition, some other factors potentially affect cross-border mergers but are not present to the same extent in domestic mergers, such as cultural differences, geographic differences, and country-level governance differences. Cultural or geographic differences can increase the costs of combining two firms. Governance-related differences across countries can motivate mergers if the combined firm has better protection for target firm shareholders because of higher governance standards in the country of the acquiring one. Taxes are potentially important in motivating cross-border mergers, if the acquirer has a lower rate or if the companies' countries have a tax treaty, combining the firms can potentially lower the firms' total tax liability.

Cross–border acquisitions are an important corporate strategy that enables firms to extend their current businesses to new markets, leverage their current capabilities, and diversify into related markets. Zhu et al. (2011) suggest that two major motivations, namely, strategic market entry hypothesis and the market for corporate control hypothesis compete for cross-border acquisitions. They suggest that domestic partial acquisitions dominate and serve the market for corporate control hypothesis extensively, while the strategic market entry hypothesis motivates and is more relevant rationale for cross-border acquisitions.

Strategic market entry hypothesis proposes that an acquisition is a rapid way of entering new markets in new countries. Acquirer enters the market cross border by acquiring an already established company. This way, the acquirer can take advantage of distribution channels, a qualified labor force, management experience, local knowledge and an established brand name (reputation). In addition to being fast in acquiring a stake in a particular market, it is a way to gain entry without adding additional capacity.

In the asset seeking perspective, cross-border acquisitions are viewed as a means to acquire strategic assets available with the target firms. Acquires intend to seek technology based resources and skills in target firm that are superior or not available with the domestic firms in a particular product market. Asset-seeking hypothesis is related to acquirers' strategy to improve competitiveness as they grow. That is how firms improve their capability. By acquiring an existing foreign company, the acquirer gains access to resources and technologies, such as patent-protected technologies and, superior management and marketing skills.

In sum, domestic partial acquisitions and cross-border partial acquisitions are motivated by different hypotheses. Cross-border acquisitions, thus, give acquiring firms access to key strategic resources that may not be available in their domestic market, and thereby, enhance their capabilities to be competitive. Cross-border acquisitions are, thus, likely to add more value in comparison to domestic acquisitions, suggesting there are real benefits from international investments.

1.2 Description of the Problem

Although the existing literature on M&A is perhaps one of the largest bodies of work in finance research, there seems to be no consensus on returns for acquiring firms. A number of different theories exist to explain the value impact of M&As. Some studies suggest that M&As create synergies by reducing costs through economies of scale, adopting more efficient technology and combining R&D facilities.

When an acquisition is announced, a considerable amount of information is revealed about the potential transaction, this information can be used to assess the stock market reaction to an M&A announcement.

In view of the above, the present study attempts to examine the market reaction related to M&A announcements and financial performance post-M&A. Precisely, it aims to evaluate the impact of mergers and acquisitions on short-term abnormal returns as well as on long-term financial performance. It also aims to assess the managements' views about the motives for undertaking mergers and acquisitions. Besides, the study also intends to understand the corporate governance practices of the acquiring firms and their impact both on the short-term and long-term performance.

1.3 Objectives and Significance

1.3.1 Objectives of the Study

The security returns around the announcement represent investors' expectation of M&A benefits whereas post-M&A financial performance represents actual economic benefits generated by M&A. The objective of the proposed research study is to gain an insight into both the short-term and the long-term performance of acquiring firms in the Indian context. The study consists of four parts. The objective of the first part is to evaluate the market reaction on announcement of M&A. The objective of the second part is to know the managerial views about motives for undertaking M&A. The objective of the third part is to understand long-term financial performance of M&A. The objective of the forth part is to develop corporate governance index of acquiring firms and the impact of corporate governance score on short-term and long-term performance of M&A.

To know the managerial views and motives, two surveys have been conducted. The first survey attempts to get an insight into the corporate governance practices of the acquiring firms by developing a corporate governance index. The second survey covers three major dimensions, namely, management view on motives for M&A, management views on sources of synergy from M&A and motives of merger of wholly owned subsidiary.

The market reaction is assessed in terms of the change in stock returns. Using event study methodology and pretest posttest research design, the stock prices and financial performance, before and after M&A, have been evaluated.

1.3.2 Significance of the Study

Despite plethora of literature on the implications of mergers and acquisitions, the empirical evidence on returns to the shareholders of the acquirer firm is not conclusive. In other words, the results of existing studies in finance and business strategy indicate that wealth effects of shareholders of the acquiring firms are mixed. The empirical findings on the subject are varied. While some studies report negative cumulative average abnormal returns, others document zero or positive cumulative average abnormal returns. In a review paper on performance of the acquiring firm, Bruner (2002) suggests that these mixed results make the conclusions regarding the acquirer firms' performance more complex.

The empirical work indicates that value is created by M&A activities. Moreover, the management also believes that the decisions to initiate strategies of M&A are based on certain motives. This observation, by and large, holds true in respect of markets across countries.

In India, few comprehensive studies have been undertaken in the past on the subject of managerial views, motives, impact on the share prices and financial performance of M&A (Rani et al. 2013, 2014). Further, much of the recent academic attention on corporate governance has been focused on corporate accounting scandals and their prevention. Corporate governance and merger strategy, however, has not been the focus.

The number of studies on share price performance exclusively due to announcement of mergers and acquisitions is limited and is industry specific in Indian context. To the best of our knowledge, an in-depth research related to the impact of mergers and acquisitions on the shareholders wealth in short-term in India has not been observed. Investigations using event study methodology have exclusively focused on developed security markets viz., United States, Canada, Japan and European nations. Existing studies of mergers in India are very few. Moreover, the studies based on Indian security markets have focused either on specific industries (Rani et al. 2012 (Pharmaceutical Industry); Chakraborty 2010 (Financial Industry); Anand and Singh 2008 (Banking Sector)) or have analyzed a very small sample size (Mann and Kohli 2009). Recently, Kohli and Mann (2011); Gubbi et al. (2010); Barai and Mohanty (2010) have analyzed abnormal returns to the announcements of mergers and acquisitions by conducting event study on large sample but have not tested the robustness of returns by any nonparametric test. Moreover, these empirical investigations have focused on comparing premerger and postmerger performance on case to case basis.

Further, extant literature has investigated the impact of control acquired in context of international acquisitions only. The present study is a modest attempt to fill this conspicuous gap.

Another significant feature of this study is that it attempts to evaluate the impact of the non-contaminated (mergers and acquisitions) sample by manually verifying rigorous sample selection criterion. This makes the study significant as the findings show, in a way, the exclusive impact of announcements of M&A.

In addition, on a methodological level, the present study has demonstrated the use of seven major significance tests to check the robustness of average abnormal returns and cumulative average abnormal returns. The use of seven main test statistics for assessing significance levels of average abnormal return and cumulative average abnormal return has proved to be useful, since these test statistics take into account effects due to event-induced variance and offer, therefore, an alternative evaluation of significance.

1.4 Scope of the Study

1. The study is confined to the analysis of acquiring companies that undertook the move of mergers and acquisitions and are listed on Bombay Stock Exchange (BSE).
2. It covers a period starting from January 1, 2003 to December 31, 2015.
3. The management survey is carried out for acquiring companies that were engaged in M&A activities during the specified time period; these companies are geographically spread throughout the country (India).

1.5 Methodology of the Study

The present study uses event study methodology[1] to examine the impact of mergers and acquisitions announcements on stock returns (Brown and Warner 1980; Bowman 1983; Doukas and Travlos 1988; Peterson 1989; Henderson Jr 1990; Morck and Yeung 1992; Markides and Ittner 1994; MacKinlay 1997; McWilliams and Siegel 1997; Serra 2004; Wells 2004; Kothari and Warner 2007; Konchitchki

---

[1]Event study methodology is one of the most popular statistical research designs in the area of finance. It is used to examine the market's response to a well-defined event by examining the security prices around such event.

and O'Leary 2011). The stock returns behavior around these announcements is likely to enable the researcher to ascertain the short-term wealth creation by mergers and acquisitions.

This study is a hypothesis testing research study. Two experimental designs have been followed, viz. 'before- and-after design' and 'after-only design'. To ascertain the magnitude of the change in the financial performance of mergers and acquisitions, pretest posttest research design[2] has been used. It attempts to gain new insights into the acquirers' performance. The study endeavors to test the performance of the acquiring firms in short-term and long-term by evaluating the financial performance during two periods of time; one before merger and acquisition and the other after the merger and acquisition. As a result, the study would also provide an insight into the validity of the synergy hypothesis for Indian corporates.

The present study uses questionnaire-based survey research method to get an insight into the managerial views and motives related to employing mergers and acquisitions and corporate governance practices of the acquirers. Two national surveys for Indian companies have been conducted to achieve this objective. Corporate governance index of the acquiring companies has been developed to get insights into the corporate governance practices of the acquirers. The impact of corporate governance practices of acquirers on performance of M&A has been examined using one-group 'after-only' experimental research design. In this case also, the short-term as well as long-term impacts are evaluated by examining variability of returns at one point in time; 'after-only' the announcement of M&A.

The whole data set has been analyzed primarily through statistical software SAS system for windows 9.1 and Eventus version 8 for event study. In addition, the present study has made extensive use of statistical software Statistical Package for Social Sciences 16.0 (SPSS) for analysis of primary as well as secondary data.

1.6 Organization of the Study

The study has been organized into eight chapters. Chapter 1 relates to the background. Chapter 2 presents the research methodology used to carry out the study. The core of the study is available in Chaps. 3, 4, and 5. Chapter 3 discusses the short-term impact of mergers and acquisitions. Chapter 4 presents the impact of mergers and acquisitions on long-term financial performance of acquirers. Chapter 5 describes the survey of management view on motives for mergers and acquisitions. Chapter 6 is devoted to the development of corporate governance index. Chapter 7 contains the impact of corporate governance score on abnormal returns and financial performance. Chapter 8 presents the concluding observations.

[2]Pretest posttest (also called before and after research design) is an experimental research design in which test units are subjected to an intervention. To observe change in a variable, both pretest and posttest values of the variable are measured and further statistically tested to draw inferences about the population.

1.7 Concluding Observations

This chapter provides a brief outline of the study. It briefly explains the motives of acquirers for undertaking mergers and acquisitions; it outlines the major hypotheses for adopting the strategy of mergers and acquisitions as proposed by earlier researchers. Further, it outlines how corporate governance affects mergers and acquisitions. Moreover, the main objectives, significance of the study, and methodology adopted to achieve these objectives have been summarized.

References

Anand, M., & Singh, J. (2008). Impact of merger announcements on shareholders' wealth: Evidence from Indian private sector banks. *Vikalpa, 33*(1), 35–54.

Andrade, G., Mitchell, M. & Stafford, E. (2001). New evidence and perspectives on mergers. *Journal of Economic Perspectives, 15*(2), 103–20.

Barai, P., & Mohanty, P. (2010). Short term performance of Indian acquirers–effects of mode of payment, industry relatedness and status of target. Retrieved November 12, 2011, from SSRN: http://ssrn.com/abstract=1697564.

Baysinger, B. D., & Hoskisson, R. E. (1990). The composition of boards of directors and strategic control: Effects on corporate strategy. *Academy of Management Review, 15*(1), 72–87.

Berkovitch, E., & Narayanan, M. (1993). Motives for takeovers: An empirical investigation. *Journal of Financial and Quantitative Analysis, 28*(3), 347–62.

Bowman, Robert G. (1983). Understanding and conducting event studies. *Journal of Business Finance & Accounting, 10*(4), 561–584.

Bradley, M., Desai, A., & Kim, E. H. (1988). Synergistic gains from corporate acquisitions and their division between the stockholders of target and acquiring firms. *Journal of Financial Economics, 21*(1), 3–40.

Brown, S. J., & Warner, J. B. (1980). Measuring security price performance. *Journal of Financial Economics, 8*(3), 205–258.

Bruner, R. F. (2002). Does M&A Pay? A survey of evidence for the decision maker. *Journal of Applied Finance*, 12 (Spring/Summer), 48–68.

Chakraborty, M. (2010). The wealth effects of takeover announcement for firms in the financial services sector in India. *Journal of Emerging Market Finance, 9*(2), 199–227.

DePamphilis, Donald. (2001). *Mergers, acquisitions, and other restructuring activities.* London: Academic Press.

Doukas, J., & Travlos, N. G. (1988). The effect of corporate multinationalism on shareholders' Wealth: Evidence from international acquisitions. *Journal of Finance, 43*(5), 1161–1175.

Gaughan, P. A. (2014). *Mergers, acquisitions, and corporate restructuring* (5th ed.). New York: Wiley.

Gubbi, S., Aulakh, P., Ray, S., Sarkar, M. B., & Chittoor, R. (2010). Do international acquisitions by emerging economy firms create shareholder value? The case of Indian firms. *Journal of International Business Studies, 41*(3), 397–418.

Henderson Jr, G. V. (1990). Problems and solutions in conducting event studies. *Journal of Risk and Insurance, 57*(2), 282–306.

Holmstrom, B., & Kaplan, S.N. (2001). Corporate governance and merger activity in the United States: Making sense of the 1980s and 1990s. *Journal of Economic Perspectives, 15*(2), 121–144.

Jensen, M. (1986). Agency costs of free cash flow, corporate finance, and takeovers. *American Economic Review, 76*(2), 323–329.

Kiymaz, H. (2004). Cross-border acquisitions of US financial institutions: Impact of macroeconomic factors. *Journal of Banking & Finance, 28*(6), 1413–1439.
Kohli, R., & Mann, B. J. S. (2012). Analyzing determinants of value creation in domestic and cross-border acquisitions in India. *International Business Review, 21*(6), 998–1016.
Konchitchki, Y., & O'Leary, Daniel E. (2011). Event study methodologies in information systems research. *International Journal of Accounting Information Systems, 12*(3), 99–115.
Kothari, S. P., & Warner, J. B. (2007). Econometrics of event studies. Chapter 1. In *Handbook of corporate finance- empirical corporate finance*. Elsevier B.V.
MacKinlay, A. C. (1997). Event studies in economics and finance. *Journal of Economic Literature, 35*(1), 13–39.
Mann, B. S., & Kohli, R. (2009). Impact of mode of payment and insider ownership on target and acquirer's announcement returns in India. *Vikalpa, 34*(4), 51–66.
Manne, Henry G. (1965). Mergers and the market for corporate control. *Journal of Political Economy, 73*(2), 110–20.
Markides, C. C., & Ittner, C. D. (1994). Shareholder benefits from corporate international diversification: evidence from U.S. international acquisitions. *Journal of International Business Studies, 25*(2), 343–366.
Marris, R. (1964). *Theory of Managerial Capitalism*. London: Macmillan.
McWilliams, A., & Siegel, D. (1997). Event studies in management research: Theoretical and empirical issues. *Academy of Management Journal, 40*(3), 626–57.
Morck, R., & Yeung, B. (1992). Internationalization: An event study test. *Journal of International Economics, 33*(1/ 2), 41–56.
Mueller, D. C., & Yurtoglu, B. B. (2007). Corporate governance and the returns to acquiring firms' shareholders. *Managerial and Decision Economics, 28*(8), 879–896.
Peterson, P. P. (1989). Event studies: A review of issues and methodology. *Quarterly Journal of Business and Economics, 28*(3), 36–66.
Rani, N., Yadav, S. S., & Jain, P. K. (2012). Impact of mergers and acquisitions on returns to shareholders of acquiring firms: Indian economy in perspective. *Journal of Financial Management and Analysis, 25*(1), 1–26.
Rani, N., Yadav, Surendra S., & Jain, P. K. (2013). Market response to the announcement of mergers and acquisitions: An empirical study from India. *VISION: The Journal of Business Perspective, 17*(1), 1–16.
Rani, N., Yadav, Surendra S., & Jain, P. K. (2014). The Impact of Cross-border and Domestic Acquisitions on Acquirer Shareholders' Wealth in India. *International Journal of Business and Management, 9*(3) March, 88–110.
Roll, R. (1986). The hubris hypothesis of corporate takeovers. *Journal of Business, 59*, 197–216.
Serra, A. P. (2004). Event study tests—A brief survey. *Gestão. Org-RevistaElectrónica de GestãoOrganizacional, 2*(3), 248–255.
Seth, A. (1990). Value creation in acquisitions: A re-examination of performance issues. *Strategic Management Journal, 11*(2), 99–115.
Seth, A., Song, K. P., & Pettit, R. (2000). Synergy, managerialism or hubris: an empirical examination of motives for foreign acquisitions of US firms. *Journal of International Business Studies, 31*(3), 387–405.
Shleifer, A., & Vishney, R. W. (1989). Management entrenchment: The case of manager specific investments. *Journal of Financial Economics, 25*(1), 123–39.
Shleifer, A., & Vishney, R. W. (2003). Stock market driven acquisitions. *Journal of Financial Economics, 70*(3), 295–311.
Wells, William H. (2004). A beginner's guide to event studies. *Journal of Insurance Regulation, 22*(4), 61–70.
Williamson, O. E. (1984). Corporate governance. *Yale Law Journal, 93*(7), 1197–1230.
Zhu, P., Jog, V., & Otchere, I. (2011). Partial acquisitions in emerging markets: A test of the strategic market entry and corporate control hypotheses. *Journal of Corporate Finance, 17*(2), 288–305.

Chapter 2
Research Methodology

Abstract This chapter presents the research methodology followed in the study to assess the impact of mergers and acquisitions on financial performance. It also enumerates the research objectives, hypotheses, sources of primary data (based on questionnaire survey, personal interviews, emails and telephonic calls) and secondary data (drawn from Bombay Stock exchange, SEBI, Prowess database Centre for Monitoring Indian Economy, Thomson Security Data Corporation (SDC) Platinum M&A database), data analysis (primarily in terms of abnormal returns, major financial ratios), event study methodology, statistical techniques used in the study and research model.

Keywords Event methodology · Financial performance · Financial ratios · Abnormal return · Parametric test · Nonparametric test · Acquisitions · Mergers · Cross-border acquisitions

2.1 Introduction

This chapter contains the research objectives and hypotheses to be tested in the study. It explains the detailed research methodology that has been proposed in order to address these research objectives. It presents the data used to test these hypotheses. There are virtually no comprehensive studies that examine the short-term as well as long-term performance of M&A with a focus on corporate governance, management opinion and motives of M&A. Therefore, this study aims to capture the managerial views on motives of M&A; impact of mergers and acquisitions on stock returns as well as financial performance of acquirers with a focus on corporate governance in Indian context. The present research study uses both primary data (representing the managerial views on motives of M&A and corporate governance survey) and secondary data (related to stock market comprising of stock prices data and financial performance).

This chapter is organized into six sections. Section 2.2 (divided into Sects. 2.2.1 and 2.2.2) presents research objectives and hypotheses to be tested. Section 2.3 is

N. Rani et al., *Mergers and Acquisitions*, India Studies in Business and Economics, DOI 10.1007/978-981-10-2203-6_2

divided into three subsections. Section 2.3.1 provides a brief on the proposed research methodology used to address the objectives of the study. Section 2.3.2 delineates the scope of the study. Section 2.4 describes the event study methodology in detail. The data used, for empirically examining the objectives for the present study, is summarized in Sect. 2.5. An equally important aspect of this research study is sample selection criteria; it is provided in Sect. 2.6. The concluding observations are listed in the last Sect. 2.7.

2.2 Research Objectives and Hypotheses

2.2.1 Research Objectives

The present study has specifically identified the following objectives:

Objective 1: To measure the effect of the announcement of mergers and acquisitions on stock returns of acquiring firms by

1.1 Ascertaining the magnitude and the direction of the abnormal returns for entire sample.
1.2 Conducting analysis of the abnormal returns for subsamples on the basis of

   (i) Domestic and cross-border M&A.
   (ii) Method of payment (cash, stock).
   (iii) Form of target firm acquired (listed, unlisted).
   (iv) Status of target firm (remains wholly owned subsidiary, absorbed with the operations of the acquirer).
   (v) Stake of acquisitions (partial/majority control, complete control).
   (vi) Origin of target firm (developed market, emerging market).

Objective 2: To gain insight into managerial views about motives and sources of synergies of M&A.

Objective 3: To measure the magnitude and the direction of change in the financial performance of the acquiring firms post-M&A.

Objective 4: To gain insight into corporate governance practices of acquirers by developing a corporate governance index.

Objective 5: To ascertain the impact of corporate governance on stock returns due to the announcement of mergers and acquisitions and financial performance.

2.2.2 Hypotheses

To achieve the above-stated objectives, the following hypotheses have been formulated in this study:

2.2.2.1 Hypotheses Related to the Short-Term Performance of M&A

Hypothesis I: There is significant average abnormal return (AAR) during the event window due to announcement of mergers and acquisitions.
Hypothesis II: There is significant cumulative average abnormal return (CAAR) during the event window due to announcement of mergers and acquisitions.

2.2.2.2 Hypotheses Related to Financial Performance of M&A

Hypothesis III: The mean level of profitability ratio (based on investments, sales, expenses) for the post-merger and acquisition period is significantly different from mean level of profitability ratio (based on investments, sales, and expenses) from pre-merger and acquisition period.
Hypothesis IV: The mean level of efficiency ratio for the post-merger and acquisition period is significantly different from mean level of efficiency ratio from pre-merger and acquisition period.
Hypothesis V: The mean level of liquidity ratio for the post-merger and acquisition period is significantly different from mean level of liquidity ratio from pre-merger and acquisition period.
Hypothesis VI: The mean level of leverage ratio for the post-merger and acquisition period is significantly different from mean level of leverage ratio from pre-merger and acquisition period.

2.2.2.3 Hypotheses Related to Corporate Governance Index

Hypothesis VII: Acquiring firms with better corporate governance (as reflected in high corporate governance index) have better abnormal returns in short term.
Hypothesis VIII: Acquiring firms with better corporate governance (as reflected in high corporate governance index) have better firm performance.
Hypothesis IX: Acquiring firms with better corporate governance (as reflected in high corporate governance index) have higher firm value post-M&A.

2.3 Research Methodology and Scope

2.3.1 Research Methodology

The objectives of the study have been addressed using a comprehensive approach; it has been demonstrated in Fig. 2.1. From the figure, it may be deciphered that the objectives 1, 3, and 5 have been addressed using secondary data and objectives 2 and 4 have been responded to using primary data.

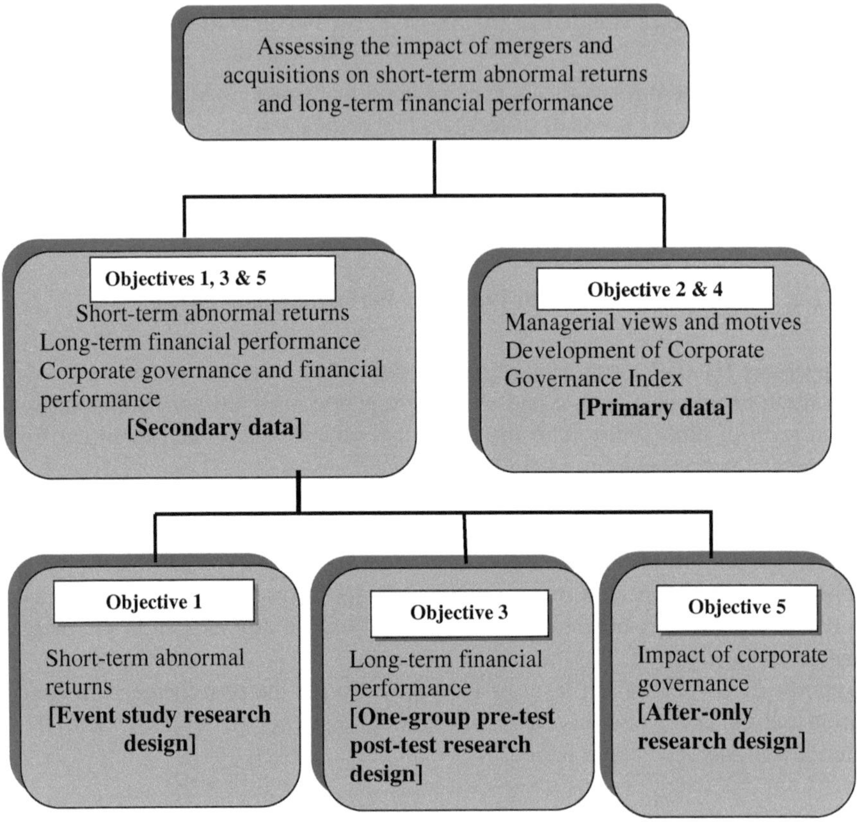

Fig. 2.1 Outline of research methodology

Objective 1 evaluates the impact of mergers and acquisitions on short-term abnormal returns. The objective has been achieved using event study methodology. Event study methodology is one of the most popular statistical research designs in the area of finance (Brown and Warner 1980; Bowman 1983; Brown and Warner 1985; Henderson 1990; Peterson 1989; McWilliams and Siegel 1997; MacKinlay 1997; McWilliams and McWilliams 2000; Serra 2004; Wells 2004; Weston et al. 2004; Kothari and Warner 2007; Tabak 2010; Konchitchki and O'Leary 2011). It is used to examine the market's response to a well-defined event by examining the security prices around such event. The secondary data (stock prices of the companies that announced mergers and acquisitions) has been examined using event study methodology. This enables a researcher to assess if there are any abnormal returns earned by the investors due to these events. The abnormal return is the differences between the observed return and the expected return on a particular day, calculated by a return model (chosen by the researcher).

For objectives 2 and 4, survey research methodology has been used to collect primary data. Survey research, as a mode of enquiry, enables the researcher to know the views and opinions of the respondents of the questionnaire. The present work conducted two questionnaire-based surveys to gauge the managerial perception about these decisions.

Objective 3 has been dealt with using one-group pre test, post test research design and ratio analysis. In one-group pre test, post test research design, the changes in financial performance (due to mergers and acquisitions decisions) have been measured 5 years prior to and after the M&A.

Objective 5 evaluates the impact of corporate governance on short-term abnormal returns due to mergers and acquisitions and financial performance. 'After-only research design' has been used to address the objective.

2.3.2 *Scope of the Study*

1. The study is confined to the analysis of companies (listed on BSE) that have undertaken mergers and acquisitions. The scope of the study is limited to analyze the performance of acquiring firms.
2. It covers a time span of more than 13 years starting from January 1, 2003 to December 31, 2015. January 1, 2003 has been chosen as it precedes the effective dates of relevant provisions of SEBI Clause 49 enacted by Stock Exchanges in India. The reference period for the study includes the 5 years before and 5 years after the M&A.
3. The management survey has been carried out for companies that completed mergers and acquisitions during the specified time period; these companies are located all over India.

2.4 Event Study Methodology

Event study methodology in the finance literature has become a standard methodology in evaluating the stock price reaction to a specific event (McWilliams and Siegel 1997). The event study methodology is used to investigate the market's response to a well-defined event by examining the security prices around such event. The methodology assesses whether specific events create abnormal stock returns as stock returns move in response to market-specific factors or several firm specific factors such as announcements of earnings, mergers and acquisitions, etc. The information about the event is released through the financial press, corporate releases or directly providing it to the stock exchanges where the security is listed. The investigation enables a researcher to assess if there are any abnormal returns earned by the security holders due to these events.

The methodology is based on the fundamental idea that stock prices represent the discounted value of firms' future stream of profits. Hence, the change in the equity value of firm observed due to stock market's response to the announcement of mergers and acquisitions may be considered as a measure of the (discounted) additional profits that they are expected to accrue as a consequence of mergers and acquisitions (Duso et al. 2010). The event study methodology uses average abnormal stock market reaction as a gauge of value creation or value destruction. Based on the announcement-period stock market response, it may be concluded whether mergers and acquisitions create value for shareholders of acquiring firms or not.

2.4.1 *Mechanics of Event Study*

The following steps comprise the mechanics of event study:

2.4.1.1 Event Definition and Date of Announcement

The *event* is the action that the researcher would like to study. The event is expected to convey some information that potentially influences the stock prices. The events defined for this research study are the announcements of mergers and acquisitions.

The first step in the event study methodology is to define the event as the date on which the acquisition is first announced to the public. Day 0 is defined as the day the announcement first appears in any newspaper. For this purpose of the study, the announcement day has been defined as the day when the Stock Exchange is informed about the board approval of the merger and acquisition deal. These dates are verified (manually) from the archives of corporate announcements of stock exchange.

In majority of cases, the stock exchanges are informed the same day on which the acquisition is first announced to the public. Intent date and the actual date have also been verified (manually). In a few cases, the intent of acquisition is announced before the approval date (almost 10 trading days), to capture the effect of this leakage event window of 20 days before the announcement has been observed. The day 0 has been defined as the board approval date as it facilitates the verification of a clean window from the archives of Bombay Stock Exchange. The most critical assumption of event study methodology is that there is no confounding event during the event window.

2.4.1.2 Estimation Period

An *estimation window* is the period used for estimating the expected returns. The *estimation period* is defined as the period prior to the occurrence of the event and the event window. The expected returns (also called normal returns) are calculated using a time period other than the event window. For the present study, the

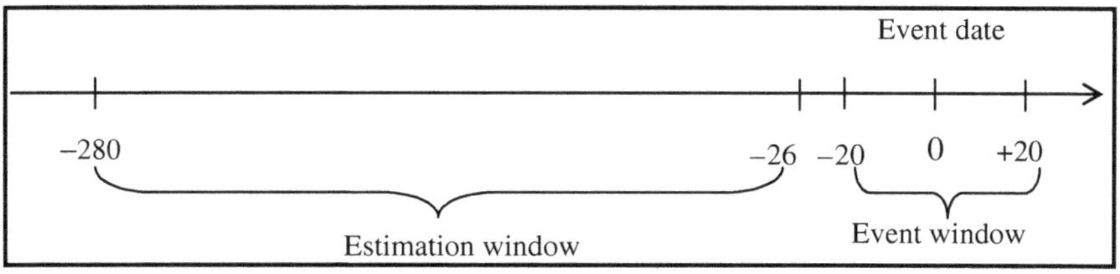

Fig. 2.2 Return analysis time line for event study research design

estimation window is from the day -280 to the day -26 (from 25 to 280 days prior to the event window), thus comprising of 255 trading days. This ensures that estimates of the normal return model are not influenced by the event-related returns.

Figure 2.2 depicts the event window and estimation window. It is imperative for the estimation window and event window not to overlap.

2.4.1.3 Event Window Period

An *event window* is the period in which an event occurs; during this period, the security prices of the relevant firms are examined. The event window for this study is chosen as –20, through 0, to +20. Here, 0 depicts the announcement date, –20 is the 20 days time period prior to announcement date and +20 is the 20 days time period after the announcement date. To conduct an in-depth analysis, the event window has been further broken into smaller windows. The event period surrounds the date of the announcement of acquisition during which the stock market's response to the announcement is investigated. In order to account for early share price reactions (induced by the anticipation of stock market of an upcoming announcement before and potentially slow information processing after the event), the cumulative abnormal returns over alternate windows are considered. Fama et al. (1969) suggest that event date may be uncertain. Therefore, it is desired to consider abnormal return which might appear before and after the defined date. This interval is known as event window.

The abnormal returns over varying windows, namely, (−20, −2), (−15, −2), (−10, −2), (−5, −2) (−5, 0) (−1, 0), (−1, +1), (−2, +2), (−5, +5) (−10, +10), (−20, +20), (+2, +5), (+2, +10), (+2, +15) and (+2, +20) have been observed to capture the leakage effect. The dates are verified (manually) from the archives of corporate announcements of Bombay Stock Exchange (BSE) to ascertain the clean period data. It has been checked (manually) that there is no contamination of information and confounding event during the event window.

Long-term event windows have not been examined in the study due to two reasons: first, using a long-event window severely reduces the power of the test statistic and leads to false inferences (Brown and Warner 1980, 1985; McWilliams and Siegel 1997). Second problem is the difficulty of controlling for confounding events. Also, long-event windows increase the likelihood of contemporaneous and inter-temporal correlations of residuals resulting in significant underestimates of standard errors (Salinger 1992).

2.4.1.4 Estimation Model and Definition of Abnormal Return

The estimation model is the model used to estimate the expected returns. The traditional single factor market model has been considered to estimate the expected returns. It involves the regression of a stock's returns against a market index. For the present study, the value weighted market index—BSE SENSEX[1] has been used for regression.

The key issue in event studies is what portion of the price movement is actually caused by the event of interest. In other words, it is required to extract the impact of the one particular event on stock returns. This leads to the concept of abnormal returns. The abnormal return is the differences between the actual return and the expected return on a particular day.

The abnormal return of the jth stock (AR_{jt}) is obtained by subtracting the normal or expected returns in absence of the event $E(R_{jt})$, from the actual return in the event period, (R_{jt}) as per following Eq. (2.4.1):

$$\mathrm{AR}_{jt} = R_{jt} - E\left(R_{jt}\right) \tag{2.4.1}$$

The market model approach relates the return of a security to the return of the market portfolio as per the market model Eq. (2.4.2):

$$R_{jt} = \alpha_j + \beta_{\mathrm{m}t} + \varepsilon_{jt} \tag{2.4.2}$$

where $t = -280, \ldots, -26$, α_j is a constant term for the jth stock, β_j is the beta of the jth stock, $R_{\mathrm{m}t}$ is the market returns, and ε_{jt} is an error term.

The parameters of the model are estimated by using the time-series data from the estimation period that precedes each individual announcement. The parameters estimated from the market model are then used in the calculation of abnormal returns for each day in the event window. The estimated parameters are then matched with the actual returns in the event period. The daily excess return, i.e., abnormal return of firm j for the day t (AR_{jt}) is estimated from actual returns during the event period and the estimated coefficients from the estimation period as per Eq. (2.4.3)

[1]BSE SENSEX (Bombay Stock Exchange Sensitivity Index) is a 'Market Capitalisation—Weighted' Index of 30 component stocks representing a sample of large well established and financially sound companies. It is reckoned as a benchmark index of the Indian capital market.

$$\mathrm{AR}_{jt} = R_{jt} - \left(\hat{\alpha} + \hat{\beta} R_{\mathrm{m}t}\right) \tag{2.4.3}$$

where $t = -20, \ldots, +20$.

The average abnormal return (AAR_t) for each day in the event window is calculated as per Eq. (2.4.4):

$$\mathrm{AAR}_t = \frac{1}{N} \sum_{j=1}^{N} \mathrm{AR}_{jt} \tag{2.4.4}$$

where N is the number of firms.

2.4.1.5 Definition of Cumulative Abnormal Return (CAR)

The cumulative abnormal return for a given security is simply the sum of daily abnormal returns over the event window. Over an interval of two or more trading days beginning with day T_1 and ending with day T_2, the cumulative average abnormal return (CAAR) is calculated as per Eq. (2.4.5)

$$\mathrm{CAAR}_{T_1 T_2} = \frac{1}{N} \sum_{j=1}^{N} \sum_{t=T_1}^{T_2} \mathrm{AR}_{jt} \tag{2.4.5}$$

2.4.1.6 Definition of Precision-Weighted Cumulative Abnormal Return

The study also reports precision-weighted cumulative average abnormal return (PWCAAR). The precision-weighted average is constructed using the relative weights of each stock (Cowan 2007). The precision-weighted return weight each stock in inverse proportion to its standard deviation. The precision-weighted CAAR (as a weighted average of the original *CARs*) preserves the sample interpretation of CAAR (Cowan 2007). The precision-weighted cumulative average abnormal return (PWCAAR) is a better measure than CAAR and average standardized cumulative abnormal return. The precision-weighted cumulative average is calculated as specified in Eq. (2.4.6)

$$\mathrm{PWCAAR}_{T_1 T_2} = \sum_{J=1}^{N} \sum_{t=T_2}^{T_2} \omega_j \mathrm{AR}_{jT} \tag{2.4.6}$$

where,

$$\omega_j = \frac{\left(\sum_{t=T_1}^{T_2} \delta_{\mathrm{AR}_{jt}}^2\right)^{-\frac{1}{2}}}{\sum_{i=1}^{N}\left(\sum_{t=T_1}^{T_2} \delta_{\mathrm{AR}_{it}}^2\right)^{-\frac{1}{2}}}$$

where,

$$\delta_{\mathrm{AR}_{jt}}^2 = \frac{\sum_{k=T_{D_b}}^{T_{D_e}} (\mathrm{AR}_{jk})^2}{D_j - 2}\left[1 + \frac{1}{D_j} + \frac{(R_{\mathrm{m}t} - \bar{R}_{\mathrm{m}})^2}{\sum_{k=T_{D_b}}^{T_{D_e}} (R_{\mathrm{m}k} - \bar{R}_m)^2}\right]$$

D_j is the number of non-missing estimation period returns for firm j. $R_{\mathrm{m}t}$ is the return on the market index on day t in the event window, $R_{\mathrm{m}k}$ is the return on the market index on day k in the estimation window. $\overline{R_{\mathrm{m}}}$ is the mean market return over estimation period. k represents the trading day in estimation period.

2.4.1.7 Hypotheses for Announcement Effects

The null hypotheses being tested are

H_{01}: The average abnormal return to the shareholders of acquiring company on the announcement of acquisition is zero.

H_{02}: The cumulative average abnormal return to the shareholders of acquiring company for the event window period around the announcements of acquisition is zero.

2.4.2 Statistical Significance of Abnormal Returns

There are numerous tests for evaluating the statistical significance of abnormal returns. Several studies have developed tests to control for specific problems that occur with event studies. Each of them tests the null hypothesis that abnormal returns are zero, but they differ in the necessary assumptions about the statistical properties of (abnormal) returns. The parametric tests implicitly assume that the residuals follow normal distribution. When the assumption of normality of abnormal returns is violated, parametric tests are not well specified. In addition to parametric statistics, event studies typically use a nonparametric test. A nonparametric test is normally used in conjunction with parametric test (in event study) to verify that the results are not driven by outliers. Nonparametric statistics do not require as stringent assumptions about return distributions as parametric tests. Kang and Stulz (1996) documented specific robustness issues in event studies using Asia-Pacific financial market data. In order to obtain robust results, a wide variety of statistical tests have been applied. These tests are well specified and more powerful in random samples of Asia-Pacific financial market data (Corrado and Truong 2008; Corrado and Zivney 1992; Campbell et al. 2010). We use the following four widely used parametric and three nonparametric test statistics commonly used in event studies to test for the significance of average abnormal returns and cumulative abnormal returns over the event period:

2.4.2.1 Parametric Tests

Four parametric test statistics, namely, Crude dependence adjustment test (Brown and Warner 1980), Cross-sectional standard deviation test (Brown and Warner, 1985), Patell's test (1976) corrected by Mikkelson and Partch (1988) and Standardized cross-sectional test (Boehmer et al. 1991) have been conducted to test for the significance of average abnormal returns and cumulative abnormal returns over the event period.

The Crude Dependence Adjustment Test (CDA)

The test incorporates the sample time-series standard deviation. Brown and Warner describe the test as featuring a 'crude dependence adjustment.' That is, the test compensates for potential dependence of returns across security events by estimating the standard deviation using the time series of sample mean returns from the estimation period. Crude dependence adjustment test uses a single variance estimate for the entire sample. Therefore, the time-series standard test does not take account of the unequal return variances across securities. This test avoids the potential problem of cross-sectional correlation of security return. To account for the dependence across firms' average residuals, in event time, Brown and Warner (1985) suggest that the standard deviation of average residuals should be estimated from the time series of the average abnormal returns over the estimation period. The estimated variance of AAR_t is given as per Eq. (2.4.2.1):

$$\hat{\sigma}^2_{AAR} = \frac{\sum_{t=-280}^{-26}\left(AAR_t - \overline{AAR}\right)^2}{254} \tag{2.4.2.1}$$

where the market model parameters are estimated over the estimation period of 255 days and

$$\overline{AAR} = \frac{\sum_{t=-280}^{-26} AAR_t}{255}$$

The test statistics for day t in event time is given as per Eq. (2.4.2.2)

$$t = \frac{\mathrm{AAR}_t}{\hat{\sigma}_{\mathrm{AAR}}} \tag{2.4.2.2}$$

The test statistics for $CAAR_{T_1,T_2}$ is given as per Eq. (2.4.2.3):

$$t = \frac{CAAR_t}{(T_2 - T_1 + 1)^{\frac{1}{2}}\hat{\sigma}_{\mathrm{AAR}}} \tag{2.4.2.3}$$

Cross-Sectional Standard Deviation Test (CSS)

This test uses a daily cross-sectional standard deviation instead of sample time-series standard deviation. The test statistics for the day t in event time is given as per Eq. (2.4.2.4)

$$t = \frac{\mathrm{AAR}_t}{\hat{\sigma}_{\mathrm{AAR}_t}/\sqrt{N}} \tag{2.4.2.4}$$

where,

$$\hat{\sigma}^2_{\mathrm{AAR}_t} = \frac{1}{N-1}\sum_{i=1}^{N}\left(\mathrm{AR}_{it} - \frac{1}{N}\sum_{j=1}^{\mathrm{N}}\mathrm{AR}_{jt}\right)^2$$

The test statistics for $CAAR_{T_1,T_2}$ is given as per Eq. (2.4.2.5):

$$t_{\mathrm{CAAR}} = \frac{CAAR_{T_1T_2}}{\hat{\sigma}_{\mathrm{CAAR}_{T_1,T_2}}/\sqrt{N}} \tag{2.4.2.5}$$

where the estimated variance of CAAR_{T_1,T_2} is

$$\hat{\sigma}^2_{\mathrm{CAAR}_{\mathrm{T}_1,\mathrm{T}_2}} = \frac{1}{\mathrm{N}-1}\sum_{i=1}^{\mathrm{N}}\left(\mathrm{CAR}_{i,\mathrm{T}_1,\mathrm{T}_2} - \frac{1}{\mathrm{N}}\sum_{j=1}^{\mathrm{N}}\mathrm{CAR}_{j,\mathrm{T}_1,\mathrm{T}_2}\right)^2$$

Patell's Test

Patell (1976) proposes a test statistic where the event period abnormal returns are standardized by the standard deviation of the estimation period abnormal returns. The Patell Z test is an example of a standardized abnormal return approach, which estimates a separate standard error for each security event and assumes cross-sectional independence. This standardization reduces the effect of stocks with large returns standard deviation on the test. Patell test statistics assumes cross-sectional independence in abnormal returns; it also assumes that there is no event-induced change in the variance of event period abnormal returns. The standardized abnormal return (SAR) for each security is calculated as per Eq. (2.4.2.6):

$$\mathrm{SAR}_{jt} = \frac{\mathrm{AR}_{jt}}{\delta_{\mathrm{AR}_{jt}}} \tag{2.4.2.6}$$

where,

$$\delta^2_{\mathrm{AR}_{jt}} = \frac{\sum_{k=T_{D_b}}^{T_{D_e}} \left(\mathrm{AR}_{jk}\right)^2}{D_j - 2}\left[1 + \frac{1}{D_j} + \frac{\left(R_{\mathrm{m}t} - \bar{R}_m\right)^2}{\sum_{k=T_{D_b}}^{T_{D_e}} \left(R_{\mathrm{m}k} - \bar{R}_{\mathrm{m}}\right)^2}\right]$$

Under the null hypothesis, each SAR_{jt} follows a Student's t distribution with $D_j - 2$ degrees of freedom. Total standardized abnormal return (TSAR) across the sample is given as per Eq. (2.4.2.7):

$$\mathrm{TSAR}_{jt} = \sum_{j=1}^{N} \mathrm{SAR}_{jt} \tag{2.4.2.7}$$

The expected value of TSAR_t is zero. The variance of TSAR_t is given as per Eq. (2.4.2.8):

$$Q_t = \sum_{j=1}^{N} \frac{D_j - 2}{D_j - 4} \tag{2.4.2.8}$$

The test statistic for the null hypothesis that $\mathrm{CAAR}_{T_1,T_2} = 0$ is given as per Eq. (2.4.2.9):

$$Z_{T_1T_2} = \frac{1}{\sqrt{N}} \sum_{j=1}^{N} Z^j_{T_1T_2} \tag{2.4.2.9}$$

where,

$$Z^j_{T_1T_2} = \frac{1}{\sqrt{Q^j_{T_1T_2}}} \sum_{t=T_1}^{T_2} \mathrm{SAR}_{jt}$$

and

$$Q^j_{T_1T_2} = (T_2 - T_1 + 1)\frac{D_j - 2}{D_j - 4}$$

under cross-sectional independence of the $Z^j_{T_1,T_2}$ and other assumptions, Z_{T_1,T_2} follows the standard normal distribution under the null hypothesis.

The Patell test statistics for cumulative abnormal return for event window is not adjusted for serial dependence. Mikkelson and Partch (1988) corrected the Patell test for the possible serial correlation of abnormal returns of each security within the window. The serial correlation occurs as all the abnormal returns are functions of the same market model intercept and slope estimators.

The corrected test statistic for the null hypothesis that CAAR = 0 is given as per Eq. (2.4.2.10)

$$Z_{\text{CAAR}} = N^{-\frac{1}{2}} \sum_{j=1}^{N} \frac{\text{CAR}_{T_{1j},T_2}}{\delta_{\text{CAR}_{T_{1j},T_2}}} \tag{2.4.2.10}$$

where

$$\delta^2_{\text{CAR}_{T_1,T_2}} = \frac{\sum_{k=T_{D_b}}^{T_{D_e}} \text{AR}^2_{jk}}{D_j - 2} \left\{ L \left[1 + \frac{L}{D_j} + \frac{\left(\sum_{t=T_1}^{T_2} R_{mt} - L\bar{R}_m \right)^2}{\sum_{k=1}^{D_j} \left(R_{mk} - \bar{R}_m \right)^2} \right] \right\}$$

where L is the length of the event period in trading days, $L = T_2 - T_1 + 1$. D_j is the number of non-missing trading day returns in the D-day interval T_{D_b} through T_{D_e} used to estimate the parameter of the firm j.

Standardized Cross-Sectional Test (SCS)

Standardized cross-sectional test developed by Boehmer et al. (1991) incorporates the information from both estimation and the event period. The event period abnormal returns are first standardized by estimation period standard deviation. The cross-sectional technique is then applied to the standardized abnormal returns. The test is same as Patell test except that there is a final adjustment in the place of analytical variance of the total standardized abnormal return.

For day t in the event period, the test statistics is given in Eq. (2.4.2.11)

$$Z_t = \frac{\text{TSAR}_t}{N^{\frac{1}{2}}(\delta_{\text{SAR}_t})} \tag{2.4.2.11}$$

where

$$\delta^2_{\text{SAR}_t} = \frac{1}{N-1} \sum_{i=1}^{N} \left(\text{SAR}_{it} - \frac{1}{N} \sum_{j=1}^{N} \text{SAR}_{jt} \right)^2$$

Define the standardized cumulative abnormal return for stock j as in Eq. (2.4.2.12)

$$\mathrm{SCAR}_{T_{1j},T_{2j}} = \left(\frac{\mathrm{CAR}_{T_{1j},T_{2j}}}{\delta_{\mathrm{CAR}_{T_{1j},T_{2j}}}}\right) \tag{2.4.2.12}$$

Then the standardized cross-sectional test for the null hypothesis that CAAR = 0 is given in Eq. (2.4.2.13)

$$Z_t = \frac{\sum_{i=1}^{N} \mathrm{SCAR}_{T_{1j},T_{2j}}}{N^{\frac{1}{2}}\left(\delta_{\mathrm{SCAR}_{\left(T_{1j},T_{2j}\right)}}\right)} \tag{2.4.2.13}$$

where

$$\delta^2_{\delta_{\mathrm{SCAR}_{\left(T_{1j},T_{2j}\right)}}} = \frac{1}{N-1}\sum_{i=1}^{N}\left(\mathrm{SCAR}_{T_{1j},T_{2j}} - \frac{1}{N}\sum_{j=1}^{N}\mathrm{SCAR}_{T_{1j},T_{2j}}\right)^2$$

2.4.2.2 Nonparametric Tests

Three nonparametric test statistics, namely, generalized sign test (Cowan 1992), rank test (Corrado 1989) and jackknife test (Giaccotto and Sfiridis 1996) have been conducted to test for the significance of average abnormal returns and cumulative abnormal returns over the event period.

Generalized Sign Test (Gsign Z)

The generalized sign test is a refined version of the sign test by allowing the null hypothesis having positive abnormal residuals to be different from 0.5 (Cowan, 1992). The sign test is a simple binomial test to ascertain whether the frequency of positive abnormal residuals equals 50 % or not. The generalized sign test adjusts for the fraction of positive abnormal returns in the estimation period instead of assuming 0.5. The generalized sign test compares the proportion of positive abnormal returns around an event to the proportion from a period unaffected by the event.

In this way, the generalized sign test takes account of a possible asymmetric return distribution under the null hypothesis. The generalized sign test does not require symmetry of the cross-sectional abnormal return distribution and becomes relatively more powerful as the length of the event window increases. The generalized sign test is correctly specified when the variance of the stock return increases during the event window.

The generalized sign test examines whether the number of stocks with positive cumulative abnormal returns in the event window exceeds the number expected in the absence of abnormal performance or not. The number expected is based on the proportion of positive abnormal returns in the 255 day estimation period as calculated in Eq. (2.4.2.14)

$$\hat{p} = \frac{1}{n}\sum_{j=1}^{n}\frac{1}{255}\sum_{t=1}^{255} S_{jt} \tag{2.4.2.14}$$

where

$$S_{jt} = \begin{Bmatrix} 1 & \text{if } \mathrm{AR}_{jt} > 0 \\ 0 & \text{otherwise} \end{Bmatrix}$$

The following statistic has an approximate unit normal distribution with parameter $\hat{p}$:

$$Z_G = \frac{w - n\hat{p}}{\sqrt{n\hat{p}(1-\hat{p})}} \tag{2.4.2.15}$$

where w is the number of stocks in the event window for which the cumulative abnormal return is positive.

The null and alternative hypotheses of interest are:

The null hypothesis for generalized sign test is that there is no difference between the proportion of positive returns in the event window and its proportion of positive returns in the estimation period.

The alternative hypothesis, for any level of abnormal performance, is that the proportion of positive returns in the event window is different from proportion of positive returns in the estimation period.

Rank Test

The rank test (Corrado 1989) procedure considers the combined estimation period and event period as a single set of returns, and assigns a rank based on return to each daily for each firm. The rank statistic has been denoted as T_R. For day zero, the test statistics is specified in Eq. (2.4.2.16)

$$Z_{\mathrm{rank}} = \left[\left(\frac{1}{N}\sum_{j=1}^{N} k_{j0}\right) - \tilde{k}\right] / S_k \tag{2.4.2.16}$$

where k_{j0} is the rank of security event j's day zero abnormal return in security event j's combined 255 day estimation period and 19-day event period (in the case of

(+2, +20)) time series, k is the expected rank defined below, and sk is the time series standard deviation of the sample mean abnormal return ranks.

Each security event's non-missing returns have been ranked with the lowest rank being one. E_j represents the number of non-missing returns of security j in the event period; if there is no missing return, $E_j = E =$ post – pre + 1 and $D =$ length of estimation window. The mean rank across the combined estimation and event period is

$$\tilde{k} = \frac{D+E+1}{2}$$

The rank test statistic for the null hypothesis relating to the event window (T1, T2) is given in Eq. (2.4.2.17)

$$Z_{\text{rank}} = (T_2 - T_1 + 1)^{\frac{1}{2}} \left\{ \frac{\overline{K_{T_1T_2}} - \widetilde{\mathrm{K}}}{\left[\sum_{t=1}^{D+E} \left(\overline{K}_t - \widetilde{\mathrm{K}}\right)^2 / D+E\right]^{\frac{1}{2}}} \right\} \tag{2.4.2.17}$$

where,

$\overline{K}_{T_1T_2} = \frac{1}{T_2 - T_1 + 1} \sum_{t=T_1}^{T_2} \frac{1}{n} \sum_{j=1}^{n} K_{jt}$ is the average rank across the n securities and $T_2 - T_1 + 1$ days of the event window and $\bar{K}_t = (1/n) \sum_{j=1}^{n} K_{jt}$ is the average rank across n securities on day t of the $D + E$ day combined estimation and event period.

Jackknife Test

The jackknife test by Giaccotto and Sfiridis (1996) computes the standardized abnormal return for each stock j, computed using the event period sample standard deviation. The standardized abnormal return for day t is given in Eq. (2.4.2.18)

$$\hat{\theta} = \frac{\mathrm{AR}_{jt}}{\tilde{\sigma}\mathrm{AR}_{jt}} \tag{2.4.2.18}$$

where

$$\tilde{\sigma}_{\mathrm{AR}_{jt}} = \left\{ \sum_{t=T_b}^{T_e} \frac{\left(\mathrm{AR}_{jt} - \mathrm{AAR}_j^2\right)}{E_j} \right\}^{\frac{1}{2}}$$

and AAR_j is the average abnormal return of stock j during the event period of $E = T_e - T_b + 1$ days. If there is an event-induced variance on day t, then $\tilde{\sigma}_{\mathrm{AR}_{jt}}$ is a biased estimator of $\sigma_{AR_{jt}}$ and $\hat{\theta}$ is a biased statistic. Giaccotto and Sfiridis (1996) propose reducing the bias by jackknifing the $\hat{\theta}$ values.

The first step of the jackknife is to sequentially delete one abnormal return AR_{jt_s} from $\tilde{\sigma}_{AR_{jt}}$ and recompute $\tilde{\sigma}_{AR_{jt}}$, using the new value in turn to recompute $\hat{\theta}$ using Eq. (2.4.2.18). This latter value is named as $\hat{\theta}_{(-d)}$ and pseudo-values are formed using $\hat{\theta}_{(-d)}$ in the next step as per Eq. (2.4.2.19)

$$\theta_{(-d)} = (E_j)\hat{\theta} - (E_j - 1)\hat{\theta}_{(-d)} \tag{2.4.2.19}$$

The jackknife estimator for stock j on day t is the mean of the pseudo-values as per Eq. (2.4.2.20):

$$\theta_{jt} = \frac{1}{E_j}\sum_{t=T_b}^{T_e} \theta(-s) \tag{2.4.2.20}$$

To gain efficiency, the estimates are averaged across the sample of stocks as in Eq. (2.4.2.21).

$$\bar{\theta}_t = \frac{1}{N}\sum_{j=1}^{N} \theta_{jt} \tag{2.4.2.21}$$

Finally, the jackknife test statistic for the sample of stock on day t is given in Eq. (2.4.2.22)

$$t_{\text{jacknife}} = \frac{\bar{\theta}_t}{S_{\text{jacknife}}/\sqrt{N}} \tag{2.4.2.22}$$

where,

$$S_{\text{jacknife}} = \left[\frac{1}{N-1}\sum_{i=1}^{N} \left(\theta_{jt} - \bar{\theta}_t\right)^2\right]^{\frac{1}{2}}$$

To test the significance of the cumulative average abnormal returns over the window from day T_1 through day T_2 define as given in Eq. (2.4.2.23)

$$\hat{\theta}_{T_1T_2} = \frac{\sum_{t=T_1}^{T_2} AR_{jt}}{(T_2 - T_1 + 1)^{\frac{1}{2}}\tilde{\sigma}_{AR_{jt}}} \tag{2.4.2.23}$$

Sequentially delete one abnormal return AR_{jt_s} from equation $\tilde{\sigma}_{AR_{jt}}$ and recompute $\tilde{\sigma}_{AR_{jt}}$, using the new value in turn to recompute $\hat{\theta}$ using Eq. (2.4.2.23). Name this latter value as in Eq. (2.4.2.24)

$$\theta_{(-d),T_1T_2} = (E_j)\hat{\theta}_{T_1T_2} - (\mathrm{E}_j - 1)\hat{\theta}_{(-d),T_1T_2} \tag{2.4.2.24}$$

The jackknife estimator for stock j in window (T_1, T_2) is the mean of the pseudo-values given in Eq. (2.4.2.25)

$$\theta_{j,T_1T_2} = \frac{1}{E_j}\sum_{t=E_b}^{E_e} \theta_{(-d)} \tag{2.4.2.25}$$

The estimates are averaged across the sample of stocks as per Eq. (2.4.2.26):

$$\overline{\theta}_{T_1T_2} = \frac{1}{N}\sum_{j=1}^{N} \theta_{T_1T_2} \tag{2.4.2.26}$$

The jackknife test statistic for CAAR for the sample of stocks in window (T_1, T_2) is given in Eq. (2.4.2.27)

$$t_{\text{jacknife}} = \frac{\overline{\theta}_{T_1T_2}}{S_{\text{jacknife},T_1T_2}/\sqrt{N}} \tag{2.4.2.27}$$

where

$$S_{\text{jacknife},T_1T_2} = \left[\frac{1}{N-1}\sum_{i=1}^{N} \left(\theta_{j,T_1T_2} - \overline{\theta_{T_1T_2}}\right)^2\right]^{\frac{1}{2}}$$

The distribution of $t_{\text{jackknife}}$ under the null hypothesis is approximately normal with mean zero and unit variance.

2.5 Data Description

The present study covers a period of 13 years from January 1, 2003 to December 31, 2015. There were 11,683 mergers and acquisitions announcements during this period.

Table 2.1 provides the year-wise sample distribution of mergers and acquisitions. It has been observed that the maximum announcements happened in the year 2006 (9.9 %) followed by 2010 (9.73 %) and 2007 (9.72 %). However, the maximum number of completed mergers and acquisitions happened in the year 2007 (10.5 %) followed by 2008 (10.2 %) and 2006 (9.1 %). The relevant data in the Table also reveal that a substantial number (37.4 %) of acquisitions announcements are either still pending or withdrawn subsequently.

Table 2.1 Year-wise distribution of mergers and acquisitions announcements, 2003–2015

S. No.		Year													Grand total	Percentage
		2003	2004	2005	2006	2007	2008	2009	2010	2011	2012	2013	2014	2015		
1	Total announcements of M&A	507	570	1003	1157	1136	1131	1058	1137	790	810	705	800	902	11,683	100
2	Rumors, news of acquisitions withdrawn subsequently and pending	198	228	411	501	395	392	398	488	273	303	276	272	321	4365	37.4
3	M&A completed	310	349	602	668	770	748	660	649	517	507	429	528	581	7318	62.6
	Total announcements of M&A	507	570	1003	1157	1136	1131	1058	1137	790	810	705	800	902		
	Percentage of total announcements	4.34	4.88	8.59	9.90	9.72	9.68	9.06	9.73	6.76	6.93	6.03	6.85	7.72		
	Percentage of total M&A completed	4.2	4.8	8.2	9.1	10.5	10.2	9.0	8.9	7.1	6.9	5.9	7.2	7.9		

Source Thomson SDC Platinum Database

Table 2.2 summarizes the stake-wise sample distribution of mergers and acquisitions; it is evident from the Table that almost half (49.2 %) of acquisitions are acquisitions of minor stake as where nearly two-fifth (39.1 %) are acquisitions of complete stake and more than one-tenth (11.7 %) acquisitions are of partial/majority control.

The study has attempted to analyze the primary as well as secondary data related to mergers and acquisitions. The primary data has been collected using a questionnaire sent to Director (Finance) of companies that were engaged in merger and acquisition activities during a specified time period. The companies are located all over India. The questionnaire captures the opinion on the three major aspects, namely, management view on motives for M&A, management views on sources of synergy from M&A and motives of merger of wholly owned subsidiary.

The secondary data has been collected from various sources; these include the Thomson SDC database on mergers and acquisitions, Prowess databases of Centre for Monitoring Indian Economy (CMIE), websites of Bombay Stock Exchange, National Stock Exchange, Securities and Exchange Board of India (SEBI), Electronic Data Information Filing and Retrieval System (EDIFAR) website of SEBI, Economic Times, Business Standard and Moneycontrol. Besides, relevant data were also extracted from the annual reports and websites of the companies. As per the research methodology, these two types of data have been further used for analysis.

2.6 Sample Selection Criteria

To ascertain that the present research study captures the impact of merger and acquisition announcements and provides valid estimates of the measures, certain sample selection criteria (McWilliams and Siegel 1997) have been considered. As per the criteria, certain announcements other than M&A should not have taken place during the chosen event window of 41 days (20 days prior to announcement, 1 day for the announcement and 20 days after the announcement). This ensures that event window is not contaminated with any other type of announcement, thereby capturing the exclusive effect of the M&A announcements. The firm is included in the sample only when criteria as stated below are fulfilled.

The shares are ordinary common shares.

(i) There are no announcements or ex-dates of cash dividend within the event window.
(ii) There are no announcements or ex-dates of stock splits and stock dividends/bonus issues during the event window.
(iii) There is no announcement of capital investment in a new project, credit rating and financial results during the event window.
(iv) As a part of normal course of business, a company receives orders from various customers. It has been observed that if the order is of a substantial

Table 2.2 Stake-wise distribution of mergers and acquisitions announcements, 2003–2015

S. No.		Year													Grand total	Percentage
		2003	2004	2005	2006	2007	2008	2009	2010	2011	2012	2013	2014	2015		
1	Acquisitions of minor stake	186	195	290	314	397	341	352	294	251	228	216	262	275	3601	49.2
2	Acquisitions of major/partial control stake	21	37	69	69	83	91	72	94	84	69	51	66	47	853	11.7
3	Acquisitions of complete stake	103	117	243	285	290	316	236	261	182	210	162	200	259	2864	39.1
	Total	310	349	602	668	770	748	660	649	517	507	429	528	581	7318	100
	Percentage	3.6	4.1	8.5	10.0	10.1	11.0	8.2	9.1	6.4	7.3	5.7	7.0	9.0		

Source Thomson SDC Platinum Database

value and from prestigious customers, some companies provide this information to Bombay Stock Exchange expecting a positive change in the stock prices of the company. To make our sample free from this issue, the companies that made such announcement during the event window are eliminated.

(v) There are no announcement of issuance of new shares by way of domestic or international offering in the form of Public Offer, Preferential Issue, Foreign Currency Convertible Bonds (FCCB), American Depository Receipts (ADR) and Global Depository Receipts (GDR).

(vi) The firms must have daily price information available from the Prowess database, Bombay Stock Exchange or the Capitaline database. The firms having non-synchronous trading have been eliminated from the sample.

(vii) The firms must have financial information available in 'Prowess' database.

Therefore, in this study while the universe for the M&A announcements is 11,683, the sample for short-term abnormal returns (event study) is 800. The unit of analysis for this study is acquiring firms in India.

The long-term performance of only those firms have been analyzed whose data is available before and after M&A. Extreme values have been excluded from the data to deal with the influence of outliers. After analyzing data for outliers, the values beyond three standard deviations have been dropped from the analysis. Due to unavailability of some data and inconsistency in some data collected, the number of firms utilized for long-term analysis of financial performance (ratio analysis) varied: 402 firms for 1 year before and after M&A, 401 firms for 1 year before and 2 year mean after M&A (−1, 2), 391 firms for 1 year before and 3 year mean after M&A (−1, 3), 361 firms for 1 year before and 4 year mean after M&A (−1, 4), 351 firms for 1 year before and 5 year mean after M&A (−1, 5), the mean of 2 years before and after M&A (−2, 2) of 401 firms, the mean of 3 years before and after M&A (−3, 3) of 398 firms, the mean of 4 years before and after M&A (−4, 4) of 387 firms, the mean of 5 years before and after M&A(−5, 5) of 360 firms have been analyzed.

2.7 Concluding Observations

This chapter discusses the objectives of the study, hypotheses to be tested and provides a description of the research methodology being used for the present work. The chapter also delineates the basis of the sample selection criteria. The proposed sample selection criterion differentiates this research work from the earlier works as it attempts to provide the non contaminated (mergers and acquisitions) sample by manually verifying rigorous sample selection criterion. This enables the researchers to determine the true impact of these decisions without contamination of data (McWilliams and Siegel 1997). The mechanics of the event study methodology, hypotheses and various tests used to check the robustness of the results have been explained in the chapter.

References

Boehmer, E., Musumeci, J., & Poulsen, A. (1991). Event study methodology under conditions of event-induced variance. *Journal of Financial Economics, 30*(2), 253–272.

Bowman, R. G. (1983). Understanding and conducting event studies. *Journal of Business Finance & Accounting, 10*(4), 561–584.

Brown, S. J., & Warner, J. B. (1980). Measuring security price performance. *Journal of Financial Economics, 8*(3), 205–258.

Brown, S. J., & Warner, J. B. (1985). Using daily stock returns: the case of event studies. *Journal of Financial Economics, 14*(1), 3–31.

Campbell, C. J., Cowan, A. R., & Salotti, V. (2010). Multi-country event study methods. *Journal of Banking & Finance, 34*(12), 3078–3090.

Corrado, C. (1989). A nonparametric test for abnormal security-price performance in event studies. *Journal of Financial Economics, 23*(2), 385–395.

Corrado, C. J., & Truong, C. (2008). Conducting event studies with Asia-Pacific security market data. *Pacific-Basin Finance Journal, 16*(5), 493–521.

Corrado, C. J., & Zivney, T. L. (1992). The specification and power of the sign test in event study hypothesis tests using daily stock returns. *Journal of Financial and Quantitative Analysis, 27*(3), 465–478.

Cowan, A. R. (1992). Nonparametric event study tests. *Review of Quantitative Finance and Accounting, 1*(4), 343–358.

Cowan, A. R. (2007). Eventus 8.0 Users Guide, Standard Edition 2.1. Ames Lowa: Cowan Research LC.

Duso, T., Gugler, K., & Yurtoglu, B. (2010). Is the event study methodology useful for merger analysis? A comparison of stock market and accounting data. *International Review of Law and Economics, 30*(2), 186–192.

Fama, E. F., Fisher, L., Jensen, M., & Roll, R. (1969). The adjustment of stock prices to new information. *International Economic Review, 10*(1), 1–21.

Giaccotto, C., & Sfiridis, James M. (1996). Hypothesis testing in event studies: The case of variance changes. *Journal of Economics and Business, 48*(4), 349–370.

Henderson, Jr, & Glenn, V. (1990). Problems and solutions in conducting event studies. *Journal of Risk and Insurance, 57*(2), 282–306.

Kang, J. K., & Stulz, R. M. (1996). How different is Japanese corporate finance? An investigation of the information content of new security issues. *Review of Financial Studies, 9*(1), 109–139.

Konchitchki, Y., & O'Leary, Daniel E. (2011). Event study methodologies in information systems research. *International Journal of Accounting Information Systems, 12*(3), 99–115.

Kothari, S. P., & Warner, J. B. (2007). Econometrics of event studies. Chapter 1 in Handbook of Corporate Finance-Empirical Corporate Finance. Elsevier B.V.

MacKinlay, A. C. (1997). Event studies in economics and finance. *Journal of Economic Literature, 35*(1), 13–39.

McWilliams, A., & Siegel, D. (1997). Event studies in management research: theoretical and empirical issues. *Academy of Management Journal, 40*(3), 626–657.

McWilliams, T. P., & McWilliams, Victoria, B. (2000). Another Look at Theoretical and Empirical Issues in Event Studies Methodology. *The Journal of Applied Business Research, 16*(3), 1–11.

Mikkelson, W. H., & Partch, M. M. (1988). Withdrawn security offerings. *Journal of Financial and Quantitative Analysis, 23*(2), 119–134.

Patell, J. M. (1976). Corporate forecasts of earning per share and stock price behavior: empirical tests. *Journal of Accounting Research, 14*(2), 246–276.

Peterson, P. P. (1989). Event studies: A review of issues and methodology. *Quarterly Journal of Business and Economics, 28*(3), 36–66.

Salinger, M. (1992). Standard errors in event studies. *Journal of Financial and Quantitative Analysis, 27*(1), 39–53.

Serra, A. P. (2004). Event study tests—a brief survey. *Gestão. Org-RevistaElectrónica de GestãoOrganizacional, 2*(3), 248–255.

Tabak, D. (2010). Use and misuse of event studies to examine market efficiency. Insight in Economics, NERA Economic Consultancy. http://www.nera.com/content/dam/nera/publications/archive2/PUB_Use_Misuse_of_Event_Studies_0410_final.pdf

Wells, William H. (2004). A beginner's guide to event studies. *Journal of Insurance Regulation, 22*(4), 61–70.

Weston, J. F., Mitchell, M. L., & Mulherin, J. H. (2004). *Takeovers, restructuring, and corporate governance* (4th ed.). New Delhi: Pearson Education.

Chapter 3
Short-Term Performance of Mergers and Acquisitions

Abstract Mergers and acquisitions (M&A) are one of the mechanisms by which firms gain access to new resources; via resource redeployment, they increase revenues and reduce cost. Stock market reactions to mergers and acquisitions announcements could help to predict mergers and acquisitions profitability. The present chapter attempts to examine the market response associated with mergers and acquisitions announcements using event study methodology. The effects of these announcements appear to be a good indicator of future success. The empirical research presents evidence that the market, usually, reacts positively to the M&A announcements that are not contaminated by any other contemporaneous firm-specific announcements. The study finds evidence that shareholders of acquiring Indian companies engaging in mergers and acquisitions experience a statistically significant positive abnormal return on announcement day as well as statistically cumulative abnormal returns over multiday event windows. The empirical findings suggest that mergers and acquisitions result in wealth creation for shareholders of the Indian acquirers.

Keywords Event study · Earn-outs · Cross-border acquisitions · Abnormal returns · Shareholders · Short-run performance · India · Event study · Cumulative abnormal return · Shareholders wealth effect · Domestic acquisitions · Emerging market multinational

3.1 Introduction

Short-term effects are of interests for immediate trading opportunities they create; moreover, stock market reactions to mergers and acquisitions announcements could help to predict mergers and acquisitions profitability. The effects of these announcements appear to be a good indicator of future success. The most statistically reliable evidence on whether mergers and acquisitions create wealth for shareholders is documented by conducting event studies. Various studies use the event methodology to analyze the short-term effects of mergers and acquisitions

N. Rani et al., *Mergers and Acquisitions*, India Studies in Business and Economics, DOI 10.1007/978-981-10-2203-6_3

(Asquith 1983; Dodd 1980; Dennis and McConnell 1986; Pettway and Yamada 1986; Sicherman and Pettway 1987; Schipper and Smith 1983; Schipper and Thompson 1983; Mitchell et al. 2004; Davidson et al. 1989). Based on the announcement-period stock market response, the empirical studies attempt to ascertain whether mergers and acquisitions create value for shareholders of acquiring firms or not. Assuming informational efficiency of the stock market, the acquirer's stock price reaction to an acquisition announcement provides an unbiased estimate of the acquisition's profitability from the perspective of acquiring firm's shareholders.

In view of this, the present chapter attempts to examine the market response associated with mergers and acquisitions announcements using event study methodology. The chapter has been organized into nine sections. Section 3.2 provides a detailed description of sample selection to examine short-term performance of M&A. Section 3.3 is divided into two subsections, namely, Sects. 3.3.1 and 3.3.2. These two subsections present the analysis of short-term performance and frequency distribution of abnormal returns of entire sample. The returns of subsamples based on cross-border M&A and domestic M&A have been discussed in Sect. 3.4. This section is further divided into Sects. 3.4.1 and 3.4.2 depicting the impact of announcement of cross-border M&A and domestic M&A on short-term returns; the cross-border effect has been examined in Sect. 3.4.3. Section 3.5 presents the analysis of short-term performance of subsamples segregated on the basis of control (per cent of stake of target firm) acquired. The section is divided into four subsections. Two subsections, namely, Sects. 3.5.1 and 3.5.2 describe the analysis of short-term performance of subsample segregated on the basis of control. Section 3.5.3 examines the performance of acquisition complete control of target firm to be totally absorbed with the acquirer's operations and Sect. 3.5.4 analyzes the control effect on returns. Section 3.6 looks into the listing effect on returns. The section is further divided into three subsections. Sections 3.6.1 and 3.6.2 describe the impact of acquisitions of unlisted firms and listed firms, respectively. Section 3.6.3 analyzes the listing effect. Section 3.7 describes the payment effect on returns. The section is further divided into three subsections, namely, Sects. 3.7.1, 3.7.2, 3.7.3, and 3.7.4. Sections 3.7.1, 3.7.2, and 3.7.3 present the impact of acquisitions financed with cash payments, stock payments, and combination of cash and stock/earn-outs, respectively. Section 3.7.4 examines the payment effect on returns. Geography effect of cross-border acquisitions on acquirers' return is discussed in Sect. 3.8. The section is divided into three subsections. The two subsections, namely, Sects. 3.8.1 and 3.8.2 discuss the impact of cross-border acquisitions of target firms from developed and emerging markets, respectively. Section 3.8.1 is further divided into two subsections, namely, Sects. 3.8.1.1 and 3.8.1.2; these subsections examine the impact of cross-border acquisitions of target firms from US and non-US developed markets. Section 3.8.3 analyzes the geography effect. The concluding observations are summarized in Sect. 3.9.

3.2 Description of Sample Selection and Sample Characteristics

Table 3.1 contains the details of selection of final sample of mergers and acquisitions for the study. Various filters (presented in Sect. 2.6) have been used to obtain the sample with a clean-period event window. These filters reduce the dataset to 800 announcements comprising 346 cross-border and 454 domestic acquisitions. Yearly distribution of the sample acquisitions as well as distribution according to different features of the transaction has been detailed in Tables 3.2 and 3.3, respectively.

Yearwise distribution of acquisitions presented in Table 3.2 shows that the trend of both type of M&A has shown increasing trend from year 2003 to 2008 with highest number of M&A reported in year 2007 for both. Declining trend is witnessed for M&A activities over the period 2009 onward.

Distribution of acquisitions according to features of transaction in Table 3.3 depicts that cash is the most frequently used form of financing in both the sets of acquisitions.

Contrary to the domestic acquisitions, stock payments are rarely used for cross-border acquisitions. Acquisitions of unlisted target firms are higher in comparison to the acquisitions of listed target firms.

Table 3.1 Sample selection

Total number of announcements	11,683
Less acquisitions excluded	
Rumors, news of acquisitions withdrawn/denial subsequently, and pending acquisitions	4365
Minor acquisitions	3601
Acquisitions of stake by promoters, inter-se transfer among associate companies, and preferential allotments	231
Increase in stake and reannouncements for open offers	127
Acquisition by financial companies	165
Acquisitions by unlisted companies and investor groups	213
Acquisitions of business, assets, divisions, and brands	245
Trading data not available	265
Confounding events	594
More than one type of acquisition in one announcements	145
Multiple acquisitions in one announcement	333
Formation of subsidiary, restructuring, and reorganization	162
Date could not be verified	437
Selected in sample (11,683–10,883)	800

Source Thomson Security Data Corporation (SDC) Platinum M&A database, year 2003–2015

Table 3.2 Yearwise sample distribution of cross-border and domestic M&A, 2003–2015

Year	Cross-border M&A	Domestic M&A	Total
2003	17	22	39
2004	20	27	47
2005	44	48	92
2006	63	86	149
2007	87	91	178
2008	66	86	152
2009	7	18	25
2010	12	21	33
2011	6	15	21
2012	8	13	21
2013	7	8	15
2014	3	10	13
2015	6	9	15
Total	346	454	800

Table 3.3 Sample distribution of cross-border and domestic M&A according to features

Feature	Cross-border M&A	Domestic M&A	Total M&A
Cash-financed M&A	326	319	645
Stock-financed M&A	7	130	137
M&A with mixed financing	13	5	18
M&A of unlisted firms	313	410	713
M&A of listed firms	30	53	83
M&A of Govt/State firms	2	2	4
Acquisitions of partial/majority controlling stake	87	122	209
Acquisitions of complete stake	253	198	451
Target firms to be absorbed with the operations of acquirer	5	135	140

3.3 Analysis of Short-Term Performance of Entire Sample

3.3.1 Impact of Announcement of M&A on Stock Returns

Table 3.4 reports the results of the event study conducted to examine the impact of announcements of merger and acquisition on stock returns. It depicts the average abnormal returns (AAR), corresponding to *t*-statistic values, median abnormal

Table 3.4 Abnormal returns and test statistics on and around M&A announcements (N = 800)

Day	Abnormal return			Positive: negative	Parametric tests				Nonparametric tests		
	Average (%)	Cumulative average (%)	Median (%)		CDA t	CSS t	Patell Z	SCS Z	GSign Z	Rank Z	Jackknife Z
−20	−0.08	−0.08	−0.30	356:434	−0.632	−0.746	−0.214	−0.214	−0.389	−0.166	−0.852
−19	−0.04	−0.12	−0.20	373:427	−0.282	−0.348	0.208	0.205	0.501	0.057	−0.675
−18	−0.14	−0.26	−0.22	367:425	−1.028	−1.251	−1.056	−0.978	0.527	−0.529	−1.392
−17	−0.03	−0.29	−0.23	363:433	−0.248	−0.314	−0.581	−0.594	0.112	−0.09	−1.311
−16	−0.02	−0.31	−0.23	361:437	−0.127	−0.159	−0.097	−0.096	−0.095	0	−0.11
−15	0.21	−0.09	−0.11	381:415	1.62	1.774	1.989[a]	1.837	1.393	1.582	1.415
−14	0.13	0.04	−0.16	370:426	0.997	1.104	1.322	1.218	0.61	0.691	1.019
−13	0.01	0.05	−0.03	389:404	0.073	0.083	0.478	0.46	2.064[a]	0.882	0.38
−12	−0.22	−0.17	−0.28	363:431	−1.65	−1.897	−1.419	−1.314	0.177	−0.708	−1.83
−11	0.00	−0.16	−0.25	367:426	0.035	0.039	0.389	0.384	0.495	−0.133	−0.129
−10	0.03	−0.13	−0.30	352:440	0.256	0.286	0.291	0.274	−0.543	−0.156	−0.356
−9	0.11	−0.02	−0.17	372:424	0.861	0.996	1.634	1.525	0.753	1.065	0.696
−8	−0.06	−0.07	−0.20	361:432	−0.426	−0.504	−0.223	−0.221	0.067	0.017	−0.799
−7	0.26	0.19	−0.14	373:422	1.975[a]	2.206[a]	1.781	1.661	0.857	1.453	1.433
−6	0.28	0.47	−0.05	389:405	2.130[a]	2.397[a]	2.110[a]	1.924	2.030[a]	1.607	2.321[a]
−5	0.16	0.63	−0.04	386:405	1.216	1.409	0.801	0.807	1.917	1.098	0.943
−4	0.16	0.79	−0.18	373:415	1.219	1.404	1.31	1.314	1.088	1.018	0.944
−3	0.31	1.10	0.00	397:396	2.349[a]	2.624[b]	2.658[b]	2.593[b]	2.634[b]	2.412[a]	2.243[a]
−2	0.40	1.50	−0.05	394:402	2.999[b]	3.563[b]	2.973[b]	3.107[b]	2.319[a]	2.587[a]	3.311[b]
−1	0.43	1.93	−0.01	394:400	3.247[b]	3.608[b]	2.779[b]	2.606[b]	2.387[a]	2.293[a]	2.610[b]
0	1.30	3.23	0.72	486:316	9.822[b]	9.061[b]	11.884[b]	8.770[b]	8.408[b]	8.123[b]	9.488[b]
1	0.10	3.33	−0.12	380:415	0.732	0.76	0.744	0.652	1.355	0.481	0.057
2	−0.04	3.29	−0.31	350:444	−0.271	−0.296	−0.322	−0.297	−0.75	−0.617	−0.639
3	−0.11	3.18	−0.35	346:448	−0.828	−0.93	−0.419	−0.392	−1.035	−0.846	−0.982

(continued)

Table 3.4 (continued)

Day	Abnormal return			Positive: negative	Parametric tests				Nonparametric tests		
	Average (%)	Cumulative average (%)	Median (%)		CDA t	CSS t	Patell Z	SCS Z	GSign Z	Rank Z	Jackknife Z
4	−0.13	3.05	−0.37	345:448	−0.984	−1.194	−1.665	−1.745	−1.074	−1.272	−2.183[a]
5	−0.16	2.89	−0.46	333:460	−1.224	−1.373	−1.403	−1.313	−1.93	−1.606	−2.305[a]
6	−0.24	2.65	−0.41	348:448	−1.838	−2.087[a]	−1.819	−1.728	−0.956	−1.302	−2.116[a]
7	−0.10	2.55	−0.33	348:447	−0.762	−0.967	−0.553	−0.566	−0.924	−0.447	−0.804
8	−0.06	2.49	−0.24	367:427	−0.43	−0.504	−0.836	−0.82	0.462	−0.657	−1.048
9	−0.05	2.44	−0.35	346:447	−0.351	−0.39	−0.592	−0.541	−1.003	−0.704	−1.083
10	−0.23	2.21	−0.35	337:453	−1.753	−2.142[a]	−1.675	−1.719	−1.551	−1.17	−2.313[a]
11	−0.16	2.06	−0.28	357:435	−1.171	−1.434	−0.795	−0.817	−0.186	−0.359	−1.309
12	−0.14	1.91	−0.23	355:436	−1.086	−1.269	−1.392	−1.415	−0.297	−0.622	−1.89
13	0.18	2.10	−0.28	361:428	1.395	1.602	1.624	1.563	0.197	0.851	0.988
14	−0.03	2.07	−0.30	346:446	−0.244	−0.277	−0.395	−0.38	−0.971	−0.21	−0.857
15	0.09	2.16	−0.14	375:421	0.681	0.761	0.475	0.445	0.966	0.564	−0.051
16	−0.23	1.93	−0.43	329:465	−1.717	−2.002[a]	−2.312[a]	−2.298[a]	−2.247[a]	−1.79	−2.906[b]
17	−0.14	1.79	−0.29	347:446	−1.054	−1.317	−1.556	−1.647	−0.932	−0.842	−1.811
18	−0.06	1.73	−0.25	358:435	−0.454	−0.525	0.011	0.011	−0.147	−0.103	−0.77
19	−0.05	1.68	−0.22	365:427	−0.343	−0.424	−0.531	−0.557	0.385	0.15	−0.49
20	−0.03	1.66	−0.16	373:420	−0.197	−0.191	−0.807	−0.802	0.923	−0.033	−1.495

[a, b]Denote significance at 5 and 1 %, respectively

returns (MAR), the number of the positive and negative abnormal returns, cumulative average abnormal returns (CAAR) for each day in the event window.

In addition, Figs. 3.1 and 3.2 graphically depict the value of AAR and CAAR corresponding to each day of the event window.

Table 3.4 depicts that during the 20-day preannouncement window, starting from day $t(-7)$ to day $t(-1)$, there is a pattern of positive average abnormal returns. The returns are positive for 13 days while they are negative for only 7 days. Out of these fourteen positive AAR values, two values are statistically significant at 5 % level of significance. The negative returns are not significant on either of the 7 days. The AAR on announcement day (0) is 1.30 %; this is the maximum and highly significant (at 1 % level). In fact, it has been noted that on that day 479 out of the total of 800 companies observed positive AARs. During the post-announcement window from day (0, 1) to day (0, 20), the pattern of positive AARs changes to negative pattern of returns. It has been observed that the AARs are negative for 17 days and positive for only 3 days.

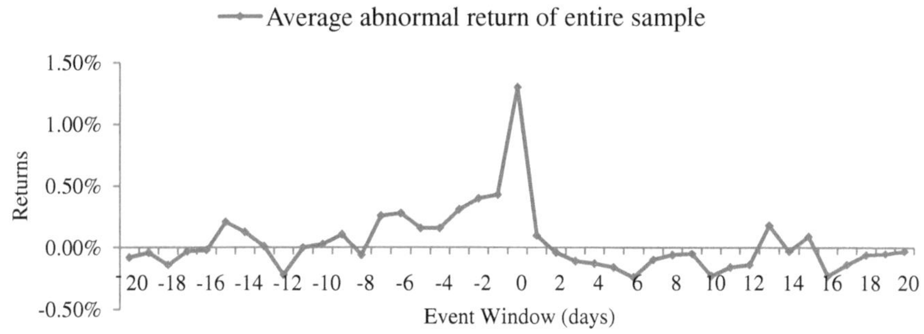

Fig. 3.1 Average abnormal returns during the event window

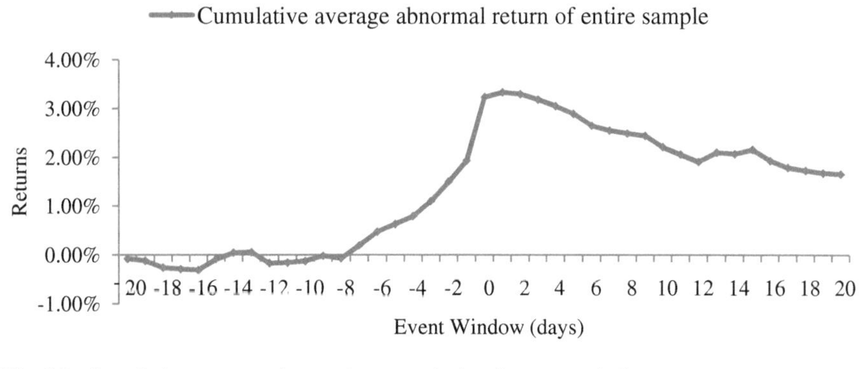

Fig. 3.2 Cumulative average abnormal returns during the event window

The observed results indicate that the investors perceive the announcement of M&A to be beneficial for them. Although the change of positive reaction prior to and on the announcement day to negative reaction after the announcement day indicates that the investors overreacted initially to these announcements but later a correction (to this overreaction by the investors) takes place quickly. Such findings lead to conclusion that the null hypothesis of zero average abnormal returns during the event window is rejected.

Besides, the returns are cumulated over the event window to assess the net magnitude of the overall returns. Table 3.4 also presents the cumulative average abnormal return (CAAR) for each day during the 41-day event window. The results indicate that CAAR starts becoming positive from day *t*(−7); observe positive pattern till day *t*(+21). The CAAR value of day *t*(−7) starts from 0.19 % reaches to a peak of almost 3.33 % on day (0, 1) and settles at 1.66 % on day (0, 20). This decline of 1.67 % value in CAAR value is due to the fact that AAR values are mostly positive till day (0, 1) and are, by and large, negative during the post-announcement window.

Further, cumulative average abnormal return (CAAR) and precision-weighted average abnormal return (PWCAAR) values over various size event windows are calculated; this is to determine the important periods for investment perspective. Table 3.5 reports the average abnormal return, CAAR, PWCAAR, and median abnormal return. Additionally, it presents proportion of positive and negative average abnormal return. Moreover, it provides the results of parametric and nonparametric tests conducted to measure statistical significance for average abnormal returns and cumulative average abnormal returns.

For various preannouncement event windows (−20, −2), (−15, −2), (−10, −2), (−5, −2), and (−5, 0), the CAAR values are 1.49, 1.80, 1.66, 1.02, and 2.75 %, respectively; these values are quite impressive. The CAAR is maximum (2.75 %) and highly significant for window (−5, −0) making it the most important event window. Moreover, the announcement effect of M&A can be measured by evaluating the (−1, 0), (0, +1), and (−5, 0) event windows. The AAR values of 0.43 % on day *t*(−1), 1.30 % on day (0, 0), and 0.10 % on day (0, +1) indicate that an investor can gain a substantial CAAR of 1.82 % if the shares of the issuing company are purchased 1 day prior to the announcement day and sold 1 day after the announcement day. Furthermore, the negative AARs from day (1, 20), results in negative CAAR values of −0.44, −1.11, −1.17, and −1.66 % for (+2, +5), (+2, +10), (+2, +15), and (+2, +20) event windows, respectively. Finally, the CAAR values of 1.82, 2.18, 2.41, 2.36, and 1.65 % for the event windows (−1, +1), (−2, +2), (−5, +5), (−10, +10), and (−20, +20), respectively, signify that the short-term impact of M&A announcements is remarkable for the investors. The results across windows (−1, +1), (−2, +2), (−5, +5), and (−10, +10) are statistically significant at 1 % indicating that the null hypothesis of zero cumulative abnormal returns during these event windows is rejected.

Table 3.5 Cumulative average abnormal returns (CAARs) for M&A announcements across various event windows ($N = 800$)

Event window	Average abnormal return			Positive: negative	Parametric tests				Nonparametric tests		
	Cumulative (%)	Precision-weighted (%)	Median (%)		CDA t	CSS t	Patell Z	SCS Z	GSign Z	Rank Z	Jackknife Z
(−20, −2)	1.49	1.37	0.44	413:387	2.587[b]	2.685[b]	3.271[b]	2.838[b]	3.497[b]	2.910[b]	1.262
(−15, −2)	1.80	1.56	0.69	418:382	3.627[b]	3.902[b]	4.279[b]	3.945[b]	3.852[b]	3.585[b]	2.619[b]
(−10, −2)	1.66	1.31	0.40	414:386	4.165[b]	4.603[b]	4.434[b]	4.199[b]	3.568[b]	3.7[b]	3.088[b]
(−5, −2)	1.02	0.75	0.22	410:390	3.862[b]	4.334[b]	3.831[b]	3.732[b]	3.284[b]	3.557[b]	3.203[b]
(−5, 0)	2.75	2.18	1.52	474:326	8.460[b]	8.811[b]	9.056[b]	8.193[b]	7.831[a, b]	7.156[b]	7.537[b]
(−1, 0)	1.73	1.45	0.90	494:306	9.215[b]	8.785[b]	10.316[b]	8.176[b]	9.186[a, b]	7.365[b]	8.618[b]
(0, 0)	1.30	1.18	0.72	484:316	9.822[b]	9.061[b]	11.838[b]	8.756[b]	8.408[b]	8.123[b]	9.437[b]
(0, +1)	1.39	1.24	0.67	459:341	7.444[b]	6.770[b]	8.865[b]	6.713[b]	6.696[a, b]	6.084[b]	6.636[b]
(0, +5)	0.96	0.84	0.05	403:397	2.947[b]	2.953[b]	3.524[b]	2.967[b]	2.786[b]	1.741	1.754
(+2, +5)	−0.44	−0.39	−0.91	347:453	−1.648	−1.747	−1.923[a]	−1.816	−1.312	−2.170[a]	−2.913[b]
(+2, +10)	−1.11	−0.92	−1.81	313:487	−2.798[b]	−2.870[b]	−3.080[b]	−2.761[b]	−3.650[a, b]	−2.873[b]	−3.530[b]
(+2, +15)	−1.17	−0.98	−2.40	316:482	−2.356[a]	−2.335[a]	−2.599[b]	−2.278[a]	−3.294[a, b]	−2.244[a]	−3.255[b]
(+2, +20)	−1.66	−1.28	−2.55	322:478	−2.877[b]	−2.815[b]	−3.360[b]	−2.283[a]	−2.969[b]	−2.527[a]	−4.039[b]
(−1, +1)	1.82	1.51	1.04	462:338	7.936[b]	7.398[b]	8.838[b]	6.998[b]	6.944[a, b]	6.291[b]	6.960[b]
(−2, +2)	2.18	1.76	1.38	468:332	7.355[b]	7.232[b]	8.004[b]	6.766[b]	7.405[a, b]	5.754[b]	6.380[b]
(−5, +5)	2.41	1.86	1.09	440:360	5.478[b]	5.792[b]	5.754[b]	5.242[b]	5.415[a, b]	4.122[b]	3.914[b]
(−10, +10)	2.36	1.89	0.59	420:380	3.893[b]	3.960[b]	4.227[b]	3.665[b]	3.994[a, b]	2.919[b]	2.288[a]
(−20, +20)	1.65	1.73	0.65	414:386	1.944	1.922	2.397[b]	2.094[a]	3.604[a, b]	1.963	−0.087

[a, b]Denote significance at 5 and 1 %, respectively

The above results lead to the conclusion that although the announcement of M&A induces positive reaction, this reaction is temporary in nature and gets diluted soon. Though the results of the announcement day are statistically significant, the reaction is not very strong; it gets nullified within a short time period. This clearly indicates that the initial overreaction is followed by a strong correction. The results vary for different event windows; in some cases, the null hypothesis is rejected while in others it is not.

The positive returns observed on announcement and during pre-event window are in sync with the expectation of the Indian managers to realize synergies and synergy hypothesis. Perhaps, this may be due to the reason that companies acquire another company for strategic reason so as to exploit economies of scale and scope, and leverage available resources and capabilities, thus creating more scope for value creation. Mergers and acquisitions provide an opportunity to the acquiring company to combine and judiciously utilize intangible resources of both the companies on a broader scale.

These findings are consistent with the conclusions drawn by Rani et al. (2015); Kohli and Mann (2011), Barai and Mohanty (2010), Gubbi et al. (2010), Karels et al. (2011), Zhu and Malhotra (2008), Anand and Singh (2008). However, these findings, in Indian context, are in contrast with the findings of hubris hypothesis (Roll 1986).

The negative abnormal returns in the post-event window are probably supported by the behavioral hypothesis which states that acquiring companies experience negative abnormal returns over post-event windows (Mueller and Yurtoglu 2007; Shleifer and Vishney 2003).

3.3.2 *Frequency Distribution of Abnormal Returns*

To reveal frequency distribution of average abnormal returns on the announcement day, AAR ranges from −11 to +25 % along with standard deviation of 4.05 (Fig. 3.3).

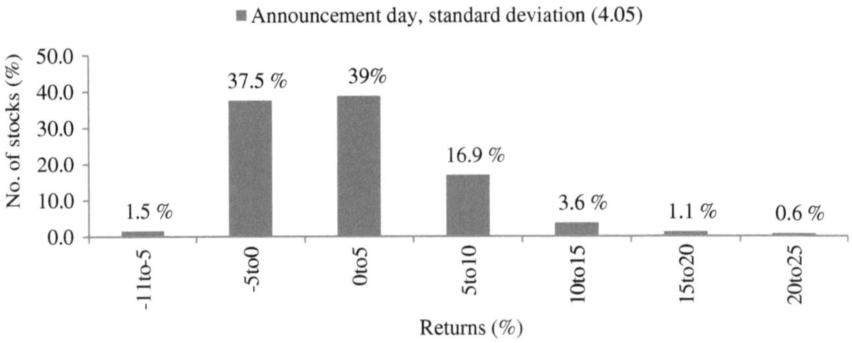

Fig. 3.3 Frequency distribution of average abnormal returns on the announcement day

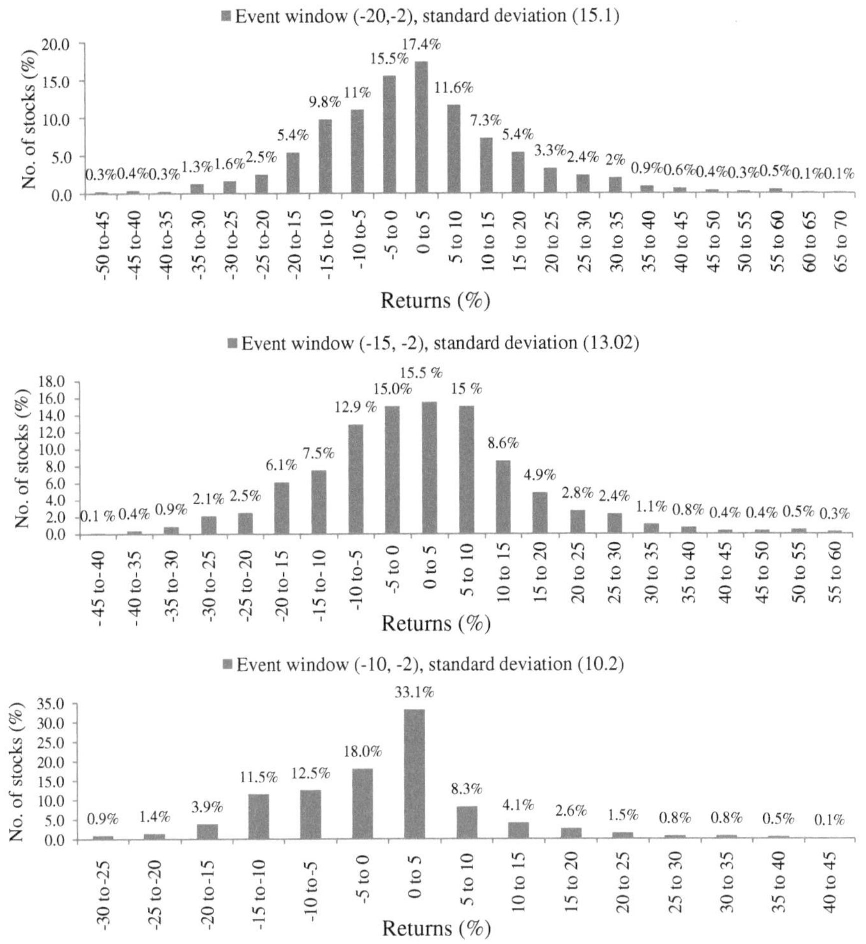

Fig. 3.4 Frequency distribution of CAAR on pre-event windowsEvent window [(−20, +2), (−15, −2), and (−10, −2)]

Shareholders of more than 60.6 % stocks experience positive abnormal return on the announcement day.

Figure 3.4 reveals the frequency distribution of CAAR over pre-event windows (−20, −2), (−15, −2), and (−10, −2). The range of CAAR vary from −50 to 70 %, −45 to 60 %, and −30 to 45 % over pre-event windows (−20, −2), (−15, −2), and (−10, −2), respectively. The standard deviation of CAAR is 15.1, 13.02, and 10.2

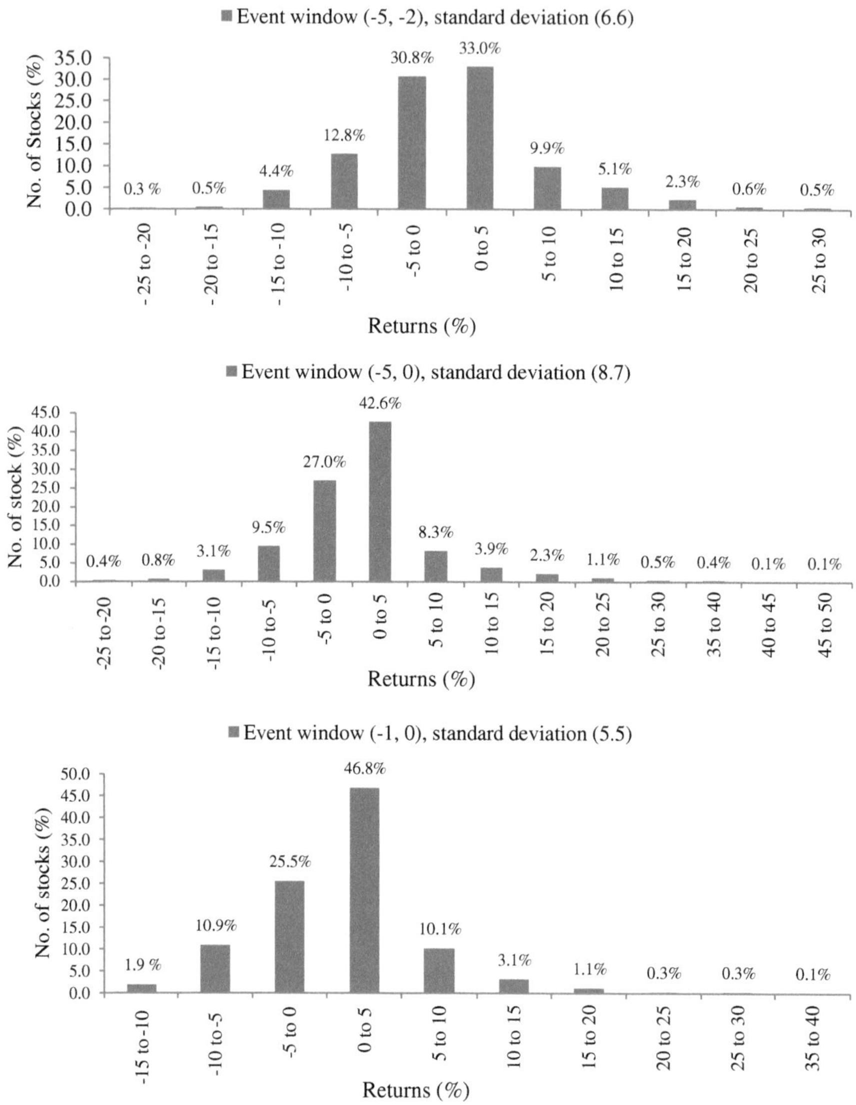

Fig. 3.5 Frequency distribution of CAAR on pre-event windows [(−5, +2), (−5, 0), and (−1, 0)]

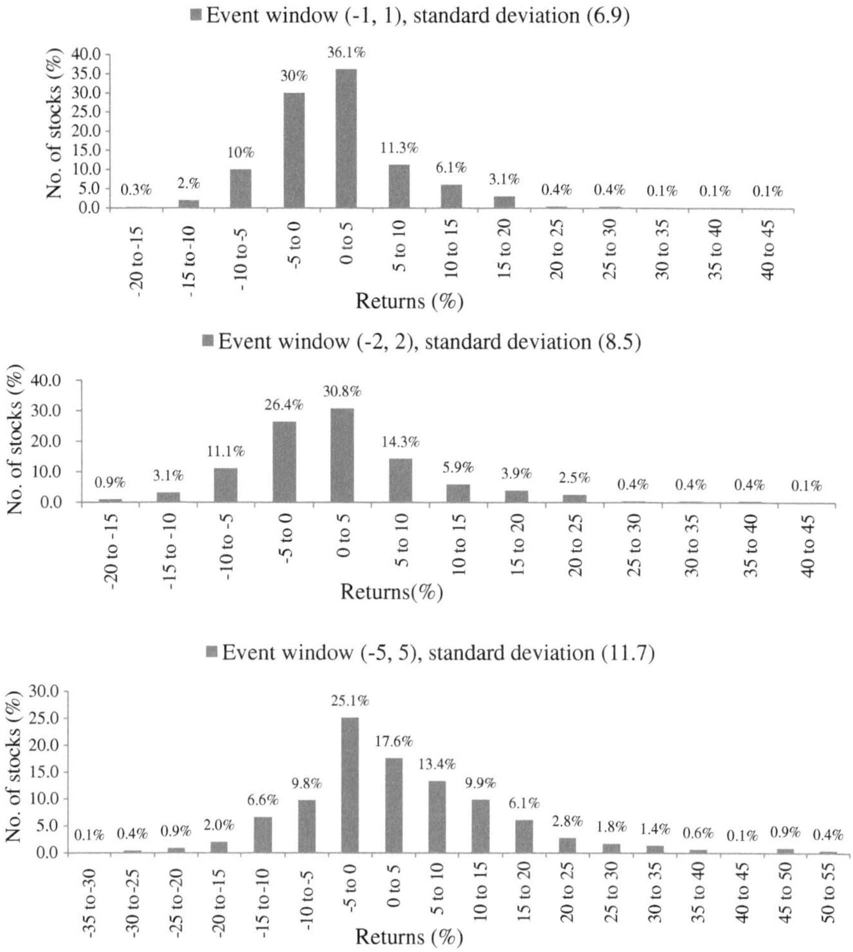

Fig. 3.6 Frequency distribution of CAAR on event windows [(−1, +1), (−2, +2), and (−5, +5)]

over pre-event windows (−20, −2), (−15, −2), and (−10, −2), respectively. The findings also indicate the problem of high variance in abnormal returns for event windows as well as pre-event window and post-event window. The high variation in cumulative abnormal returns for various event windows is also evident from the range and standard deviation of CAAR for various event windows as depicted in Figs. 3.4, 3.5, 3.6, 3.7, 3.8, and 3.9.

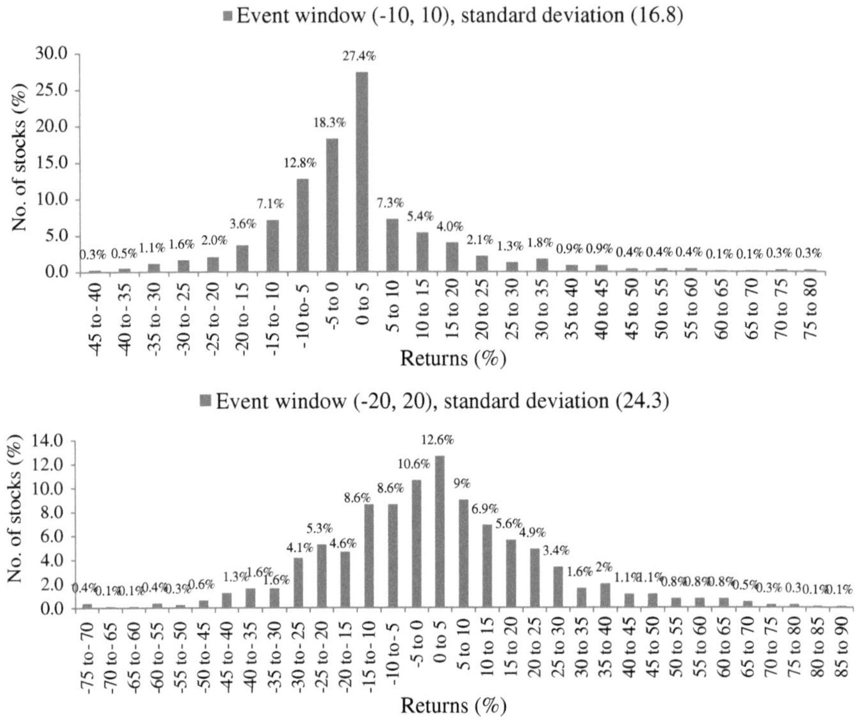

Fig. 3.7 Frequency distribution of CAAR on event windows [(−10, +10) and (−20, +20)]

The standard deviation of CAAR is 6.9, 8.5, 11.7, 16.8, and 24.3 for event widows of 3 days (−1, 1), 5 days (−2, +2), 11 days (−5, +5), 21 days (−10, +10), and 41 days (−20, +20), respectively. It may be noted from these results that variance in CAAR increases with the increase in event duration (Fig. 3.7).

Frequency distribution of CAAR reveals that the problem of high variance is observed during the longer pre-event, post-event, and event windows.

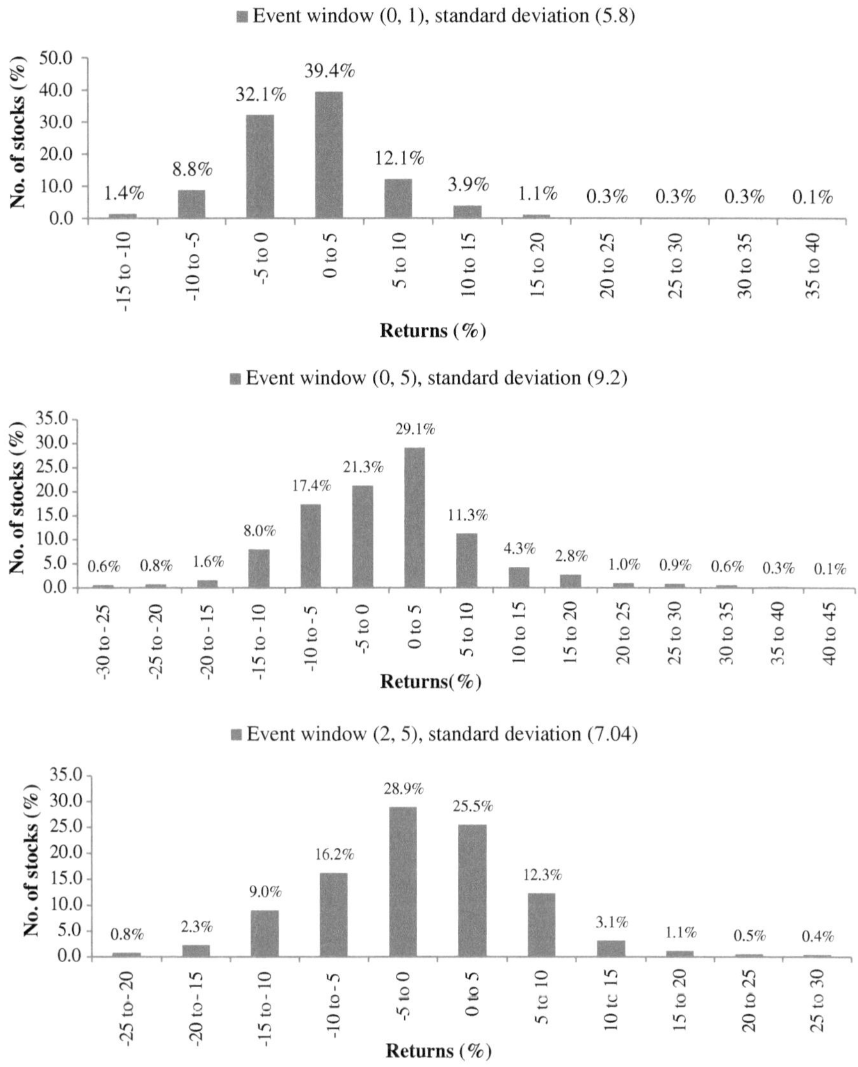

Fig. 3.8 Frequency distribution of CAAR on post-event windows [(0, +1), (0, +5), and (+2, +5)]

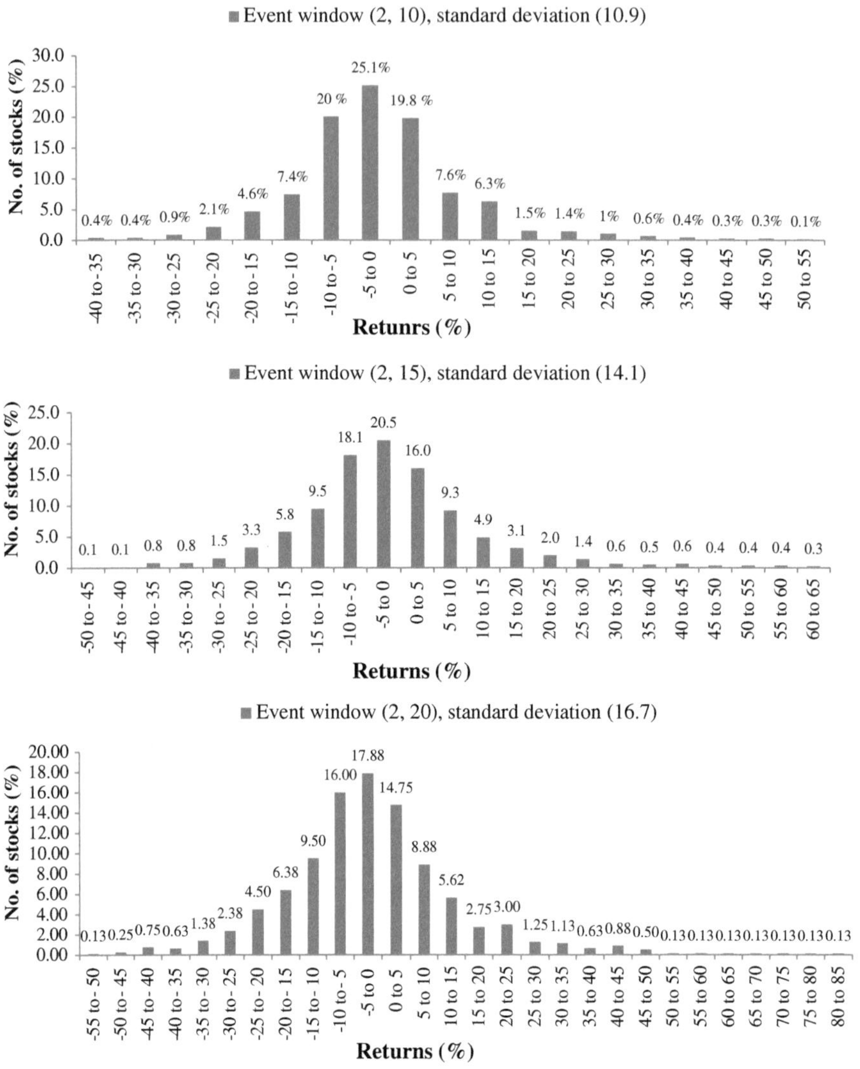

Fig. 3.9 Frequency distribution of CAAR on post-event windows [(+2, +10), (+2, +15), and (+2, +20)]

3.4 Analysis of Cross-Border Effect

Cross-border acquisitions are an important corporate strategy that enables firms to extend their current businesses to new markets, leverage their current capabilities, and diversify into related markets. In addition, cross-border acquisitions can be an important mechanism for corporate governance convergence (Wang and Xie 2009).

Zhu et al. (2011) suggest that two major motivations, namely, strategic market entry hypothesis and the market for corporate control hypothesis compete for cross-border acquisitions. Blonigen (1997) argues that cross-border acquisitions are motivated by a desire to acquire a complementary asset to gain access to new ideas and technology, thus, resulting into research and development synergies. Firm specific advantages would arise from the capacity to acquire, or the efficient coordination of, the complementary assets owned by the cross-border target firms. Gubbi et al. (2010) also opine that Indian firms use cross-border acquisitions for strategic assets-seeking in order to facilitate strategic and organizational transformation of the firms.

Domestic partial acquisitions and cross-border partial acquisitions are motivated by different hypotheses. Cross-border acquisitions, thus, give acquiring firms access to key strategic resources that may not be available in their domestic market, and thereby, enhance their capabilities to be competitive. Cross-border acquisitions are, thus, likely to add more value in comparison with domestic acquisitions, suggesting there are real benefits from international investment. Empirical work documents variation in returns for acquirers in domestic and cross-border acquisitions (Cakici et al. 1996; Aw and Chatterjee 2004; Conn et al. 2005; Lowinski et al. 2004; Campa and Hernando 2004; Goergen and Renneboog 2004; Moeller and Schlingemann 2005; Francis et al. 2008; Rani et al. 2012, 2015, 2015a).

3.4.1 Analysis of Short-Term Performance of Cross-Border M&A

Table 3.6 reports the abnormal returns to the acquirer's shareholders on the announcement day and multiperiod event windows for cross-border M&A. It contains average abnormal return, cumulative average abnormal return, precision-weighted average abnormal return, and median abnormal return. Additionally, it presents proportion of positive and negative average abnormal returns. Moreover, it provides the results of parametric and nonparametric tests conducted to measure statistical significance for average abnormal returns and cumulative average abnormal returns.

It is evident from the Table that acquirer's shareholders earn average abnormal return of 1.69 % on the announcement day for cross-border M&A; the value is significant at 1 %. The proportion of stocks having positive return on the announcement day is more than 67 %. The proportion of stocks having positive return is significant at 1 %. Moreover, the value of precision-weighted average abnormal returns and median abnormal returns are 1.50 and 1.10 %, respectively.

Relevant data contained in Table 3.6 also shows that the acquirer's shareholders experience CAAR of 2.99 % during event windows of 11 days (−5, +5) and 2.78 % of 5 days (−2, +2). CAAR during pre-event window of 19 days (−20, −2) is 1.99 %. CAAR during the short-event window of 2 days (−1, 0) and 3 days (−1, +1) is 2.07 and 2.32 %, respectively. The maximum CAAR of almost 3 % (3.06 %)

Table 3.6 Abnormal returns to the shareholders of acquiring firms (cross-border M&A, N = 346) on the announcement day and during multidays event windows, 2003–2015

Event window	Average abnormal return			Positive: negative	Parametric tests				Nonparametric tests		
	Cumulative (%)	Precision-weighted (%)	Median (%)		CDA t	CSS t	Patell Z	SCS Z	GSign Z	Rank Z	Jackknife Z
(−20, −2)	1.99	2.02	1.13	186:160	2.487[a]	2.583[b]	2.962[b]	3.449[b]	3.165[b]	2.685[b]	2.002[a]
(−15, −2)	1.74	1.73	0.89	185:161	2.534[a]	2.862[b]	3.285[b]	3.433[b]	3.057[b]	2.712[b]	2.349[a]
(−10, −2)	1.35	1.22	−0.04	171:175	2.441[a]	2.971[b]	2.967[b]	2.981[b]	1.545	2.215[a]	2.154[a]
(−5, −2)	1.00	0.78	0.41	181:165	2.709[b]	3.239[b]	2.947[b]	2.853[b]	2.625[b]	2.842[b]	2.745[b]
(−5, 0)	3.06	2.53	1.95	220:126	6.801[b]	7.502[b]	6.894[b]	7.647[b]	6.837[b]	6.342[b]	7.013[b]
(−1, 0)	2.07	1.77	1.12	234:112	7.949[b]	7.602[b]	6.736[b]	9.273[b]	8.349[b]	6.966[b]	7.472[b]
(0, 0)	1.69	1.50	1.10	232:114	9.210[b]	7.972[b]	7.413[b]	11.158[b]	8.133[b]	7.889[b]	8.307[b]
(0, +1)	1.95	1.69	1.26	221:125	7.491[b]	6.814[b]	6.189[b]	8.845[b]	6.945[b]	6.302[b]	6.609[b]
(0, +5)	1.62	1.39	0.69	188:158	3.591[b]	3.739[b]	3.513[b]	4.218[b]	3.381[b]	2.737[b]	3.097[b]
(+2, +5)	−0.33	−0.29	−0.59	157:189	−0.899	−0.978	−0.976	−1.089	0.033	−1.104	−1.645
(+2, +10)	−1.44	−1.15	−1.46	134:212	−2.604[b]	−2.940[b]	−2.572[a]	−2.835[b]	−2.451[a]	−2.759[b]	−3.468[b]
(+2, +15)	−1.54	−1.15	−1.83	139:207	−2.237[a]	−2.525[a]	−2.074[a]	−2.268[a]	−1.911	−2.069[a]	−2.859[b]
(+2, +20)	−2.45	−1.93	−2.65	142:204	−3.054[b]	−3.363[b]	−2.985[b]	−3.254[b]	−1.587	−2.780[b]	−3.789[b]
(−1, +1)	2.32	1.95	1.57	222:124	7.289[b]	7.119[b]	6.147[b]	8.356[b]	7.053[b]	6.279[b]	6.640[b]
(−2, +2)	2.78	2.29	1.73	223:123	6.773[b]	7.113[b]	6.174[b]	7.585[b]	7.161[b]	5.981[b]	6.549[b]
(−5, +5)	2.99	2.42	2.26	209:137	4.898[b]	5.560[b]	4.962[b]	5.406[b]	5.649[b]	4.327[b]	4.641[b]
(−10, +10)	2.23	1.99	1.52	193:153	2.648[b]	3.114[b]	2.966[b]	3.216[b]	3.921[b]	2.017[a]	2.024[a]
(−20, +20)	1.87	2.00	1.16	192:154	1.586	1.748	2.042[a]	2.380[b]	3.813[b]	1.633	0.754

[a], [b]Denote significance at 5 and 1 %, respectively

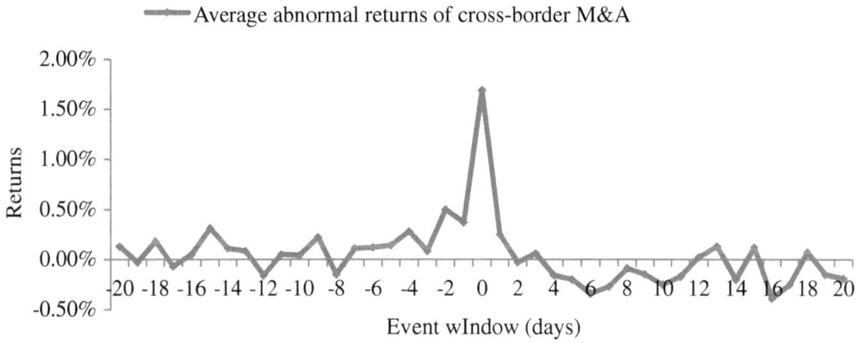

Fig. 3.10 AAR of cross-border M&A over event window (−20, +20)

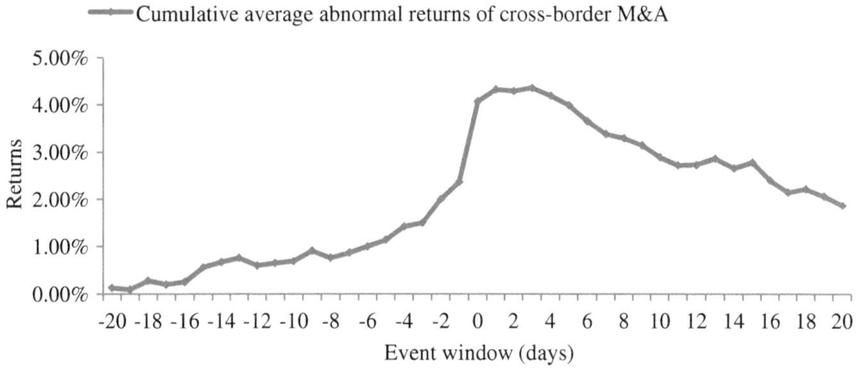

Fig. 3.11 CAAR of cross-border M&A over event window (−20, +20)

is observed during pre-event window of 6 days (−5, 0). All these results are significant at 1 %.

One notable finding is that the positive CAAR along with impressive precision-weighted CAAR sustain for longer event windows of 21 days (−10, +10) and 41 days (−20, +20). Moreover, these results are significant at 1 %.

But acquisitions reduce wealth significantly during post-event window of 19 days (+2, +20). The negative abnormal returns are 2.45 % (significant at 1 %) for the post-event window (+2, +20) (Figs. 3.10 and 3.11).

3.4.2 Analysis of Short-Term Performance of Domestic M&A

Table 3.7 presents the results of the event study conducted to assess the market reaction to announcements of domestic M&A. This table shows the average

Table 3.7 Abnormal returns to the shareholders of acquiring firms (domestic M&A, $N = 454$) on the announcement day and during multidays event windows, 2003–2015

Event window	Average abnormal return			Positive: negative	Parametric tests				Nonparametric tests		
	Cumulative (%)	Precision-weighted (%)	Median (%)		CDA t	CSS t	Patell Z	SCS Z	GSign Z	Rank Z	Jackknife Z
(−20, −2)	1.11	0.77	−0.11	227:227	1.458	1.418	1.331	1.121	1.878	1.912	0.096
(−15, −2)	1.84	1.39	0.54	233:221	2.808[b]	2.759[b]	2.682[b]	2.386[a]	2.444[a]	2.929[b]	1.55
(−10, −2)	1.89	1.39	0.80	242:211	3.600[b]	3.558[b]	3.283[b]	2.990[b]	3.388[b]	3.579[b]	2.264[a]
(−5, −2)	1.04	0.73	0.09	228:225	2.981[b]	3.034[b]	2.594[b]	2.403[a]	2.067[a]	2.763[b]	1.961[a]
(−5, 0)	2.50	1.85	1.05	253:200	5.836[b]	5.531[b]	5.344[b]	4.841[b]	4.426[b]	4.962[b]	4.222[b]
(−1, 0)	1.47	1.15	0.66	257:194	5.918[b]	5.285[b]	5.591[b]	4.832[b]	4.900[b]	4.687[b]	4.950[b]
(0, 0)	1.00	0.87	0.34	247:202	5.707[b]	5.163[b]	5.957[b]	4.944[b]	4.049[b]	4.971[b]	5.239[b]
(0, +1)	0.97	0.82	0.26	235:216	3.920[b]	3.356[b]	4.038[b]	3.306[b]	2.820[b]	3.347[b]	3.051[b]
(0, +5)	0.45	0.32	−0.33	214:239	1.054	0.972	0.994	0.794	0.746	0.063	−0.176
(+2, +5)	−0.52	−0.49	−1.25	186:264	−1.479	−1.448	−1.603	−1.565	−1.773	−2.290[a]	−2.410[a]
(+2, +10)	−0.86	−0.71	−2.12	177:275	−1.644	−1.509	−1.612	−1.439	−2.705[b]	−1.789	−1.946
(+2, +15)	−0.88	−0.81	−2.81	177:275	−1.35	−1.179	−1.469	−1.252	−2.705[b]	−1.48	−2.031[a]
(+2, +20)	−1.06	−0.67	−2.55	179:274	−1.391	−1.207	−1.618	−0.745	−2.556[a]	−1.234	−2.367[a]
(−1, +1)	1.44	1.11	0.41	238:214	4.742[b]	4.052[b]	4.433[b]	3.769[b]	3.057[b]	3.690[b]	3.506[b]
(−2, +2)	1.72	1.26	0.70	244:209	4.383[b]	3.916[b]	4.001[b]	3.484[b]	3.577[b]	3.148[b]	3.038[b]
(−5, +5)	1.97	1.33	0.22	230:223	3.383[b]	3.237[b]	2.917[b]	2.610[b]	2.256[a]	2.212[a]	1.514
(−10, +10)	2.47	1.79	−0.15	226:227	3.071[b]	2.739[b]	2.804[b]	2.311[a]	1.878	2.567[a]	1.424
(−20, +20)	1.48	1.47	−0.61	222:232	1.323	1.164	1.103	1.127	1.456	1.46	−0.601

[a, b]Denote significance at 5 and 1 %, respectively

abnormal returns, cumulative average abnormal returns, precision-weighted average abnormal returns, median abnormal returns, and the number of the positive versus negative abnormal returns. Additionally, it provides the results of parametric and nonparametric tests conducted to measure statistical significance for average abnormal returns and cumulative average abnormal returns. Moreover, Figs. 3.12 and 3.13 graphically depict the values of AAR and CAAR of domestic M&A during the 41-day event window, respectively.

It is evident from the Table that acquirer shareholders earn average abnormal return of 1 % on the announcement day for domestic M&A; the value is significant at 1 %. The proportion of stocks having positive return on the announcement day is more than 54 %. The proportion of stocks having positive return is significant at 1 %. Moreover, the value of precision-weighted average abnormal returns and median abnormal returns are 0.87 and 0.34 %, respectively. CAAR of domestic

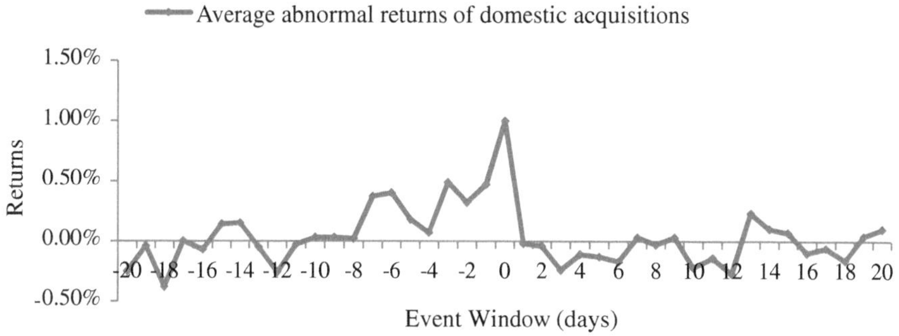

Fig. 3.12 AAR of domestic M&A over event window (−20, +20)

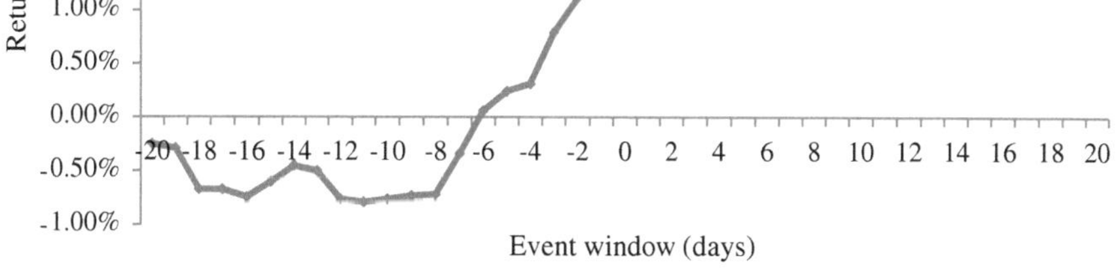

Fig. 3.13 CAAR of domestic M&A over event window (−20, +20)

acquisitions during pre-event window of 19 days (−20, −2) is positive (1.11 %) and remains positive till *t*(+5).

Relevant data contained in Table 3.7 also shows that the acquirer's shareholders experience CAAR of 1.72 % of 5 days (−2, +2) and 1.97 % during event windows of 11 days (−5, +5). CAAR during the short-event window of 2 days (−1, 0) and 3 days (−1, +1) is 1.47 and 1.44 %, respectively. The maximum CAAR of almost 3 % (2.5 %) is observed during pre-event window of 6 days (−5, 0). All these results are significant at 1 %.

In the case of domestic M&A also, the market, in general, reacts positively to M&A announcements. Later, a mild correction in market price of the acquiring company takes place as almost all the CAAR values during the post-event window of 7, 13, and 19 days are negative; although not significant. From the above findings, it is reasonable to conclude that the null hypothesis of zero abnormal returns on the announcement day has been rejected; though during the event window, the null hypothesis of zero abnormal returns is rejected for most of the windows.

Lowinski et al. (2004), Campa and Hernando (2004), Conn et al. (2005), Moeller and Schlingemann (2005) have also observed positive cumulative average abnormal return for domestic acquisitions.

3.4.3 Cross-Border Effect

Independent t-test has been conducted to measure the difference between mean CAR of cross-border acquisition and mean CAR of domestic acquisitions; the results are tabulated in Table 3.8.

It is apparent that mean difference is positive during eleven windows. However, the difference is significant (*p*-value = 0.02 < 0.05) only for the announcement day and event window (0, +1). These results provide some support to the hypothesis that returns to acquirer's shareholders of the cross-border acquisitions is higher than the domestic acquisitions. Further, Figs. 3.14 and 3.15 exhibit the trend of average abnormal returns and cumulative average abnormal returns of cross-border and domestic acquisitions for (−20, +20) including both pre-event window and post-event window.

It is clear from the graph (Fig. 3.15) of CAAR that cross-border acquisitions enhance wealth over entire 41 days (−20, +20) period, whereas domestic acquisitions generate lower wealth and start reducing in comparison to cross-border acquisitions.

The positive returns observed on announcement and during pre-event window for cross-border acquisitions and domestic acquisitions are in sync with the expectation of the Indian managers to realize synergies and synergy hypothesis. The plausible reason is that companies acquire another company for strategic reason with intent to exploit economies of scale and scope, and leverage available resources and capabilities, thus creating more scope for value creation. Campa and Hernando (2004),

Table 3.8 Independent samples t-test for difference of mean CAR (cross-border M&A, domestic M&A)

Event window	Mean CAR (%) of cross-border M&A (*N* = 346)	Mean CAR (%) of domestic M&A (*N* = 454)	Mean difference (%)	*t*-value	Significance value
(−20, −2)	1.99	1.11	0.88	0.8	0.43
(−15, −2)	1.74	1.84	−0.10	−0.11	0.91
(−10, −2)	1.35	1.89	−0.54	−0.78	0.43
(−5, −2)	1.00	1.04	−0.04	−0.11	0.92
(−5, 0)	3.06	2.50	0.56	0.91	0.36
(−1, 0)	2.07	1.47	0.60	1.54	0.12
(0, 0)	1.69	1.00	0.69	2.41[a]	0.02
(0, +1)	1.95	0.97	0.98	2.4[a]	0.02
(0, +5)	1.62	0.45	1.17	1.83	0.07
(+2, +5)	−0.33	−0.52	0.19	0.38	0.70
(+2, +10)	−1.44	−0.86	−0.58	−0.76	0.45
(+2, +15)	−1.54	−0.88	−0.66	−0.68	0.50
(+2, +20)	−2.45	−1.06	−1.39	−1.21	0.23
(−1, +1)	2.32	1.44	0.88	1.83	0.07
(−2, +2)	2.78	1.72	1.06	1.81	0.07
(−5, +5)	2.99	1.97	1.02	1.26	0.21
(−10, +10)	2.23	2.47	−0.24	−0.21	0.84
(−20, +20)	1.87	1.48	0.39	0.23	0.82

[a], [b]Denote significance at 5 and 1 %, respectively

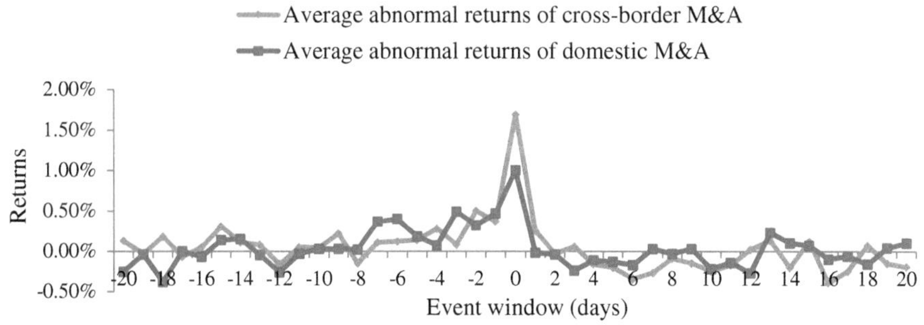

Fig. 3.14 AAR of cross-border and domestic M&A over event window (−20, +20)

Lowinski et al. (2004), Conn et al. (2005), Markides and Ittner (1994), Markides and Oyon (1998), Eun et al. (1996) have also observed wealth gains for shareholders of acquiring firms of cross-border acquisitions. Cakici et al. (1996), Goergen and Renneboog (2004) have observed significant positive performance for US acquirer firms. Eun et al. (1996), Kang (1993) observe higher gains for Japanese acquirers

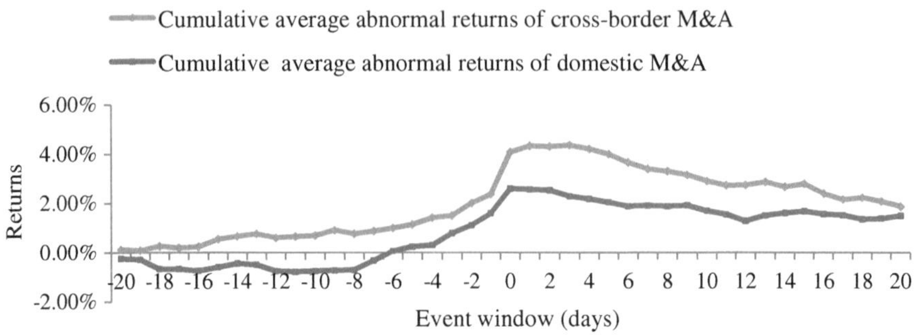

Fig. 3.15 CAAR of cross-border and domestic M&A over event window (−20, +20)

targeting acquisitions in US compared to domestic acquirers there. Kose et al. (2010), Zhu (2011), Zhu et al. (2011) document positive returns for the acquirer of cross-border acquisitions.

Further, Indian firms use cross-border acquisitions with intent to have strategic assets in order to facilitate strategic and organizational transformation of the firms. Moreover, access to developed markets for products, resources, and capabilities enable Indian firms to leapfrog to the global league and thus create greater value than what could be achieved by acquiring a domestic firm (Gubbi et al. 2010). Further, over the years, Indian firms, especially, in technology intensive industries like pharmaceutical sector and information technology had established their base as low cost product or service providers on mass scale. The cross-border acquisitions complement the acquiring firms with necessary technological, management expertise and international customer base to compete in overseas markets.

3.5 Analysis of Control Effect

Empirical evidence on benefits of acquisition of controlling stake has been suggested by Beamish and Banks (1987), Chari et al. (2010), Geringer and Hebert (1989), Nenova (2003), Dyck and Zingales (2004). These studies document that the level of control is one of the factors in determining the success of acquisition.

Chen (2008) argues that complete acquisitions are driven mostly by procurements of capabilities, whereas partial/majority control acquisitions are motivated by other strategic considerations. Acquirers can procure competitive assets from indigenous firms, such as advanced technologies and reputed brands (Anand and Delios 2002; Chen and Zeng 2004). Acquirers can use acquisitions to achieve other strategic goals, such as speedy entry into rapidly growing industries, or consolidation of market power in concentrated sectors (Caves and Mehra 1986; Hennart and Park 1993). The strategic considerations for partial/majority control acquisitions are market power consolidation in concentrated sectors, capacity control in mature industries, and speedy entry into rapidly growing markets.

Caves (1996) documents that only with dominant positions can companies fully reflect their economic rationale, strategic ability, and resource commitment during the course of entry and operations in cross-border acquisitions. Chari et al. (2010) have examined the impact of acquiring majority control of the target firm and the acquiring firm's stock returns in the cross-border acquisitions in emerging markets. The study observes that the acquisition of majority control in the emerging markets is associated with significant increases in the stock returns of the acquiring firm as well as of target firm. This finding confirms that acquiring majority control is beneficial to the shareholders both of acquiring and target firms.

Acquirers obtain complete access to the resources of the target firm through 100 % acquisitions. Access to complementary resources is a major motive for acquisitions (Harrison et al. 2001) as it provides acquirers with otherwise hard to obtain organizationally embedded resources. If, the acquirer has full control over the target, it can reorganize the latter according to its needs (Kiymaz 2004). If the entire company is not acquired, other shareholders can hinder actions by the acquirer (Butz 1994). Further, the integration of the company acquired across border might be hindered by cultural differences. In addition, cultural differences might also lead to communication and coordination problems. Therefore, acquirers choose to acquire full equity of the targets deliberately to avoid the hassles of managing co-ownership.

A partial acquisition represents a unique form of corporate restructuring because it alters the ownership structure of target firm, and, therefore, alters the form of control over the target's management. The proportion of the partial target that is owned by other shareholders is reduced by the increase in ownership by the partial acquirer.

Partial acquisitions provide access to resources held by the target firm, including capabilities embedded in business practices. Moreover, partial acquisitions often initiate a dynamic process leading to full control over local firms (Meyer and Tran 2006), thus giving access to a wider range of resources. Further, partial ownership also serves other motives such as minimizing capital commitments or reducing investment risks, acquirers can choose to acquire only a partial stake in domestic firms and then use speedy entry. This implies that acquisitions can be made to control capacity expansions in mature industries.

3.5.1 Analysis of Short-Term Performance of Acquisitions of Partial/Majority Control

Table 3.9 reveals the abnormal returns for the acquisitions of partial/majority control of target firm. Average abnormal return is 1.7 % on the announcement day. Precision-weighted average abnormal return and median abnormal return are 1.57 and 0.79 %, respectively; the results are significant at 1 %.

Table 3.9 Abnormal returns to the shareholders of acquiring firms (partial/majority control acquisitions $N = 209$) on the announcement day and during multidays event windows, 2003–2015

Event window	Average abnormal return			Positive: negative	Parametric tests				Nonparametric tests		
	Cumulative (%)	Precision-weighted (%)	Median (%)		CDA t	CSS t	Patell Z	SCS Z	GSign Z	Rank Z	Jackknife Z
(−20, −2)	0.36	0.27	−0.21	104:105	0.325	0.362	0.347	0.319	1.403	1.094	0.175
(−15, −2)	0.88	0.72	0.69	109:100	0.929	0.995	0.967	0.962	2.098[a]	1.334	0.72
(−10, −2)	1.63	1.35	0.33	108:101	2.146[a]	2.444[a]	2.215[a]	2.399[a]	1.959	2.751[b]	2.316[a]
(−5, −2)	0.72	0.60	0.09	106:103	1.421	1.781	1.424	1.693	1.681	2.082[a]	1.752
(−5, 0)	2.76	2.29	0.77	114:95	4.450[b]	4.531[b]	4.663[b]	4.287[b]	2.794[b]	4.470[b]	4.264[b]
(−1, 0)	2.04	1.73	0.91	128:81	5.698[b]	4.822[b]	6.139[b]	4.856[b]	4.740[b]	4.797[b]	4.795[b]
(0, 0)	1.70	1.57	0.79	131:78	6.740[b]	5.617[b]	7.877[b]	5.691[b]	5.158[b]	6.002[b]	5.495[b]
(0, +1)	1.73	1.55	0.92	128:81	4.834[b]	4.045[b]	5.469[b]	4.147[b]	4.740[b]	4.284[b]	3.994[b]
(0, +5)	1.15	0.99	0.40	107:102	1.856	1.857	2.021[a]	1.75	1.82	1.367	1.468
(+2, +5)	−0.58	−0.56	−0.82	90:119	−1.145	−1.207	−1.392	−1.208	−0.544	−1.355	−1.223
(+2, +10)	−0.80	−0.71	−1.36	86:123	−1.054	−1.1	−1.173	−1.028	−1.1	−0.547	−1.332
(+2, +15)	−0.50	−0.77	−1.64	93:116	−0.526	−0.531	−1.012	−0.918	−0.127	−0.053	−1.268
(+2, +20)	−1.81	−1.91	−1.69	95:114	−1.643	−1.701	−2.138[a]	−1.916	0.152	−0.887	−2.434[a]
(−1, +1)	2.06	1.71	0.99	124:85	4.708[b]	3.930[b]	4.934[b]	3.929[b]	4.184[b]	3.949[b]	3.987[b]
(−2, +2)	1.99	1.67	1.06	121:88	3.527[b]	3.305[b]	3.717[b]	3.190[b]	3.767[b]	3.365[b]	3.231[b]
(−5, +5)	2.20	1.71	0.91	115:94	2.625[b]	2.739[b]	2.569[b]	2.388[a]	2.933[b]	2.501[a]	2.337[a]
(−10, +10)	2.89	2.26	1.08	112:97	2.494[a]	2.594[b]	2.511[b]	2.242[a]	2.516[a]	2.936[b]	2.017[a]
(−20, +20)	0.61	−0.04	0.45	105:104	0.377	0.382	0.097	−0.031	1.542	1.209	−0.499

[a], [b]Denote significance at 5 and 1 %, respectively

It is also evident from the Table that partial/majority control acquisitions generate maximum wealth 2.76 % during event window (−5, 0). CAAR during the short-event window of 2 days (−1, 0), (0, +1), 3 days (−1, +1), and 5 days (−2, +2) are 2.04, 1.73, 2.06, and 1.99 %, respectively; the results are also significant.

Notable finding is that partial/majority control acquisition of target firm as a subsidiary generates positive CAAR of 2.2 % and 2.89 during the longer event window of 11 days (−5, +5) and 21 days (−10, +10); moreover, the results are significant.

But acquisitions reduce wealth during all the post-event window of (0, +5) onward; however, the results are not significant. The negative abnormal returns are 1.81 % for the post-event window (+2, +20).

AAR of partial/majority control acquisition during event window (−20, +20) is portrayed in Fig. 3.16. The trend shown in graph corroborates the above finding. It is obvious from the graph of CAAR of partial/majority control acquisition during event window (−20, +20) depicted in Fig. 3.17 that CAAR reaches maximum on day (0, +5) and starts falling after that.

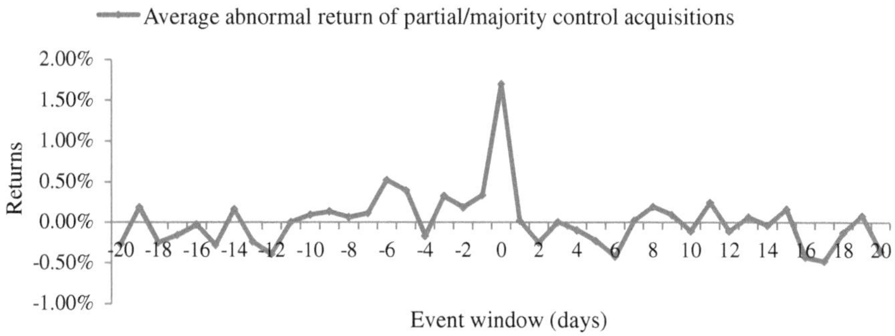

Fig. 3.16 AAR of partial/majority control acquisitions over event window (−20, +20)

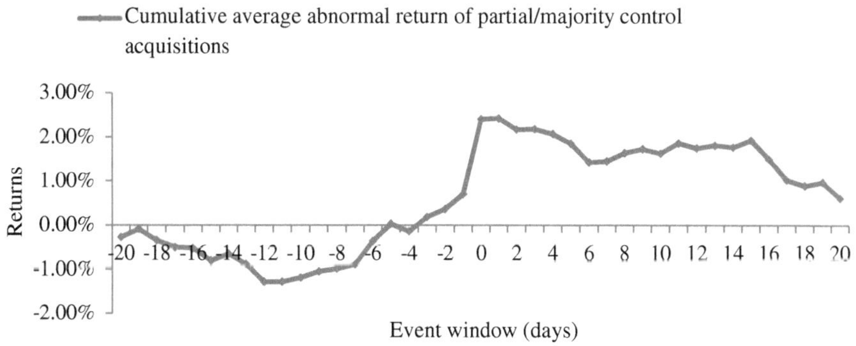

Fig. 3.17 CAAR of partial/majority control acquisitions over event window (−20, +20)

3.5.2 Analysis of Short-Term Performance of Acquisitions of Complete Control

As illustrated in Table 3.10, notable finding is that complete acquisition of target firm as a wholly owned subsidiary generates positive CAAR of 2.52 % along with quiet impressive PWCAAR of 2.12 % during the pre-event window of 6 days (−5, 0); moreover, the results are significant at 1 %. The relevant data contained in the Table 3.15 shows that the acquirer's shareholders of complete acquisitions earn 1.20 and 1.07 % average abnormal return and precision-weighted average abnormal return, respectively, on the announcement day. The CAAR during the event window of 3 days (−1, +1), 5 days (−2, +2), and 11 days (−5, +5) is 1.87, 2.21, and 2.47 %, respectively; moreover, the returns are significant.

The most noteworthy finding is that the acquirer's shareholders earn 3.03, 2.47, and 2.32 % during the longer event windows of 41 days (−20, +20), 21 days (−10, +10), and 11 days (−5, +5), respectively; moreover, the returns are significant.

In the case of complete acquisitions, the market, in general, reacts positively to announcements and remains positive during the entire event window. Later, a mild correction in market price of the acquiring company takes place as the CAAR values 5 days after the announcement period are negative. From the above findings, it would be reasonable to conclude that the null hypothesis of zero abnormal returns on the announcement day has been rejected in the case of complete acquisitions. AAR plotted in Fig. 3.18 also supports the above conclusion as AAR is positive for 18 out of 23 days till day *t*(+2). The trend of CAAR displayed in Fig. 3.19 shows that the complete acquisitions generate shareholders' wealth for a longer period.

3.5.3 Analysis of Short-Term Performance of Acquisitions of Target Firm to Be Observed with Acquirer's Operations

Table 3.11 presents the abnormal returns (for the acquisitions of target firm) to be absorbed totally with the acquirer. It is obvious that acquirer's shareholders experience return of 1.52 % over event window of 2 days (−1, 0); the results are significant at 1 %. It may be noted from the Table, CAAR is positive for only 5 days (−2, +2), in the case, target firm is totally absorbed with the acquirer. However, CAAR is positive for all pre-event window and event windows of 3 days (−1, +1), 5 days (−2, +2), 11 days (−5, +5), and 21 days (−10, +10); the results are significant only for small event window of 5 days.

The above results lead to conclusion that although the announcement of acquisition of target firm to be totally absorbed with the operations of acquiring firm induces positive reaction, this reaction is temporary in nature and gets diluted soon. Though the results of the event window of 6 days (−5, 0) day are statistically significant at 1 %, the reaction is not very strong; it gets nullified within 1 day. This

Table 3.10 Abnormal returns to the shareholders of acquiring firms (complete acquisitions, N = 451) on the announcement day and during multidays event windows, 2003–2015

Event window	Average abnormal return			Positive: negative	Parametric tests				Nonparametric tests		
	Cumulative (%)	Precision-weighted (%)	Median (%)		CDA t	CSS t	Patell Z	SCS Z	GSign Z	Rank Z	Jackknife Z
(−20, −2)	2.31	2.11	1.04	241:209	3.365[b]	3.175[b]	3.899[b]	3.352[b]	3.416[b]	2.937[b]	2.356[a]
(−15, −2)	2.22	1.96	0.67	236:214	3.766[b]	3.753[b]	4.238[b]	3.906[b]	2.943[b]	3.257[b]	3.075[b]
(−10, −2)	1.49	1.27	0.35	231:219	3.155[b]	3.348[b]	3.412[b]	3.192[b]	2.470[a]	2.527[a]	2.397[a]
(−5, −2)	0.90	0.73	0.41	236:214	2.851[b]	3.068[b]	2.897[b]	2.821[b]	2.943[b]	2.631[b]	2.465[a]
(−5, 0)	2.54	2.12	1.55	276:174	6.592[b]	6.685[b]	6.956[b]	6.380[b]	6.729[b]	5.674[b]	6.141[b]
(−1, 0)	1.65	1.39	0.90	280:170	7.386[b]	6.620[b]	7.948[b]	5.996[b]	7.108[b]	6.107[b]	6.465[b]
(0, 0)	1.20	1.07	0.68	268:182	7.627[b]	6.643[b]	8.612[b]	6.259[b]	5.972[b]	6.291[b]	6.951[b]
(0, +1)	1.43	1.26	0.66	258:192	6.417[b]	5.778[b]	7.210[b]	5.443[b]	5.026[b]	5.346[b]	5.649[b]
(0, +5)	1.13	1.07	0.31	238:212	2.921[b]	2.819[b]	3.568[b]	3.004[b]	3.132[b]	1.968	2.176[a]
(+2, +5)	−0.30	−0.18	−0.60	201:247	−0.965	−0.969	−0.726	−0.686	−0.284	−1.37	−1.861
(+2, +10)	−1.05	−0.74	−1.45	180:269	−2.223[a]	−2.225[a]	−2.002[a]	−1.814	−2.317[a]	−2.629[b]	−2.913[b]
(+2, +15)	−1.04	−0.56	−2.07	181:268	−1.763	−1.701	−1.208	−1.061	−2.223[a]	−1.971[a]	−2.206[a]
(+2, +20)	−1.14	−0.42	−2.22	183:267	−1.664	−1.546	−1.383	−0.566	−2.074[a]	−2.106[a]	−2.670[b]
(−1, +1)	1.87	1.58	1.08	262:188	6.866[b]	6.314[b]	7.408[b]	5.741[b]	5.404[b]	5.719[b]	5.885[b]
(−2, +2)	2.21	1.87	1.52	265:185	6.282[b]	6.136[b]	6.787[b]	5.779[b]	5.688[b]	5.153[b]	5.853[b]
(−5, +5)	2.47	2.12	1.83	255:195	4.726[b]	4.920[b]	5.190[b]	4.836[b]	4.742[b]	3.747[b]	3.952[b]
(−10, +10)	2.32	2.11	1.14	241:209	3.208[b]	3.314[b]	3.727[b]	3.367[b]	3.416[b]	2.095[a]	2.128[a]
(−20, +20)	3.03	3.44	1.18	246:205	3.009[b]	2.892[b]	3.768[b]	3.104[b]	3.842[b]	2.112[a]	1.457

[a], [b]Denote significance at 5 and 1 %, respectively

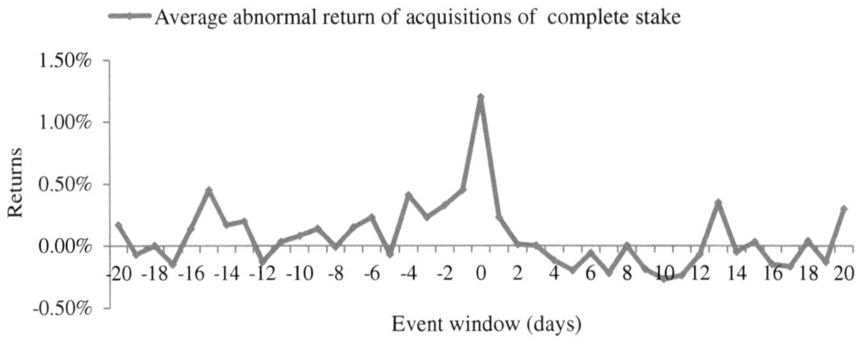

Fig. 3.18 AAR of acquisitions of complete control over event window (−20, +20)

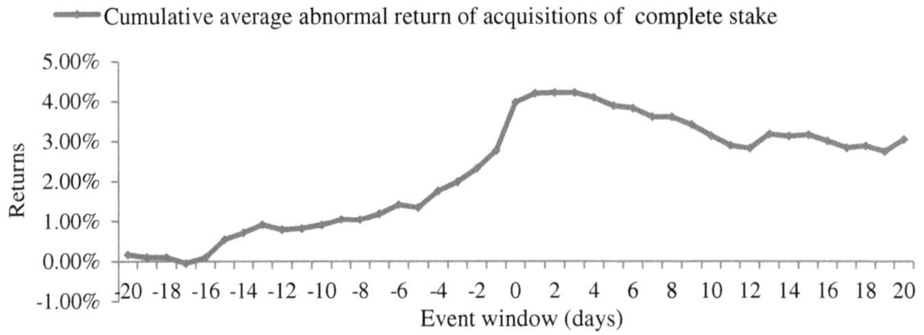

Fig. 3.19 CAAR of acquisitions of complete control over event window (−20, +20)

clearly indicates that the initial overreaction is followed by a strong correction. Moreover, even though the market reacts positively to announcement of acquisition of target firm to be totally absorbed with the acquirer's operations, the reaction is not as strong as that for complete acquisitions. The results vary for different event windows; in some cases, the null hypothesis is rejected while in others it is not.

AAR portrayed in Fig. 3.20 also support the above conclusion, it is evident from the Graph that AAR is positive only for 11 days and negative for 30 days during event window. The trend of CAAR depicted in Fig. 3.21 shows that the positive reaction gets nullified within a short duration.

3.5.4 *Control Effect*

Independent t-test has been conducted to measure the difference between mean CAR of complete acquisition of target firm as a subsidiary and mean CAR of partial/majority control acquisitions of target firm as a wholly owned subsidiary; the results are tabulated in Table 3.12. It is apparent that mean difference is positive for

Table 3.11 Abnormal returns to the shareholders of acquiring firms (target firm to be totally absorbed with the acquirer's operations, $N = 140$) on the announcement day and during multidays event windows, 2003–2015

Event window	Average abnormal return			Positive: negative	Parametric tests				Nonparametric tests		
	Cumulative (%)	Precision-weighted (%)	Median (%)		CDA t	CSS t	Patell Z	SCS Z	GSign Z	Rank Z	Jackknife Z
(−20, −2)	0.56	0.29	−0.91	67:73	0.388	0.363	0.412	0.204	0.515	1.274	−0.947
(−15, −2)	1.82	1.36	0.64	72:68	1.455	1.449	1.431	1.17	1.363	2.330[a]	0.21
(−10, −2)	2.23	1.38	0.69	74:66	2.224[a]	2.044[a]	1.720[a]	1.438	1.702	2.323[a]	0.623
(−5, −2)	1.88	1.14	−0.40	67:73	2.818[b]	2.498[a]	2.100[a]	1.753	0.515	2.567[a]	1.222
(−5, 0)	3.38	2.26	1.99	83:57	4.135[b]	3.670[b]	3.370[b]	2.893[b]	3.229[b]	4.008[b]	2.234[a]
(−1, 0)	1.52	1.18	0.74	83:55	3.224[b]	3.213[b]	2.882[b]	2.815[b]	3.409[b]	3.312[b]	3.082[b]
(0, 0)	1.01	0.93	0.81	80:60	3.035[b]	2.826[b]	3.161[b]	2.643[b]	3.074[b]	3.634[b]	3.294[b]
(0, +1)	0.78	0.62	0.12	70:68	1.647	1.32	1.660[a]	1.18	1.187	1.705	1.02
(0, +5)	0.12	−0.38	−1.09	57:83	0.147	0.126	−0.328	−0.483	−1.182	−0.594	−1.043
(+2, +5)	−0.65	−0.95	−1.79	52:87	−0.974	−0.909	−1.518	−1.707	−1.960[a]	−1.933	−2.033[a]
(+2, +10)	−1.78	−2.04	−3.87	45:95	−1.773	−1.492	−2.300[a]	−2.066[a]	−3.218[b]	−2.511[a]	−1.662
(+2, +15)	−2.58	−3.03	−5.18	42:98	−2.067[a]	−1.69	−2.786[b]	−2.327[a]	−3.727[b]	−2.626[b]	−2.051[a]
(+2, +20)	−3.11	−3.72	−4.74	43:97	−2.136[a]	−1.739	−2.905[b]	−2.431[a]	−3.557[b]	−2.117[a]	−1.952
(−1, +1)	1.29	0.89	0.95	74:65	2.233[a]	1.912	1.899[a]	1.522	1.786	1.998[a]	1.309
(−2, +2)	2.35	1.43	1.41	81:59	3.145[b]	2.607[b]	2.550[b]	1.907	2.890[b]	2.306[a]	1.33
(−5, +5)	2.52	1.03	−0.33	69:71	2.274[a]	1.989[a]	1.328	0.988	0.854	1.426	0.179
(−10, +10)	1.73 %	0.30	−1.77	66:74	1.133	0.886	0.377	0.181	0.345	0.632	−0.177
(−20, +20)	−1.26	−2.33	−2.54	63:77	−0.59	−0.481	−1.096	−1.012	−0.164	−0.033	−1.48

[a], [b]Denote significance at 5 and 1 %, respectively

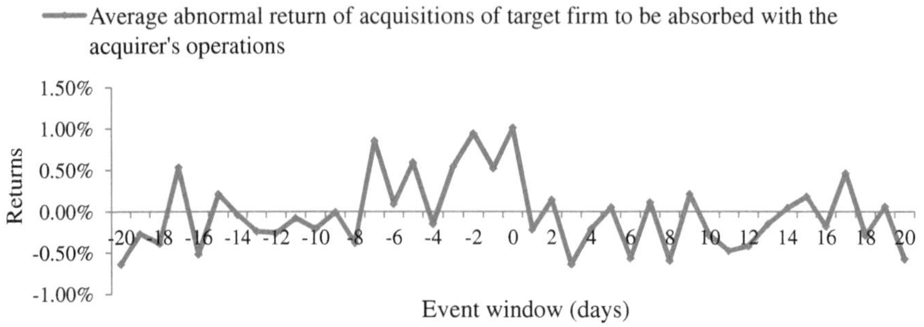

Fig. 3.20 AAR of acquisitions of target firm to be observed with acquirer's operation over event window (−20, +20)

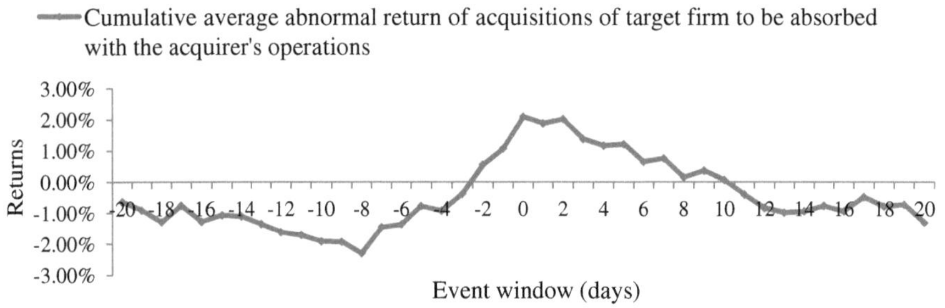

Fig. 3.21 CAAR of acquisitions of target firm to be observed with acquirer's operation over event window (−20, +20)

the longest event window of 41 days. The *t*-statistics shows that difference is also significant at 5 % level (*p*-value = 0.036 < 0.05).

On the basis of these results, it may be concluded that complete acquisition of target as a wholly owned subsidiary generates higher abnormal returns than the acquisition of partial/majority control.

Independent t-test has been conducted to measure the difference between mean CAR of complete acquisition of target firm as a wholly owned subsidiary and mean CAR of acquisitions of target firm to be totally absorbed with the operations of acquiring firm; the results are tabulated in Table 3.13. It is apparent that mean difference is positive for most of the event windows. The *t*-statistics shows that difference is also significant for event window of 41 days (*p*-value = 0.009 < 0.01) and the post-event windows of 17 days (*p*-value = 0.009 < 0.01) and 19 days (*p*-value = 0.011 < 0.05).

On the basis of the above findings, it is reasonable to conclude that complete acquisition of target firm as a wholly owned subsidiary generates higher abnormal returns than the complete acquisition of target firm to be totally absorbed with the operations of the acquirer. It may also be concluded that complete acquisition of target firm as a wholly owned subsidiary generates maximum abnormal returns;

Table 3.12 Independent samples t-test for difference of mean CAR (complete acquisitions, partial/majority control acquisitions)

Event Window	Mean CAR (%) of acquisitions complete control ($N = 451$)	Mean CAR (%) of acquisitions partial/majority control ($N = 209$)	Mean difference	t-value	Significance value
(−20, −2)	2.31	0.36	1.95	1.8	0.072
(−15, −2)	2.22	0.88	1.34	1.39	0.165
(−10, −2)	1.49	1.63	−0.14	−0.09	0.930
(−5, −2)	0.90	0.72	0.18	0.18	0.857
(−5, 0)	2.54	2.76	−0.22	−0.42	0.674
(−1, 0)	1.65	2.04	−0.39	−0.75	0.455
(0, 0)	1.20	1.70	−0.50	−1.5	0.134
(0, +1)	1.43	1.73	−0.30	−0.57	0.569
(0, +5)	1.13	1.15	−0.02	−0.43	0.666
(+2, +5)	−0.30	−0.58	0.28	1	0.316
(+2, +10)	−1.05	−0.80	−0.25	−0.3	0.766
(+2, +15)	−1.04	−0.50	−0.54	−0.78	0.434
(+2, +20)	−1.14	−1.81	0.67	1.39	0.166
(−1, +1)	1.87	2.06	−0.19	−0.15	0.877
(−2, +2)	2.21	1.99	0.22	0.29	0.769
(−5, +5)	2.47	2.20	0.27	0.62	0.537
(−10, +10)	2.32	2.89	−0.57	−0.19	0.850
(−20, +20)	3.03	0.61	2.42	2.1[a]	0.036

[a, b]Denote significance at 5 and 1 %, respectively

complete acquisition of target firm to be totally absorbed with the operations of the acquirer earns minimum abnormal returns. Figure 3.22 also corroborates the conclusion. It is obvious from the graphs of CAAR portrayed in Fig. 3.23 that the acquisitions of complete control as a wholly owned subsidiary and partial/majority control earn positive abnormal returns for the entire event window of 41 days (−20, +20).

The advantages of acquiring complete control of a firm arise from assets owned and capacity to acquire complimentary assets. Lack of requisite voting power[1] to

[1]A special resolution is passed (to be passed with 2/3rd of majority) to change the name of a company, alterations to the memorandum or articles of association, or a reduction of capital of the company, etc. A special resolution requires 75 % shareholders of a company present or by appointment of a proxy to vote in favor at a general meeting of the company to alter a company's constitution.

Table 3.13 Independent samples t-test for difference of mean CAR (complete acquisitions, acquisitions of target firm to be totally absorbed with the acquirer's operations)

Event Window	Mean CAR (%) of acquisitions of complete control (*N* = 451)	Mean CAR (%) of acquisitions of complete control of target firm to be totally absorbed with the acquirer's operations (*N* = 140)	Mean difference	*t*-value	Significance value
(−20, −2)	2.31	0.56	1.75	1.12	0.266
(−15, −2)	2.22	1.82	0.40	0.4	0.690
(−10, −2)	1.49	2.23	−0.74	−0.26	0.796
(−5, −2)	0.90	1.88	−0.98	−0.16	0.875
(−5, 0)	2.54	3.38	−0.84	−0.21	0.837
(−1, 0)	1.65	1.52	0.13	0.55	0.580
(0, 0)	1.20	1.01	0.19	0.16	0.874
(0, +1)	1.43	0.78	0.65	0.68	0.500
(0, +5)	1.13	0.12	1.01	1.76	0.081
(+2, +5)	−0.30	−0.65	0.35	1.77	0.077
(+2, +10)	−1.05	−1.78	0.73	1.77	0.079
(+2, +15)	−1.04	−2.58	1.54	2.65[b]	0.009
(+2, +20)	−1.14	−3.11	1.97	2.55[a]	0.011
(−1, +1)	1.87	1.29	0.58	0.9	0.368
(−2, +2)	2.21	2.35	−0.14	−0.6	0.548
(−5, +5)	2.47	2.52	−0.05	−1.42	0.157
(−10, +10)	2.32	1.73	0.59	1.59	0.113
(−20, +20)	3.03	−1.26	4.29	2.66[b]	0.009

[a], [b]Denote significance at 5 and 1 %, respectively

pass a special resolution, less autonomy, and difficulty in integration process post-acquisitions also seems to be a factor for lower abnormal returns in the case of partial/majority control acquisitions. Further, the problems of post-acquisitions integration in the case of complete acquisitions of target firm to be totally absorbed with the acquirer's operations may be a reason for negative market reaction in the case of absorptions. Zhu et al. (2011), Spencer et al. (2001) also observe that long-term performance of partial acquired firms is highly dependent on corporate control characteristics of the target and the acquiring firms. Aybar and Ficici (2009), Rani et al. (2011) also find support for the positive impact of the stake pursued in the acquisition of target firm.

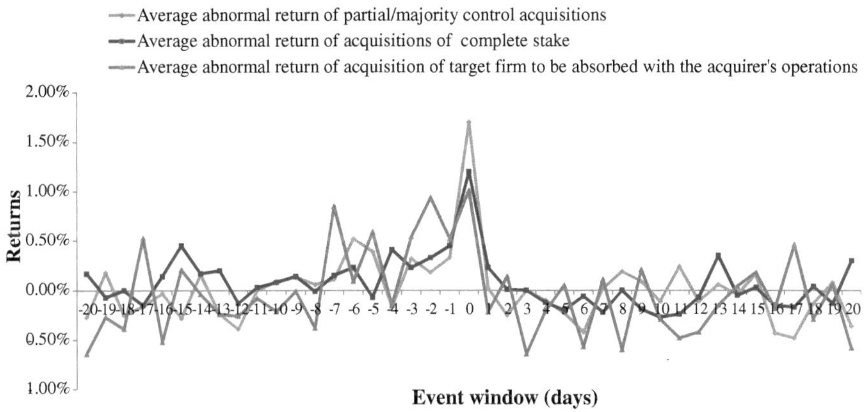

Fig. 3.22 AAR of acquisitions of (partial/majority control, complete control, and target firm to be observed with acquirer's operation) over event window (−20, +20)

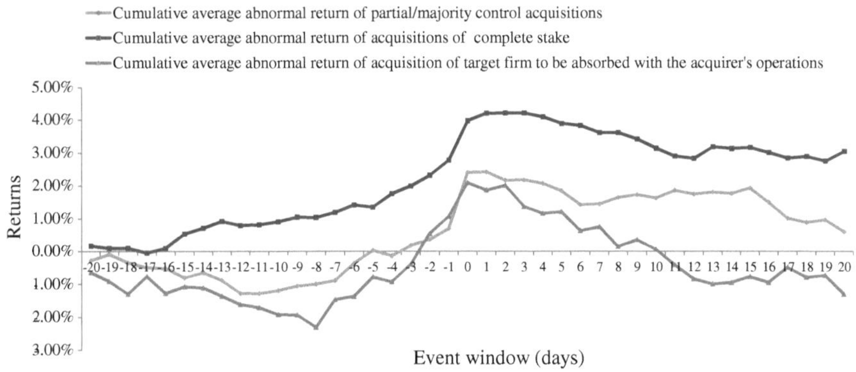

Fig. 3.23 CAAR of acquisitions of (partial/majority control, complete control, and target firm to be observed with acquirer's operation) over event window (−20, +20)

3.6 Analysis of Listing Effect

The form of target firms (unlisted or listed) may influence the post-M&A performance of the acquiring firms.

Empirical literature has also emphasized the public or private status of the target also impacts the acquirer returns. Extant literature in this context reveals that the acquirers of unlisted firms make valuable acquisitions. The positive results are not observed in the case of acquirers of publicly listed target firms (Firth 1980; Jensen and Ruback 1983; Travlos 1987; Jarrell et al. 1988; Franks and Harris 1989; Hansen and Lott 1996; Chang 1998; Andrade et al. 2001; Ang and Kohers 2001;

Fuller et al. 2002; Conn et al. 2005; Faccio et al. 2006; Draper and Paudyal 2006; Alexandridis et al. 2010).

Draper and Paudyal (2006) proposed three possible hypotheses for higher gains of unlisted target acquisition. They are:

(1) The managerial motive hypothesis,
(2) The illiquidity hypothesis, and
(3) The bargaining power hypothesis.

These three hypotheses explain the major reasons of lower returns for acquisition of listed firms as: (i) that agency problems are more likely for acquirers of listed firms but do not apply to acquirers of privately held and unlisted target firms, (ii) lack of liquidity of unlisted firms reduce their bargaining power of target firms which, in turn, (iii) leads to reduction in their bargaining power to negotiate higher premiums from the acquirers. This creates value for acquirers.

3.6.1 Analysis of Short-Term Performance of M&A of Unlisted Firms

Table 3.14 illustrates the short-term performance of acquisitions of unlisted target firms. The acquirer shareholders earn 1.30, 1.19, and 0.72 % average abnormal return, precision-weighted average abnormal return, and median abnormal return on the announcement day; moreover, the results are highly significant. Shareholders of as much as 61 % stocks experience positive abnormal returns on the announcement day. The maximum CAAR of 2.65 %, PWCAAR of 2.12 %, and median abnormal return of 1.43 % are observed during the pre-event window (−5, 0); the results are significant at 1 %.

Notable finding is that acquisition of unlisted target firm generates positive CAAR during all the event windows as well as pre-event windows. But acquisitions reduce wealth during all the post-event window of (0, +5) onward; however, the results are not significant. The negative abnormal returns are 1.55 % for the post-event window (+2, +20). During the post-announcement windows (+2, +5), (+2, +10), (+2, +15), and (+2, +20), there is a consistent fall in the CAAR values indicating that the positive reaction is almost nullified by the negative reaction (the peak value of CAAR decline from 3.40 % on day (0, +2) to and settles at 1.81 % on day (0, +20)). AAR of acquisition of unlisted target firm during event window (−20, +20) is portrayed in Fig. 3.24. The trend shown in graph corroborates the above finding. It is obvious from the graph of CAAR of acquisition of unlisted target firm during event window (−20, +20) depicted in Fig. 3.25 that CAAR reaches maximum on day (0, +2) and starts falling after that (Figs. 3.24, 3.25 and Table 3.14).

Table 3.14 Abnormal returns to the shareholders of acquiring firms of M&A of (unlisted firms, $N = 713$) on the announcement day and during multidays event windows, 2003–2015

Event window	Average abnormal return			Positive: negative	Parametric tests				Nonparametric tests		
	Cumulative (%)	Precision-weighted (%)	Median (%)		CDA t	CSS t	Patell Z	SCS Z	GSign Z	Rank Z	Jackknife Z
(−20, −2)	1.59	1.44	0.46	368:344	2.560[a]	2.668[b]	3.223[b]	2.820[b]	3.348[b]	3.020[b]	1.436
(−15, −2)	1.87	1.59	0.71	374:338	3.515[b]	3.798[b]	4.089[b]	3.782[b]	3.800[b]	3.774[b]	2.662[b]
(−10, −2)	1.69	1.34	0.35	365:347	3.955[b]	4.356[b]	4.262[b]	4.033[b]	3.123[b]	3.783[b]	3.037[b]
(−5, −2)	0.98	0.69	0.22	365:347	3.428[b]	3.907[b]	3.306[b]	3.228[b]	3.123[b]	3.278[b]	2.836[b]
(−5, 0)	2.65	2.12	1.43	420:292	7.584[b]	8.002[b]	8.241[b]	7.428[b]	7.262[b]	6.802[b]	6.840[b]
(−1, 0)	1.67	1.44	0.87	438:272	8.312[b]	8.053[b]	9.649[b]	7.560[b]	8.698[b]	7.146[b]	7.967[b]
(0, 0)	1.30	1.19	0.72	434:279	9.161[b]	8.505[b]	11.22[b]	8.213[b]	8.099[b]	7.930[b]	8.962[b]
(0, +1)	1.41	1.24	0.69	408:302	6.995[b]	6.361[b]	8.282[b]	6.231[b]	6.436[b]	5.943[b]	6.243[b]
(0, +5)	1.05	0.92	0.06	359:353	3.021[b]	3.029[b]	3.633[b]	3.039[b]	2.671[b]	2.050[a]	1.838
(+2, +5)	−0.35	−0.30	−0.74	313:396	−1.237	−1.309	−1.375	−1.3	−0.69	−1.692	−2.451[a]
(+2, +10)	−1.09	−0.89	−1.66	282:429	−2.554[a]	−2.645[b]	−2.782[b]	−2.474[a]	−3.093[b]	−2.546[a]	−3.177[b]
(+2, +15)	−1.06	−0.85	−2.32	288:423	−1.981[a]	−1.971[a]	−2.119[a]	−1.854	−2.641[b]	−1.814	−2.828[b]
(+2, +20)	−1.55	−1.13	−2.48	289:423	−2.501[a]	−2.444[a]	−2.887[b]	−1.866	−2.598[b]	−2.160[a]	−3.526[b]
(−1, +1)	1.78	1.49	1.04	410:301	7.214[b]	6.782[b]	8.174[b]	6.405[b]	6.548[b]	6.109[b]	6.391[b]
(−2, +2)	2.13	1.72	1.34	415:297	6.679[b]	6.655[b]	7.371[b]	6.197[b]	6.886[b]	5.610[b]	5.859[b]
(−5, +5)	2.40	1.86	1.06	390:322	5.086[b]	5.405[b]	5.420[b]	4.934[b]	5.004[b]	4.147[b]	3.636[b]
(−10, +10)	2.38	1.93	0.58	372:340	3.642[b]	3.751[b]	4.059[b]	3.550[b]	3.649[b]	3.119[b]	2.300[a]
(−20, +20)	1.81	1.93	0.70	370:343	1.986[a]	1.990[a]	2.511[b]	2.203[a]	3.462[b]	2.238[a]	0.221

[a], [b]Denote significance at 5 and 1 %, respectively

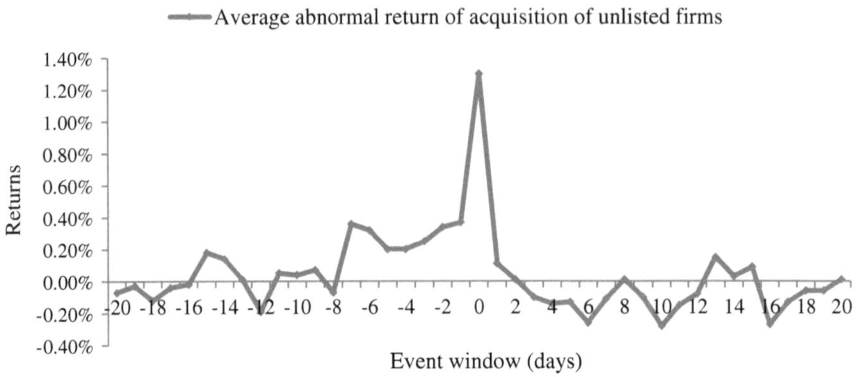

Fig. 3.24 AAR of M&A of unlisted firms over event window (−20, +20)

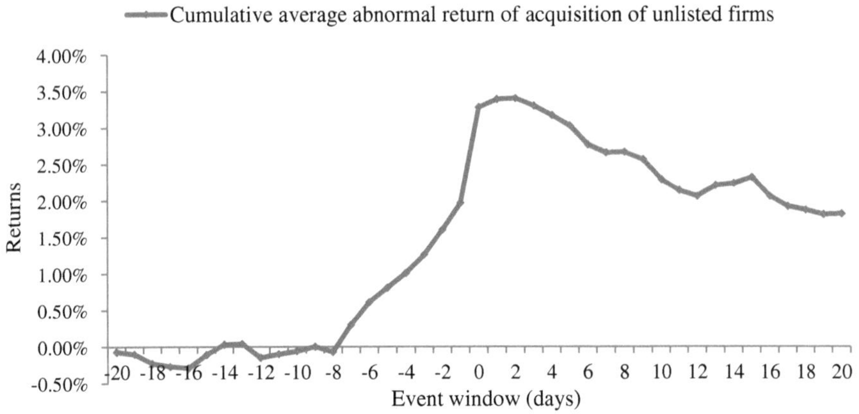

Fig. 3.25 CAAR of M&A of unlisted firms over event window (−20, +20)

3.6.2 Analysis of Short-Term Performance of M&A of Listed Firms

As illustrated in Fig. 3.26, the acquisition of listed target firms does not generate significant abnormal returns for all the event windows. The AAR is positive as well as significant on announcement day. The relevant data contained in the Table 3.15 shows that the CAAR values of 2.01 and 1.71 % for the event window (−5, +5) and (−10, +10) though positive, are not statistically significant.

During the post-announcement windows (0, +5), (+2, +5), (+2, +10), (+2, +15), and (+2, +20), there is a consistent fall in the CAAR values indicating that even positive reaction for a small event window is almost nullified by the negative reaction (the peak value of CAAR declines from 2.80 % on day *t*(0) to −0.49 % on day *t*(+20)) (Fig. 3.27).

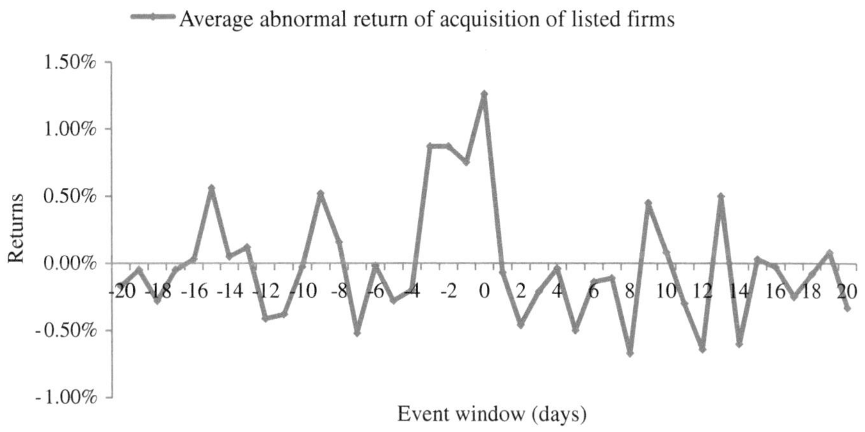

Fig. 3.26 AAR of M&A of listed firms over event window (−20, +20)

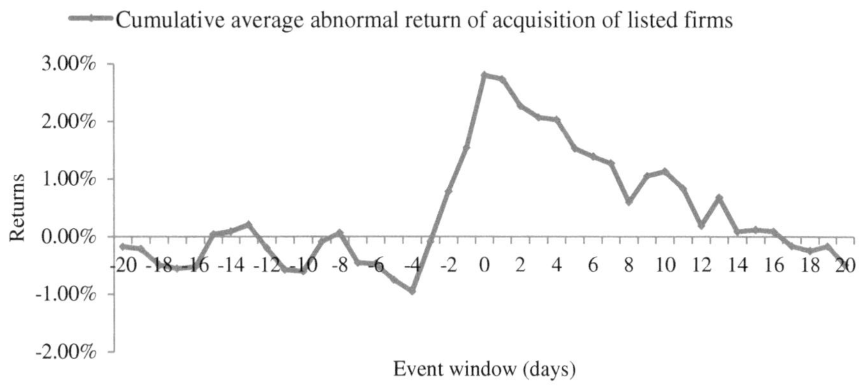

Fig. 3.27 CAAR of M&A of listed firms over event window (−20, +20)

3.6.3 Listing Effect

Independent t-test has been conducted to measure the difference between mean CAR of acquisition of unlisted target firms and mean CAR of acquisitions of unlisted target firms; the results are tabulated in Table 3.16. It is apparent that mean difference is positive for all the windows except pre-event window (−15, −2). Still, the difference is not significant for any event window. However, it is important to note that unlisted target firms, on the whole, perform better than their public counterparts.

Table 3.15 Abnormal returns to the shareholders of acquiring firms of M&A of (listed firms, $N = 83$) on the announcement day and during multidays event windows, 2003–2015

Event window	Average abnormal return			Positive: negative	Parametric tests				Nonparametric tests		
	Cumulative (%)	Precision-weighted (%)	Median (%)		CDA t	CSS t	Patell Z	SCS Z	GSign Z	Rank Z	Jackknife Z
(−20, −2)	0.80	1.00	0.08	42:41	0.493	0.498	0.785	0.635	1.003	0.615	−0.23
(−15, −2)	1.31	1.52	1.68	42:41	0.942	0.978	1.389	1.222	1.003	0.565	0.366
(−10, −2)	1.36	1.14	0.78	46:37	1.226	1.438	1.323	1.25	1.885	0.949	0.674
(−5, −2)	1.26	1.13	0.42	42:41	1.703	1.725	1.929[a]	1.891	1.003	1.873	1.436
(−5, 0)	3.27	2.56	2.03	51:32	3.609[b]	3.554[b]	3.541[b]	3.439[b]	2.988[b]	3.179[b]	3.070[b]
(−1, 0)	2.01	1.43	0.92	51:32	3.844[b]	3.292[b]	3.405[b]	3.004[b]	2.988[b]	2.858[b]	3.080[b]
(0, 0)	1.26	1.10	0.91	48:35	3.402[b]	2.972[b]	3.685[b]	2.928[b]	2.327[a]	3.093[b]	2.817[b]
(0, +1)	1.19	1.29	0.49	46:37	2.281[a]	2.131[a]	3.070[b]	2.438[a]	1.885	2.202[a]	2.112[a]
(0, +5)	−0.01	0.21	−0.04	41:42	−0.008	−0.009	0.287	0.268	0.783	−0.619	0.049
(+2, +5)	−1.20	−1.08	−1.59	29:54	−1.623	−1.849	−1.820[a]	−1.891	−1.864	−2.315[a]	−1.8
(+2, +10)	−1.60	−1.45	−2.95	28:55	−1.441	−1.479	−1.618	−1.674	−2.085[a]	−2.379[a]	−1.949
(+2, +15)	−2.61	−2.48	−3.35	26:57	−1.887	−1.959	−2.227[a]	−2.126[a]	−2.526[a]	−2.684[b]	−2.289[a]
(+2, +20)	−3.22	−3.03	−3.55	29:54	−1.996[a]	−2.130[a]	−2.319[a]	−2.192[a]	−1.864	−2.529[a]	−2.700[b]
(−1, +1)	1.95	1.62	1.05	48:35	3.037[b]	2.755[b]	3.159[b]	2.801[b]	2.327[a]	2.345[a]	2.600[b]
(−2, +2)	2.35	1.96	1.66	50:33	2.843[b]	2.610[b]	2.962[b]	2.717[b]	2.768[b]	2.096[a]	2.430[a]
(−5, +5)	2.01	1.67	1.74	47:36	1.634	1.853	1.715[a]	1.734	2.106[a]	0.958	1.352
(−10, +10)	1.71	1.32	0.62	45:38	1.007	0.997	1.001	0.861	1.665	−0.05	0.212
(−20, +20)	−0.48	−0.43	−0.19	41:42	−0.201	−0.186	−0.193	−0.177	0.783	−0.669	−1.084

[a], [b]Denote significance at 5 and 1 %, respectively

Table 3.16 Independent samples t-test for difference of mean CAR (unlisted firms, listed firms)

Event Window	Mean CAR (%) M&A of unlisted firms ($N = 713$)	Mean CAR (%) M&A of listed firms ($N = 83$)	Mean difference	t-value	Significance value
(−20, −2)	1.59	0.80	0.79	0.32	0.75
(−15, −2)	1.87	1.31	0.56	0.17	0.86
(−10, −2)	1.69	1.36	0.33	0.05	0.96
(−5, −2)	0.98	1.26	−0.28	−0.81	0.42
(−5, 0)	2.65	3.27	−0.62	−0.42	0.68
(−1, 0)	1.67	2.01	−0.34	0.33	0.74
(0, 0)	1.30	1.26	0.04	0.25	0.80
(0, +1)	1.41	1.19	0.22	0.52	0.60
(0, +5)	1.05	−0.01	1.06	0.67	0.50
(+2, +5)	−0.35	−1.20	0.85	1.39	0.17
(+2, +10)	−1.09	−1.60	0.51	0.73	0.46
(+2, +15)	−1.06	−2.61	1.55	1.58	0.12
(+2, +20)	−1.55	−3.22	1.67	1.41	0.16
(−1, +1)	1.78	1.95	−0.17	−0.35	0.73
(−2, +2)	2.13	2.35	−0.22	−0.46	0.64
(−5, +5)	2.40	2.01	0.39	0.12	0.91
(−10, +10)	2.38	1.71	0.67	0.31	0.75
(−20, +20)	1.81	−0.48	2.29	0.95	0.34

[a], [b]Denote significance at 5 and 1 %, respectively

The graph of AAR displayed in Fig. 3.28 reveals that AAR is positive for 21 days for unlisted target firm and 11 days for listed target firms. In addition, the CAAR portrayed in Fig. 3.29 shows that abnormal returns are positive in the case of acquisition of unlisted target firms. In marked contrast, the CAAR is positive for a shorter duration for acquisition of listed target firms.

Lack of liquidity of unlisted firms reduces their bargaining power which, in turn, reduces their bargaining power to negotiate higher premiums from the acquirers. This creates value for acquirers. Further, agency problems are more likely for acquirers of listed firms but do not apply to acquirers of privately held and unlisted target firms which may be a major reason of lower returns for acquisition of listed firms. The plausible reason for better performance of unlisted target could also be explained by the fact that these firms are relatively small compared to public companies that are generally owned by a small group of people, monitoring and control can be exercised effectively thereby leading to a reduction in agency cost and better wealth gains. This finding is consistent with the conclusions of various studies by Draper and Paudal (2006), Conn et al. (2005), Fuller et al. (2002), Chang (1998).

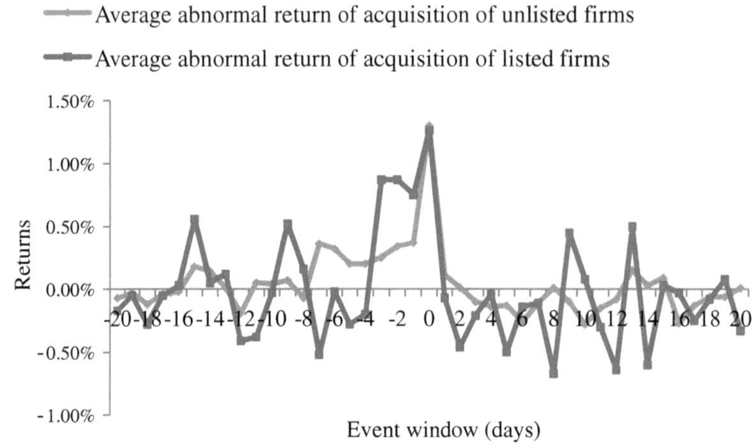

Fig. 3.28 AAR over event window (−20, +20) based on the type of target firm (unlisted, listed) acquired

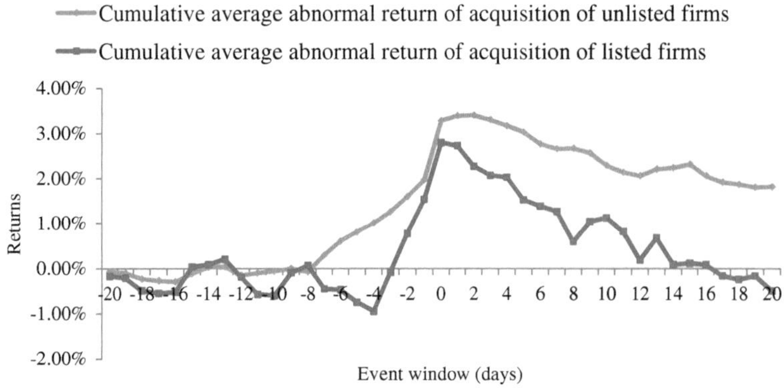

Fig. 3.29 CAAR over event window (−20, +20) based on the type of target firm (unlisted, listed) acquired

3.7 Analysis of Payment Effect

In making an acquisition, the acquiring firm can pay either in cash or stock. The mode of payment can influence the acquirer's performance. Most empirical studies agree that the method of payment plays an important role in explaining acquiring firms' stock return. The stock market reacts differently to the announcement of acquisitions on the basis of mode of financing being used. In an acquisition, the acquirer can pay the claims of the shareholders of target firm either by paying cash or by issuing stock or by a combination of both cash and stock. Asquith, Bruner, and Mullins (1987), Huang and Walkling (1987), Travlos (1987), Yook (2003), and

Heron and Lie (2002) observed that acquisitions financed with stock generate negative returns to the acquirer shareholders on acquisition announcement, whereas returns for acquisitions, financed with cash, generate either zero or very marginal positive return.

Many hypotheses have been put forward to explain the theoretical rationale why the share prices are influenced by the choice of the payment method.

The "free cash flow" hypothesis contends that acquisitions, being paid for in cash, reduce the agency costs and convey positive signal to market (Jensen 1986; Masse et al. 1990). Free cash flow hypothesis proposes that cash transactions result in positive abnormal returns.

Asymmetric information hypothesis (also known as the information content hypothesis) states that an offer to pay in shares for an acquisition will be seen by market participants as a signal that the stocks are overvalued (Myers and Majluf 1984). A stock offer enables an acquirer to share the risk of not realizing the expected future growth opportunities with the target firm in the post-acquisition period. Hansen (1987) supports asymmetric information hypothesis with a different point of view. He argues that when an acquirer is not able to assess the true value of the assets of the target firm, it will finance such an acquisition with stock. He proposes that the stock financing has a "contingent pricing effect" and enables the acquirer to share the risk of overvaluation of the target firm with that of the target firm shareholders in the post-acquisition period. Stock offers convey a negative signal to the market that the acquirer is not confident about the valuation of the target company and wants to share the risk of overvaluation with the target company's shareholders in the post-acquisition period.

A few studies have investigated the impact of asymmetric information on the choice of mode of payment (cash or stock) by the acquiring firms (Fishman 1989; Eckbo et al. 1990). The acquiring firm may experience the risk of overpaying the target firm under high information asymmetry. If the payment is made in cash, the target firms will accept the offer only when the offer value exceeds the firm's intrinsic value (known to the target but not known to the acquirer). The risk of overpayment is much higher in this case. If the payment is made in the acquiring firm's stock, the value of the offer is determined by the combined value of the acquirer and the target as well as the synergy resulting from the acquisition. Because of the "contingent pricing effect" (Hansen 1987) in the stock payment, the cost of overpayment is reduced, as any of such cost will be absorbed by the combined firms and, thus, partly shared by the target firms. Therefore, it is expected that higher information asymmetry will lead to lower cash payment or more stock swaps in the acquisition. Asymmetric information hypothesis concludes that stock transactions lead to negative abnormal returns around the announcement date.

Extant literature establishes that cash offers, internationally, are accompanied with higher returns to the acquirer firm shareholders than the stock offers. The rationale suggested is that cash is usually employed in financing an acquisition when the acquirer has less information asymmetry about the true value of the target company's assets.

Contrary to the above hypotheses examined by Myers and Majluf (1984), Jensen (1986), Martin (1996) reports that stock transactions are no longer observed as a negative signal by the market participants. He suggested the investment opportunity hypothesis and the risk-sharing hypothesis.

The investment opportunity hypothesis proposes that firms with excellent future investment opportunities should not pay in cash for acquisitions. Cash transactions often have to be financed with new debt. Cash flows, however, should not be used for debt service payments since this reduces the amount of discretionary cash flows available in the future (Jung et al. 1996; Martin 1996).

The risk-sharing hypothesis proposes that it could be beneficial to pay in stock especially in high-risk transactions, because in this case, the target firm will have an incentive to make a success of the takeover transaction (Rappaport and Sirower 1999; Martin 1996). Martin (1996) examines this hypothesis and observes that the acquirer is more likely to use stock to finance an acquisition when the acquirer's growth opportunities are higher.

The risk-sharing hypothesis and the investment opportunity hypothesis conclude that stock transactions are no longer observed as a negative signal by the market participants.

3.7.1 Analysis of Short-Term Performance of M&A Financed with Cash

Table 3.17 contains the results of the impact of announcements of M&A, financed with cash payment, across various event windows by reporting the CAAR values and their corresponding test statistic values. The CAAR values across various preannouncement event windows (−20, −2) (−15, −2) (−10, −2), (−5, −2), and (−5, −0) are 1.62, 1.84, 1.47, 0.78, and 2.54 %, respectively; the CAAR values are also significant at 1 % level. This announcement effect during the event windows (−1, 0), (0, +1), (−1, +1), (−2, +2), (−5, +5), and (−10, +10) has been interpreted by analyzing the CAAR values of 1.77, 1.49, 1.93, 2.20, 2.38, and 2.21 %, respectively. These values are highly significant at 1 % indicating that null hypothesis of zero CAAR has been rejected.

During the post-announcement windows (+2, +5), (+2, +10), (+2, +15), and (+2, +20), there is a mild fall in the CAAR values indicating that the positive reaction is somewhat diluted by the negative reaction (the peak value of CAAR decline from 3.56 % on day *t*(+1) to 1.69 % on day *t*(+20)). The CAAR value of 1.69 % for the event window (−20, +20) is statistically significant as per GSign test.

The graph portrayed in Fig. 3.30 depicts that AAR is positive for 21 days during event window. Figure 3.31 corroborates the conclusion that strong positive market reaction generates high abnormal returns and after announcement starts falling and remains positive during the entire event window.

Table 3.17 Abnormal returns to the shareholders of acquiring firms of M&A (financed with cash, $N = 645$) on the announcement day and during multidays event windows, 2003–2015

Event window	Average abnormal return			Positive: negative	Parametric tests				Nonparametric tests		
	Cumulative (%)	Precision-weighted (%)	Median (%)		CDA t	CSS t	Patell Z	SCS Z	GSign Z	Rank Z	Jackknife Z
(−20, −2)	1.62	1.52	0.61	337:307	2.604[b]	2.747[b]	3.306[b]	2.944[b]	3.557[b]	2.812[b]	2.002[a]
(−15, −2)	1.84	1.62	0.76	339:305	3.442[b]	3.713[b]	4.071[b]	3.799[b]	3.716[b]	3.284[b]	3.027[b]
(−10, −2)	1.47	1.18	0.30	329:315	3.429[b]	3.921[b]	3.658[b]	3.548[b]	2.924[b]	3.118[b]	3.021[b]
(−5, −2)	0.78	0.61	0.28	333:311	2.724[b]	3.174[b]	2.770[b]	2.843[b]	3.241[b]	2.894[b]	2.865[b]
(−5, 0)	2.54	2.05	1.47	382:262	7.284[b]	7.766[b]	7.841[b]	7.431[b]	7.119[b]	6.596[b]	7.327[b]
(−1, 0)	1.77	1.46	0.90	399:245	8.763[b]	8.077[b]	9.700[b]	7.692[b]	8.465[b]	7.331[b]	8.062[b]
(0, 0)	1.33	1.17	0.72	388:255	9.334[b]	8.430[b]	10.944[b]	8.135[b]	7.636[b]	7.835[b]	8.743[b]
(0, +1)	1.49	1.29	0.75	374:270	7.401[b]	6.800[b]	8.576[b]	6.512[b]	6.486[b]	6.260[b]	6.743[b]
(0, +5)	1.17	1.08	0.40	340:304	3.341[b]	3.460[b]	4.186[b]	3.579[b]	3.795[b]	2.514[a]	2.670[b]
(+2, +5)	−0.33	−0.20	−0.60	289:353	−1.145	−1.23	−0.937	−0.869	−0.17	−1.347	−2.039[a]
(+2, +10)	−1.19	−0.86	−1.45	258:385	−2.780[b]	−2.930[b]	−2.701[b]	−2.410[a]	−2.662[b]	−2.625[b]	−3.613[b]
(+2, +15)	−1.25	−0.90	−2.21	262:381	−2.350[a]	−2.421[a]	−2.239[a]	−1.975[a]	−2.345[a]	−2.049[a]	−3.314[b]
(+2, +20)	−1.86	−1.20	−2.29	265:379	−2.993[b]	−3.051[b]	−3.054[b]	−1.980[a]	−2.142[a]	−2.551[a]	−4.360[b]
(−1, +1)	1.93	1.58	1.07	378:266	7.817[b]	7.251[b]	8.617[b]	6.835[b]	6.803[b]	6.574[b]	7.072[b]
(−2, +2)	2.20	1.80	1.44	383:261	6.893[b]	6.978[b]	7.585[b]	6.568[b]	7.199[b]	5.951[b]	6.769[b]
(−5, +5)	2.38	1.97	1.35	367:277	5.036[b]	5.548[b]	5.601[b]	5.282[b]	5.932[b]	4.366[b]	4.615[b]
(−10, +10)	2.21	1.88	1.19	348:296	3.383[b]	3.690[b]	3.867[b]	3.486[b]	4.428[b]	2.807[b]	2.377[a]
(−20, +20)	1.69	2.01	1.02	341:304	1.847	1.946	2.536[b]	2.271[a]	3.835[b]	1.955	0.294

[a], [b]Denote significance at 5 and 1 %, respectively

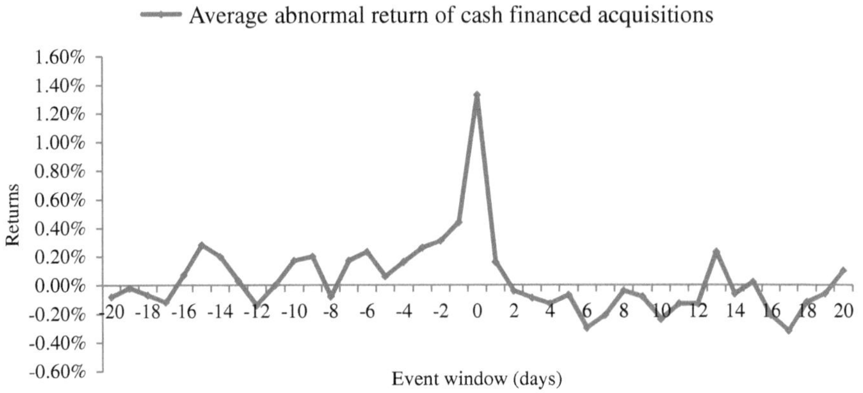

Fig. 3.30 AAR over event window (−20, +20) of M&A financed with cash

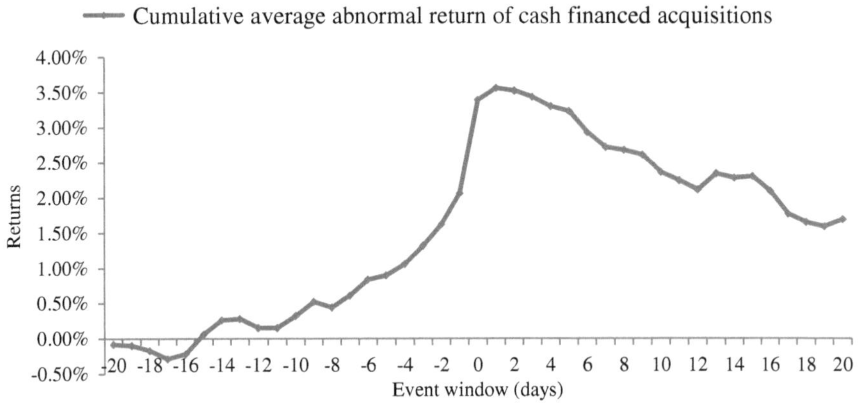

Fig. 3.31 CAAR over event window (−20, +20) of M&A financed with cash

3.7.2 Analysis of Short-Term Performance of M&A Financed with Stock

Table 3.18 reveals that market reacts negatively to the announcement of acquisitions financed with stock. The shareholders of acquiring companies experience negative abnormal returns during pre-event window (−20, −2), however, the results are not statistically significant. During pre-event window (−15, −2), (−10, −2), and (−5, −2), the average abnormal returns are positive but the median abnormal returns are negative; they are also not significant. The market starts reacting positively near the announcement day and generates 0.78 % return on the announcement day.

During the post-announcement windows (+2, +5), (+2, +10), (+2, +15), and (+2, +20), there is a consistent fall in the CAAR values indicating that the negative

Table 3.18 Abnormal returns to the shareholders of acquiring firms of M&A (financed with stock, N = 137) on the announcement day and during multidays event windows, 2003–2015

Event window	Average abnormal return			Positive: negative	Parametric tests				Nonparametric tests		
	Cumulative (%)	Precision-weighted (%)	Median (%)		CDA t	CSS t	Patell Z	SCS Z	GSign Z	Rank Z	Jackknife Z
(−20, −2)	−0.69	−9.52	−1.95	65:72	−0.458	−0.369	0.186	−1.054	−0.287	0.707	−1.684
(−15, −2)	0.42	−4.75	−0.68	69:68	0.319	0.292	1.045	−0.934	0.546	1.786	−0.721
(−10, −2)	0.64	−3.12	−0.57	75:62	0.609	0.549	2.305[a]	−0.919	0.713	1.475	−0.624
(−5, −2)	1.01	−3.28	−0.64	67:70	1.451	1.344	2.678[b]	−0.895	−0.378	1.783	0.138
(−5, 0)	2.09	−4.43	0.97	80:57	2.448[a]	2.231[a]	3.569[b]	−0.833	2.379[a]	2.946[b]	0.844
(−1, 0)	1.10	−1.41	0.55	78:57	2.233[a]	2.235[a]	2.417[b]	−0.751	2.718[b]	2.580[a]	1.925
(0, 0)	0.78	0.72	0.76	77:57	2.240[a]	2.132[a]	2.437[a]	1.994[a]	2.647[b]	2.855[b]	2.577[b]
(0, +1)	0.38	−2.54	−0.03	68:67	0.778	0.638	1.828[a]	−0.928	0.872	1.033	0.306
(0, +5)	−0.97	−6.95	−1.30	52:85	−1.135	−0.935	−0.604	−1.099	−1.453	−1.47	−1.928
(+2, +5)	−1.35	−4.82	−1.91	50:86	−1.946	−1.734	−1.976[a]	−1.212	−2.050[a]	−2.530[a]	−2.772[b]
(+2, +10)	−2.76	−15.34	−3.98	46:91	−2.648[b]	−2.216[a]	−1.203	−1.115	−3.453[b]	−3.004[b]	−2.292[a]
(+2, +15)	−3.72	−23.01	−5.61	49:88	−2.860[b]	−2.301[a]	−1.151	−1.106	−3.786[b]	−2.930[b]	−2.605[b]
(+2, +20)	−4.83	−30.04	−5.66	50:87	−3.185[b]	−2.571[a]	−1.16	−1.107	−3.952[b]	−2.678[b]	−2.653[b]
(−1, +1)	0.72	−3.85	0.45	67:69	1.201	1.004	1.695[a]	−0.917	1.461	1.301	0.361
(−2, +2)	1.39	−4.84	0.87	73:64	1.784	1.454	2.446[b]	−0.896	2.046[a]	1.48	0.175
(−5, +5)	0.38	−10.79	−1.51	63:74	0.327	0.271	1.294	−1.013	−0.12	0.229	−1.204
(−10, +10)	−1.41	−19.63	−3.78	61:76	−0.884	−0.646	1.401	−1.051	−0.62	−0.509	−1.531
(−20, +20)	−0.69	−9.52	−1.95	63:74	−2.157[a]	−1.653	−0.117	−1.084	−0.787	−0.99	−2.506[a]

[a], [b]Denote significance at 5 and 1 %, respectively

reaction turns more strong (the peak value of negative CAAR rises from 0.06 % on day $t(+2)$ to 4.93 % on day $t(+20)$). The CAAR values of 1.98, 0.94, and 1.28 % for the event windows (−5, 0), (−1, 0), and (−2, +2), though positive, are not statistically significant. The extent of negative median abnormal returns during the post-event window is noticeable.

Figure 3.32 depicts that AAR is positive only for 13 days during the event window. Figure 3.33 corroborates the conclusion that negative market reaction generates negative abnormal returns and, after announcement, starts falling more sharply and remains negative during the entire event window.

Shareholders of the acquiring firm perceive higher chances of dilution of earnings per share (EPS) of the stock of the acquiring firm in case acquisition is financed with the stock. Issue of new stock may erode the wealth of the existing shareholders by diluting EPS. On the basis of above findings it is reasonable to conclude that

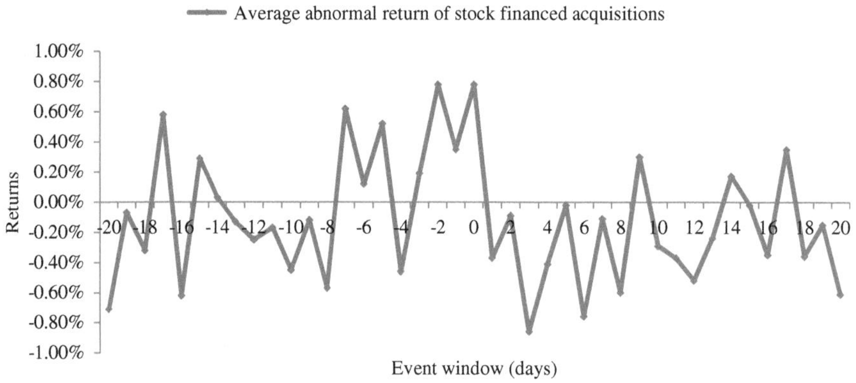

Fig. 3.32 AAR over event window (−20, +20) of M&A financed with stock

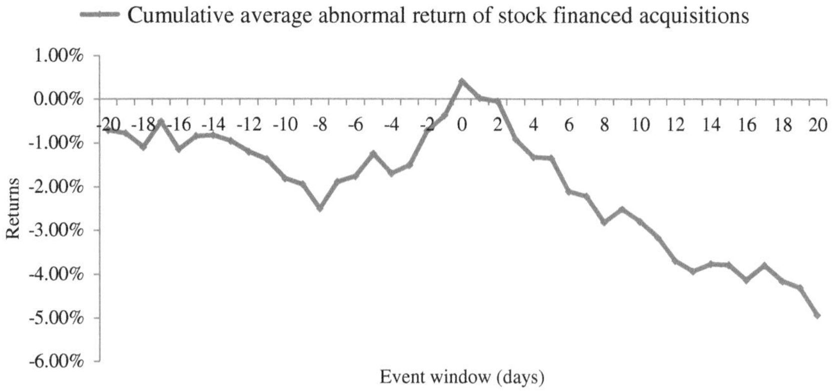

Fig. 3.33 CAAR over event window (−20, +20) of M&A financed with stock

"Issuance of new stock for M&A is a bad news for the market." The finding is in agreement with financial theory (Myers and Majluf 1984) suggesting that issuance of stock is viewed negatively by capital markets. The results are also in line with the empirical evidence with respect to stock issues (DeAngelo et al. 1984; Hansen 1987; Jensen 1986).

3.7.3 Analysis of Short-Term Performance of M&A Financed with Mixed Payment/Earn-Outs

This section explores the influence of innovative mode of financing like combination of cash and stock or earn-out offers used in the acquisitions.[2] Average abnormal returns on the announcement day and cumulative average abnormal returns (CAARs) for various event windows have been analyzed for all acquisitions, financed with a combination of cash and stock or earn-outs. The results indicate that acquisitions generate statistically significant positive abnormal returns when earn-outs are used as a mode of payment for acquisition.

It is obvious from the data summarized in Table 3.19 that shareholders of acquiring companies earn substantial return of 3.49 % on the announcement day. Median abnormal returns are 3.60 %. Returns are positive for more than 78 % stocks. Moreover, the results are statistically significant.

The study documents that the shareholders of acquiring Indian corporates employing mixed financing or earn-outs as a mode of payment experience positive abnormal return of 3.49 % (statistically significant) on the announcement day.

The relevant data shows that the acquirers experience 3.82 % cumulative average abnormal return over the event window of 3 days (−1, 1). The notable finding is that the median cumulative abnormal return is 3.39 %. More than 78 % stocks have positive returns. The results are statistically significant at 5 %. The abnormal returns are also quite impressive of more than 6 % during the pre-event window as well as multidays event window of 6 days (−5, 0), 2 days (1, 0), and 3 days (−1, +1). Moreover, they are statistically also significant.

The cumulative average abnormal returns are also positive for longer event windows of 11 days (−5, +5), 21 days (−10, +10), and 41 days (−20, +20). The positive and impressive returns (6.69 %) over the longer window of 41 days are noteworthy.

Figure 3.34 presents the average abnormal return for the entire event window. The graph portrayed in Fig. 3.35 supports the conclusion that shareholders of

---

[2]Earn-out refers to two-part contractual financing structure in mergers and acquisitions where the target firm must "earn" part of the valuation based on the performance of the business following the acquisition. In an earn-out, part of the acquisition price is paid after closing based on the target firm's ability to attain certain predefined financial goals.

Table 3.19 Abnormal returns to the shareholders of acquiring firms of M&A (financed with earn-outs, combinations, N = 18) on the announcement day and during multidays event windows, 2003–2015

Event window	Average abnormal return			Positive: negative	Parametric tests				Nonparametric tests		
	Cumulative (%)	Precision-weighted (%)	Median (%)		CDA t	CSS t	Patell Z	SCS Z	GSign Z	Rank Z	Jackknife Z
(−20, −2)	4.55	4.84	3.82	10:08	1.165	0.999	1.507	1.277	0.869	1.371	0.49
(−15, −2)	2.79	3.51	2.13	9:09	0.831	1.045	1.27	1.378	0.395	1.084	0.629
(−10, −2)	2.52	2.89	0.20	9:09	0.937	1.117	1.304	1.354	0.395	1.145	0.835
(−5, −2)	1.74	2.30	0.33	9:09	0.973	0.932	1.565	1.089	0.395	0.879	0.436
(−5, 0)	6.24	6.51	4.65	11:07	2.841[b]	2.150[a]	3.590[b]	1.714	1.342	2.118[a]	1.691
(−1, 0)	4.49	4.18	3.46	14:4	3.545[b]	2.640[b]	4.005[b]	1.793	2.762[b]	2.426[a]	2.371[a]
(0, 0)	3.49	3.60	2.83	14:4	3.892[b]	2.974[b]	4.875[b]	2.369[a]	2.762[b]	2.929[b]	2.735[b]
(0, +1)	2.81	2.81	3.03	14:4	2.216[a]	2.428[a]	2.685[b]	2.191[a]	2.762[b]	1.654	2.218[a]
(0, +5)	0.19	0.21	0.58	10:08	0.085	0.071	0.111	0.095	0.869	−0.849	−0.062
(+2, +5)	−2.62	−2.60	−3.42	4:14	−1.464	−1.377	−1.763[a]	−1.636	−1.972[a]	−2.209[a]	−1.549
(+2, +10)	−2.24	−2.33	−5.30	7:11	−0.832	−0.746	−1.044	−0.815	−0.552	−1.492	−1.104
(+2, +15)	−1.68	−2.10	−5.05	5:13	−0.502	−0.44	−0.748	−0.65	−1.499	−1.033	−0.716
(+2, +20)	−1.68	−2.98	−6.40	6:12	−0.429	−0.322	−0.918	−0.682	−1.025	−1.135	−0.806
(−1, +1)	3.82	3.39	3.69	15:3	2.458[a]	2.378[a]	2.648[b]	1.675	3.236[b]	1.64	2.236[a]
(−2, +2)	2.23	1.99	2.87	11:07	1.11	1.001	1.211	0.816	1.342	0.528	0.637
(−5, +5)	2.94	3.08	0.71	9:09	0.988	0.81	1.263	0.833	0.395	0.054	0.36
(−10, +10)	4.10	3.92	3.83	10:08	0.998	0.801	1.171	0.778	0.869	0.393	0.397
(−20, +20)	6.69	5.11	1.97	10:08	1.166	0.784	1.117	0.749	0.869	0.604	0.163

[a, b]Denote significance at 5 and 1 %, respectively

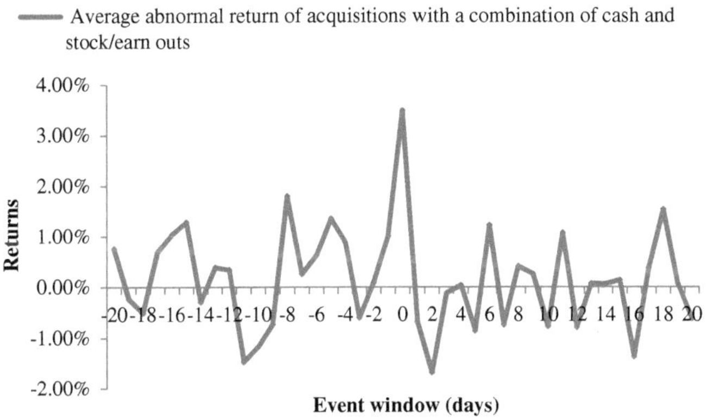

Fig. 3.34 AAR of M&A financed with a combination of cash and stock/earn-outs over event window (−20, +20)

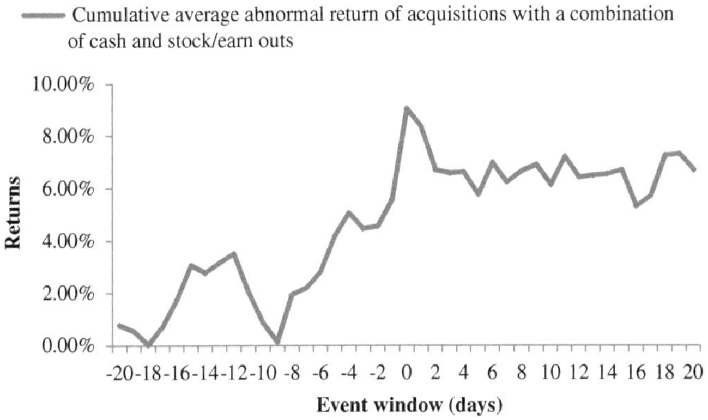

Fig. 3.35 CAAR of M&A financed with a combination of cash and stock/earn-outs over event window (−20, +20)

acquiring companies experience substantial gain when acquisition is financed with some combination or earn-outs.

3.7.4 *Payment Effect*

Independent t-test has been conducted to measure the difference between mean CAR of acquisitions when cash and stock is employed as mode of payment; the results are tabulated in Table 3.20.

Table 3.20 Independent samples t-test for difference of mean CAR (cash payment, stock payment)

Event window	Mean CAR (%) Cash payment (N = 645)	Mean CAR (%) Stock payment (N = 137)	Mean difference (%)	t-value	Significance value
(−20, −2)	1.62	−0.69	2.31	1.17	0.24
(−15, −2)	1.84	0.42	1.42	0.57	0.57
(−10, −2)	1.47	0.64	0.83	0.65	0.51
(−5, −2)	0.78	1.01	−0.23	−0.96	0.34
(−5, 0)	2.54	2.09	0.45	0.17	0.87
(−1, 0)	1.77	1.10	0.67	0.93	0.35
(0, 0)	1.33	0.78	0.55	0.27	0.79
(0, +1)	1.49	0.38	1.11	0.43	0.67
(0, +5)	1.17	−0.97	2.14	1.94	0.05
(+2, +5)	−0.33	−1.35	1.02	2.29[a]	0.02
(+2, +10)	−1.19	−2.76	1.57	0.77	0.44
(+2, +15)	−1.25	−3.72	2.47	0.97	0.33
(+2, +20)	−1.86	−4.83	2.97	0.7	0.48
(−1, +1)	1.93	0.72	1.21	0.91	0.37
(−2, +2)	2.20	1.39	0.81	0.38	0.70
(−5, +5)	2.38	0.38	2.00	1.3	0.20
(−10, +10)	2.21	−1.41	3.62	0.47	0.64
(−20, +20)	1.69	−0.69	2.38	1.42	0.16

[a, b]Denote significance at 5 and 1 %, respectively

It is apparent that mean difference is positive for all the windows except pre-event window of 4 days (−5, −2). However, the difference is significant for event window [(+2, +5) (p-value = 0.02 < 0.05)] (Tables 3.21 and 3.22).

Figure 3.36 depicts that AAR is positive for 21 days in the case of cash-financed acquisitions, only for 13 days in the case of stock-financed acquisitions and for 25 days in the case of mixed financing/earn-outs acquisitions during the event window.

Figure 3.37 corroborates the conclusion that market reaction is positive for cash-financed acquisitions and negative for stock-financed acquisitions. Shareholders of the acquiring firm perceive lower possibility of dilution of earnings per share (EPS) of the stock of the acquiring firm in case acquisition is financed with cash. Issue of new stock may erode the wealth of the existing shareholders by diluting EPS.

Table 3.21 Independent samples t-test for difference of mean CAR (cash payment, mixed payment/earn-outs)

Event window	Mean CAR (%) Cash payment ($N = 645$)	Mean CAR (%) Mixed payment/earn-outs ($N = 18$)	Mean difference	t-value	Significance value
(−20, −2)	1.62	4.55	−2.93	−1.04	0.297
(−15, −2)	1.84	2.79	−0.95	−1.11	0.268
(−10, −2)	1.47	2.52	−1.05	−1.03	0.302
(−5, −2)	0.78	1.74	−0.96	−1.65	0.100
(−5, 0)	2.54	6.24	−3.70	−0.42	0.673
(−1, 0)	1.77	4.49	−2.72	−0.92	0.36
(0, 0)	1.33	3.49	−2.16	−0.4	0.689
(0, +1)	1.49	2.81	−1.32	−1.42	0.157
(0, +5)	1.17	0.19	0.98	0.23	0.821
(+2, +5)	−0.33	−2.62	2.29	1.51	0.132
(+2, +10)	−1.19	−2.24	1.05	0.92	0.356
(+2, +15)	−1.25	−1.68	0.43	0.72	0.474
(+2, +20)	−1.86	−1.68	−0.18	−0.96	0.339
(−1, +1)	1.93	3.82	−1.89	−1.20	0.231
(−2, +2)	2.20	2.23	−0.03	−0.31	0.755
(−5, +5)	2.38	2.94	−0.56	−0.76	0.446
(−10, +10)	2.21	4.10	−1.89	−0.55	0.581
(−20, +20)	1.69	6.69	−5.00	−0.39	0.695

[a, b]Denote significance at 5 and 1 %, respectively

The acquisitions, financed with cash, experience higher returns than the acquisitions financed with stock. This could be a signal in favor of "asymmetric information hypothesis and free cash flow hypothesis."

On the basis of above findings, it is reasonable to conclude that "Issuance of new stock is a bad news for the market." The study also has managerial application in indicating mergers and acquisition strategies are the source of value creation for an emerging economy like India when earn-outs or a mixed method of financing is employed to mitigate the risk of valuation and adverse selection.

Table 3.22 Independent samples t-test for difference of mean CAR (stock payment, mixed payment/earn-outs)

Event window	Mean CAR (%) Stock payment ($N = 137$)	Mean CAR (%) Mixed payment/earn-outs ($N = 18$)	Mean difference	t-value	Significance value
(−20, −2)	−0.69	4.55	−5.24	−1.32	0.191
(−15, −2)	0.42	2.79	−2.37	−1.11	0.268
(−10, −2)	0.64	2.52	−1.88	−0.61	0.54
(−5, −2)	1.01	1.74	−0.73	−1.02	0.3094
(−5, 0)	2.09	6.24	−4.15	−2.2[a]	0.0295
(−1, 0)	1.10	4.49	−3.39	−2.47[a]	0.015
(0, 0)	0.78	3.49	−2.71	−2.79[b]	0.006
(0, +1)	0.38	2.81	−2.43	−1.22	0.2252
(0, +5)	−0.97	0.19	−1.16	−0.04	0.9678
(+2, +5)	−1.35	−2.62	1.27	0.94	0.347
(+2, +10)	−2.76	−2.24	−0.52	−0.49	0.6273
(+2, +15)	−3.72	−1.68	−2.04	−0.22	0.8261
(+2, +20)	−4.83	−1.68	−3.15	−0.18	0.858
(−1, +1)	0.72	3.82	−3.10	−1.43	0.1538
(−2, +2)	1.39	2.23	−0.84	−0.05	0.959
(−5, +5)	0.38	2.94	−2.56	−0.13	0.899
(−10, +10)	−1.41	4.10	−5.51	−0.22	0.828
(−20, +20)	−0.69	6.69	−7.38	−0.73	0.467

[a, b]Denote significance at 5 and 1 %, respectively

3.8 Analysis of Geography Effect

One of the sources of benefits of cross-border acquisitions is the geographical diversification that enables acquiring firms to internationalize and use their strategic advantages in overseas markets. The benefits of intercountry diversification are not same for all the international markets in which the acquiring firm acquires target firms. Regional domicile hypothesis considers geographic influence on the performance of acquiring firms. A disaggregated analysis has been conducted on the basis of geographic origin of target firms to examine the performance of the acquirers of cross-border acquisitions. The sample of cross-border acquisition has been segregated for target firms from developed markets and emerging markets. The target firms from developed markets have been further segregated in acquisitions of US and non-US target firms.

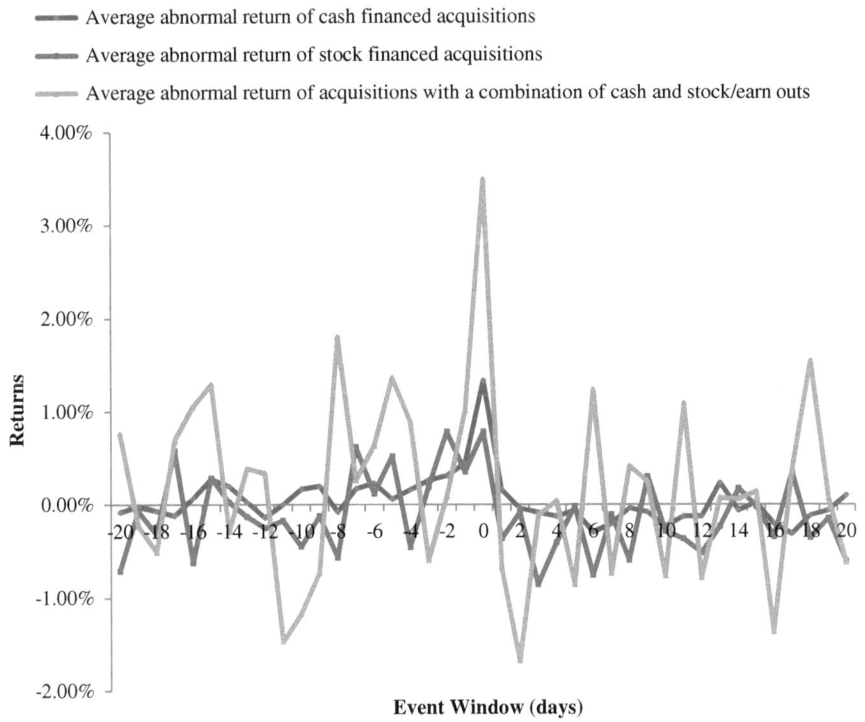

Fig. 3.36 AAR over event window (−20, +20) of M&A based on mode of payment (cash, stock, mixed/earn-outs)

3.8.1 Analysis of Short-Term Performance of Acquisitions of Target Firms from Developed Markets

Table 3.23 presents the data relating to the impact of announcements of cross-border acquisitions of target firms from developed markets across various event windows by reporting the CAAR values and their corresponding test statistic values. The CAAR values across various preannouncement event windows (−20, −2), (−15, −2), (−10, −2), (−5, −2), and (−5, 0) are 1.62, 1.45, 1, 0.93, and 3.15 %, respectively. The CAAR values for the last window are significant at 1 % level. This announcement effect during the event windows (−1, 0), (0, +1), (−1, +1), (−2, +2), (−5, +5), and (−10, +10) has been interpreted by analyzing the CAAR values of 2.22, 2.07, 2.5, 3.07, 3.19, and 2.21 %, respectively. These values are highly significant at 1 % indicating that null hypothesis of zero CAAR has been rejected.

During the post-announcement windows (+2, +5), (+2, +10), (+2, +15), and (+2, +20), there is a consistent fall in the CAAR values indicating that the positive reaction is almost nullified by the negative reaction (the peak value of CAAR

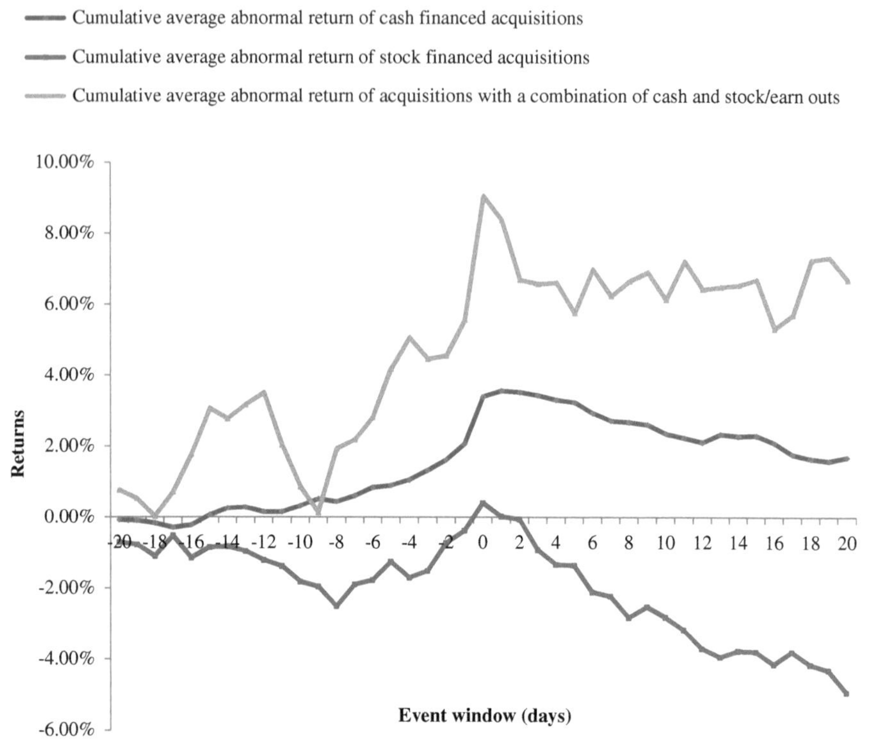

Fig. 3.37 CAAR over event window (−20, +20) of M&A based on method of payment (cash, stock)

decline from 4.31 % on day $t(+3)$ to 1.7 % on day $t(+20)$). The CAAR values of 1.70 % for the event window, and (−20, +20), though positive, are not statistically significant.

Figure 3.38 depicts that AAR is positive for 21 days during event window. Figure 3.39 corroborates the conclusion that strong positive market reaction generates high abnormal returns and, after announcement, starts falling and remains positive during the entire event window.

3.8.1.1 Analysis of Short-Term Performance of Acquisitions of US Target Firms

Table 3.24 depicts the abnormal returns for the cross-border acquisitions of target firms from US. It is revealed from the data contained in the Table that positive market reaction is strong on the announcement and the windows around the announcement. This announcement effect during the event windows (−5, 0), (−1, 0), (0, +1), (−1, +1) (−2, +2), and (−5, +5) has been interpreted by analyzing

Table 3.23 Abnormal returns to the shareholders of acquiring firms of cross-border acquisitions (developed markets $N = 291$) on the announcement day and during multidays event windows, 2003–2015

Event window	Average abnormal return			Positive: negative	Parametric tests				Nonparametric tests		
	Cumulative (%)	Precision-weighted (%)	Median (%)		CDA t	CSS t	Patell Z	SCS Z	GSign Z	Rank Z	Jackknife Z
(−20, −2)	1.62	1.60	0.47	151:140	1.835	1.95	2.479[b]	2.237[a]	2.259[a]	1.846	1.31
(−15, −2)	1.45	1.43	0.45	152:139	1.909	2.163[a]	2.564[b]	2.485[a]	2.377[a]	2.001[a]	1.599
(−10, −2)	1.00	0.89	−0.26	138:153	1.643	2.047[a]	1.934[a]	2.011[a]	0.728	1.263	1.198
(−5, −2)	0.93	0.65	0.02	146:145	2.290[a]	2.705[b]	2.128[a]	2.215[a]	1.671	2.062[a]	2.081[a]
(−5, 0)	3.15	2.61	2.02	189:102	6.343[b]	6.861[b]	7.145[b]	6.216[b]	6.734[b]	5.692[b]	6.454[b]
(−1, 0)	2.22	1.98	1.28	202:89	7.749[b]	7.303[b]	9.436[b]	6.630[b]	8.265[b]	6.942[b]	7.494[b]
(0, 0)	1.80	1.64	1.22	200:91	8.859[b]	7.453[b]	11.016[b]	7.030[b]	8.030[b]	7.638[b]	7.956[b]
(0, +1)	2.07	1.84	1.43	185:106	7.214[b]	6.449[b]	8.741[b]	5.972[b]	6.263[b]	6.041[b]	6.366[b]
(0, +5)	1.84	1.62	0.66	157:134	3.699[b]	3.725[b]	4.448[b]	3.624[b]	2.966[b]	2.775[b]	3.357[b]
(+2, +5)	−0.23	−0.21	−0.56	132:159	−0.571	−0.605	−0.734	−0.641	0.022	−0.873	−1.183
(+2, +10)	−1.28	−1.02	−1.31	115:176	−2.108[a]	−2.328[a]	−2.281[a]	−2.022[a]	−1.980[a]	−2.229[a]	−2.768[b]
(+2, +15)	−1.46	−1.10	−1.84	116:175	−1.923	−2.123[a]	−1.970[a]	−1.772	−1.862	−1.78	−2.319[a]
(+2, +20)	−2.42	−1.83	−2.76	117:174	−2.739[b]	−2.922[b]	−2.797[b]	−2.497[a]	−1.745	−2.352[a]	−3.143[b]
(−1, +1)	2.50	2.18	1.88	190:101	7.103[b]	6.852[b]	8.486[b]	6.090[b]	6.852[b]	6.191[b]	6.594[b]
(−2, +2)	3.07	2.57	2.00	191:100	6.760[b]	7.001[b]	7.713[b]	6.225[b]	6.970[b]	5.884[b]	6.640[b]
(−5, +5)	3.19	2.59	2.55	178:113	4.746[b]	5.257[b]	5.248[b]	4.695[b]	5.439[b]	3.950[b]	4.504[b]
(−10, +10)	2.21	2.01	1.74	166:125	2.381[a]	2.739[b]	2.939[b]	2.644[b]	4.026[b]	1.708	1.858
(−20, +20)	1.70	1.91	1.02	159:132	1.306	1.401	2.065[a]	1.727	3.202[b]	1.33	0.656

[a], [b]Denote significance at 5 and 1 %, respectively

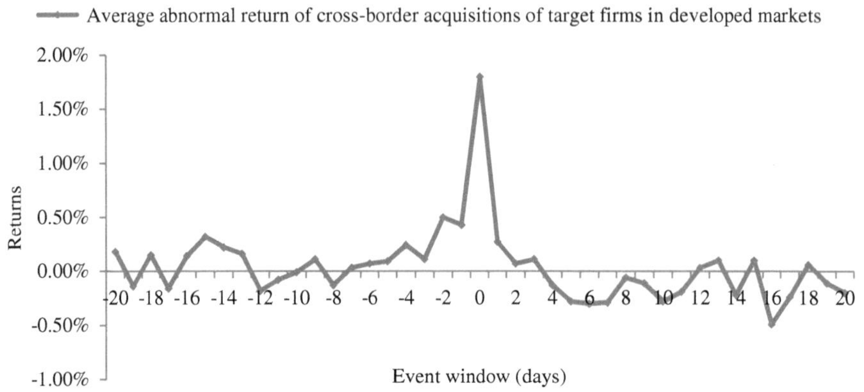

Fig. 3.38 AAR over event window (−20, +20) of cross-border acquisitions from developed markets

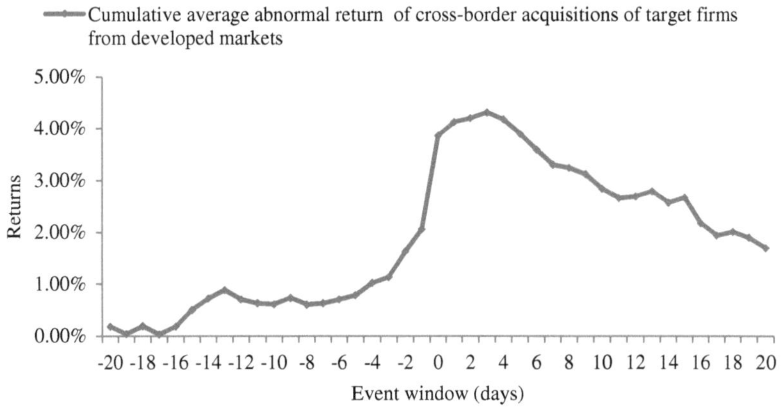

Fig. 3.39 CAAR over event window (−20, +20) of cross-border acquisitions from developed markets

the CAAR values of 3.20, 2.57, 2.6, 3.04, 3.60, and 3.44 %, respectively. These values are highly significant at 1 % indicating that null hypothesis of zero CAAR has been rejected.

The acquirer's shareholders experience negative abnormal returns during pre-event window (−20, −2); however, the results are not statistically significant. During the post-announcement windows (+2, +5), (+2, +10), (+2, +15), and (+2, +20), there is a consistent fall in the CAAR values indicating that the negative reaction turns more strong (the peak value of positive CAAR decline from 2.78 % on day *t*(+2) to 0.33 % on day *t*(+20)). The CAAR values of 1.61 % (−10, +10) though positive, are not statistically significant.

Table 3.24 Abnormal returns to the shareholders of acquiring firms of cross-border acquisitions from US (N = 130) on the announcement day and during multidays event windows, 2003–2015

Event window	Average abnormal return			Positive: negative	Parametric tests				Nonparametric tests		
	Cumulative (%)	Precision-weighted (%)	Median (%)		CDA t	CSS t	Patell Z	SCS Z	GSign Z	Rank Z	Jackknife Z
(−20, −2)	−0.37	−0.20	−2.30	57:73	−0.31	−0.31	−0.173	−0.185	−0.422	−0.128	−1.057
(−15, −2)	0.91	1.09	0.39	66:64	0.874	0.967	1.268	1.233	1.162	1.068	0.243
(−10, −2)	0.31	0.48	−0.84	58:72	0.367	0.429	0.679	0.658	−0.246	0.593	−0.108
(−5, −2)	0.63	0.46	−0.62	59:71	1.13	1.213	1.011	1.106	−0.07	1.159	0.848
(−5, 0)	3.20	2.69	2.04	84:46	4.711[b]	4.800[b]	4.711[b]	4.506[b]	4.331[b]	4.127[b]	4.788[b]
(−1, 0)	2.57	2.22	1.49	96:34	6.562[b]	5.439[b]	6.734[b]	4.457[b]	6.444[b]	5.510[b]	5.687[b]
(0, 0)	2.13	1.80	1.38	91:39	7.692[b]	5.480[b]	7.699[b]	4.472[b]	5.564[b]	5.879[b]	5.716[b]
(0, +1)	2.60	2.07	1.75	92:38	6.641[b]	4.831[b]	6.249[b]	3.828[b]	5.740[b]	5.122[b]	4.689[b]
(0, +5)	2.37	1.77	1.17	71:59	3.491[b]	3.009[b]	3.097[b]	2.454[a]	2.043[a]	2.296[a]	2.554[a]
(+2, +5)	−0.23	−0.29	−0.66	58:72	−0.42	−0.37	−0.625	−0.529	−0.246	−0.809	−0.841
(+2, +10)	−1.73	−1.41	−1.65	51:79	−2.087[a]	−1.972[a]	−2.024[a]	−1.831	−1.479	−2.234[a]	−2.688[b]
(+2, +15)	−2.15	−1.88	−2.32	53:77	−2.078[a]	−2.046[a]	−2.143[a]	−1.992[a]	−1.127	−1.88	−2.513[a]
(+2, +20)	−2.33	−2.03	−2.29	53:77	−1.933	−1.8	−1.965[a]	−1.849	−1.127	−1.694	−2.431[a]
(−1, +1)	3.04	2.49	2.18	94:36	6.339[b]	5.101[b]	6.163[b]	3.987[b]	6.092[b]	5.286[b]	5.019[b]
(−2, +2)	3.60	2.93	2.90	87:43	5.815[b]	5.177[b]	5.624[b]	4.209[b]	4.860[b]	4.960[b]	5.165[b]
(−5, +5)	3.44	2.66	2.69	82:48	3.739[b]	3.608[b]	3.448[b]	3.054[b]	3.979[b]	2.971[b]	3.179[b]
(−10, +10)	1.61	1.52	0.49	68:62	1.27	1.263	1.433	1.215	1.514	0.924	0.449
(−20, +20)	0.33	0.22	0.37	67:63	0.188	0.179	0.208	0.124	1.338	0.19	−0.808

[a], [b]Denote significance at 5 and 1 %, respectively

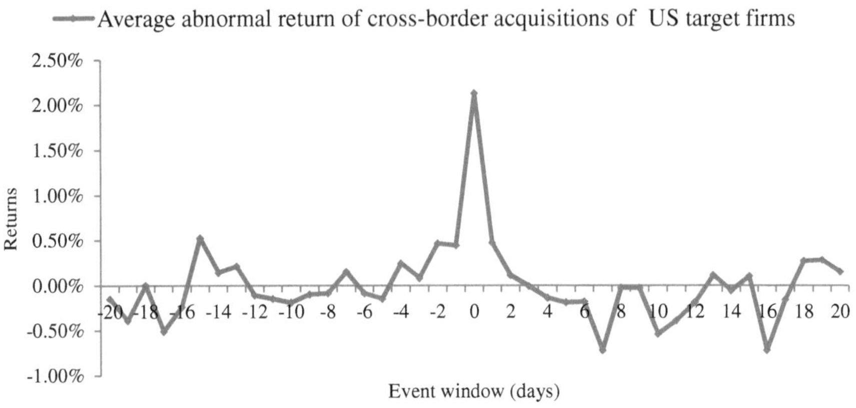

Fig. 3.40 AAR over event window (−20, +20) of cross-border acquisitions of US firms

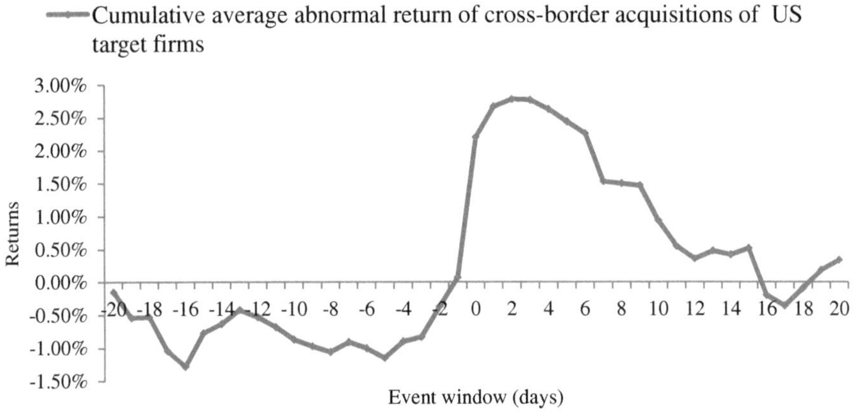

Fig. 3.41 CAAR over event window (−20, +20) of cross-border acquisitions of US firms

Figure 3.40 depicts that AAR is positive for 14 days during the event window. Figure 3.41 corroborates the conclusion that market reaction generates positive abnormal returns and, after announcement, starts falling more sharply.

3.8.1.2 Analysis of Short-Term Performance of Acquisitions of Target Firms from Non-US Developed Markets

Table 3.25 illustrates the impact of announcements of cross-border acquisitions of target firms from non-US developed markets across various event windows by reporting the CAAR values and their corresponding test statistic values. The CAAR values across various preannouncement event windows (−20, −2), (−15, −2),

Table 3.25 Abnormal returns to the shareholders of acquiring firms of cross-border acquisitions (non-US developed markets, $N = 161$) on the announcement day and during multidays event windows, 2003–2015

Event window	Average abnormal return			Positive: negative	Parametric tests				Nonparametric tests		
	Cumulative (%)	Precision-weighted (%)	Median (%)		CDA t	CSS t	Patell Z	SCS Z	GSign Z	Rank Z	Jackknife Z
(−20, −2)	3.24	2.94	2.60	94:67	2.484[a]	2.855[b]	3.487[b]	3.075[b]	3.420[b]	2.727[b]	2.590[b]
(−15, −2)	1.89	1.69	0.60	86:75	1.689	1.994[a]	2.307[a]	2.210[a]	2.152[a]	1.909	1.852
(−10, −2)	1.56	1.19	−0.03	80:81	1.742	2.330[a]	1.990[a]	2.163[a]	1.202	1.277	1.642
(−5, −2)	1.17	0.79	0.79	87:74	1.964[a]	2.549[a]	1.952[a]	1.941	2.311[a]	1.919	1.981[a]
(−5, 0)	3.12	2.56	1.99	105:56	4.257[b]	4.910[b]	5.373[b]	4.373[b]	5.162[b]	4.488[b]	4.425[b]
(−1, 0)	1.94	1.81	1.04	106:55	4.597[b]	4.901[b]	6.635[b]	4.909[b]	5.321[b]	5.060[b]	4.938[b]
(0, 0)	1.53	1.52	1.04	109:52	5.112[b]	5.064[b]	7.893[b]	5.503[b]	5.796[b]	5.725[b]	5.533[b]
(0, +1)	1.64	1.67	0.84	93:68	3.881[b]	4.293[b]	6.137[b]	4.664[b]	3.261[b]	4.117[b]	4.315[b]
(0, +5)	1.41	1.51	0.51	86:75	1.926	2.252[a]	3.196[b]	2.659[b]	2.152[a]	1.937	2.204[a]
(+2, +5)	−0.23	−0.16	−0.21	74:87	−0.386	−0.489	−0.424	−0.38	0.251	−0.539	−0.829
(+2, +10)	−0.92	−0.72	−1.06	64:97	−1.024	−1.312	−1.248	−1.087	−1.333	−1.223	−1.25
(+2, +15)	−0.90	−0.53	−1.52	63:98	−0.804	−0.991	−0.722	−0.638	−1.492	−0.896	−0.824
(+2, +20)	−2.49	−1.69	−2.76	64:97	−1.915	−2.319[a]	−1.994[a]	−1.707	−1.333	−1.873	−2.022[a]
(−1, +1)	2.05	1.96	1.45	96:65	3.970[b]	4.590[b]	5.871[b]	4.658[b]	3.736[b]	4.188[b]	4.317[b]
(−2, +2)	2.63	2.31	1.80	104:57	3.942[b]	4.725[b]	5.315[b]	4.588[b]	5.004[b]	4.035[b]	4.244[b]
(−5, +5)	3.00	2.55	2.48	96:65	3.025[b]	3.813[b]	3.957[b]	3.557[b]	3.736[b]	3.019[b]	3.191[b]
(−10, +10)	2.70	2.37	2.90	98:63	1.971[a]	2.604[b]	2.664[b]	2.511[a]	4.053[b]	1.618	2.124[a]
(−20, +20)	2.80	3.17	2.01	92:69	1.462	1.757	2.590[b]	2.221[a]	3.103[b]	1.714	1.645

[a], [b]Denote significance at 5 and 1 %, respectively

(−10, −2), (−5, −2), and (−5, 0) are 3.24, 1.89, 1.56, 1.17, and 3.12 %, respectively. The CAAR value for the last window is maximum significant at 1 % level.

This announcement effect during the event windows (−1, 0), (0, +1), (−1, +1), (−2, +2), (−5, +5), and (−10, +10) has been interpreted by analyzing the CAAR values of 1.94, 1.64, 2.05, 2.63, 3, and 2.47 %, respectively. These values are highly significant at 1 % indicating that null hypothesis of zero CAAR has been rejected.

During the post-announcement windows (+2, +5), (+2, +10), (+2, +15), and (+2, +20), there is a consistent fall in the CAAR values indicating that the positive reaction is almost nullified by the negative reaction (the peak value of CAAR decline from 5.55 % on day $t(+3)$ to 2.80 % on day $t(+20)$). The CAAR values of 2.80 % for the event window (−20, +20), though positive, are not statistically significant.

Figure 3.42 depicts that AAR is positive for 23 days during event window. Figure 3.43 corroborates the conclusion that strong positive market reaction for target firms from non-US developed markets generates high positive abnormal returns and remains positive during the entire event window.

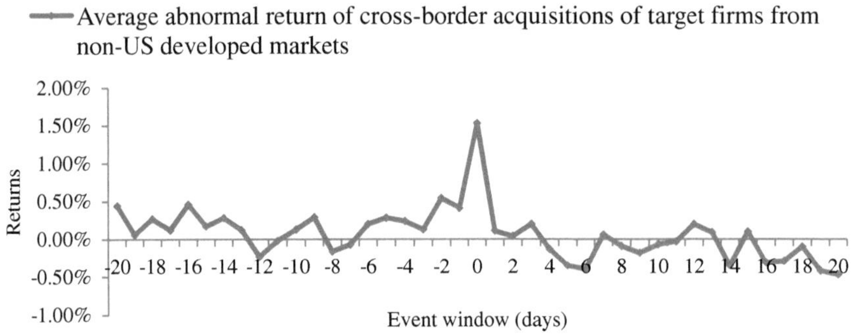

Fig. 3.42 AAR over event window (−20, +20) of cross-border acquisitions of target firms from non-US developed markets

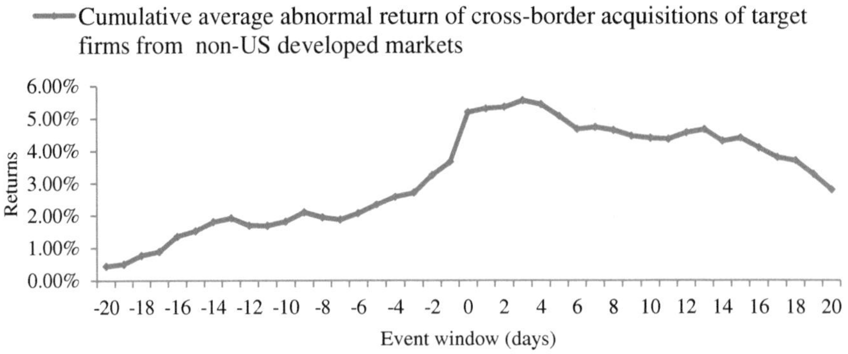

Fig. 3.43 CAAR over event window (−20, +20) of cross-border acquisitions of target firms from non-US developed markets

3.8.2 Analysis of Short-Term Performance of Cross-Border Acquisitions of Target Firms from Emerging Markets

Table 3.26 illustrates the impact of announcements of cross-border acquisitions of target firms from emerging markets. The CAAR values across various preannouncement event windows (−20, −2), (−15, −2), (−10, −2), (−5, −2), and (−5, 0) are 3.98, 3.20, 3.07, 1.36, and 2.46 %, respectively. The CAAR values for the pre-event windows are significant at 5 % level.

This announcement effect during the event windows (−1, 0) and (0, +1) has been interpreted by analyzing the CAAR values of 1.10 and 1.16 %, respectively. These values are significant at 5 % indicating that null hypothesis of zero CAAR has been rejected.

During the post-announcement windows (+2, +5), (+2, +10), (+2, +15), and (+2, +20), there is decline in the CAAR values. The peak value of CAAR declined from 5.11 % on day (0, +1) to 4.76 % on day (0, +20). The CAAR values of 1.67, 2.11, 3.47, and 2.74 % for the event windows (−1, +1) (−2, +2), (−5, +5), (−10, +10), and (−20, +20), though positive, are not statistically significant.

Figure 3.44 depicts that AAR is positive for 20 days during event window. Figure 3.45 corroborates the conclusion that strong positive market reaction for target firms from emerging markets generates high positive abnormal returns and remains positive during the entire event window.

3.8.2.1 Geography Effect

Independent t-test has been conducted to measure the difference between mean CAR of acquisitions of target firm from developed markets and emerging markets. The results are tabulated in Table 3.27.

It is apparent from the relevant data contained in Table 3.27 that mean difference of CAR acquisitions of target firm from developed markets and emerging markets vary for different event windows; in some cases, the difference is positive while in others it is negative. However, the difference is significant for the announcement day ($p = 0.008 < 0.01$) and event windows around the announcement (−1,0) ($p = 0.008 < 0.01$), (−1, +1) ($p = 0.0171 < 0.05$) (−2, +2) ($p = 0.033 < 0.05$).

Figure 3.46 depicts that AAR is positive for 20 days in the case of acquisitions of target firms from emerging markets and 22 days for acquisitions of target firms from developed markets. Figure 3.47 depicts that abnormal returns of acquisitions from developed as well as emerging markets are positive during the event window.

It is noted that though the abnormal returns of cross-border acquisitions from developed markets and emerging markets vary for different event windows, the difference is not statistically significant.

In addition, independent t-test has also been conducted to measure the difference between mean CAR of acquisitions of target firm from US and non-US developed markets; the results are tabulated in Table 3.28.

Table 3.26 Abnormal returns to the shareholders of acquiring firms of cross-border acquisitions (emerging markets $N = 52$) on the announcement day and during multidays event windows, 2003–2015

Event window	Average abnormal return			Positive: negative	Parametric tests				Nonparametric tests		
	Cumulative (%)	Precision-weighted (%)	Median (%)		CDA t	CSS t	Patell Z	SCS Z	GSign Z	Rank Z	Jackknife Z
(−20, −2)	3.98	4.01	2.06	33:19	2.487[a]	1.857	2.849[b]	1.960[a]	2.636[b]	2.757[b]	1.852
(−15, −2)	3.20	3.15	2.20	31:21	2.331[a]	2.125[a]	2.612[b]	2.339[a]	2.079[a]	2.347[a]	1.990[a]
(−10, −2)	3.07	2.87	0.82	31:21	2.787[b]	2.491[a]	2.960[b]	2.523[a]	2.079[a]	2.832[b]	2.276[a]
(−5, −2)	1.36	1.44	0.81	32:20	1.851	1.926	2.227[a]	2.218[a]	2.358[a]	2.686[b]	1.924
(−5, 0)	2.46	2.05	1.10	29:23	2.734[b]	2.943[b]	2.591[b]	2.960[b]	1.522	3.267[b]	2.556[a]
(−1, 0)	1.10	0.61	0.68	30:22	2.118[a]	2.054[a]	1.338	1.274	1.8	1.859	1.316
(0, +1)	1.16	0.84	0.59	30:22	3.173[b]	2.845[b]	2.587[b]	2.299[a]	1.8	2.772[b]	2.387[a]
(0, 0)	1.20	0.83	0.47	33:19	2.322[a]	1.959	1.807[a]	1.453	2.636[b]	2.048[a]	1.565
(0, +5)	0.45	0.27	0.53	29:23	0.505	0.581	0.346	0.322	1.522	0.647	0.044
(+2, +5)	−0.75	−0.56	−0.65	25:27	−1.024	−1.117	−0.854	−0.843	0.407	−0.655	−1.106
(+2, +10)	−1.94	−1.53	−2.04	19:33	−1.763	−1.924	−1.564	−1.6	−1.264	−1.801	−1.892
(+2, +15)	−1.53	−1.03	−1.53	23:29	−1.114	−1.224	−0.835	−0.823	−0.15	−0.975	−1.419
(+2, +20)	−2.37	−2.13	−2.50	24:28	−1.485	−1.737	−1.508	−1.635	0.129	−1.7	−2.117[a]
(−1, +1)	1.14	0.60	1.00	30:22	1.793	1.721	1.075	0.95	1.8	1.59	1.077
(−2, +2)	1.08	0.78	1.03	30:22	1.321	1.348	1.086	0.926	1.8	1.691	0.872
(−5, +5)	1.75	1.49	0.99	29:23	1.436	1.683	1.389	1.481	1.522	2.055[a]	1.148
(−10, +10)	2.27	1.95	0.02	26:26	1.348	1.518	1.32	1.387	0.686	1.276	0.747
(−20, +20)	2.74	2.47	1.28	31:21	1.167	1.295	1.203	1.16	2.079[a]	1.15	0.363

[a, b]Denote significance at 5 and 1 %, respectively

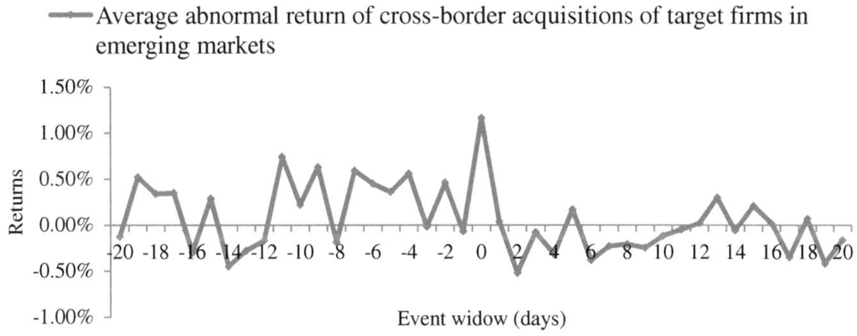

Fig. 3.44 CAAR over event window (−20, +20) of cross-border acquisitions from emerging markets

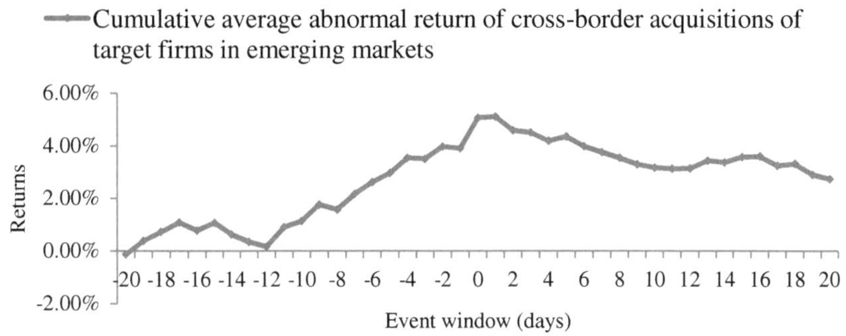

Fig. 3.45 CAAR over event window (−20, +20) of cross-border acquisitions from emerging markets

Independent t-test shown in Table 3.28 indicates that mean difference between CAR of acquisitions of target firms from US and non-US developed markets also vary for different event windows; in some cases, the difference is positive while in others it is negative. However, the difference is significant for event window (−20, −2) ($p = 0.043 < 0.05$).

Figure 3.48 depicts that AAR is positive for only 17 days in the case of acquisitions of target firms from US and 24 days for acquisitions of target firms from non-US developed markets during the event window. Figure 3.49 depicts that abnormal returns of acquisitions from developed markets as well as emerging is positive during the event window.

On the basis of above findings, it may be concluded that though the abnormal returns of cross-border acquisitions from non-US developed markets are higher than that for US target firms, the difference is statistically significant only for one window.

Table 3.27 Independent samples t-test for difference of mean CAR of cross-border acquisitions (developed markets, emerging markets)

Event window	Mean CAR (%) of acquisitions of developed market target firms (N = 291)	Mean CAR (%) of acquisitions of emerging market target firms (N = 52)	Mean difference (%)	t-value	Significance value
(−20, −2)	1.62	3.98	−2.36	−1.34	0.1855
(−15, −2)	1.45	3.20	−1.75	−1.41	0.1632
(−10, −2)	1.00	3.07	−2.07	−1.84	0.0704
(−5, −2)	0.93	1.36	−0.43	−1.73	0.0885
(−5, 0)	3.15	2.46	0.69	0.42	0.6783
(−1, 0)	2.22	1.10	1.12	2.71[b]	0.008
(0, 0)	1.80	1.16	0.64	2.15[a]	0.0341
(0, +1)	2.07	1.20	0.87	1.79	0.0764
(0, +5)	1.84	0.45	1.39	1.49	0.1409
(+2, +5)	−0.23	−0.75	0.52	0.32	0.7478
(+2, +10)	−1.28	−1.94	0.66	0.45	0.6542
(+2, +15)	−1.46	−1.53	0.07	0.27	0.7891
(+2, +20)	−2.42	−2.37	−0.05	−0.32	0.749
(−1, +1)	2.50	1.14	1.36	2.43[a]	0.0171
(−2, +2)	3.07	1.08	1.99	2.17[a]	0.033
(−5, +5)	3.19	1.75	1.44	0.7	0.4839
(−10, +10)	2.21	2.27	−0.06	0.01	0.9882
(−20, +20)	1.70	2.74	−1.04	−0.27	0.7906

[a, b]Denote significance at 5 and 1 %, respectively

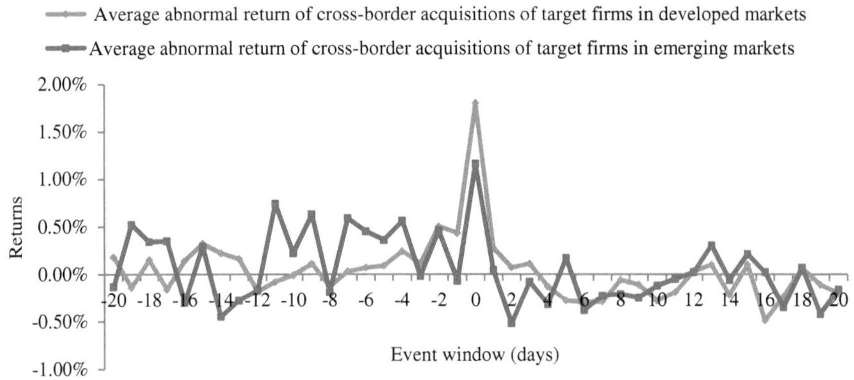

Fig. 3.46 AAR over event window (−20, +20) of cross-border acquisitions (developed markets, emerging markets)

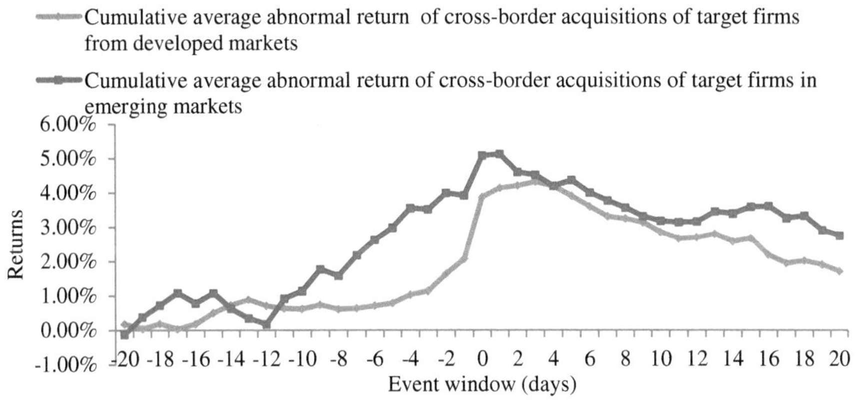

Fig. 3.47 CAAR over event window (−20, +20) of cross-border acquisitions (developed markets, emerging markets)

Table 3.28 Independent samples t-test for difference of mean CAR of cross-border acquisitions (US, non-US developed markets)

Event Window	Mean CAR (%) acquisitions of non-US developed market target firms (N = 161)	Mean CAR (%) acquisitions of US target firms (N = 130)	Mean difference	t-value	Significance value
(−20, −2)	3.24	−0.37	3.61	2.04[a]	0.0427
(−15, −2)	1.89	0.91	0.98	0.43	0.6639
(−10, −2)	1.56	0.31	1.25	0.52	0.6005
(−5, −2)	1.17	0.63	0.54	0.22	0.8246
(−5, 0)	3.12	3.20	−0.08	−0.14	0.8921
(−1, 0)	1.94	2.57	−0.63	−0.41	0.6838
(0, 0)	1.53	2.13	−0.60	−0.05	0.9609
(0, +1)	1.64	2.60	−0.96	−0.06	0.9512
(0, +5)	1.41	2.37	−0.96	−0.15	0.8836
(+2, +5)	−0.23	−0.23	0.00	0.26	0.7957
(+2, +10)	−0.92	−1.73	0.81	0.51	0.6128
(+2, +15)	−0.90	−2.15	1.25	1.1	0.2729
(+2, +20)	−2.49	−2.33	−0.16	−0.45	0.6531
(−1, +1)	2.05	3.04	−0.99	−0.37	0.7151
(−2, +2)	2.63	3.60	−0.97	−0.45	0.6559
(−5, +5)	3.00	3.44	−0.44	−0.04	0.9677
(−10, +10)	2.70	1.61	1.09	0.46	0.6474
(−20, +20)	2.80	0.33	2.47	1.46	0.146

[a, b]Denote significance at 5 and 1 %, respectively

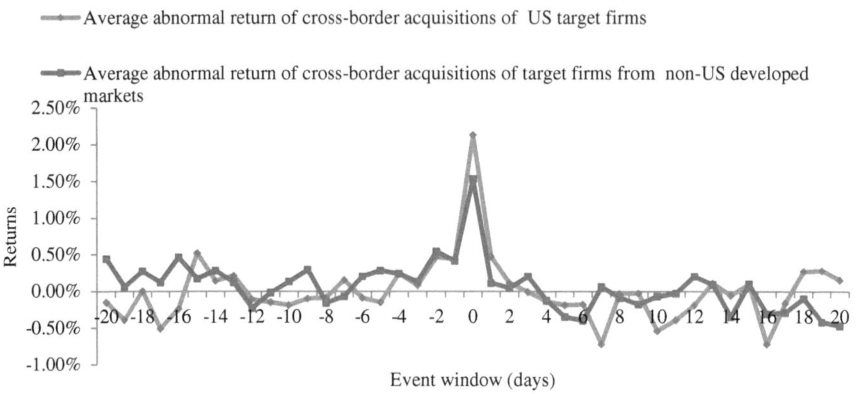

Fig. 3.48 AAR over event window (−20, +20) of cross-border acquisitions (US, non-US developed markets)

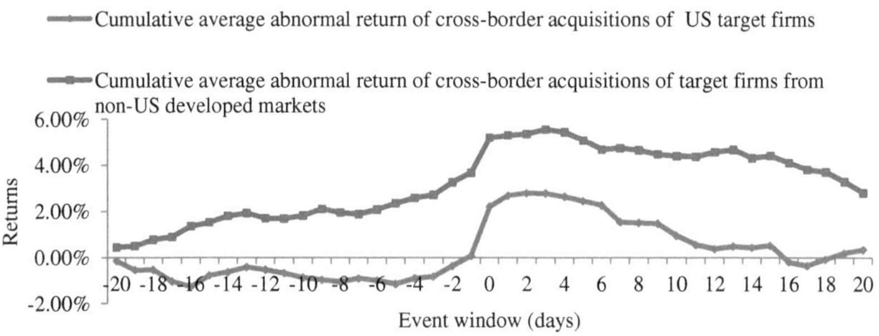

Fig. 3.49 CAAR over event window (−20, +20) of cross-border acquisitions (US, non-US developed markets)

3.9 Concluding Observations

The empirical research presents evidence that the market, usually, reacts positively to the M&A announcements that are not contaminated by any other contemporaneous firm specific announcements. The study finds evidence that shareholders of acquiring Indian companies engaging in mergers and acquisitions experience a statistically significant positive abnormal return on announcement day as well as statistically cumulative abnormal returns over multi- day event windows. The empirical findings suggest that mergers and acquisitions result in wealth creation for shareholders of the Indian acquirers. The gains are significantly positive during the event windows of 2, 3, 5, 11, and 41 days surrounding the announcement.

Although the positive reaction has been observed in all the subsamples, the stock return behavior differs. The magnitude of the excess returns is much larger for cross-border acquisitions, unlisted target firms, cash payment, complete control on the target firm as wholly owned subsidiary and target firms from non-US developed markets in comparison to that for domestic acquisitions, listed target firms, stock payment, partial control, and US target firms. These findings are consistent with other studies on the same subject.

As per the findings of the current study, the most beneficial investment window for the investors is (−5, 0), as the returns provided to the investors during this window are maximum. In the case of entire sample, the return is 2.75 % and, for the cross-border acquisitions, it is 3.06 %. The complete acquisition of target firm as a wholly owned subsidiary generates maximum return of 3.03 % during event window (−20, +20). This implies that investors associate information content with M&A announcements. The M&A can be treated as a tool to augment the wealth of the shareholders.

Keeping the investment perspective in mind, an investor can earn substantial returns if he purchases the shares within 5 days before the news of M&A comes to the market and sells 1 day after the announcement. An investor can also gain if the shares of the acquiring company are purchased 2 days prior to the announcement day and sold 2 days after the announcement day. Conclusion may be summed up as "EARLIER HE SELLS MORE HE GAINS" and "ISSUANCE OF STOCK FOR M&A IS NOT A GOOD NEWS".

References

Alexandridis, G., Petmezas, D., & Travlos, N. G. (2010). Gains from mergers and acquisitions around the world: new evidence. *Financial Management, 39*(4), 1671–1694.

Anand, J., & Delios, A. (2002). Absolute and relative resources as determinants of international acquisitions. *Strategic Management Journal, 23*(2), 119–134.

Anand, M., & Singh, J. (2008). Impact of merger announcements on shareholders' wealth: evidence from Indian private sector banks. *Vikalpa, 33*(1), 35–54.

Andrade, G., Mitchell, M., & Stafford, E. (2001). New evidence and perspectives on mergers. *Journal of Economic Perspectives, 15*(2), 103–120.

Ang, J., & Kohers, N. (2001). The takeover market for private companies: the US experience. *Cambridge Journal of Economics, 25*(6), 723–748.

Asquith, P. (1983). Merger bids, uncertainty, and stockholder returns. *Journal of Financial Economics, 11*(1–4), 51–83.

Asquith, P., Bruner, R., & Mullins, D, Jr. (1987). Merger returns and the form of financing. *Proceedings of the Seminar on the Analysis of Security Prices, 34*(1), 115–146.

Aw, M., & Chatterjee, R. (2004). The performance of UK firms acquiring large cross-border and domestic takeover targets. *Applied Financial Economics, 14*(5), 337–349.

Aybar, B., & Ficici, A. (2009). Cross-border acquisitions and firm value: An analysis of emerging-market multinationals. *Journal of International Business Studies, 40*(8), 1317–1338.

Barai, P., & Mohanty, P. (2010). Short term performance of Indian acquirers–effects of mode of payment, industry relatedness and status of target. Available at SSRN. Retrieved November 12, 2011, from http://ssrn.com/abstract=1697564

Beamish, P. W., & Banks, J. C. (1987). Equity joint ventures and the theory of the multinational enterprise. *Journal of International Business Studies, 18*(2), 1–16.

Blonigen, B. (1997). Firm-specific assets and the link between exchange rates and foreign direct investment. *American Economic Review, 87*(3), 447–465.

Butz, D. A. (1994). How do large minority shareholders wield control? *Managerial and Decision Economics, 15*(4), 291–298.

Cakici, N., Hessel, C., & Tandon, K. (1996). Foreign acquisitions in the United States: effect on shareholder wealth of foreign acquiring firms. *Journal of Banking & Finance, 20*(2), 307–329.

Campa, J. M., & Hernando, I. (2004). Shareholder value creation in European M&As. *European Financial Management, 10*(1), 47–81.

Caves, R. E. (1996). *Economic analysis and the multinational corporation* (2nd ed.). Cambridge: Cambridge University Press.

Caves, R. E., & Mehra, S. K. (1986). Entry of foreign multinationals into U.S. manufacturing industries. In M. E. Porter (Ed.), *Competition in global industries* (pp. 449–481). Boston MA: Harvard Business School Press.

Chang, S. (1998). Takeovers of privately held targets, methods of payment, and bidder returns. *Journal of Finance, 53*(2), 773–784.

Chari, A. P., Ouimet, P. P., & Tesar, L. (2010). The value of control in emerging markets. *Review of Financial Studies, 23*(4), 1741–1770.

Chen, Shih-Fen S. (2008). The motives for international acquisitions: capability procurements, strategic considerations, and the role of ownership structures. *Journal of International Business Studies, 39*(3), 454–471.

Chen, S. F., & Zeng, M. (2004). Japanese investors' choice of acquisitions vs startups in the US: The role of reputation barriers and advertising outlays. *International journal of Research in Marketing, 21*(2), 123–136.

Conn, R. L., Cosh, A., Guest, P. M., & Hughes, A. (2005). Impact on UK acquirers of domestic, cross-border, public and private acquisitions. *Journal of Business Finance and Accounting, 32*(5/6), 815–870.

Davidson, W. N., Dutia, D., & Cheng, L. (1989). A re-examination of the market reaction to failed mergers. *The Journal of Finance, 44*(4), 1077–1088.

DeAngelo, H., DeAngelo, L., & Rice, E. M. (1984). Going private: Minority freezeouts and stockholder wealth. *Journal of Law and Economics, 27*(2), 367–402.

Dennis, D. K., & McConnell, J. J. (1986). Corporate mergers and security returns. *Journal of Financial Economics, 16*(2), 143–188.

Dodd, P. (1980). Merger proposals, management discretion and stockholder wealth. *Journal of Financial Economics, 8*(2), 105–137.

Draper, P., & Paudyal, K. (2006). Acquisitions: private vs. public. *European Financial Management, 12*(1), 57–80.

Dyck, A., & Zingales, L. (2004). The private benefits of control. *Journal of Finance, 59*(2), 533–596.

Eckbo, B. E., Giammarino, R. M., & Heinkel, R. L. (1990). Asymmetric information and the medium of exchange in takeovers. *Review of Financial Studies, 3*(4), 651–676.

Eun, C. S., Kolodny, R., & Scheraga, C. (1996). Cross-border acquisitions and shareholder wealth: tests of synergy and internalization hypotheses. *Journal of Banking & Finance, 20*(9), 1559–1582.

Faccio, M., McConnell, J. J., & Stolin, D. (2006). Returns to acquirers of listed and unlisted targets. *Journal of Financial and Quantitative Analysis, 41*(1), 197–220.

Firth, M. (1980). Takeovers: shareholder returns and the theory of the firm. *Quarterly Journal of Economics, 94*(2), 235–260.

Fishman, M. (1989). Pre-emptive bidding and the role of the medium of exchange in acquisitions. *Journal of Finance, 44*(1), 41–58.

Francis, B. B., Hasan, I., & Sun, X. (2008). Financial market integration and the value of global diversification: evidence for acquirers in cross-border mergers and acquisitions. *Journal of Banking & Finance, 32*(8), 1522–1540.

Franks, J. R., & Harris, R. S. (1989). Shareholder wealth effects of corporate takeovers: the UK experience 1955–1985. *Journal of Financial Economics, 23*(2), 225–249.

Fuller, K., Netter, J., & Stegemoller, M. (2002). What do returns to acquiring firms tell us?: Evidence from firms that make many acquisitions. *Journal of Finance, 57*(4), 1763–1794.

Geringer, J. M., & Hebert, L. (1989). Control and performance of international joint ventures. *Journal of International Business Studies, 20*(2), 235–254.

Goergen, M., & Renneboog, L. (2004). Shareholder wealth effects of European domestic and cross-border takeover bids. *European Financial Management, 10*(1), 9–45.

Gubbi, S., Aulakh, P., Ray, S., Sarkar, M. B., & Chittoor, R. (2010). Do international acquisitions by emerging economy firms create shareholder value? The case of Indian firms. *Journal of International Business Studies, 41*(3), 397–418.

Hansen, R. G. (1987). A theory for the choice of exchange medium in mergers and acquisitions. *Journal of Business, 60*(1), 75–95.

Hansen, R. G., & Lott, J. (1996). Externalities and corporate objectives in a world with diversified shareholders/consumers. *Journal of Financial and Quantitative Analysis, 31*(1), 43–68.

Harrison, J. S., Hitt, M. A., Hoskisson, R. E., & Ireland, R. D. (2001). Resource complementarity in business combinations: extending the logic of organizational alliances. *Journal of Management, 27*(6), 679–690.

Hennart, J. F., & Park, Y. R. (1993). Greenfield vs acquisition: The strategy of Japanese investors in the United States. *Management Science, 39*(9), 1054–1070.

Heron, R., & Lie, E. (2002). Operating performance and the method of payment in takeovers. *Journal of Financial and Quantitative Analysis, 37*(1), 137–155.

Huang, Y., & Walkling, R. (1987). Target abnormal returns associated with acquisition announcements: payment, acquisition form, and managerial resistance. *Journal of Financial Economics, 19*(2), 329–350.

Jarrel, G., Brickley, J., & Natter, J. (1988). The market for corporate control: the empirical evidence since 1980. *Journal of Economic Perspectives, 2*(2), 49–68.

Jensen, M. (1986). Agency costs of free cash flow, corporate finance, and takeovers. *American Economic Review, 76*(2), 323–329.

Jensen, M., & Ruback, R. (1983). The market for corporate control: the scientific evidence. *Journal of Financial Economics, 11*(1–4), 5–50.

Jung, K., Kim, Y., & Stulz, R. (1996). Timing, investment opportunities, managerial discretion, and the security issue decision, *Journal of Financial Economics, 42*(2), 159–185.

Kang, J. (1993). The international market for corporate control. *Journal of Financial Economics, 34*(3), 345–371.

Karels, G. V., Lawrence, E., & Yu, J. (2011). Cross-border mergers and acquisitions between industrialized and developing countries. *International Journal of Banking and Finance, 8*(1). Retrieved September 21, 2011, from http://epublications.bond.edu.au/ijbf/vol8/iss1/3

Kiymaz, H. (2004). Cross-border acquisitions of US financial institutions: Impact of macroeconomic factors. *Journal of Banking & Finance, 28*(6), 1413–1439.

Kohli, R., & Mann, B. J. S. (2011). Analyzing determinants of value creation in domestic and cross-border acquisitions in India. *International Business Review, 21*(6), 998–1016.

Kose, J., Steven, F., Nguyen, D., & Vasudevan, G. K. (2010). Investor protection and cross-border acquisitions of private and public targets. *Journal of Corporate Finance, 16*(3), 259–275.

Lowinski, F., Schiereck, D., & Thomas, T. W. (2004). The effects of cross-border acquisitions on shareholder wealth: evidence from Switzerland. *Review of Quantitative Finance and Accounting, 22*(4), 315–330.

Markides, C., & Oyon, D. (1998). International acquisitions: do they create value for shareholders? *European Management Journal, 16*(2), 125–135.

Markides, C. C., & Ittner, C. D. (1994). Shareholder benefits from corporate international diversification: evidence from U.S. international acquisitions. *Journal of International Business Studies, 25*(2), 343–366.

Martin, K. J. (1996). The method of payment in corporate acquisitions, investment opportunities and managerial ownership. *Journal of Finance, 51*(4), 1227–1246.

Masse, I., Hanrahan, R., & Kushner, J. (1990). The effect of the method of payment on stock returns in Canadian tender offers and merger proposals for both target and bidding firms. *Quarterly Journal of Business and Economics, 29*(4), 102–124.

Meyer, K. E., & Tran, Y. T. T. (2006). Market penetration and acquisition strategies for emerging Economies. *Long Range Planning, 39*(2), 263–290.
Mitchell, M., Pulvino, T., & Stafford, E. (2004). Price pressure around mergers. *Journal of Finance, 59*(1), 31–63.
Moeller, S. B., & Schlingemann, F. P. (2005). Global diversification and bidder gains: a comparison between cross-border and domestic acquisitions. *Journal of Banking & Finance, 29*(3), 533–564.
Mueller, D. C., & Yurtoglu, B. B. (2007). Corporate governance and the returns to acquiring firms' shareholders. *Managerial and Decision Economics, 28*(8), 879–896.
Myers, S. C., & Majluf, N. S. (1984). Corporate financing and investment decisions when firms have information that investors do not have. *Journal of Financial Economics, 13*(2), 187–221.
Nenova, T. (2003). The value of corporate voting rights and control: A cross-country analysis. *Journal of Financial Economics, 68*, 328–351.
Pettway, R. H., & Yamada, T. (1986). Mergers in Japan and their impacts upon stockholders' wealth. *Financial Management, 15*(4), 43–52.
Rani, N., Yadav, Surendra S., & Jain, P.K. (2011). Impact of Mergers and Acquisitions on Shareholders' Wealth in Short-Run: An Empirical Study of Indian Pharmaceutical Industry. *International Journal of Global Business and Competitiveness, 6*(1), 40–52.
Rani, N., Yadav, Surendra. S., & Jain, P. K. (2012). Impact of mergers and acquisitions on returns to shareholders of acquiring firms: Indian economy in perspective. *Journal of Financial Management and Analysis, 25*(1), 1–26.
Rani, N., Yadav, S. S., & Jain, P. K. (2015). Innovative mode of financing and abnormal returns to shareholders of Indian acquiring firms. In Sushil & G. Chroust (Ed.), *Systemic flexibility and business agility* (pp. 367–383). Springer.
Rani, N., Yadav, Surendra S., & Jain, P. K. (2015a). Impact of cross-border acquisitions' announcements on shareholders' wealth: Evidence from India. *Global Business and Economic Review., 17*(4), 360–382.
Rappaport, A., & Sirower, M. (1999). Stock or cash? The trade-offs for buyers and sellers in mergers and acquisitions. *Harvard Business Review, 77*(6), 147–158.
Roll, R. (1986). The hubris hypothesis of corporate takeovers. *Journal of Business, 59*, 197–216.
Schipper, K., & Smith, A. (1983). Effects of restructuring on shareholders wealth: The case of voluntary spinoffs. *Journal of Financial Economics, 12*(4), 437–467.
Schipper, K., & Thompson, R. (1983). Evidence on the capitalized value of merger activity for acquiring firms. *Journal of Financial Economics, 11*(1–4), 85–119.
Shleifer, A., & Vishny, R. W. (2003). Stock market driven acquisitions. *Journal of Financial Economics, 70*(3), 295–311.
Sicherman, N. W., & Pettway, R. H. (1987). Acquisition of divested assets and shareholders' wealth. *Journal of Finance, 42*(5), 1261–1273.
Spencer, C., Akhigbe, A., & Madura, J. (2001). Financial decisions and signaling for partially acquired firms. *Journal of Financial Research, 24*, 99–118.
Travlos, N. (1987). Corporate takeover bids method of payment, and bidding firms' stock returns. *Journal of Finance, 42*(4), 943–963.
Wang, C., & Xie, F. (2009). Corporate governance transfer and synergistic gains from mergers and acquisitions. *Review of Financial Studies, 22*(2), 829–858.
Yook, K. C. (2003). Larger return to cash acquisitions: signalling effect or leverage effect? *Journal of Business, 76*(3), 477–498.
Zhu, P. (2011). Persistent performance and interaction effects in sequential cross-border mergers and acquisitions. *Journal of Multinational Financial Management, 21*(1), 18–39.
Zhu, P., & Malhotra, S. (2008). Announcement effect and price pressure: An empirical study of cross-border acquisitions by Indian firms. *International Research Journal of Finance and Economics*, 13 (Feburary), 24–41.
Zhu, P., Jog, V., & Otchere, I. (2011). Partial acquisitions in emerging markets: A test of the strategic market entry and corporate control hypotheses. *Journal of Corporate Finance, 17*(2), 288–305.

Chapter 4
Financial Performance Analysis of Mergers and Acquisitions

Abstract Mergers and acquisitions (M&A) have long been used as a strategy for corporate growth and expansion. But, does the financial performance of the acquiring firm (in long term) really improve following mergers and acquisitions? This chapter addresses the major questions related to the long-term performance of the acquiring firm.

Keywords Financial performance · Operating performance · Liquidity · Leverage · Financial ratios

4.1 Introduction

The question of whether M&As improves corporate performance is one that has been addressed by many researchers. Various accounting studies have examined the reported financial results to assess post-merger performance of corporates. These studies (Ravenscraft and Scherer 1987; Switzer 1996; Ramaswamy and Waegelein 2003; Ghosh 2001; Parrino and Harris 1999; Manson et al. 2000; Sharma and Ho 2002; Healy et al. 1992; Yeh and Hoshino 2000; Rahman and Limmack 2004; Gugler et al. 2003; Ghosh and Jain 2000; Pawaskar 2001; Cosh et al. 1998; Mueller 1986; Ramakrishnan 2008) have focused on the accounting statements of the acquirers pre-merger and post-merger to observe how financial performance changes. Studies of mergers and acquisitions in India are very few. Moreover, these empirical investigations have focused on comparing pre-merger and post-merger performance on case-to-case basis.

The present chapter seeks to measure the impact of M&A on long-term performance of the acquiring firms. It investigates profitability as well as operating performance of the acquiring firms. This study uses long-term pre-and post-mergers and acquisitions financial data to assess firms' operating performance. Ratio analysis has been carried out to examine long-term financial performance of the acquiring firm. The chapter measures and compares the pre-and post-merger and acquisition financial performance of acquiring companies in terms of profitability,

N. Rani et al., *Mergers and Acquisitions*, India Studies in Business and Economics, DOI 10.1007/978-981-10-2203-6_4

operating efficiency, leverage, and liquidity. A sufficiently long period is required to analyze and understand the impact of a merger and acquisition since efficiency improves over a long time horizon. Hence, financial performance of Indian acquirers for 10 years period—5 years prior to and 5 year subsequent to the mergers and acquisitions—has been analyzed.

Year 0, i.e., the year of merger and acquisition has been excluded from the analysis as its inclusion may cause distortions due to change in financial reporting caused due to adjustments in accounting. In order to provide a holistic view of the long-term profitability and performance of mergers and acquisition, various accounting measures have been investigated in the study. This chapter explains various measures of pre-and post-mergers and acquisitions profitability and operational efficiency used in the study. To determine the significant difference over pre- and post-merger and acquisition, two-sample paired t-test has been conducted for each measure used in the study. The null hypothesis for each test is that the mean level for the post-merger and acquisition period is not significantly different from the mean from pre-merger and acquisition period. A positive *t*-value indicates a higher mean value for post-merger and acquisition period and vice versa.

The chapter has been organized into six sections. Section 4.2 presents the paired t-test and the distribution of the sample used in the study. Financial ratios used in the study to analyze the long-term performance have been discussed in Sect. 4.3. The discussion on empirical results of paired samples t-test is delineated in Sect. 4.4. Section 4.5 comprises of analysis of sources of performance of M&A; this section is divided into Sects. 4.5.1 and 4.5.2 describing the Du Pont analysis based on operating profit margin and operating cash flow ratio respectively. Section 4.6 contains the concluding observations.

4.2 Paired Samples t-Test

The crucial research question that is investigated by examining the major fourteen financial ratios is: "Is post-merger and acquisition performance of acquiring firm better than the performance of the acquiring firm in pre-merger and acquisition period?" The selected accounting ratios for sample companies over a period of 5 years before (−5, −4, −3, −2, −1) and 5 years after (1, 2, 3, 4, 5) the merger and acquisition event have been calculated. Paired samples t-test has been carried out on 14 ratios to assess the difference in post-M&A performance and pre-M&A performance. The paired samples t-test compares the mean of two variables from the same group. It determines whether the difference between the means of the two variables is significantly different from zero. In this study, the two variables are mean ratios of the acquired firm before and after the merger and acquisition. The paired samples t-test, thus, determines whether there is significant change in the variable 'pre and post-merger and acquisition'. The paired samples t-test compares the mean of two variables before and after an event from the same group. The performance of those firms has been analyzed whose data is available pre-M&A and post-M&A. The performance of 14 ratios has been analyzed for 1 year pre-M&A and post-the event, i.e., M&A (−1, 1), 1 year pre- and 2 year mean post-M&A (−1, 2), 1 year pre-M&A and 3 year mean post-M&A (−1, 3), 1 year pre-M&A and 4 year mean post-M&A (−1, 4), 1 year pre- and 5 year mean post-M&A (−1, 5). In addition, mean of 2 years pre-M&A and post-M&A (−2, 2), mean of 3 years pre-M&A and post-M&A (−3, 3), mean of 4 years pre-M&A and post-M&A (−4, 4) and mean of 5 years pre-M&A and post-M&A (−5, 5) have been compared.

A positive and significant difference in profitability ratios and efficiency ratios indicates a better performance for the post-M&A period. A negative and significant difference in expense ratios indicates operating economies for the post-M&A period.

Table 4.1 presents the distribution of sample across years. It is evident from the table that the maximum 35 % of mergers and acquisition took place in the year 2007. The final sample consists of 61.3 % firms in manufacturing sector, 24.6 % firms in services sector, 8.4 % in construction and real estate, 5.7 % in mining, electricity and diversified sector as exhibited in Fig. 4.1.

Table 4.1 Distribution of sample across years, 2003–2015

Year	Number of mergers and acquisitions studied	Data on ratios available
2003	29 (5.9 %)	22 (5.5 %)
2004	25 (5.1 %)	20 (5 %)
2005	49 (10 %)	36 (9 %)
2006	109 (22.2 %)	91 (22.6 %)
2007	172 (35 %)	144 (35.8 %)
2008	90 (18.3 %)	77 (19.2 %)
2009	4 (0.8 %)	3 (0.7 %)
2010	4 (0.8 %)	3 (0.7 %)
2011	5 (1 %)	3 (0.7 %)
2012	1 (0.2 %)	1 (0.2 %)
2013	2 (0.4 %)	2 (0.5 %)
2014	1 (0.2 %)	0 (0 %)
2015	1 (0.2 %)	0 (0 %)
Total	491 (100 %)	402 (100 %)

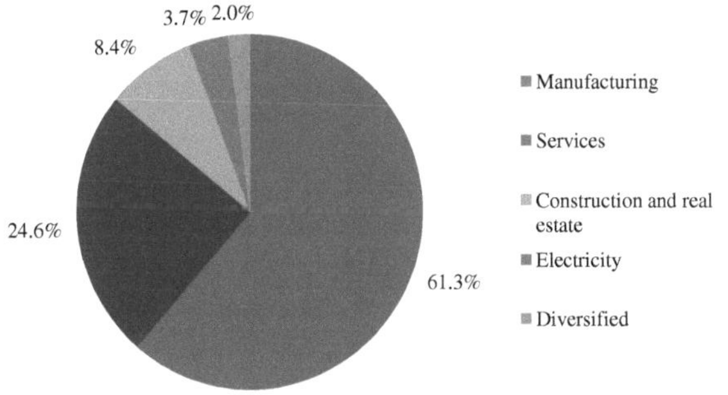

Fig. 4.1 Sector-wise distribution of sample

Extreme values have been excluded from the data to deal with the influence of outliers. After analyzing data for outliers, the values beyond three standard deviations have been dropped from the analysis. Only those firms have been retained in analysis for which data is available in pairs relating to before and after M&A. The mean difference of 14 ratios has been analyzed in following pairs:

(i) 1 year pre-M&A and post-M&A (−1, 1).
(ii) 1 year pre-M&A and 2 years post-M&A (−1, 2).
(iii) 1 year pre-M&A and 3 year mean post-M&A (−1, 3).
(iv) 1 year pre-M&A and 4 years mean post-M&A (−1, 4).
(v) 1 year pre-M&A and 5 years mean post-M&A (−1, 5).
(vi) 2 years mean pre-M&A and post-M&A (−2, 2).
(vii) 3 years mean pre-M&A and post-M&A (−3, 3).
(viii) 4 years mean pre-M&A and post-M&A (−4, 4).
(ix) 5 years mean pre-M&A and post-M&A (−5, 5).

Due to these inconsistencies, the number of firms utilized for long-term analysis of financial performance (ratio analysis) varied, i.e., 402 firms for 1 year before and after M&A (−1,1), 401 firms for 1 year before and 2 year mean after M&A (−1, 2), 391 firms for 1 year before and 3 year mean after M&A (−1, 3), 361 firms for 1 year before and 4 year mean after M&A (−1, 4), 351 firms for 1 year before and 5 year mean after M&A (−1, 5), the mean of 2 years before and after M&A (−2, 2) of 401 firms, the mean of 3 years before and after M&A (−3, 3) of 398 firms, the mean of 4 years before and after M&A (−4, 4) of 387 firms, the mean of 5 years before and after M&A (−5, 5) of 360 firms have been analyzed.

4.3 Financial Ratios

Ratio analysis is an effective technique to assess the financial performance. Given this fact, the technique has been used in the study. The improvement in post-M&A period can arise from various sources such as better operating margins, greater assets productivity or lower labor costs etc. Hence, primarily fourteen ratios pertaining to profitability, efficiency, leverage and liquidity have been used in the study.

4.3.1 Profitability Ratios

Profitability has been measured in terms of rate of return (ROR) on investment and sales, and on the two major concepts of investment, namely, return on equity funds (ROE), and return on capital employed (ROCE). These rates have been computed based on average assets, average capital employed, and average equity funds; the average is based on their respective values at the beginning and end of the year.

Return on the basis of sales has been computed in terms of operating profit margin based on sales (OPM_S), operating profit margin based on assets (OPM_A) and net profit margin (NPM). Better margin in post-merger and acquisition period indicates the managerial ability to realize the expected synergies and run the business profitably. Actual economic gains from assets are captured by operating cash flows. The change in acquisition-related performance of the acquirer is examined by comparing operating performance before and after the acquisition. For this purpose, operating cash flow profit ratio (OCFR) based on sales as well as assets has also been calculated. This definition of operating performance is not affected by depreciation, goodwill, etc. (Healy et al. 1992).

4.3.1.1 Return on Equity Funds (ROE)

ROE indicates the return for the equity owners.

$$\text{ROE} = \frac{\text{Profit after taxes} - \text{preference dividend}}{\text{Average equity funds}} \tag{4.3.1}$$

Equity fund = paid-up equity capital + reserves and surpluses + retained profit − accumulated losses.

4.3.1.2 Return on Capital Employed (ROCE)

ROCE also determines how efficiently the financial resources are deployed by acquiring companies. ROCE indicates how efficiently the long-term funds of the owners and lenders are being used and focus directly on operating efficiency.

$$\text{ROCE} = \frac{\text{Profit before interest and taxes (PBIT)}}{\text{Average long} - \text{term assets used} + \text{net working capital}} \tag{4.3.2}$$

Capital work-in-progress has been excluded.

4.3.1.3 Operating Profit Margin (OPM)

OPM based on sales indicates the magnitude of operating profit in terms of sales.

$$\text{OPM}_\text{S} = \frac{\text{Profit before interest and taxes (PBIT)} - \text{non operating income}}{\text{Net sales}} \tag{4.3.3}$$

The level of economic benefits generated by assets is represented by operating profits. In addition to operating profit margin on sales, operating profit ratio based on assets has also been calculated. Operating profit margin based on assets has also been calculated by dividing pretax operating profits with average operating assets to measure change in post-M&A performance. This measure can be compared across time and firms. Total assets have been used net of preliminary expenses, fictitious assets, and miscellaneous expenses.

$$\mathrm{OPM_A} = \frac{\text{Profit before interest and taxes (PBIT)} - \text{nonoperating income}}{\text{Average of (total assets} - \text{preliminery expenses} - \text{fictitious assets} - \text{miscell.expenses)}} \quad (4.3.4)$$

The change in operating performance attributable to M&A is the comparison of the post-M&A and pre-M&A OPM.

4.3.1.4 Net Profit Margin (NPM)

NPM determines the relationship of reported net profit after taxes to sales.

$$\mathrm{NPM} = \frac{\text{Profit after taxes}}{\text{Net sales}} \quad (4.3.5)$$

4.3.1.5 Operating Cash Flow Ratio Based on Sales ($\mathrm{OCFR_S}$)

Operating cash flow ratio based on sales $\mathrm{OCFR_S}$ has been calculated as

$$\mathrm{OCFR_S} = \frac{\text{PBIT} - \text{nonoperating income} + \text{depreciation} + \text{amortisation} + \text{any non cash expenditure}}{\text{Net sales}} \quad (4.3.6)$$

4.3.1.6 Operating Cash Flow Ratio Based on Assets ($\mathrm{OCFR_A}$)

Pretax operating cash flows scaled by assets are used to measure the change in performance measures.

$$\mathrm{OCFR_A} = \frac{\text{PBIT} - \text{nonoperating income} + \text{depreciation} + \text{amortisation} + \text{any non cash expenditure}}{\text{Average of (total assets} - \text{preliminery expenses} - \text{fictitious assets} - \text{miscell.expenses)}} \quad (4.3.7)$$

4.3.2 *Expense Ratios*

In addition to above profitability ratios, four expense ratios have been calculated to measure various operating economies expected from mergers and acquisitions. The source of operating economies could be realized through reduced manufacturing cost due to large scale, labor expense, marketing expenses, and research and development expenses.

Expense ratios, namely, cost of goods sold ratio (COGR), labor-related expense ratio (LRE), selling, general and administration expense ratio (SRE), and research and development expense ratio (RDE) have been analyzed. In case of expense ratios, a negative *t*-value indicates a lower mean value for post-merger and acquisition period. In other words, a lower mean value of expense ratio in post-M&A period reveals that mergers and acquisitions have generated expected economies.

4.3.2.1 Cost of Goods Sold Ratio (COGR)

$$\text{CGSR} = \frac{\text{Cost of goods sold}}{\text{Net sales}} \tag{4.3.8}$$

4.3.2.2 Labor Related Expense Ratio (LRE)

$$\text{LRE} = \frac{\text{Labour related expenses}}{\text{Net sales}} \tag{4.3.9}$$

4.3.2.3 Selling, General, and Administration Expense Ratio (SRE)

$$\text{SGR} = \frac{\text{Selling, general and administration expenses}}{\text{Net sales}} \tag{4.3.10}$$

4.3.2.4 Research and Development Expense Ratio (RDE)

$$\text{RDE} = \frac{\text{R\&D expenses}}{\text{Net sales}} \tag{4.3.11}$$

4.3.3 Efficiency Ratios

Efficiency ratios assess the operational performance of acquirers before and after M&A. Efficiency in utilization of resources has been determined on the basis of three dimensions, namely, total assets turnover ratio (TATR), fixed assets turnover ratio (FATR), and current assets turnover ratio (CATR). High turnover ratio in post-merger and acquisition period is indicative of better utilization of available resources whereas low turnover ratio in post-merger and acquisition period shows presence of idle capacity and under-utilization of available resources.

Total assets turnover indicates the efficiency with which the firm uses its assets to generate sales. This measure is probably of the greatest interest to management because it indicates whether firm's operations have been financially efficient (Gitman 2009, p. 82) Accordingly, total assets turnover ratio (TATR) has been computed by dividing net sales to average total assets. Total assets have been used net of preliminary expenses, fictitious assets and miscellaneous expenses. Fixed assets turnover ratio (FATR) has been computed by dividing net sales by average fixed assets. Current assets turnover ratio (CATR) has been computed by dividing net sales by average current assets.

4.3.3.1 Total Assets Turnover Ratio (TATR)

Total assets turnover ratio (TATR) has been computed by dividing net sales by average total assets. Total assets have been used net of preliminary expenses, fictitious assets, and miscellaneous expenses.

$$\text{TATR} = \frac{\text{Net Sales}}{\text{Average of (total assets} - \text{preliminery expenses} - \text{fictitious assets} - \text{miscell.expenses}} \tag{4.3.12}$$

4.3.3.2 Fixed Assets Turnover Ratio (FATR)

Fixed assets turnover ratio (FATR) has been computed by dividing net sales by average fixed assets.

$$\text{FATR} = \frac{\text{Net sales}}{\text{Average fixed assets}} \tag{4.3.13}$$

4.3.3.3 Current Assets Turnover Ratio (CATR)

Current assets turnover ratio (CATR) has been computed by dividing net sales by average current assets.

$$\text{CATR} = \frac{\text{Net sales}}{\text{Average current assets}} \tag{4.3.14}$$

4.3.4 *Liquidity Ratio*

Liquidity has been assessed by current ratio (CR). CR takes into account five items of current assets, i.e., cash and bank balances, sundry debtors, inventories, loans and advances, and stock of other current assets.

$$\text{CR} = \frac{\text{Current assets}}{\text{Current liabilities}} \tag{4.3.15}$$

4.3.5 *Leverage Ratio*

Leverage ratios are based on comprehensive measure of total external obligations (long-term debt plus current liabilities) to total assets. The total debt to assets (DA) ratio shows the proportion of a company's assets which are financed through external borrowing.

$$\text{DA} = \frac{\text{Total debt}}{\text{Total assets}} \tag{4.3.16}$$

4.4 Empirical Results of Paired Samples t-Test

The objective of the present chapter is to compare the financial performance of acquirers before and after M&A in terms of profitability, efficiency, expenses, liquidity, and leverage. It is hypothesized that acquirers have posted better post-M&A financial performance vis-à-vis pre-M&A performance. The financial performance is based on the four major groups of ratios, namely, profitability, efficiency, leverage, and liquidity.

4.4.1 Analysis of Pre-M&A and Post-M&A Profitability Ratios

4.4.1.1 Profitability Ratios Related to Investment

It is hypothesized that profitability position of acquirers has improved during post-M&A period. The paired sample t-test values for comparison of means of profitability ratio based on investment (ROE and ROCE) before and after M&A have been presented in Table 4.2. The relevant data contained in the table shows that mean profitability in terms of rate of return on investment (ROCE and ROE) has shown improvement in post-M&A period. The paired sample t-test for comparison of means (−1, 7) reveals that ROE exhibits increase of 2.92 % (significant at 5 %) during post-M&A period. Positive mean difference in ROE has been observed for majority (61.1 %) of acquirers. As expected, the profitability of the acquirers has increased over post-M&A period. It is evident from Table 4.2 that ROCE has improved to the extent of more than 7 % after M&A. Paired t-test has identified the significant positive difference in mean ROCE after and before M&A

Table 4.2 Paired samples t-test of profitability ratios (related to investment) pre-M&A and post-M&A

Paired sample (pre-M&A, post-M&A)	Mean ratio post-M&A	Mean ratio pre-M&A	Mean difference	Positive: negative	*t*-value	Degree of freedom	Significance
A: Return on equity (ROE)							
(−1, +1)	16.6	16.03	0.57	192:210	0.706	401	0.480
(−1, +2)	15.9	15.4	0.5	187:214	0.658	400	0.511
(−1, +3)	14.94	14.89	0.05	172:219	0.054	390	0.957
(−1, +4)	15.19	12.45	2.74	220:141	1.97[a]	360	0.049
(−1, +5)	15.43	12.51	2.92	201: 150	2.28[a]	350	0.023
(−2, +2)	15.85	15.68	0.18	213:188	0.212	400	0.832
(−3, +3)	14.63	13.94	0.69	214:187	0.659	397	0.510
(−4, +4)	13.54	13.39	0.15	199:187	0.131	386	0.896
(−5, +5)	14.31	12.54	1.77	176:184	1.616	359	0.107
B: Return on capital employed (ROCE)							
(−1, +1)	21.6	19.1	2.5	229:173	3.74[b]	401	0.000
(−1, +2)	22.1	18.6	3.5	223:178	3.86[b]	400	0.000
(−1, +3)	21.8	19.5	2.3	216:175	2.28[a]	390	0.023
(−1, +4)	23.7	18.3	5.4	203:158	5.29[b]	360	0.000
(−1, +5)	19.2	18.2	1.0	162:188	2.37[a]	350	0.018
(−2, +2)	21.6	19.3	2.3	227:174	2.87[b]	400	0.004
(−3, +3)	22.87	18.47	4.4	222:176	4.35[b]	397	0.000
(−4, +4)	23.16	16.19	7.3	225:162	5.08[b]	386	0.000
(−5, +5)	23.41	17.41	6.0	218:142	5.08[b]	359	0.000

[a], [b]Denote significance at 5 and 1 %, respectively

for all the pairs compared. The percentage increase is 2.5, 2.3, 4.4, 7.3, and 6 % during 1, 2, 3, 4, and 5 years, respectively. Positive mean difference in ROCE has been observed in the case of more than two-third acquirers for all the pairs.

4.4.1.2 Profitability Ratios Related to Sales

Table 4.3 presents the paired sample t-test for comparison of means of profitability ratio based on sales (OPM_S and NPM) before and after M&A. Operating profit margin based on assets has also been presented in the Table.

Table 4.3 Paired samples t-test of pre-M&A and post-M&A profitability ratios (related to sales)

Paired sample (pre-M&A, post-M&A)	Mean ratio post-M&A	Mean ratio pre-M&A	Mean difference	Positive: negative	*t*-value	Degree of freedom	Significance
A: Operating profit margin based on sales (OPM_S)							
(−1, +1)	14.39	12.76	1.63	234:168	2.19[a]	401	0.029
(−1, +2)	14.60	12.87	1.73	212:189	2.34[a]	400	0.020
(−1, +3)	13.57	13.43	0.14	199:192	0.19	390	0.844
(−1, +4)	14.14	13.61	0.53	183:178	0.78	360	0.437
(−1, +5)	14.43	13.17	1.26	177:174	1.23	350	0.222
(−2, +2)	13.3	12.1	1.2	218:183	1.81	400	0.071
(−3, +3)	13.5	11.4	2.1	213:185	1.97[a]	397	0.049
(−4, +4)	14.01	12.33	1.68	208:179	0.403	386	0.687
(−5, +5)	13	9	4	198:162	2.06[a]	359	0.041
B: Operating profit margin based on assets (OPM_A)							
(−1, +1)	10.38	10.22	0.16	206:196	0.434	401	0.665
(−1, +2)	10.26	9.49	0.77	196:205	1.97[a]	400	0.049
(−1, +3)	9.84	9.46	0.38	191:200	0.939	390	0.348
(−1, +4)	9.78	9.1	0.68	185:176	1.67	360	0.095
(−1, +5)	9.15	8.66	0.49	181:170	1.02	350	0.311
(−2, +2)	9.8	9	0.8	208:193	2.01[a]	400	0.046
(−3, +3)	9.8	8.85	0.95	203:195	2.08[a]	397	0.039
(−4, +4)	9.58	8.71	0.87	211:176	1.79	386	0.075
(−5, +5)	9.36	9.09	0.27	171:189	0.605	359	0.546
A: Net profit margin (NPM)							
(−1, +1)	9.66	9.25	0.41	229:173	0.597	401	0.551
(−1, +2)	9.59	9.53	0.06	208:193	0.109	400	0.913
(−1, +3)	10.36	9.02	1.34	189:202	1.164	390	0.245
(−1, +4)	10.06	9.37	0.7	174:187	0.806	360	0.421
(−1, +5)	10.79	8.75	2.04	187:164	1.286	350	0.199
(−2, +2)	9.8	8.6	1.2	209:192	1.71	400	0.081
(−3, +3)	8.4	8.3	0.1	210:188	0.11	397	0.916
(−4, +4)	10.14	6.27	3.87	208:179	1.22	386	0.225
(−5, +5)	7.01	6.52	0.49	194:166	0.312	359	0.755

[a], [b]Denote significance at 5 and 1 %, respectively

The relevant data contained in the Table shows that NPM has exhibited impressive improvement for all the pairs. Mean NPM has increased by 2.04 % during 1 year before and 5 years after M&A. The positive mean difference has been observed in NPM for all the pairs compared. Positive mean difference has been found in the case of 53 % acquirers.

The positive mean difference of 1.63 and 1.73 % has been observed in OPM based on sales for 1 and 2 years before and after M&A respectively. One significant finding may be noted from the relevant data presented in Table 4.3 that operating profit margin based on assets (OPM_A) has shown only marginal improvement (up to 1 %). The findings may be attributed to the advent of recessionary conditions existing since 2008.

Table 4.4 shows that the paired sample t-test for comparison of means provides a test-statistics of 2.48 ($p = 0.014 < 0.05$), 2.36 ($p = 0.019 < 0.05$), and 2.28 ($p = 0.023 < 0.05$) for OCFRS for 1 year pre- and 3 year mean post-M&A difference, 1 year pre- and 4 year mean post-M&A difference and 1 year pre- and 5 year mean post-M&A difference, respectively. Further, the mean difference is positive for all the pairs. The firms' performance appears to have improved significantly in fifth year after M&A as indicated by positive and significant mean difference post-M&A. The improvement seems to be higher as the years progress

Table 4.4 Paired samples t-test of pre-M&A and post-M&A profitability ratios (related to sales)

Paired sample (pre-M&A, post-M&A)	Mean ratio post-M&A	Mean ratio pre-M&A	Mean difference	Positive: negative	*t*-value	Degree of freedom	Significance
A: Operating cash flow ratio based on sales ($OCFR_S$)							
(−1, +1)	15.47	14.98	0.49	232:170	1.26	401	0.208
(−1, +2)	18.28	17.74	0.54	204:197	0.96	400	0.340
(−1, +3)	20.11	16.92	3.19	200:191	2.48[a]	390	0.014
(−1, +4)	18.74	16.37	2.37	181:180	2.36[a]	360	0.019
(−1, +5)	21.59	16.79	4.81	181:170	2.28[a]	350	0.023
(−2, +2)	17.6	16.98	0.62	207:194	1.08	400	0.282
(−3, +3)	18.58	16.71	1.87	205:193	2.03[a]	397	0.043
(−4, +4)	21.5	11.55	9.9	189:198	1.52	386	0.130
(−5, +5)	18.6	15.1	3.5	180:180	1.93	359	0.054
B: Operating cash flow ratio based on assets ($OCFR_A$)							
(−1, +1)	13	12.76	0.24	200:202	0.46	401	0.65
(−1, +2)	12.91	12.49	0.42	198:203	1.07	400	0.29
(−1, +3)	13	12.1	0.9	187:204	1.87	390	0.062
(−1, +4)	12.61	12.20	0.41	170:191	0.998	360	0.319
(−1, +5)	12.49	12.10	0.39	150:201	0.682	350	0.496
(−2, +2)	12.78	12.18	0.06	191:210	1.44	400	0.15
(−3, +3)	12.46	12.31	0.15	186:212	0.34	397	0.74
(−4, +4)	12.14	12.04	0.1	182:205	0.211	386	0.833
(−5, +5)	12.32	11.77	0.6	158:202	1.16	359	0.247

[a, b]Denote significance at 5 and 1 %, respectively

post-M&A. This validates our hypothesis that M&A in India have resulted in improved long-term operating performance.

The paired test is also carried out for operating cash flow ratio based on assets. The test statistic related to OCFR based on assets is insignificant. This indicates that the mean difference in OCFR based on assets post- and pre-M&A is due to chance and it cannot be inferred that M&A has led to a significant improvement in acquirers' OCFR based on assets. Perhaps, longer time for larger assets base following post-M&A is required to generate expected returns.

4.4.1.3 Profitability Ratios Related to Expenses

Other profitability ratios related to sales are expense ratios; they are computed dividing expenses by sales. Four major expense ratios, namely, COGR, LRE, SGR, and RDE have been calculated to assess the impact of M&A on profitability of acquirers. The empirical results of expense ratios have been presented in Table 4.5.

The significant finding, as revealed by expense ratios, is that nearly two-third (66 %) acquirers have achieved economy in their selling, general, and administrative expenses in third, fourth year, and fifth years post-M&A as reflected in

Table 4.5 Paired samples t-test of pre-M&A and post-M&A expense ratios

Paired sample (pre-M&A, post-M&A)	Mean ratio post-M&A	Mean ratio pre-M&A	Mean difference	Positive: negative	*t*-value	Degree of freedom	Significance
A: COGR							
(−1, +1)	69.02	69.06	0.03	224:178	−0.064	401	0.949
(−1, +2)	70.50	70.54	−0.04	224:177	−0.087	400	0.931
(−1, +3)	71.04	71.37	−0.33	222:169	−0.625	390	0.533
(−1, +4)	72.02	73.71	−1.69	201:160	−1.17	360	0.245
(−1, +5)	72.7	74.9	−2.28	198:153	−1.05	350	0.294
(−2, +2)	71.3	71.5	−0.18	218:183	−0.417	400	0.677
(−3, +3)	71.4	71.6	−0.2	237:161	−0.280	397	0.779
(−4, +4)	72.26	73.06	−0.8	239:148	−0.402	386	0.688
(−5, +5)	73.05	72.74	0.31	225:135	0.303	359	0.762
B: LRE							
(−1, +1)	8.36	9.06	−0.7	114:288	−4.9[a]	401	0.000
(−1, +2)	9.75	9.86	−0.11	233:168	−0.690	400	0.490
(−1, +3)	10.03	10.59	−0.56	217:174	−1.705	390	0.089
(−1, +4)	9.83	10.43	−0.6	199:162	−1.98[a]	360	0.049
(−1, +5)	10.28	10.80	−0.52	187:164	−0.87	350	0.383
(−2, +2)	10.01	10.12	−0.11	167:234	−0.61	400	0.544
(−3, +3)	11.03	11.12	−0.09	213:185	−0.334	397	0.738
(−4, +4)	12.14	12.04	0.1	200:187	0.163	386	0.870
(−5, +5)	10.64	11.16	−0.52	195:165	−0.929	359	0.353

(continued)

Table 4.5 (continued)

Paired sample (pre-M&A, post-M&A)	Mean ratio post-M&A	Mean ratio pre-M&A	Mean difference	Positive: negative	*t*-value	Degree of freedom	Significance
D: SGR							
(−1, +1)	5.59	6.2	−0.61	184:218	−6.8[b]	401	0.000
(−1, +2)	5.98	6.74	−0.75	176:225	−6.5[b]	400	0.000
(−1, +3)	5.87	7.25	−1.38	155:236	−4.61[b]	390	0.000
(−1, +4)	5.97	7.42	−1.45	133:228	−5.26[b]	360	0.000
(−1, +5)	5.96	7.35	−1.39	120:231	4.71[b]	350	0.000
(−2, +2)	6.21	6.75	−0.54	160:240	−4.48[b]	400	0.000
(−3, +3)	6.45	7.55	−1.1	151:248	−4.86[b]	397	0.000
(−4, +4)	7.73	8.44	−1.1	134:253	−0.66	386	0.500
(−5, +5)	4.87	7.73	−2.86	226:134	−0.502	359	0.616
E: RDE							
(−1, +1)	1.3	1.6	−0.3	184:218	−0.458	401	0.647
(−1, +2)	1.02	1.34	−0.32	287:114	−3.39[b]	400	0.001
(−1, +3)	1.03	1.28	−0.25	276:135	−2.89[a]	390	0.004
(−1, +4)	1.11	1.36	−0.25	216:145	−2.64[a]	360	0.009
(−1, +5)	1.18	1.34	−0.16	199:152	1.74	350	0.082
(−2, +2)	1.05	0.96	−0.09	171:230	−1.48	400	0.141
(−3, +3)	0.74	0.72	0.02	188:210	0.34	397	0.734
(−4, +4)	1.17	1.51	0.34	189:198	−3.17[b]	386	0.002
(−5, +5)	1.48	1.55	−0.07	195:165	−0.577	359	0.565

[a], [b]Denote significance at 5 and 1 %, respectively

significant negative difference of SGR. The significant negative difference in SGR may be due to the marketing economies realized post-M&A. Higher volume of sales, avoidance of duplication of distribution, and advertising expenses may be the reason.

Acquirers also seem to have achieved operational economies in their manufacturing expenses, as reflected in negative difference of COGR for almost all pairs of comparison. The negative difference in COGR may be due to the economies of scale realized, post-M&A. Higher volume of raw material and large scale of economies post-M&A may be the reason.

The relevant data in Table 4.5 also reveals that the acquirers have also been able to gain economy in research and development expenses (RDE) in post-M&A period (reflected in negative mean difference); perhaps, this has been achieved due to the elimination of duplicate efforts in research and development at the level of each firm (acquirer and target firm) after M&A. There is significant negative difference in the labor expense ratio in the first and fourth year post-M&A. Labor cost appears to have reduced post-M&A in comparison to before M&A as indicated by negative difference for all the pairs.

Paired t-test has also identified negative difference in terms of other expense ratios, i.e., COGR, LRE, and SGR in all the pairs before and after M&A.

4.4.2 Analysis of Pre-M&A and Post-M&A Efficiency Ratios

Efficiency ratios have been used to assess the operational performance of acquirers before and after M&A.

Analysis has been carried out primarily on the basis of assets turnover ratios (fixed, total, and current). It is hypothesized that efficiency of acquirers has shown improvement in utilization of resources after M&A.

The relevant data contained in Table 4.6 suggests that the TATR and CATR of both period (before and after M&A) is less than one for the entire period of study

Table 4.6 Paired samples t-test of pre-M&A and post-M&A efficiency ratios

Paired sample (pre-M&A, post-M&A)	Mean ratio post-M&A	Mean ratio pre-M&A	Mean difference	Positive: negative	*t*-value	Degree of freedom	Significance
A: FATR							
(−1, +1)	4.43	4.06	0.37	233:169	3.52[b]	401	0.000
(−1, +2)	4.93	4.47	0.46	228:174	3.12[b]	400	0.002
(−1, +3)	5.14	4.51	0.63	223:168	3.74[b]	390	0.000
(−1, +4)	4.64	4.00	0.64	200:161	4.7[a]	360	0.000
(−1, +5)	4.51	4.17	0.34	186:165	2.37[a]	350	0.018
(−2, +2)	4.53	4.22	0.31	234:167	2.44[a]	400	0.015
(−3, +3)	4.84	4.37	0.47	235:163	2.75[b]	397	0.006
(−4, +4)	5.4	4.6	0.8	227:160	3.31[b]	386	0.001
(−5, +5)	5.15	4.15	1	219:141	4.63[b]	359	0.000
B: TATR							
(−1, +1)	0.85	0.847	0.003	191:211	0.021	401	0.983
(−1, +2)	0.78	0.84	−0.06	168:233	−0.365	400	0.000
(−1, +3)	0.82	0.89	−0.07	154:237	−4.98[b]	390	0.000
(−1, +4)	0.80	0.87	−0.07	137:224	−4.72[b]	360	0.000
(−1, +5)	0.84	0.90	−0.06	129:222	−3.68[b]	350	0.000
(−2, +2)	0.82	0.87	−0.05	144:257	−3.53[b]	400	0.000
(−3, +3)	0.82	0.84	−0.02	150:238	−1.5	397	0.135
(−4, +4)	0.82	0.89	−0.07	154:233	−3.38[b]	386	0.001
(−5, +5)	0.81	0.87	−0.06	145:215	−3.15[b]	359	0.002
C: CATR							
(−1, +1)	0.88	0.87	0.01	190:212	0.73	401	0.466
(−1, +2)	0.85	0.87	−0.02	184:217	−1.93	400	0.055
(−1, +3)	0.87	0.92	−0.05	182:209	−3.11[b]	390	0.002
(−1, +4)	0.86	0.92	−0.06	160:201	−4.55[b]	360	0.000
(−1, +5)	0.74	0.93	−0.19	128:223	−7.19[b]	350	0.000
(−2, +2)	0.89	0.91	−0.02	174:227	−1.80	400	0.072
(−3, +3)	0.91	0.87	−0.04	159:239	−2.27[a]	397	0.024
(−4, +4)	0.88	0.94	−0.06	152:235	−3.18[b]	386	0.002
(−5, +5)	0.731	0.727	0.004	225:135	0.303	359	0.762

[a], [b]Denote significance at 5 and 1 %, respectively

(10 years); evidently, the TATR and CATR, *prima-facie*, do not seem to be satisfactory and is indicative of under-utilization of resources before as well as after M&A.

In contrast, fixed assets turnover ratio (FATR) has presented better picture of efficiency in utilization of fixed assets before as well as after M&A. There is an improvement, duly corroborated by paired t-test showing significant positive difference in FATR for all the pairs. Moreover, the positive mean difference in FATR has been observed in the case of majority (56 %) of acquiring firms.

4.4.3 Analysis of Pre-M&A and Post-M&A Liquidity Ratios

A comparison has been made between liquidity position before and after M&A, *prima-facie,* Indian acquiring firms seem to have adequate and satisfactory level of liquidity position before as well as after M&A as reflected in mean current ratio. The corporate firms in India have access to short-term borrowings in the form of bank borrowings, overdraft, and cash credit limits from banks (Jain and Yadav 2000). These facilities enable management to operate on lesser margin of working capital reflected in lower current ratio. The mean current ratio is quite high 2.6, 2.87, 2.96, 3.12, and 2.93 before 1, 2, 3, 4, and 5 years respectively. The acquirer firms seem to have excessive inventories for the current requirements before M&A. High current ratio is indicative of slack management practices and poor credit management in terms of overextended accounts receivable also.

In light of this, acquiring firms have managed liquidity better during post-M&A phase, as reflected in significant negative difference implying decrease in CR which seems to be in order/desirable, given the fact that current ratio was higher than normative norm of 2:1. Mean current ratio for 5 year before M&A is 2.74 which quite high; it has reduced to 2.19 in fifth year after M&A (Table 4.7). The negative difference is significant; three-forth (75 %) firms have negative current ratio. The t-test has also revealed significant negative difference for all the pairs of mean current ratio (Table 4.7). On the basis of empirical results, it may be concluded that liquidity and credit management practices have improved significantly after M&A.

4.4.4 Analysis of Pre-M&A and Post-M&A Leverage Ratios

Total debt constitutes a significant source of financing total assets of acquiring firms as corroborated by debt to total assets ratio presented in Table 4.8; evidently, DA, *prima-facie,* seems to be satisfactory before as well as after M&A. Paired t-test has not identified any considerable change in leverage (DA) post-M&A. As expected, there is no change in the leverage of the acquirers over the post-M&A period. Based on these findings, it may be concluded that M&A has no impact on the leverage of acquiring firms before and after M&A.

Table 4.7 Paired samples t-test of pre-M&A and post-M&A liquidity ratios

Paired sample (pre-M&A, post-M&A)	Mean ratio post-M&A	Mean ratio pre-M&A	Mean difference	Positive: negative	*t*-value	Degree of freedom	Significance
(−1, +1)	2.5	2.6	−0.1	192:210	−1.84	401	0.067
(−1, +2)	2.6	2.7	−0.1	193:208	−2.34[a]	400	0.020
(−1, +3)	2.6	2.8	−0.2	184:207	−3.28[b]	390	0.001
(−1, +4)	2.4	2.6	−0.2	154:207	−3.43[b]	360	0.001
(−1, +5)	2.19	2.74	−0.55	122:229	−7.35[b]	350	0.000
(−2, +2)	2.63	2.87	−0.24	184:217	−3.83[b]	400	0.000
(−3, +3)	2.68	2.96	−0.32	169:229	−3.6[b]	397	0.000
(−4, +4)	2.68	3.12	−0.44	142:245	−5.07[b]	386	0.000
(−5, +5)	2.42	2.93	−0.51	110:250	−6.87[b]	359	0.000

[a, b]Denote significance at 5 and 1 %, respectively

Table 4.8 Paired samples t-test of pre-M&A and post-M&A leverage ratios

Paired sample (pre-M&A, post-M&A)	Mean ratio post-M&A	Mean ratio pre-M&A	Mean difference	Positive: negative	*t*-value	Degree of freedom	Significance
(−1, +1)	0.51	0.50	0.01	230:172	0.49	401	0.622
(−1, +2)	0.514	0.507	0.007	234:167	1.17	400	0.244
(−1, +3)	0.51	0.506	0.004	221:170	0.639	390	0.523
(−1, +4)	0.56	0.50	0.06	223:138	4.27[b]	360	0.000
(−1, +5)	0.52	0.51	0.01	207:144	1.67	350	0.096
(−2, +2)	0.52	0.50	0.02	241:160	3.27[b]	400	0.001
(−3, +3)	0.52	0.51	0.01	230:168	1.10	397	0.271
(−4, +4)	0.52	0.51	0.01	219:168	2.05[a]	386	0.041
(−5, +5)	0.53	0.52	0.01	199:161	1.26	359	0.207

[a, b]Denote significance at 5 and 1 %, respectively

4.5 Analysis of Sources of Performance

The improvement in the period, following M&A, can arise from various sources such as better operating margins, greater assets productivity, lower labor costs, or higher volume or higher sales, etc. In order to ascertain the sources of the better long-term post-M&A returns, the measure of operating performance has been decomposed into its constituents in terms of Du Pont analysis. Du Pont analysis indicates that the profitability has improved either by improving profit margin per rupees of sales or by generating more sales revenue per rupee of investment.

4.5.1 Du Pont Analysis Based on OPM

The operating profit margin, based on assets, can be decomposed into operating profit margin based on sales and total assets turnover ratio. The operating profit margin based on assets (OPM_A) calculated as operating profit (OP) divided by average total assets as per Eq. (4.5.1) may be decomposed into the operating profit margin based on sales (OPMs) and the total assets turnover ratio as per Eq. (4.5.2)

$$OPM_A = \frac{\text{PBIT} - \text{nonoperating income}}{\text{Average total assets}} \tag{4.5.1}$$

or

$$OPM_A = \frac{\text{PBIT} - \text{nonoperating income}}{\text{net sales}} \times \frac{\text{net sales}}{\text{Average total assets}} \tag{4.5.2}$$

where

$$\frac{\text{PBIT} - \text{nonoperating income}}{\text{net sales}} = \text{operating profit margin based on sale } (OPM_S)$$

and

$$\frac{\text{Net sales}}{\text{Average total assets}} = \text{Total assets turnover ratio (TATR)}$$

In Du Pont terms

$$OPM_A = OPM_S \times TATR \tag{4.5.3}$$

The operating profit margin based on sales depicts the operating profit obtained through each rupee of sales. Total assets turnover indicates the efficiency with which the firm uses its assets to generate sales. The relevant data contained in Table 4.9 shows that the operating profit margin based on sales have improved post-M&A. As we have divided the operating profit of the acquirer with the net sales of the acquirer, the significant post-M&A operating margin indicates that the acquirer appears to have generated higher operating profit per unit net sales post-M&A. The analysis indicates the possible increase in market power due to M&A in India. The better operating margin seems to be due to the lower costs as a result of economies of scale. Negative *t*-values identified by paired sample t-test on expense ratio (Table 4.5) also corroborate this finding. Further, the evidence of increase in the operating profit margin based also supports these results.

Table 4.9 Paired samples t-test of pre-M&A and post-M&A constituent ratios in terms of Du Pont

Paired sample (pre-M&A, post-M&A)	Mean ratio post-M&A	Mean ratio pre-M&A	Mean difference	Positive: negative	*t*-value	Degree of freedom	Significance
A: Operating profit margin based on assets (OPM_A)							
(−1, +1)	10.38	10.22	0.16	206:196	0.434	401	0.665
(−1, +2)	10.26	9.49	0.77	196:205	1.97*	400	0.049
(−1, +3)	9.84	9.46	0.38	191:200	0.939	390	0.348
(−1, +4)	9.78	9.1	0.68	185:176	1.67	360	0.095
(−1, +5)	9.15	8.66	0.49	181:170	1.02	350	0.311
(−2, +2)	9.8	9	0.8	208:193	2.01*	400	0.046
(−3, +3)	9.8	8.85	0.95	203:195	2.08*	397	0.039
(−4, +4)	9.58	8.71	0.87	211:176	1.79	386	0.075
(−5, +5)	9.36	9.09	0.27	171:189	0.605	359	0.546
B: Operating profit margin based on sales (OPM_S)							
(−1, +1)	14.39	12.76	1.63	234:168	2.19[a]	401	0.029
(−1, +2)	14.60	12.87	1.73	212:189	2.34[a]	400	0.020
(−1, +3)	13.57	13.43	0.14	199:192	0.19	390	0.844
(−1, +4)	14.14	13.61	0.53	183:178	0.78	360	0.437
(−1, +5)	14.43	13.17	1.26	177:174	1.23	350	0.222
(−2, +2)	13.3	12.1	1.2	218:183	1.81	400	0.071
(−3, +3)	13.5	11.4	2.1	213:185	1.97[a]	397	0.049
(−4, +4)	14.01	12.33	1.68	208:179	0.403	386	0.687
(−5, +5)	13	9	4	198:162	2.06[a]	359	0.041
C: Total assets turnover ratio							
(−1, +1)	0.85	0.847	0.003	191:211	0.021	401	0.983
(−1, +2)	0.78	0.84	−0.06	168:233	−0.365	400	0.000
(−1, +3)	0.82	0.89	−0.07	154:237	−4.98[b]	390	0.000
(−1, +4)	0.80	0.87	−0.07	137:224	−4.72[b]	360	0.000
(−1, +5)	0.84	0.90	−0.06	129:222	−3.68[b]	350	0.000
(−2, +2)	0.82	0.87	−0.05	144:257	3.53[b]	400	0.000
(−3, +3)	0.82	0.84	−0.02	150:238	−1.5	397	0.135
(−4, +4)	0.82	0.89	−0.07	154:233	−3.38[b]	386	0.001
(−5, +5)	0.81	0.87	−0.06	145:215	−3.15[b]	359	0.002

[a], [b]Denote significance at 5 and 1 %, respectively

The efficiency of utilization of assets to generate higher sales does not appear to have improved as revealed by total assets turnover ratio post-M&A. It cannot be inferred that acquirers' total assets turnover after the M&A is significantly different from pre-M&A levels. In fact, there is a marginal decrease in this ratio. Thus, we cannot conclude that M&A have led to higher total assets turnover which indicates that it is unlikely that acquirer firms have generated higher incremental sales utilizing their assets more efficiently.

4.5.2 Du Pont Analysis Based on OCFR

The operating cash flow ratio ($OCFR_A$), based on assets, can be decomposed into operating cash flow based on sales and total assets turnover ratio.

The operating cash flow ratio based on assets ($OCFR_A$) calculated as operating cash flow (OCF) divided by average total assets as per Eq. (4.5.4) may be decomposed into the operating cash flow based on sales ($OCFR_s$) and the total assets turnover ratio as per Eq. (4.5.5)

$$OCFR_A = \frac{\text{PBIT} - \text{nonoperating income} + \text{Depreciation} + \text{Amortisation} + \text{any non cash expenses}}{\text{Average total assets}} \tag{4.5.4}$$

or

$$OCFR_A = \frac{\text{PBIT} - \text{nonoperating income} + \text{Depreciation} + \text{Amortisation} + \text{any non cash expenses}}{\text{net sales}} \times \frac{\text{net sales}}{\text{Average total assets}} \tag{4.5.5}$$

where,

$$\frac{\text{PBIT} - \text{nonoperating income} + \text{Depreciation} + \text{Amortisation} + \text{any non cash expenses}}{\text{net sales}} = \text{Operating cash flow ratio based on sale}(OCFR_S)$$

$$\frac{\text{net sales}}{\text{Average total assets}} = \text{Total assets turnover ratio (TATR)}$$

and

In Du Pont terms

$$OCFR_A = OCFR_S \times TATR \tag{4.5.6}$$

The operating cash flow based on sales depicts the operating cash flow obtained through each rupee of sales. Total assets turnover indicates the efficiency with which the firm uses its assets to generate sales.

Table 4.10 shows that the operating cash flow ratio (based on sales) has improved post-M&A. As we have divided the operating cash flows of the acquirers by the net sales of the acquirer, the significant post-M&A operating cash flow indicates that the acquirers appear to have generated higher operating cash flow per unit net sales post-M&A. The Du Pont analysis indicates the increase in the operating cash flow ratio based on sales. The better operating cash flow seems to be due to the lower

Table 4.10 Paired samples t-test of pre-M&A and post-M&A constituent ratios in terms of Du Pont

Paired sample (pre-M&A, post-M&A)	Mean ratio post-M&A	Mean ratio pre-M&A	Mean difference	Positive: negative	*t*-value	Degree of freedom	Significance
A: Operating cash flow ratio based on assets ($OCFR_A$)							
(−1, +1)	13	12.76	0.24	200:202	0.46	401	0.65
(−1, +2)	12.91	12.49	0.42	198:203	1.07	400	0.29
(−1, +3)	13	12.1	0.9	187:204	1.87	390	0.062
(−1, +4)	12.61	12.20	0.41	170:191	0.998	360	0.319
(−1, +5)	12.49	12.10	0.39	150:201	0.682	350	0.496
(−2, +2)	12.78	12.18	0.06	191:210	1.44	400	0.15
(−3, +3)	12.46	12.31	0.15	186:212	0.34	397	0.74
(−4, +4)	12.14	12.04	0.1	182:205	0.211	386	0.833
(−5, +5)	12.32	11.77	0.6	158:202	1.16	359	0.247
B: Operating cash flow ratio based on sales ($OCFR_S$)							
(−1, +1)	15.47	14.98	0.49	232:170	1.26	401	0.208
(−1, +2)	18.28	17.74	0.54	204:197	0.96	400	0.340
(−1, +3)	20.11	16.92	3.19	200:191	2.48[a]	390	0.014
(−1, +4)	18.74	16.37	2.37	181:180	2.36[a]	360	0.019
(−1, +5)	21.59	16.79	4.81	181:170	2.28[a]	350	0.023
(−2, +2)	17.6	16.98	0.62	207:194	1.08	400	0.282
(−3, +3)	18.58	16.71	1.87	205:193	2.03[a]	397	0.043
(−4, +4)	21.5	11.55	9.9	189:198	1.52	386	0.130
(−5, +5)	18.6	15.1	3.5	180:180	1.93	359	0.054
C: Total assets turnover ratio							
(−1, +1)	0.85	0.847	0.003	191:211	0.021	401	0.983
(−1, +2)	0.78	0.84	−0.06	168:233	−0.365	400	0.000
(−1, +3)	0.82	0.89	−0.07	154:237	−4.98[b]	390	0.000
(−1, +4)	0.80	0.87	−0.07	137:224	−4.72[b]	360	0.000
(−1, +5)	0.84	0.90	−0.06	129:222	−3.68[b]	350	0.000
(−2, +2)	0.82	0.87	−0.05	144:257	3.53[b]	400	0.000
(−3, +3)	0.82	0.84	−0.02	150:238	−1.5	397	0.135
(−4, +4)	0.82	0.89	−0.07	154:233	−3.38[b]	386	0.001
(−5, +5)	0.81	0.87	−0.06	145:215	−3.15[b]	359	0.002

[a], [b]Denote significance at 5 and 1 %, respectively

costs as a result of economies of scale. This conclusion is also validated by evidence of negative mean difference of expense ratios presented in Table 4.5.

However, the efficiency of utilization of assets to generate higher sales does not appear to have improved as revealed by total assets turnover ratio post M&A. It cannot be inferred that acquirers' total assets turnover after the M&A is significantly different from pre-M&A levels. Thus, we cannot conclude that M&As have led to higher total assets turnover which indicates that it is unlikely that acquirer firms have generated higher incremental sales utilizing their assets more efficiently.

4.6 Concluding Observations

The objective of this chapter is to analyze the financial performance of corporates involved in M&A in India. The major hypothesis is that acquiring firms have improved their performance post-M&A. The empirical evidence validates the hypothesis that Indian acquirers have performed financially better after M&A, compared to their performance in pre-M&A period.

The study indicates that in the long term, M&As appear to have been financially beneficial for the acquiring companies. The findings suggest that profitability of acquiring firms has improved during post-M&A phase. This improvement in performance can be attributed to the mergers and acquisitions. Enhanced efficiency in utilization of fixed assets by the acquiring firms appears to have generated higher operating profits. Acquirers seem to have realized synergistic benefits of mergers and acquisitions by controlling expenses, specially selling, general and administration expenses as identified by negative (statistically significant) *t*-value of paired samples test. Better management of liquidity position during the post-M&A period has also been observed. These findings, in Indian context, are in sync with the findings of Ramakrishnan (2008), Pawaskar (2001), Selvam et al. (2009), Kumar and Bansal (2008), Rani et al. (2013, 2015), Sinha et al. (2010). However, these findings are in contrast with the findings of Kumar (2009).

However, mergers and acquisitions have not resulted in improvement in all assets turnover ratios. A reason for this may be that additional assets generate additional capacities. Initially, it may not be possible to achieve 100 % capacity utilization. Therefore, assets turnover ratio improves slowly. It appears that recession in the year 2008 resulted in low assets turnovers of acquiring firms. Further, the two constituents of the measure of operating profits (operating profit margin based on sales and total assets turnover) provide insights into sources of the economic performance. The long-term operating profit margin of the acquiring firms, on an average, appears to have improved. This means higher profit is generated per unit net sales by the acquiring firm after the M&A.

The higher profits (profit before interest and taxes and nonoperating income) are generated through the better margins. This might be due to the economies of scale obtained by the firms' larger size after M&A.

The analysis indicates the possible increase in market power due to M&A in India. Survey findings by Rani et al. (2010) on motives of mergers and acquisitions also corroborates this finding. Further, the evidence of significant increase in the operating profit margin also supports these results. However, assets turnover of the acquiring firms does not seem to have improved after M&A (also revealed by paired samples t-test); net sales per unit of asset invested have not increased after M&A. In operational terms, the efficiency/utilization of assets does not get manifested in generating higher net sales after M&A. That may be, partly, due to recessionary conditions in global economy after 2008.

On the basis of empirical results, it is reasonable to conclude that, on an average, acquiring firms in India appear to have performed better financially after M&A, compared to their performance in the pre-M&A period.

References

Cosh, A., Hughes, A., Lee, K., & Singh, A. (1998). Takeovers, institutional investment and the persistence of profits. In I. Begg & B. Henry (Eds.), *Applied economics and public policy* (pp. 107–144) Department of Applied Economics Occasional Paper No.63, Cambridge University Press, Cambridge. http://www.cbr.cam.ac.uk/pdf/wp030.pdf

Ghosh, A. (2001). Does operating performance really improve following corporate acquisition? *Journal of Corporate Finance, 7*(2), 151–178.

Ghosh, A., & Jain, P. C. (2000). Financial leverage changes associated with corporate mergers. *Journal of Corporate Finance, 6*(4), 377–402.

Gitman, L. J. (2009). *Principles of managerial finance* (XI ed.). New York: Pearsons.

Gugler, K., Mueller, D. C., & Yurtoglu, B. B. (2003). The impact of corporate governance on investment returns in developed and developing countries. *Economic Journal, 113*(491), 511–539.

Healy, P. M., Palepu, K. G., & Ruback, R. S. (1992). Does corporate performance improve after mergers? *Journal of Financial Economics, 31*(2), 135–175.

Jain, P. K., & Yadav, S. S. (2000). Financial Management Practices in Select Private Corporate Enterprises, Hindustan Publishing Company, New Delhi.

Kumar, R. (2009). Post merger corporate performance an Indian perspective. *Management Research Review, 32*(2), 145–157.

Kumar, S., & Bansal, L. K. (2008). The impact of mergers and acquisitions on corporate performance in India. *Management Decision, 46*(10), 1531–1543.

Manson, S., Powell, R., Stark, A. W., & Thomas, H. M. (2000). Identifying the sources of gains from takeovers. *Accounting Forum., 24*(4), 319–343.

Mueller, D. C. (1986). *Profits in the long run*. Cambridge, New York and Sydney: Cambridge University Press.

Parrino, J. D., & Harris, R. S. (1999). Takeovers management and replacements, and post-acquisition operating performance: Some evidence from 1980s. *Journal of Applied Corporate Finance, 11*(4), 88–97.

Pawaskar, V. (2001). Effect of mergers on corporate performance in India. *Vikalpa, 26*(1), 19–32.

Rahman, R. A., & Limmack, R. J. (2004). Corporate acquisitions and the operating performance of Malaysian companies. *Journal of Business Finance and Accounting, 31*(3&4), 359–400.

Ramakrishnan, K. (2008). Long-term post-merger performance of firms in India. *Vikalpa, 33*(2), 47–63.

Ramaswamy, K. P., & Waegelein, J. F. (2003). Firm financial performance following mergers. *Review of Quantitative Finance and Accounting, 20*(2), 115–126.

Rani, N., Yadav, Surendra, S., & Jain P. K. (2010). Corporate merger practices in India: An empirical study. In *Proceedings of Tenth Global Conference on Flexible Systems Management GLOGIFT10, Graduate School of System Design and Management Collaboration Complex*, Hiyoshi Campus, Keio University: Japan. http://ssrn.com/abstract=2043698

Rani, N., Yadav, Surendra S., & Jain, P. K. (2013). Du pont analysis of post M&A operating performance of indian acquiring firms. *International Journal of Economics and Finance, 5*(8), 65–73.

Rani, N., Yadav, Surendra S., & Jain, P. K. (2015). Financial performance analysis of mergers and acquisitions: evidence from India. *International Journal of Commerce and Management., 25*(4), 402–423.

Ravenscraft, D. J., & Scherer, F. M. (1987). *Mergers, sell-offs, and economic efficiency*. Washington, DC: The Brookings Institution.

Selvam, M., Babu, M., Indumathi, G., & Ebenezer (2009). Impact of mergers on the corporate performance of acquirer and target companies in India. *Journal of accounting and Auditing*, 5 (11), 55–64.

Sharma, D. S., & Ho, J. (2002). The impact of acquisitions on operating performance: some Australian evidence. *Journal of Business Finance and Accounting, 29*(1&2), 155–200.

Sinha, N., Kaushik, K. P., & Chaudhary, T. (2010). Measuring post merger and acquisition performance: An investigation of select financial sector organizations in India. *International Journal of Economics and Finance, 2*(4), 190–200.

Switzer, J. A. (1996). Evidence on real gains in corporate acquisitions. *Journal of Economics and Business, 48*(5), 443–460.

Yeh, T. M., & Hoshino, Y. (2000). The effects of mergers and acquisitions on Taiwanese corporations. *Review of Pacific Basin Financial Markets and Policies, 3*(2), 183–199.

Chapter 5
Survey of Management View on Motives for Mergers and Acquisitions

Abstract The objective of this chapter is to investigate motives and trend of merger activities of Indian companies during the period 2003–15. A survey has been conducted in the present research work to understand the viewpoint of Indian managers regarding motives of undertaking mergers and acquisitions (M&A). The survey findings show that the primary motivation for mergers is to achieve operating synergies.

Keywords Economies of scale and scope · Synergy · Motives · Operational synergies · Market power · Cross-selling · Subsidiary

5.1 Introduction

The existing literature as well as empirical work on motives of mergers does not offer a conclusive explanation for why mergers occur. The present chapter seeks to answer "Why do mergers take place?" As per the literature available, very few surveys have been conducted to study the managerial views about motives for undertaking mergers and acquisitions. The surveys that have been conducted are primarily for United States (US) managers.

To gauge the viewpoint of Indian managers regarding motives of undertaking mergers and acquisitions (M&A), a survey has been conducted in the present research work. The target population for the surveys is the acquiring companies that merged another company or have gone for acquisition of another company during the chosen time period and are located all over India. The surveys are expected to provide useful insights as the results of these surveys will enlighten the managers about what is expected from these transactions and what are the motives for M&A.

In the survey, the viewpoints of the respondents have been captured on three major aspects, namely, (i) management views on motives for M&A, (ii) management views on sources of synergy from M&A, and (iii) motives of merger of wholly owned subsidiary.

N. Rani et al., *Mergers and Acquisitions*, India Studies in Business and Economics, DOI 10.1007/978-981-10-2203-6_5

The chapter has been organized into four sections. Section 5.2 explains the survey research methodology. Section 5.2 is divided into three subsections, namely, (i) validity analysis, (ii) sample, and (iii) respondents' profile. Survey results and discussions constitute the subject matter of Sect. 5.3. The concluding observations have been presented in Sect. 5.4. The questionnaire used for the survey is at Appendix.

5.2 Survey Methodology

The survey has been carried out to get the responses from the Director (Finance) of the companies that adopted strategy of merger and acquisition during the specified time period; these companies are located across India. The survey plays an important role because the strategy of mergers and acquisitions are adopted by the top management of the company keeping certain objectives in mind. Therefore, the views and motives of the respondents make a basis for the expected performance both in long-term as well as short-term.

For the survey, structured questionnaire has been used as a primary tool to collect the required information from the respondents. A preliminary questionnaire was developed on a set of questions based on an extensive review of the earlier researches on motives of mergers and acquisitions. Previous studies have empirically assessed importance of acquisitions as a mode of entry in foreign market (Andersen 1997; Kogut and Singh 1988), performance outcome of acquisitions like knowledge transfer and learning post-acquisition (Brouthers and Brouthers 2001; Bhagat et al. 2002) and creation of shareholder value, etc. (Ravenscraft and Scherer 1987; Gugler et al. 2003; Moeller et al. 2005; Mueller and Yurtoglu 2007).

Berkovitch and Narayanan (1993) have identified synergy, hubris, and agency as three major motives of takeovers. Mukherjee et al. (2004) showed that primary motivation for mergers and acquisitions is to achieve operating synergies.

Seth et al. (2000) lend support to the synergy hypothesis as the main motive. The study also revealed that hubris also played an important role in these deals. Eun et al. (1996) have concluded that acquisitions are synergy creating activities.

Ghosh (2004) suggests that market power is the source of value creation and a rationale for merger and acquisition activities.

Wasserstein (1998) has identified five major causes of mergers. He states that the process of merger is driven by the forces of technological change, regulatory, and political reforms, fluctuations in financial markets, the role of leadership, and the tension between scale and focus. Trautwein (1990) organized the theories of merger motives into seven groups: efficiency, monopoly, empire building, raider, valuation, and process and disturbance theory.

Kumar and Rajib (2007) observed capital structure characteristics as a main motive for the merger for both acquirer and target companies in India. They reveal that firms with tighter liquidity positions are more likely to become a target. Goold and Campbell (1998) have pointed out that shared know-how, pooled negotiated power, coordinated strategies, vertical integration, shared tangible resources, and combined business creation bring synergy for merged entity. Eccles et al. (1999) have suggested cost savings, process involvement, revenue enhancement, tax benefits, financial engineering as main sources of synergy.

The questionnaire was modified on the inputs collected from experts' opinion. The experts include top level corporate managers and academicians in the area of finance. They belonged to the organizations located in Mumbai, Delhi, and NCR (National Capital Region). A preliminary version of this survey was pretested by a personal interview of 20 CFOs, directors (finance, legal), and company secretaries. The questionnaire was firmed-up after incorporating all the improvements suggested by these experts. The survey explores four major issues involved in merger and acquisition practices in India. Part I of the questionnaire contains the first issue which involves background data. In part II three major questions related to types and motives for engaging in mergers and acquisitions have been addressed. First, what are the motives behind corporate mergers? Second, what are the sources of synergies expected form M&A? Third, what are the reasons for a wave of merger of the subsidiaries with the parent company during the sample period?

The respondents were asked to choose the three most important motives from a list of eighth motives and ninth labeled as 'Any other' and, from a list of seven motives and an eighth labeled as 'Any other' for the sources of synergies expected from mergers and acquisitions. Additionally, in Part II of the questionnaire, we have also investigated the motives behind the mergers of wholly owned subsidiaries with the parent company.

The primary source of information, about the firms that acquired or merged other companies, is Prowess[1]; it is a financial database of Indian companies. In addition, the announcement dates were collected from online archives[2] of the Bombay Stock Exchange, the National Stock Exchange, the financial dailies, like The Economic Times, The Hindu Business Line, and other financial websites like moneycontrol, etc. We checked the names and address and email of the company secretaries, chief financial officers, director finance, and head—investor relations from the websites of the acquirer companies. We could obtain the email address of 750 companies. We requested 280 companies from Mumbai, Delhi, Gurgaon, Noida, Faridabad, Chandigarh, Ludhiana, Panchkula for an appointment for a personal interview and mailed the questionnaire to the 270 companies in first round of survey. 200 more companies were contacted in the second round of survey during 2015.

A follow up questionnaire was sent to the non-responding companies after 2 months. Further, the follow-up was done by sending emails to the companies wherever email addresses were available. Interview of 168 persons were personally scheduled and 52 responses were received through mail. Though the response proportion is more than one-fourth (25.2 %), it should not be considered as

[1]This database is a product of Centre for Monitoring Indian Economy Pvt. Ltd. (CMIE).

[2]http://www.bseindia.com/stockinfo/ann.aspx.
http://www.nseindia.com/content/corporate/corp_introduction.htm.

poor/low response rate. The reason is that the survey response to the subject of finance is usually not encouraging. In general, the respondents are apprehensive and shy away from giving their opinion or providing information related to financial decision making. In fact, respondents normally consider information related to any finance matter as very sensitive and confidential. They do not realize that the opinion or information provided by them is summarized on an average basis without quoting any one in particular. Hence, as a matter of policy, most of the companies are reluctant to respond to a finance questionnaire.

The study is not free from limitations. One limitation is that our study addresses only limited number of issues in the survey. This is not a comprehensive survey on various hypotheses prevalent in the area of mergers and acquisitions. We limit the scope to the acquiring companies only.

5.2.1 Validity Analysis

The questionnaire was validated by six finance experts—including academicians and practitioners. Based on their evaluation, the questionnaire had high face validity. Thus, the questionnaire maybe deemed suitable for further analysis.

5.2.2 Sample

The sample includes acquiring companies that merged or acquired companies during period starting from January 1, 2003 and ending on December 31, 2015. The sample consists of 755 companies that completed the transactions during the time period chosen for the study.

Table 5.1 exhibits the year-wise distribution (2003–2015) of the number of M&A completed by the sample companies and the respondent companies between January 1st, 2003 and December 31st, 2015. Year–wise distribution shows that 1255 companies completed 1930 deals. But there are companies which made multiple announcements across the year. So the sample consists of 755 companies that completed 1930 mergers and acquisitions deals during the sample period. Out of 755 companies email address of 750 companies could be obtained. So, the final sample was reduced to 750 companies.

Further, 1930 mergers and acquisitions deals were completed during the time span of the study; out of these, nearly one-fifth are in the year 2007. There are 189 companies that responded for this survey; out of these, nearly one-fourth respondents announced M&A in the year 2007. It is evident from Table 5.1 that the respondent companies are fairly representative of the sample companies. Out of the above respondents, nearly two-third (65 %) are from manufacturing sector while one-forth (26 %) are from services sector. Remaining almost one-tenth (9 %) represent construction, real estate, electricity, and diversified sector (depicted in Fig. 5.1).

Table 5.1 Distribution of sample, year-wise (2003–2015)

Year	No. of acquisitions completed	No. of mergers completed	No. of companies	Number of respondent companies
2003	13	15	23	13
2004	28	20	41	13
2005	52	18	47	15
2006	213	39	146	28
2007	260	59	174	54
2008	184	28	133	44
2009	97	15	87	6
2010	99	9	80	3
2011	129	18	98	4
2012	81	22	66	2
2013	95	51	99	3
2014	89	48	97	2
2015	178	70	164	2
Total	1518	412	1255	189

Year-wise distribution of sample, 2003–2015
Source CMIE Prowess

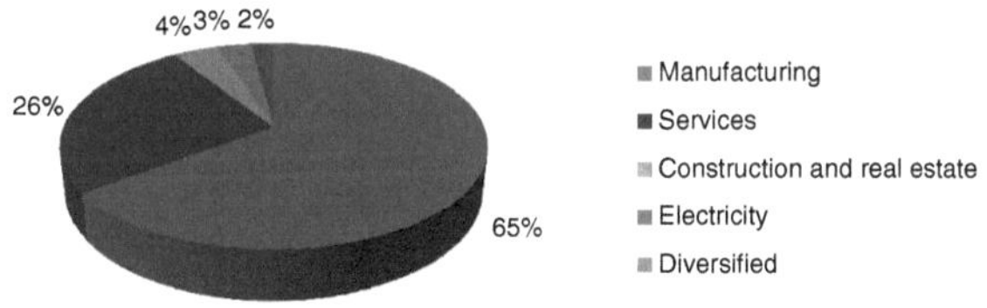

Fig. 5.1 Sector-wise distribution of the respondent companies

5.2.3 *Respondents' Profile*

Table 5.2 depicts the respondents' profile; the respondents are primarily the executives who held top level management positions in their respective companies. They include: more than one-fourth (27 %) chairman, managing directors, chief executive officers, chief financial officers and directors, almost one-third (31.7 %)

Table 5.2 Respondents' profile

Respondents designation	Number
Chairman, Executive Directors (Finance) and Chief Financial Officers	51 (27 %)
Company Secretary and Deputy General Manager	60 (31.7 %)
Vice Presidents, Head, and Chief Legal Officers	42 (22.2 %)
General Manager (Finance, Investor Relations)	36 (19.1 %)
Total	189 (100 %)

company secretary and deputy general managers, 22.2 % vice-presidents, and chief legal officers and the remaining almost one-fifth (19.1 %) are general managers (finance) and investor relation officers.

5.3 Survey Results and Discussion

The following three subsections present the results of the survey. They include the characteristics of responding firms, motives for mergers and motives for mergers of subsidiaries with the parent company. Table 5.3 depicts the results involving number of mergers (Question 1). The survey indicates that almost three-fourths (71.9 %) of the responding firms have been involved in multiple mergers. These 189 companies acquired and merged 1092 target companies during 2003–2015; out of these half (50.1 %) acquirers have acquired or merged independent companies; nearly one-third (34.2 %) acquirers have merged wholly owned subsidiaries and rest have merged group companies, associates companies, and subsidiaries (Table 5.4).

Table 5.5 reports the results involving ranking of motives of merging the other firms (Question 3). The respondents were asked to select three most important motives, in order of priority. They were given eight choices along with ninth as 'any other' option, where they could specify any other motive for

Table 5.3 Frequency distribution related to number of companies merged and acquired by sample corporates, 2003–2015

Number of M&A	*N*	%
1	53	28.1
2–4	60	31.7
5–7	35	18.5
8–10	20	10.6
11–15	13	6.9
Above 15	8	4.2
Total	189	100

Table 5.4 Involvement in mergers and acquisitions of the sample companies, 2003–2015

Type of M&A	*N*	%
Acquired or merged an independent company	547	50.1
Merger of wholly owned subsidiary	373	34.2
Merger of a group company	92	8.4
Merger of an acquired company (now subsidiary)	40	3.6
Merger of an associate company	40	3.7
Total	1092	100

Table 5.5 Management view of motives for mergers of the sample companies, 2003–2015

Motive No.	Motives for mergers	Prime motive	Second motive	Third motive	Weighted index	Rank
1	To take advantage of synergy	89	55	45	70	**1**
4	To consolidate	14	55	49	34	**2**
6	To adopt as a strategy for inorganic growth	24	34	45	31	**3**
5	To restructure organization	9	20	30	16	**4**
8	To rehabilitate a company through Board for Industrial and Financial Reconstruction (BIFR)	24	0	0	12	**5**
7	Exit of joint venture by other partner	17	0	0	9	**6**
3	To reduce tax on the combined company	4	13	10	8	**7**
2	To diversify	4	12	9	8	**7**
9	Any other (specify)	4	0	1	2	**8**

Note The weighted score = [{(Prime Motive × 3) + (Second Motive × 2) + (Third Motive × 1)} ÷ 6]

merging/acquiring other firm. A weighted index has been calculated for each motive for the purpose of ranking as per Eq. (5.3.1).

$$\text{Index} = \left[\frac{(\text{Prime motive} \times 3) + (\text{Second motive} \times 2) + (\text{Third motive} \times 1)}{6}\right] \quad (5.3.1)$$

For every statement, the number of respondents choosing it as prime motive has been multiplied by three, as secondary motive by two and as tertiary motive by one. These three numbers have been further summed up and then divided by six to get the value of the index. Using this weighted index, the statements are ranked in the descending order.

Table 5.5 reports the choices made by the respondents regarding the primary, secondary and tertiary motives for mergers. The empirical findings of the survey reveal that the primary motive of the mergers is to take advantage of synergies. The second highest-ranked motive of merger is to consolidate.

The survey findings show that the primary motivation for mergers is to achieve synergies. Synergy may arise from various sources. To investigate further, we asked another question (Q4) about the most important source of synergy.

Table 5.6 presents the ranking of sources of synergy as revealed by respondents. The respondents were asked to select three most important sources of synergy, in order of priority. They were given seven choices along with eighth as 'any other' option, where they could specify any other source of synergy arising out of merger. 'Operating economies' has been chosen by the respondents as the top ranked source of synergy. The second highest-ranked source of synergy is increased market

Table 5.6 Management view of sources of synergy from mergers of the sample companies, 2003–16

Synergy No.	Sources of synergy	Prime motive	Second motive	Third motive	Weighted index	Rank
2	Operating economies	55	45	41	23.5	**1**
4	Increased market power	54	40	45	23.2	**2**
1	Financial economies	21	34	29	14.0	**3**
6	Availing of cross-selling opportunities	15	14	31	10.0	**4**
8	Other (specify)	20	15	19	9.0	**5**
3	Enhanced managerial capabilities	15	16	9	6.7	**6**
7	Improved technology	5	20	8	5.5	**7**
5	Location economies	4	5	7	2.7	**8**

Note 1 The weighted score = [{(Prime Motive × 3) + (Second Motive × 2) + (Third Motive × 1)} ÷ 6]

Note 2 The response indicated in "Others" included linkages and integration, such as backward, forward and vertical, real estate/strategic assets, etc.

power. The findings are in agreement with Singh and Montgomery (1987); Mukherjee et al. (2004); their empirical evidence documented that synergistic gains in domestic acquisitions are derived from increase in operational efficiency and increase in market power. The results also match with Ghosh (2004) who has observed that market power is a rationale for acquiring other companies.

Keeping into consideration the trends of mergers as revealed in Table 5.4, 34 % mergers by the respondent companies are of wholly owned subsidiaries. We attempted to investigate the motive of mergers/amalgamation of wholly owned subsidiaries. Table 5.7 contains the results.

Table 5.7 Management view of motives of merger of wholly owned subsidiary sample companies, 2003–16

Motive No.	Motives of merger in case of wholly owned subsidiary	Prime motive	Second motive	Third motive	Weighted index	Rank
2	A composite scheme of arrangement for consolidation	22	21	13	20.2	1
4	A response to changes in regulatory framework	16	19	13	16.5	2
5	To eliminate duplication of compliance cost	8	10	17	10.2	3
1	To reduce complexity of organizational structure	12	6	9	9.5	4
3	Tax savings due to elimination of dividend distribution tax	6	8	9	7.2	5
6	Other (specify)	3	4	7	4	6

Note The weighted score = [{(Prime Motive × 3) + (Second Motive × 2) + (Third Motive × 1)} ÷ 6]

The respondents revealed that the primary motive has been a composite scheme of arrangement for consolidation. They opined that mergers of the wholly owned subsidiary facilitate corporate restructuring and reallocate the resources to higher valued uses.

Another important reason has been a response to the changes in regulatory framework. The results are in agreement with other studies (Jarrell and Bradley 1980; Schipper and Thompson 1983; Solvin and Sushka 1998) who investigated that regulatory changes play a key role in influencing the mergers and acquisition strategies of firms.

Parent-subsidiary mergers have not been widely investigated in the finance literature, but have implications for corporate governance. It has been observed that regulations related to corporate governance have evolved during 2003. SEBI monitors and regulates corporate governance of listed companies in India through Clause 49. This clause is incorporated in the listing agreement of stock exchanges with companies and it is compulsory for them to comply with its provisions. Some specific developments in the various clauses of listing agreement during 2001–2005 are:

(a) SEBI has amended clause 32[3] and Clause 41[4] of Listing Agreement. In lieu of the amended clause, a listed parent company is now mandatorily required to publish audited Consolidated Financial Statements in the annual report in addition to the separate financial statements.
(b) SEBI has revised Clause 49 of the Listing Agreement pertaining to corporate governance.[5] The major new provisions included in the revised Clause 49 regarding subsidiaries are:
    (i) At least one independent director of the holding company to be a director in material non-listed subsidiary company.
    (ii) The audit committee of the listed company will review the financial statements of the unlisted subsidiary, in particular, the investments made by the unlisted subsidiary company.
    (iii) The minutes of the Board meetings of the unlisted subsidiary company will be placed at the Board meeting of the listed holding company. The management should periodically bring to the attention of the Board of Directors of the listed holding company, a statement of all significant transactions, and arrangements entered into by the unlisted subsidiary company.

[3]Vide a notification SMDRP/Policy/Cir-44/01, dated, 31 August, 2001 available at http://www.sebi.gov.in/circulars/2001/CIR442001.html.

[4]Vide a notification SMD/Policy/Cir-2/2003 dated January 10, 2003 available at http://www.sebi.gov.in/circulars/2003/cir02-2003.html.

[5]Vide circular SEBI/CFD/DIL/CG/1/2004/12/10 dated October 29, 2004 available at http://web.sebi.gov.in/circulars/2004/cfdcir0104.pdf.

These changes are likely to result in an increase in administrative and compliance cost of having a number of subsidiaries. The third motive revealed by respondents is to eliminate the duplication of compliance cost. It appears that these changes in regulations have influenced the merger strategies of Indian companies.

5.4 Concluding Observations

The present chapter discusses the empirical survey of managers (management) of Indian companies engaged in mergers and acquisitions. The survey has been conducted to know their views about the motives of merging and acquiring other firms. Survey findings reveal that the primary motive of mergers and acquisitions in India during 2003–2015 has been to take advantage of synergies. Operating economies, increased market share and financial economies (lower risk leading to lower cost of capital) have been indicated in order of importance as the desired synergies to be gained through corporate mergers and acquisitions in India.

Based on the survey evidence, it is reasonable to conclude that primary motivation for mergers and acquisitions is to achieve operating synergies. For unlisted wholly owned subsidiary, motive of mergers is to achieve consolidation and a response to changing regulatory framework.

Empirical results suggest some implications for practitioners and researchers. This exploratory study suggests a need for detailed investigation of the synergy motive in Indian context. Parent-subsidiary mergers have not been widely investigated in the finance literature, but have implications for corporate governance. The present study suggests that issue should be deliberated more in Indian context. Management can merge the large number of unlisted subsidiaries to achieve consolidation and form a good governance structure. This practice will not only achieve savings in compliance cost but also improve the corporate governance standards of the company. Management of companies can adopt the strategy of merging large number of unlisted subsidiaries to improve the corporate governance structure of the companies.

Appendix

Questionnaire Survey on Mergers & Acquisitions

I. BACKGROUND INFORMATION

1. What is your current position or title? *(Pl. Specify)* ____________________________
2. What is the principal nature of your business? *(Pl. Fill in one circle)*

O Manufacturing O Wholesale/retail O Service O Mining
O Transportation O Construction O Other (*Pl. Specify*)

II. ISSUES INVOLVING MERGERS & ACQUISITIONS

1. Company was involved in _____mergers and ________acquisitions during the period January 1, 2003- December 31, 2015.

2. Company was involved in the merger/acquisition of following:

[Please tick the appropriate]

O An independent company O An associate company O A group company

O An acquired company O A wholly -owned subsidiary

3. Which of the following motives best explain your company's merger/ acquisition during the period Jan*uary 1, 2003- December 31, 2015?*

[Choose the three most important motives for merging the other firm]

Motive	***First Most Important*** *(Tick only one)*	***Second Most Important*** *(Tick only one)*	***Third Most Important*** *(Tick only one)*
1. To take advantage of synergy	O	O	O
2. To Diversify	O	O	O
3.To reduce tax on the combined company	O	O	O
4. To use free cash	O	O	O
5. To consolidate	O	O	O
6. To restructure organization	O	O	O
7. Strategic inorganic growth	O	O	O
8.To rehabilitate a company through Board for Industrial and Financial Reconstruction (BIFR)	O	O	O
9. Any other (pl. specify)	O	O	O

4. The following sources of synergies were expected from the merger/ acquisition:

[Choose the three most important sources of synergies from the merger]

Source	*First Most Important (Tick only one)*	*Second Most Important (Tick only one)*	*Third Most Important (Tick only one)*
1. Financial Synergies	O	O	O
2. Operating Synergies	O	O	O
3. Enhanced managerial capabilities	O	O	O
4. Increased Market power	O	O	O
5. Location Economies	O	O	O
6. Avail Cross-selling opportunity	O	O	O
7. Improved Technology	O	O	O
8. Any other (pl. specify)	O	O	O

5. Which of the following motives best explain your companies merger of the wholly - owned subsidiary with the parent company during the period January 1, 2003- December 31, 2015. *[Choose the three most important motives for merging the wholly-owned subsidiary]*

Motive	*First Most Important (Tick only one)*	*Second Most Important (Tick only one)*	*Third Most Important (Tick only one)*
1. To reduce complexity of organizational structure	O	O	O
2. A composite scheme of arrangement for consolidation	O	O	O
3. Tax savings due to elimination of dividend distribution tax	O	O	O
4.A response to changes in regulatory framework	O	O	O
5. To eliminate duplication of compliance cost	O	O	O
6. Any other (pl. specify)	O	O	O

Thank you for your cooperation

References

Andersen, O. (1997). Internationalization and market entry mode: a review of theories and conceptual framework. *Management International Review, 37*(2), 27–42.

Berkovitch, E., & Narayanan, M. (1993). Motives for takeovers: an empirical investigation. *Journal of Financial and Quantitative Analysis, 28*(3), 347–362.

Bhagat, R., Kedia, S., Harveston, B. L., & Triandis, H. C. (2002). Cultural variations in the cross-border transfer of organizational knowledge. *Academy of Management Review, 27*(2), 204–221.

Brouthers, K., & Brouthers, L. (2001). Explaining the national cultural distance paradox. *Journal of International Business Studies, 32*(1), 177–189.

Eccles, R. G., Lanes, K. L., & Wilson, T. C. (1999). Are you paying too much for that acquisition? *Harvard Business Review, 77*(4), 136–146.

Eun, C. S., Kolodny, R., & Scheraga, C. (1996). Cross-border acquisitions and shareholder wealth: tests of synergy and internalization hypotheses. *Journal of Banking & Finance, 20*(9), 1559–1582.

Ghosh, A. (2004). Increasing market share as a rational for corporate acquisitions. *Journal of Business Finance and Accounting, 31*(1&2), 209–247.

Goold, M., & Campbell, A. (1998). Desperately seeking synergy. *Harvard Business Review*, 131–143.

Gugler, K., Mueller, D. C., & Yurtoglu, B. B. (2003). The impact of corporate governance on investment returns in developed and developing countries. *Economic Journal, 113*(491), 511–539.

Jarrell, G. A., & Bradley, M. (1980). The economic effects of Federal and State regulations of cash tender offers. *Journal of Law and Economics, 23*(2), 371–407.

Kogut, B., & Singh, H. (1988). The effect of national culture on the choice of entry mode. *Journal of International Business Studies, 19*(3), 411–432.

Kumar, B. R., & Rajib, P. (2007). Characteristics of merging firms in India: An empirical examination. *Vikalpa, 32*(1), 27–44.

Moeller, S. B., Schlingemann, F. P., & Stulz, R. M. (2005). Wealth destruction on a massive scale: a study of acquiring firm returns in the recent merger wave. *Journal of Finance, 60*(2), 757–782.

Mueller, D. C., & Yurtoglu, B. B. (2007). Corporate governance and the returns to acquiring firms' shareholders. *Managerial and Decision Economics, 28*(8), 879–896.

Mukherjee, T. K., Kiymaz, H., & Baker, K. H. (2004). Merger motives and target valuation: A survey of evidence from CFOs. *Journal of Applied Finance, 14*(2), 7–24.

Ravenscraft, D. J., & Scherer, F. M. (1987). *Mergers, sell-offs, and economic efficiency*. Washington, DC: The Brookings Institution.

Schipper, K., & Thompson, R. (1983). Evidence on the capitalized value of merger activity for acquiring firms. *Journal of Financial Economics, 11*(1–4), 85–119.

Securities and Exchange Board of India. (2001). Amendment to the Listing Agreement. Circular (August 31, 2001). Retrieved June 1, 2016 from http://www.sebi.gov.in/cms/sebi_data/attachdocs/1300866355907.pdf

Securities and Exchange Board of India. (2003). Amendment to Listing Agreement-Clause 32 and Clause 41. Circular (January 10, 2003). Retrieved June 1, 2016 from http://www.sebi.gov.in/cms/sebi_data/pdffiles/16452_t.pdf

Securities and Exchange Board of India. (2004). Corporate Governance in listed Companies-Clause 49 of the Listing Agreement. Circular (October 29, 2004). Retrieved June 1, 2016 from http://www.sebi.gov.in/cms/sebi_data/attachdocs/1293168356651.pdf

Seth, A., Song, K. P., & Pettit, R. (2000). Synergy, managerialism or hubris: an empirical examination of motives for foreign acquisitions of US firms. *Journal of International Business Studies, 31*(3), 387–405.

Singh, H., & Montgomery, C. (1987). Corporate acquisition strategies and economic performance. *Strategic Management Journal, 8*(4), 377–386.
Solvin, M. B., & Sushka, M. E. (1998). The economies of parent-subsidiary mergers: An empirical analysis. *Journal of Financial Economics, 49*(2), 255–279.
Trautwein, F. (1990). Merger motives and prescriptions. *Strategic Management Journal, 11*(4), 283–295.
Wasserstein, B. (1998). *Big deal: The battle for control of America's leading corporations*. New York: Warner Books.

Chapter 6
Development of Corporate Governance Index

Abstract The objective of this chapter is to discuss the development of corporate governance index. Inputs from questionnaire constitute the basis for preparing corporate governance index. The questionnaire focused not only on the transparency and disclosures but broader issues like management discipline and social recognition and responsibility. Corporate Governance Score (CGS) is based on the responses of the 67 issues, categorized under seven main aspects included in the questionnaire. The chapter also presents corporate governance score of the respondent companies.

Keywords Transparency · Disclosure · Corporate social responsibility · Accountability · Fairness · Board independence · Board size

6.1 Introduction

Corporate governance has become a popular area of discussion recently throughout the world and, also, in India. The relationship between corporate governance and firm valuation has attracted particular attention among academics. The majority of prior literature on relationship between corporate governance and firm value documents a positive association between stronger corporate governance and firm valuation (Bebchuk et al. 2009; Cremers and Nair 2005; Core et al. 2006; Yermack 1996, Gompers et al. 2003). Virtually most of the previous works focus on the specific aspect of corporate governance such as Gompers et al. (2003) on takeover defenses; Yermack (1996), Lipton and Lorch (1992) on board size, Hermalin and Weisbach (1991), Bhagat and Black (2007) on board composition, Bebchuk et al. (2005) on management entrenchment, Cremers and Nair (2005), Core et al. (1999) on executive compensation.

Another set of the empirical studies analyze the impact of corporate governance in a cross-section of countries (Klapper and Love 2004; Durnev and Kim 2005). A Few studies use primary and survey-based data on firm level corporate

N. Rani et al., *Mergers and Acquisitions*, India Studies in Business and Economics, DOI 10.1007/978-981-10-2203-6_6

governance structure within a specific country (Balasubramaniam et al. 2010; Beiner et al. 2006; Black et al. 2006; Drobetz et al. 2004; Chen et al. 2007).

Empirical studies utilizing various corporate governance indices have shown that corporate governance is positively associated with firm value or stock returns (Bebchuk et al. 2005; Gompers et al. 2003; Garay and González 2008).

An important question in this regard is how corporate governance practices of acquirer firms directly influence performance outcomes of acquisitions' decisions. The question deserves attention for several reasons. Mergers and acquisitions serve as an important instrument of corporate governance to increase corporate efficiency. In fact, mergers and acquisitions are well-suited events where corporate values are tested over the time. The role of corporate governance has been explored on the financial performance and valuation post-M&A as well as measurement of the announcement effects of the acquiring firms (Carline et al. 2009; Gompers et al. 2003; Bris and Cabolis 2002; Swanstrom 2006; Malekzadeh et al. 1998; Bertrand and Mullainathan 1998; Datta et al. 2001; Roll 1986; Shleifer and Vishny 1988; Shivdasani 1993; Shleifer and Vishney 1986; Bris and Cabolis 2002; Rossi and Volpin 2004; Rani et al. 2014; Aggarwal and Williamson 2006; Dahya et al. 2008).

This chapter describes the construction of broad corporate governance Index (CGI) for the Indian public listed acquiring companies. This chapter has been organized into four sections. Section 6.2 comprises of the research design used to construct corporate governance index; this section is divided into Sects. 6.2.1, 6.2.2 and 6.2.3 explaining sample, survey design and limitations, respectively. Section 6.3 discusses development of corporate governance index. Section 6.4 reveals corporate governance score of the respondent companies. This is followed by concluding observations contained in Sect. 6.5.

6.2 Research Design and Respondents' Profile

6.2.1 Sample

As described in Sects. 5.2.2 and 5.2.3, the registered office address of the companies which made announcements of mergers and acquisitions was taken from CMIE database Prowess. Names of the executive director, CFO, CS, and legal heads were taken from the investor grievance section of the annual reports available for the companies; where the contact could not be found from the website it was checked in the contact information on the website of Bombay stock exchange. Annual convention, summits and conferences organized by Confederation of Indian Industries (CII) were also attended to meet possible respondents. A request for appointment through e-mail was sent first and a follow up through personal call was made through phone. The questionnaires were personally administered. The survey was conducted in five rounds. First round was completed during the internship at National Institute of Securities Markets (NISM), Mumbai, during October 2008–December 2008. A second round was conducted for companies having corporate offices in Mumbai in February 2009. One hundred companies in National Capital Region (NCR) and northern states were approached during June 2009–October 2009. Twenty Chennai-based companies were approached during May 2010. Final round of the data collection was conducted during January 2016–February 2016 for NCR-based and Bangalore-based companies and March 2016 for Kolkata and Mumbai-based companies.

Twenty percent respondents replied through email at first instance for the personal interview. Fourty percent responses were collected after two follow-up calls. Thirty-five percent respondents agreed to meet after fifth follow-up call. Five percent respondents agreed to meet in annual convention of CII at New Delhi and Mumbai. A total of 750 companies were approached in four phases and 189 responded to the request. Response rate is 25.2 %.

To collect data related to corporate governance measures, annual reports of the acquirers have been examined from website of companies, the brief profile section of PROWESS 3.2 data base of CMIE, Capitaline data base, Website of Ministry of Corporate Affairs and Security Exchange Board of India (SEBI) website and Electronic Data Information Filing and Retrieval System (EDIFAR) website of SEBI.

Figure 6.1 depicts the frequency distribution of respondents. Out of the above respondents, nearly two-third (65 %) are from manufacturing sector while one-forth (26 %) are from services sector, (depicted in Fig. 6.2). The largest number of the respondent acquirers in the manufacturing sector are in Pharmaceuticals (n = 31) followed by Chemicals (n = 14), Iron & steel (n = 10) and so on. Respondents' profile is described in Sect. 5.2.2.

To utilize the responses of the two groups for analysis, an independent samples t-test is conducted (presented in Chap. 7). This is to determine if there is any significant difference between the two groups in their corporate governance scores.

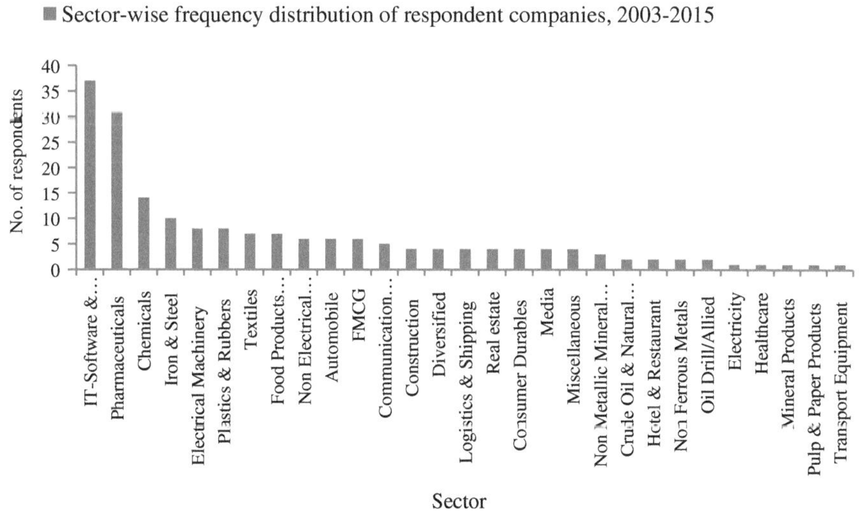

Fig. 6.1 Sector-wise frequency distribution of respondent companies, 2003–2015

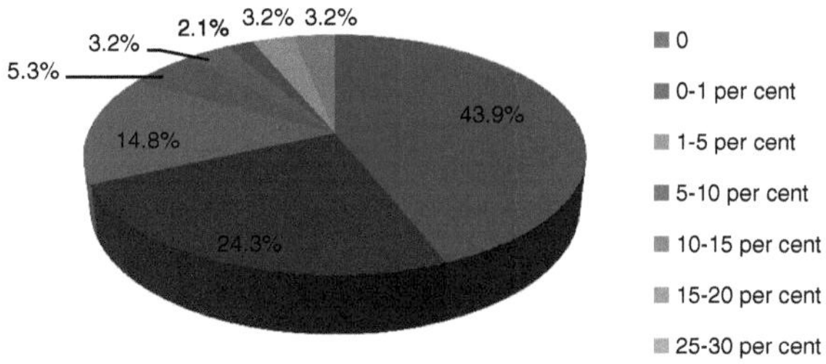

Fig. 6.2 The frequency distribution of CEO/MD's equity

6.2.2 *Survey Design*

We have designed a survey questionnaire on the broader definition of corporate governance. The questionnaire focused not only on the transparency and disclosures but broader issues like management discipline and social recognition and responsibility. The survey questionnaire has been divided into two parts. Part I of the questionnaire contains questions related to the respondent's profile; they were asked to provide their current job title and the industry classification of their firm. Part II of the questionnaire contains 67 questions.

The survey is based on the 67 broad attributes of corporate governance arranged into following seven key sub-categories.

1. Management Discipline (MDIS)
2. Transparency (TRA)
3. Independence (IND)
4. Accountability (ACC)
5. Responsibility (RES)
6. Fairness (FAI)
7. Corporate Social Responsibility, Corporate Governance Initiatives, and Recognition (CGR).

Corporate Governance Score (CGS) is based on the responses of the 67 issues categorized under seven main aspects included in the questionnaire. The respondents were asked to indicate the company's practice on different level of scales; these points have been later translated into numeric values as per the scale. The questionnaire has been designed to give a numeric, presenting overall Corporate Governance score, stated as a percentage. Corporate Governance Index (CGI) has been constructed on the basis of total scores obtained for these attributes. A higher corporate governance score indicates the good governance of the company. We are not interested in disaggregated score in each category as the categories are prone to be overlapping.

The questionnaire was validated by six practitioners (CEO Bombay Stock Exchange, Former Director SEBI, Regional Director SEBI, Director NISM, CEO Delhi Stock Exchange, and Director Confederation of Indian Industries (CII)) in the area. The questionnaire was modified as suggested by them. For example, question 56 (Does the company have non-executive directors who are independent?) in the original questionnaire was replaced with (whether the office of the chairman and chief executive officer is held by different persons?) The scale of Question 2(b), 5, 12, 13, 14, 16, 24, 25, and 33 was changed from binary to three and five point scale. Questions 15 and 39 were changed to open-ended questions to get a genuine response.

A company is required to make specified disclosures at the time of issue and make continuous disclosures as long as its securities are listed on exchanges. The standards for these disclosures, including the content, medium and time of disclosure, have been specified in the Companies Act, Disclosure and Investor Protection Guidelines, Listing Agreement, Regulations relating to insider trading and takeovers, etc. These disclosures are made through various documents such as prospectus, quarterly statements, annual reports, etc., and are disseminated through media, websites of the company and the exchanges, and through EDIFAR (Electronic Data Information Filing and Retrieval) system maintained by the regulator. Extensive information was collected from these sources before meeting the respondents. The respondents were cross-checked with the information available from public domain.

CGS has been assigned a value of 1 to governance attribute if the company meets minimally acceptable standard on that attribute and 0 otherwise in case of binary scale. The answers to these questions are also cross-checked from the information available in public domain as stated earlier. The scores are assigned in a highly conservative manner, based on the response obtained in discussion with the respondent. Primary data has been used to prepare a Corporate Governance Index (CGI). There are several minimum accepted standards that are met by all companies in the sample. These minimum standards are the mandatory requirements of SEBI Clause 49 on Corporate Governance. Our questionnaire contains 18 such questions and the minimum average score for such minimum accepted standards[1] is 26.9 % (this conforms to SEBI's requirement). On the basis of these scores', companies are classified in four quartiles. Companies in top quartile are those that have a score above 90 %. These are the companies which have gone beyond the mandatory requirements and moved ahead in pursuit of excellence in corporate governance. Companies in the bottom quartiles are those complying with the minimum mandatory standards of corporate governance.

6.2.3 *Limitations*

The survey is not free from limitations. First, although, we have tried to capture as much as information we could, yet the survey is not exhaustive, given the multi-dimensional nature of corporate governance. Our survey represents a step forward in expanding our understanding about the association between the

[1]Calculated as ((mandatory requirement/total attributes) * 100) i.e. (18/67 * 100) = 26.9 %.

corporate governance and the financial performance of the company. Second, non-response bias is another issue. Third, we tried to collect information as much as possible from public domain before meeting the respondents to elicit a genuine response, but some subjectivity may be expected. Fourth, we derive our results from the responses of the acquirer Indian companies, regulated under Indian Law. We limit our discussion and analysis to Indian companies.

6.3 Development of Corporate Governance Index

Corporate governance is a mechanism by which the principles, values, procedures, and policies of a company evolve and manifest. The essence of Corporate Governance lies in maintaining transparency, accountability and integrity of management. Corporate governance is not merely a compliance philosophy; it is continuous drive towards excellence in building the company. We have designed the questionnaire as per this broader definition of corporate governance.

6.3.1 Management Discipline (MDIS)

The first section of the survey questionnaire focuses on management discipline and practices which align the interests of the shareholders with the management

6.3.2 Transparency (TRA)

Good corporate governance demands the companies to be fair and transparent in their operations. This happens when the companies continuously disseminate information to shareholders and other classes of stakeholders about the anticipation and happening of all material developments as soon as possible. The questionnaire examines the companies' practices on the basis of 12 questions. Five of these require responses on the basis of binary scale.

6.3.3 Independence (IND)

Board constitutes an important corporate governance mechanism. Independent board is essential for sound Corporate governance. Representation of independent directors on the board is one of the important governance mechanisms to provide independent view on major corporate decisions, align shareholders' interest with management and control agency costs. Board and Board Committees like Audit

Committee, Remuneration Committee, and Nomination Committee, thus, form the key instruments for the quality of corporate governance. This section of the questionnaire scores the companies on the basis of board and board committee practices.

6.3.4 *Accountability (ACC)*

Accountability means the board is responsible and accountable to the company and its various stakeholders. The board should be effective in supervising and monitoring the activities of management. The corporate governance framework of the company should ensure the effective monitoring and accountability of the management by the board. This section of the survey rates the companies on the basis of board monitoring. This section comprises 10 questions.

6.3.5 *Responsibility (RES)*

Responsibility means the board is responsible and accountable to the company and its various stakeholders. The board should be effective in supervising and monitoring the activities of management. This section of the survey questionnaire rates the company's practices to address the situations of mismanagement by having effective internal control mechanisms. This section comprises six questions.

6.3.6 *Fairness (FAI)*

The CG framework should ensure the fair treatment of all shareholders, including minority shareholders. All the shareholders should have the access to effective redressal for violation of their rights. This section comprises nine questions.

6.3.7 *Corporate Governance Initiatives, Recognition, and Corporate Social Responsibility (CGR)*

This section rates the companies on the basis of their Corporate governance initiatives and recognition. This section comprises three questions. Table 6.1 summarizes the aspects covered to rate companies on binary scale. The respondents are asked to indicate the company's practice on binary scale (1 for Yes and 0 for No). These points are later translated into numeric values. Table 6.1 reveals that 54 questions pertaining to seven attributes of corporate governance have been rated on binary scale.

Table 6.1 Questions on binary scale

Sr. No.	Que. No.	Statement
Management discipline (MDIS)		
1	2(a)	Has the company or management publicly articulated principles of good Governance that it is committed to maintain?
2	2(c)	Does the company have a written code of conduct?
3	3	Is senior management incentivized to work towards a higher share price for the company by giving them stock option plans, etc., or any part of remuneration based on share prices?
4	6	Does the company have a policy on Employee Stock Option Plan (ESOPs)?
5	7	Does management take into consideration cost of equity for investment decisions?
6	8	Cost of equity capital in your firm is equivalent to
7	9	Cost of retained earnings in your company is equivalent to
8	10	Does management set targets related to Return on Assets (ROA)?
9	11	Does management set targets related to Return on Equity (ROE)?
10	42	Does the company's annual report include a section devoted to the company's performance in implementing corporate governance principles?
11	43	Has the company issued a "mission statement" that explicitly places a priority on good corporate governance?
12	50	Does management stick to clearly defined core businesses?
13	51	Has management diversified business into an unrelated area during last 3 years?
Transparency (TRA)		
14	44	Are the reports clear and informative?
15	45	Does the company have an English-language website where results and other announcements are updated promptly?
16	46	Are accounts presented according to internationally accepted accounting standards (IGAAP)?
17	47	Are accounts presented according to internationally accepted accounting standards (IGAAP)?
18	59	Is the data of the company uploaded and upgraded on the website of Electronic Data Information Filing and Retrieval (EDIFAR)
Independence (IND)		
19	21	Are independent directors being appointed through nomination by other board members?
20	22	Does the board include direct representatives of banks, financial/strategic investor and other large creditors of the company?
21	52	Does the company have an audit committee?
22	53	Are the members having financial/accounting background?
23	54	Does the company have a remuneration committee?
24	55	Does the company have a nomination committee?
25	56	Whether the office of the chairman and chief executive officer is held by different persons?

(continued)

Table 6.1 (continued)

Sr. No.	Que. No.	Statement
26	57	Do independent and non-executive directors account for more than 50 % of the board?
27	60	Does the company ensure that all independent directors attend at least one training program on corporate governance?
28	63	Is the Chairman of the Audit Committee an Independent Director?
29	64	Is the Chairman of the Remuneration Committee an Independent Director?
30	65	Is the Chairman of the Investors' Grievance Committee an Independent Director?
31	66	Is the Chairman of the Nomination Committee an Independent Director?
Accountability (ACC)		
32	17	Does the company have an executive or management committee that makes most of the executive decisions?
33	19	Are the statutory auditors of the company unrelated to the top management of company?
34	23	Are there any foreign nationals on the Board who are seen as providing added credibility to the Board's independence?
35	26	Does the audit committee supervise internal audit and review accounting procedures?
36	40	Is company listed on any Exchange in other Nation?
37	41	Does company follow Sarbanes Oxley Act (SOX)?
38	58	Are full board meetings held once in a quarter?
Responsibility (RES)		
39	18	Are the board members and members of the executive/management committee substantially different?
40	27	Are there mechanisms for actions of the executive/management committee in the event of mismanagement?
41	28	Kindly state whether there have been any controversies/questions over whether the share trading by Board members has been by and large fair, fully transparent and well intentioned?
42	28	Kindly state if the company has a reporting system for share traded as per insider trading regulations
43	30	Please state whether minority shareholders have ever approached any court against the company in last 5 years
Fairness (FAI)		
44	31	Kindly state whether there have been any controversies or questions raised over any decisions by senior management in the past 5 years where majority shareholders are believed to have gained at the expense of minority shareholders?
45	32	Is all necessary information for General Meetings made available prior to General Meetings?
46	34	Please State whether foreign institutional investors have a stake in the company?
47	35	Please State whether domestic institutional investors have a stake in the company?

(continued)

Table 6.1 (continued)

Sr. No.	Que. No.	Statement
48	36	Is there a whistle–blower policy in your company?
49	38	Has the company appointed an Investor Relation Officer?
50	48	Do all equity holders have the right to call General Meetings?
51	49	Are voting methods easily accessible?
Corporate governance initiatives, recognition and corporate social responsibility (CGR)		
52	1	Has the company been assessed for its Corporate Governance practices by any external rating agency like CRISIL or ICRA, etc.
53	61	Has company won any award for Corporate Governance?
54	67	Has the company or management publicly articulated its corporate social responsibility (CSR) practices?

For questions 2(a), if the company has issued a "mission statement" that explicitly places a priority on good corporate governance, we have assigned a score of 1 otherwise 0. If the companies have posted the code of contact on the website, we have assigned a score of 1; otherwise 0. Stock options are offered to management and others to align their interest with those of the shareholders. This gives an incentive to behave in ways that are likely to enhance the company's performance and hence its stock price. If the company has a Stock Option policy, it is assigned a score of 1; otherwise 0. The question numbers 7–11 focus on the management practice to know the cost of capital before taking the investment decisions. This is not only an aspect of good governance but also good management to assess the cost of capital. The question numbers 50 and 51 focus on the management practices to diversify business into non-core and unrelated areas.

The response for the question no. 14 was cross-checked with the responses from the archives of Bombay Stock Exchange

For question no. 44, we checked the annual reports and considered "No" if consolidated accounts are not presented; Directors remuneration is not disclosed or if we could find any instance of any controversy in the public domain over the past 5 years that the results announced lacked disclosure.

For question number 45, we cross-checked the following information on the website of the company before meeting the respondents: annual reports, quarterly and half yearly results, news update, investor service. If all this information was available, we assigned a score of 1; otherwise 0. For question no. 46 if the company provides two or more sets of accounts in their annual reports, we considered it meeting standards; otherwise not. For question number 47 respondents were cross-checked if the company has changed accounting policies during last 5 years and if that has raised any controversy. For question number 59, the website of Electronic Data Information Filing and Retrieval (EDIFAR) was checked before meeting the respondents.

For question 21, score of 1 is assigned if the company has a written policy to induct the independent directors otherwise 0. If the board include direct representatives of banks, financial/strategic investor and other large creditors of the company the score is 0. If the company has appointed an investor relation officer the score assigned is 1; otherwise 0. The information for the questions number 52–57 was collected from annual reports. Question number 60 is a non-mandatory requirement of SEBI Clause 49. The information is given in the annual report of the company. The information for this question was collected from annual reports.

For question 17, we checked the annual report and the website of the companies if there is a management committee different from board. We rated the company with a score 1; otherwise 0. A score of 1 is assigned if the company has a policy to rotate the auditor for question 19.

Information was gathered from public domain like websites, background section of the prowess database and the respondents were cross-questioned to get a clear response. Besides, annual reports were also investigated to obtain the information.

To cross-check the response for the questions 26 and 58, the information was obtained from the annual report. If the companies are listed on overseas exchange, they are required to comply with an additional set of disclosures, rules and regulations depending on the exchange concerned. For question 41, it is reasonable to presume that firms, listed on a United States Exchange, should have a better corporate governance ranking. Firms listed in US exchange are required to comply with USGAAP accounting standards, which might improve transparency. Second, these firms are subject to many SEC laws and regulations that protect shareholders.

For question 31, information was gathered from public domain and the profile section of Prowess (3.2) CMIE database and the respondents were cross-questioned to get a clear response.

If there is a stake by foreign institutional investors (FII)/domestic institutional investors (DII) we have assigned a score of 1. If there is no stake of FIIs or DIIs, we have assigned a score of 0 for questions 34 and 35.

For questions 48 and 49, according to Indian rules and regulations, all shareholders have the right to participate and vote at general meetings. The Companies Act encourages proxy voting by granting all shareholders the legal right to appoint a proxy. Until recently, laws in India promoted the "one share, one vote" principle. But a rule enacted in 2001 by the Ministry of Company Affairs, now permits Indian companies to issue shares with multiple voting rights as long as such shares do not exceed 25 % of share capital. Provisions for cumulative voting, particularly in the election of directors, would be a means to foster stronger minority shareholder protection. But Indian law does not have specific provisions for cumulative voting.

If a company makes a decision to adopt and disclose the level of corporate governance rating by any external rating agency, it works as a signaling to investors. Thus, market realizes the effort of the company to increase the level of corporate governance. CRISIL, a leading credit rating agency in India and one of the four largest agencies in the world, has developed a yardstick in the form of 'Governance and Value Creation Rating (GVC)' on eight point scale. ICRA is another rating agency which is engaged in corporate governance rating (CGR) in India. ICRA assigns CGR on a six point scale. If the company has taken an initiative to be rated by any external rated agency and has disclosed the rating publicly, it is assigned a score of 1 irrespective of the level of rating obtained.

If the company has won any award for Corporate Governance, it is assigned a score of 1; otherwise 0. If the company or management publicly articulated its corporate social responsibility (CSR) practices, it is assigned a score of 1; otherwise 0. The annual report of the company has been used to cross-check the corporate social responsibility (CSR) practices.

Table 6.2 presents the questions rated on three point scale. For question 16 and 33 the companies are rated as

Always: 1,
Sometimes: 0.5,
Never: 0.

The response for the question 25 is rated as

Comprehensive Review: 1,
Partial Review: 0.5,
No Review: 0.

Table 6.3 presents the questions rated on five point scale.

For question number 2(b) the companies are rated for application of principles of good governance as

No Priority: 0,
Lowest Priority: 0.25,
Low Priority: 0.5,
Priority: 0.75,
Top Priority: 1.

The response for question 5 is rated as

No comment: 0
Consolidated: 0.25
Consolidated + Performance: 0.5
Consolidated + Performance + Net Profit: 0.75
Consolidated + Performance + Net Profit + Share Price (Stock options): 1

The responses of questions numbers 12–14 are rated as

Always: 1,
Mostly: 0.75,

Table 6.2 Questions on three point scale

Sr. No.	Que. No.	Statement
Transparency (TRA)		
1	16	Does the company consistently disclose major and market-sensitive information punctually?
2	33	Whether senior management ensures that right market/price sensitive information is timely disclosed?
Accountability (ACC)		
3	25	Does the audit committee conduct a detailed review of the work of auditors?

Table 6.3 Questions on five point scale

Sr. No.	Que. No.	Statement
Management discipline (MDIS)		
1	2(b)	Application of these principles is given:
2	5	In your company, the compensation for the top executive(s) is based on
Transparency (TRA)		
3	12	Does the company publish its full year results within 3 months of the end of the financial year?
4	13	Does the company send half-yearly reports to each household of shareholders at the end of the half-year?
5	14	Does the company publish/announce quarterly reports within 1 month of the end of the quarter?
Accountability (ACC)		
6	24	What is the normal time lag between notice of the board meeting (sent along with agenda) and actual board meetings?

Occasionally: 0.5,
Sometimes: 0.25,
Never: 0.

Question 13 is a non-mandatory requirement of SEBI-Clause 49. We have cross-checked the responses from the information available in the annual reports of the company. It was checked from the annual reports and the Capitaline database that companies have not changed their annual year during last 5 years. If a company has changed the financial year once in last 5 years, it is assigned a score of 0.75. If the companies have changed twice, then they are assigned a score of 0.5.

For question 24, the response is rated as
1 day: 0,
2 days: 0.25,
3 days: 0.5,
1 week: 0.75,
More than 1 week: 1

I Table 6.4, for question 39, if the Investor relation officer reports to a board member or the chairman of shareholders grievance committee or audit committee, we have assigned a score of 1; if he reports to chief executive officer, we have assigned a score of 0.

Question 4 is related to equity-holding of CEO. Figure 6.2 reveals the frequency distribution of equity-holding of CEO of respondent companies.

Question 37 is related to board size of respondent companies. The frequency distribution of board size is shown in Fig. 6.3. The average board size of the respondent companies is 9.1. The average board size is higher than the optimal board size of six or eight directors as suggested by Jensen (1993).

Table 6.4 Factual open-ended questions

Sr. No.	Que. No.	Statement
Management discipline (MDIS)		
1	4	Please state the percentage of equity holding of CEO/MD in the company's equity?
Transparency (TRA)		
2	15	How much time, in general, management takes between the Board meeting to accept results for a period (quarterly/half-yearly/annual) and the public announcement of the results?
Accountability (ACC)		
3	20	Who recommends to the board the appointment of the auditors?
Responsibility (RES)		
4	37	How many members are on the Board? (Please specify)
Fairness (FAI)		
5	39	To whom investor relation officer reports?

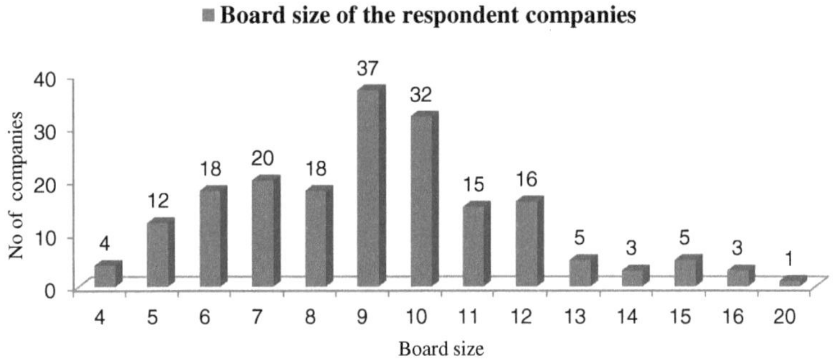

Fig. 6.3 Distribution of board size of the respondent companies

6.4 Corporate Governance Score of Respondent Companies

An equal-weighted index has been created on the basis of the score obtained in seven different sections as in Eq. (6.4.1)

$$\mathrm{CGS} = \frac{\sum_{j=1}^{15}\mathrm{MDIS} + \sum_{j=1}^{13}\mathrm{IND} + \sum_{j=1}^{11}\mathrm{TRA} + \sum_{j=1}^{10}\mathrm{ACC} + \sum_{j=1}^{10}\mathrm{FAI} + \sum_{j=1}^{5}\mathrm{RES} + \sum_{j=1}^{3}\mathrm{CGR}}{67} \tag{6.4.1}$$

Table 6.5 presents the corporate governance score of the respondent companies. Average corporate governance score of the respondent companies is 71.96.

Table 6.5 Corporate governance index of respondent companies

Company code	Year of M&A	Corporate governance score
1	2008	98.5
2	2008	98.5
3	2009	98.5
4	2006	97
5	2004	94.2
6	2007	94
7	2008	94
8	2008	91
9	2008	91
10	2006	89.6
11	2008	89.6
12	2008	89.2
13	2008	89.2
14	2008	88.1
15	2015	88.1
16	2007	86.9
17	2015	86.9
18	2005	86.6
19	2007	86.6
20	2007	86.6
21	2007	86.6
22	2010	86.6
23	2013	86.6
24	2014	86.6
25	2007	86.2
26	2008	85.8
27	2013	85.8
28	2014	85.8
29	2007	85.4
30	2013	85.4
31	2008	84.7
32	2008	84
33	2007	83.6
34	2007	83.6
35	2008	83.2
36	2007	82.8
37	2007	82.8
38	2004	82.1
39	2006	82.1
40	2012	82.1

(continued)

Table 6.5 (continued)

Company code	Year of M&A	Corporate governance score
41	2008	81.7
42	2008	81.7
43	2006	81.3
44	2007	81.3
45	2008	81.3
46	2011	81.3
47	2007	81
48	2006	80.2
49	2007	80.2
50	2008	79.9
51	2005	79.5
52	2005	79.5
53	2005	79.5
54	2011	79.5
55	2007	78.7
56	2007	78.7
57	2006	78.4
58	2008	78.4
59	2009	78.4
60	2006	78
61	2006	78
62	2008	78
63	2012	78
64	2003	77.6
65	2004	77.6
66	2004	77.6
67	2004	77.6
68	2004	77.6
69	2008	77.6
70	2008	77.6
71	2008	77.6
72	2011	77.6
73	2006	77.2
74	2003	76.9
75	2003	76.9
76	2004	76.9
77	2008	76.9
78	2006	76.1
79	2007	76.1
80	2006	75.7

(continued)

Table 6.5 (continued)

Company code	Year of M&A	Corporate governance score
81	2007	75.7
82	2007	75.4
83	2007	75
84	2005	74.6
85	2005	74.6
86	2005	74.6
87	2006	74.6
88	2005	74.3
89	2006	74.3
90	2008	74.3
91	2008	74.3
92	2003	73.9
93	2006	73.9
94	2011	73.9
95	2007	73.5
96	2007	73.5
97	2007	73.5
98	2003	73.1
99	2008	72.8
100	2007	72.4
101	2007	72.4
102	2010	72.4
103	2005	72
104	2007	72
105	2007	72
106	2008	72
107	2003	71.3
108	2006	71.3
109	2007	71.3
110	2006	70.9
111	2007	70.9
112	2007	70.9
113	2007	70.9
114	2007	70.9
115	2008	70.9
116	2010	70.9
117	2003	70.5
118	2006	70.5
119	2006	69.8
120	2004	69.4

(continued)

Table 6.5 (continued)

Company code	Year of M&A	Corporate governance score
121	2007	69.4
122	2007	69
123	2007	69
124	2007	68.7
125	2008	68.7
126	2009	68.7
127	2009	68.7
128	2007	67.9
129	2007	67.5
130	2005	67.2
131	2006	67.2
132	2009	67.2
133	2007	66.8
134	2009	66.4
135	2006	66
136	2008	66
137	2004	65.7
138	2005	65.7
139	2007	65.7
140	2008	65.4
141	2008	64.9
142	2007	64.2
143	2008	64.2
144	2004	63.4
145	2006	63.4
146	2007	63.4
147	2008	63.1
148	2007	62.7
149	2007	62.7
150	2003	62.3
151	2006	62.3
152	2007	61.6
153	2006	60.8
154	2007	60.1
155	2008	60.1
156	2008	59.3
157	2008	59
158	2003	58.6
159	2008	58.2
160	2003	57.8

(continued)

Table 6.5 (continued)

Company code	Year of M&A	Corporate governance score
161	2005	57.8
162	2005	57.8
163	2006	57.8
164	2004	57.5
165	2007	57.5
166	2007	56.7
167	2007	56.3
168	2008	55.2
169	2003	54.9
170	2006	54.9
171	2007	54.9
172	2003	54.5
173	2005	54.1
174	2006	53.7
175	2006	53.4
176	2007	52.2
177	2007	50.4
178	2008	48.1
179	2007	47
180	2004	46.3
181	2008	46.3
182	2005	44.8
183	2008	44.8
184	2008	44
185	2004	43.7
186	2008	42.9
187	2006	39.9
188	2007	37.7
189	2003	30.6
Average score		71.96

6.5 Concluding Observations

An attempt has been made to develop a corporate governance index. For the purpose of this study, corporate governance standards, as prevailing and in practice are assessed in respect of 189 companies. Information for the study was collected through a wide range of sources which included the annual reports and corporate governance reports of the respective companies. Practice of corporate governance has progressed in a big way in Indian companies as revealed by their average score.

There are several companies which made proactive initiatives in introducing good governance norms and standards even before these became mandatory. The scores obtained are used for further analysis in Chap. 7.

References

Aggarwal, R., & Williamson, R. G. (2006). Did new regulations target the relevant corporate governance attributes? Working Paper, Georgetown University. Retrieved November 03, 2007, 10:16:47 PM. from http://papers.ssrn.com/sol3/papers.cfm?abstract_id=859264

Balasubramanian, N., Black, Bernard S., & Khanna, Vikramaditya. (2010). The relation between firm-level corporate governance and market value: A case study of India. *Emerging Markets Review, 11*(4), 319–340.

Bebchuk, L., Cohen, A., & Ferrell, A. (2009). What matters in corporate governance? *Review of Financial Studies, 22*(2), 783–827.

Bebchuk, Lucian A., & Alma, C. (2005). The costs of entrenched boards. *Journal of Financial Economics, 78*(2), 409–433.

Beiner, S., Drobetz, W., Schmid, M. M., & Zimmermann, H. (2006). An integrated framework of corporate governance and firm valuation. *European Financial Management, 12*(2), 249–283.

Bertrand, M., & Mullainathan, S. (1998). Executive compensation and incentives: The impact of takeover legislation. NBER Working Paper, 6830. Retrieved November 03, 2007, 10:45:47 PM from http://ssrn.com/abstract=141883

Bhagat, S., & Black, B. (2007). The non-correlation between board independence and long-term firm performance. *Journal of Corporate Law, 27*(2), 231–272.

Black, B. S., Jang, H., & Kim, W. (2006). Predicting firms' corporate governance choices: evidence from Korea. *Journal of Corporate Finance, 12*(3), 660–691.

Bris, A., & Cabolis, C. (2002). Corporate governance convergence by contract: evidence from cross-border mergers. *Yale ICF Working Paper No. 02–32*. Retrieved on November 03, 2007, 10:16:47 PM from http://ssrn.com/abstract=321101

Carline, N. F., Linn, S. C., & Yadav, P. K. (2009). Operating performance changes associated with corporate mergers and the role of corporate governance. *Journal of Banking and Finance, 33* (10), 1829–1841.

Chen, A., Kao, L., And, Tsao M., & Wu, C. (2007). Building a corporate governance index from the perspectives of ownership and leadership for firms in Taiwan. *Corporate Governance: An International Review, 15*(2), 251–261.

Core, J., Guay, W. R., & Rusticus, T. O. (2006). Does weak governance cause weak stock returns? An examination of firm operating performance and investors' expectations. *Journal of Finance, 61*(2), 655–687.

Core, J., Holthausen, R., & Larker, D. (1999). Corporate governance, chief executive officer compensation and firm performance. *Journal of Financial Economics, 51*(3), 371–406.

Cremers, M., & Nair, V. (2005). Governance mechanisms and equity prices. *Journal of Finance, 60*(6), 2859–2894.

Dahya, J., Dimitrov, O., & McConnell, John J. (2008). Dominant shareholders, corporate boards and corporate value: a cross-country analysis. *Journal of Financial Economics, 87*(1), 73–100.

Datta, S., Iskandar-Datta, M., & Raman, K. (2001). Executive compensation and corporate acquisition decisions. *Journal of Finance, 56*(6), 2299–2336.

Drobetz, W., Schillhofer, A., & Zimmermann, H. (2004). Corporate governance and expected stock returns: evidence from Germany. *European Financial Management, 10*(2), 267–293.

Durnev, A., & Kim, E. H. (2005). To steal or not to steal: firm attributes, legal environment, and valuation. *Journal of Finance, 60*(3), 1461–1493.

Garay, U., & González, M. (2008). Corporate governance and firm value: The case of Venezuela. *Corporate Governance, 16*(3), 194–209.

Gompers, Paul A., Ishii, Joy L., & Metrick, A. (2003). Corporate governance and equity prices. *The Quarterly Journal of Economics, 118*(1), 107–155.

Hermalin, B., & Weisbach, Michael S. (1991). The effects of board composition and direct incentives on form performance. *Financial Management, 20*(4), 101–112.

Jensen, M. C. (1993). The modern industrial revolution, exit and the failure of internal control systems. *Journal of Finance, 48*(3), 831–880.

Klapper, Leora F., & Love, I. (2004). Corporate governance, investor protection, and performance in emerging markets. *Journal of Corporate Finance, 10*(5), 703–723.

Lipton, M., & Lorcsh, J. (1992). A modest approach for improved corporate governance. *Business Lawyer, 48*(1), 59–77.

Malekzadeh, A., McWilliams, V., & Sen, N. (1998). Implications of CEO structural and ownership powers, board ownership and composition, on the market's reaction to anti-takeover charter amendments. *Journal of Applied Business Research, 14*(3), 53–63.

Rani, N., Yadav, Surendra S., & Jain, P. K. (2014). Impact of corporate governance score on abnormal returns and financial performance of mergers and acquisitions. *Decision, 41*(4), 371–398.

Roll, R. (1986). The hubris hypothesis of corporate takeovers. *Journal of Business, 59*, 197–216.

Rossi, S., & Volpin, P. F. (2004). Cross-country determinants of mergers and acquisitions. *Journal of Financial Economics, 74*(2), 277–304.

Shivdasani, A. (1993). Board composition, ownership structure, and hostile takeovers. *Journal of Accounting and Economics, 16*(1–3), 167–198.

Shleifer, A., & Vishny, R. (1986). Large shareholders and corporate control. *Journal of Political Economy, 94*(3), 461–488.

Shleifer, A., & Vishny, R. (1988). Value maximization and the acquisition process. *Journal of Economic Perspectives, 2*(1), 7–20.

Swanstrom, M. (2006). Corporate governance and the abnormal returns to acquisition announcements. *Journal of Business Strategy, 23*(2), 115–129.

Yermack, D. (1996). Higher market valuation of companies with small board of directors. *Journal of Financial Economics, 40*(2), 185–211.

Chapter 7
Impact of Corporate Governance Score on Abnormal Returns and Financial Performance

Abstract The present chapter provides the empirical evidence on relationship between corporate governance score and M&A performance in Indian context. The role of corporate governance has been explored on the measurement of the announcement effects on the acquiring firms. The empirical findings indicate that companies with high corporate governance score have positive abnormal returns in the short-term, better financial performance, and higher valuations post-M&A, while companies with lower corporate governance score have lower financial performance and lower valuations post-M&A.

Keywords Financial performance · Valuation · Price to book ratio · Price-earnings ratio · Agency theory

7.1 Introduction

Corporate governance aims at resolving conflicts of interest between managers and shareholders; between large shareholders and minority shareholders, and thus mitigates agency costs. Financial transparency, operational transparency and information disclosure are extremely important elements of corporate governance. Firms with poor corporate governance practices are usually associated with a low level of financial and operational transparency, and low quality of information disclosure, which implies great information asymmetry. Agency theory suggests that firms with better corporate governance standards perform better because of lower agency costs and more effective monitoring mechanisms. Botosan (1997) noted less information asymmetry between shareholders and managers due to better corporate governance practices. Lang and Lundholm (1999) observed lower information risk associated with a higher level of transparency and higher quality of disclosure. The market for corporate control is an important corporate governance mechanism. An important question in this regard is how corporate governance practices of acquirer firms directly influence performance outcomes of acquisitions decisions.

N. Rani et al., *Mergers and Acquisitions*, India Studies in Business and Economics, DOI 10.1007/978-981-10-2203-6_7

While corporate governance has received more attention in recent years, the role that such governance plays in merger and acquisition strategy has not attracted such attention particularly in India. Much of the recent academic attention on corporate governance has been focused on corporate accounting scandals and their prevention. Corporate governance and merger strategy, however, has not been the focus. The important question of whether good corporate governance leads to higher stock returns on the announcement of M&A and consequently to higher firm valuation and better financial performance has not received attention.

The question deserves attention for several reasons. Mergers and acquisitions serve as an important instrument of corporate governance to increase corporate efficiency. The primary objective of the chapter is to investigate the relationship between corporate governance score and performance of acquiring firms in short-term as well as long-term.

The present chapter investigates the impact of corporate governance score on the abnormal returns. Further, association between corporate governance score and the financial performance of the sample acquiring firms post-merger and acquisition have been examined.

The chapter has been organized into five sections. Section 7.2 presents the analysis of corporate governance score of the respondent companies; this section is divided into Sects. 7.2.1 and 7.2.2 explaining the frequency distribution of corporate governance score and group-wise t-test respectively. Impact of corporate governance score on short-term abnormal returns has been presented in Sect. 7.3. The discussion on association between corporate governance score and post-M&A performance is delineated in Sect. 7.4; this section is divided into Sects. 7.4.1 and 7.4.2 describing the impact of corporate governance score on financial performance and valuation respectively. Section 7.5 presents the concluding observations.

7.2 Analysis of Corporate Governance Score

Corporate governance index (CGI) is constructed on the basis of total scores obtained for 67 attributes of corporate governance covered in questionnaire. Corporate governance score has been calculated for each attribute individually and total score has been used to rank the companies. Minimum accepted standards have been met by all companies in the sample. These minimum standards are the mandatory requirements of SEBI Clause 49 on Corporate Governance. Our questionnaire contains 18 such questions and the minimum average score for such minimum accepted standards[1] is 26.9 % (this conforms to SEBI's requirement).

[1]Calculated as ((mandatory requirement/total attributes) * 100) i.e. ((18/67) * 100) = 26.9 %.

Table 7.1 Year-wise Frequency distribution of corporate governance score, 2003–2015

Year	Mean CG score	Minimum CG score	Maximum CG score	Number of respondent companies
2003	64.53	30.6	77.6	13
2004	69.97	43.7	94.2	13
2005	69.51	44.8	86.6	15
2006	70.65	39.9	97	28
2007	70.24	37.7	94	54
2008	73.45	42.9	98.5	44
2009	74.65	66.4	98.5	6
2010	76.63	70.5	86.6	3
2011	78.08	73.9	81.3	4
2012	80.05	78	82.1	2
2013	85.93	85.4	86.6	3
2014	85.93	85.4	86.6	2
2015	87.5	86.9	88.1	2
Total	71.96	30.6	98.5	189

7.2.1 *Distribution of Corporate Governance Score*

A survey of 189 companies was conducted to construct a corporate governance index. We then classify companies, using quartiles based on their corporate governance score, into four governance portfolios. Mean average score for the sample is 71.96 %.

Table 7.1 shows the distribution of survey-based corporate governance score for 189 Indian public-listed firms. It is evident that mean corporate governance score has increased from 64.53 in 2003 to 87.5 in 2015. The minimum as well as maximum score has also shown improvement over time. It appears from the relevant data that Indian corporates have learned and become conscious about the importance of good corporate governance over time. Moreover, the minimum mandatory requirements have also graduated and have become stringent over the period 2003–2015.

Table 7.2 presents quartile-wise mean corporate governance score of respondent companies. Companies in upper quartile (Q_4) have score above 80 %. These are the companies which have gone beyond the mandatory requirements and moved ahead in pursuit of excellence in corporate governance. Companies in the lower quartile (Q_1) are the companies complying with the minimum mandatory standards of corporate governance. Table shows that nearly 25 % companies in the sample had scores below 54.6 %. Mean average score for the sample is 71.96 %.

Table 7.2 Mean corporate governance score of respondent companies, Quartile-wise

Quartile	Mean corporate governance score (CGS)	Number of companies
Upper quartile (Q_4)	81	47 (24.9 %)
Q_3	77	47 (24.9 %)
Q_2	69.7	47 (24.9 %)
Lower quartile (Q_1)	54.6	48 (25.3 %)
Sample	71.96	189 (100 %)

Table 7.3 Sector-wise frequency distribution of corporate governance score, 2003–2015

Sector	Mean CG score	Minimum CG score	Maximum CG score	Number of respondent companies
Manufacturing	70.98	30.6	98.5	128
Services	74.01	42.9	98.5	61
Total	71.96	30.6	98.5	189

7.2.2 Group-Wise Independent Samples t-Test

7.2.2.1 Independent Samples t-Test for Manufacturing Sector and Service Sector Groups

The respondents have been divided into two groups based on the industry they belong to, manufacturing and services. Table 7.3 reveals the sector-wise distribution of corporate governance score of the respondent companies. It is obvious from the relevant data that companies in service sector have better corporate governance score. It appears that companies in service sector are conscious for their corporate governance practices and put their corporate governance structures in place.

An independent samples t-test has been conducted to observe if there is a significant difference between the corporate governance score of these groups. Table 7.4 reports the findings of the independent samples t-test. The results illustrate that firms in service sector vis-à-vis manufacturing sector are more conscious for governance; however, the difference in corporate governance score is not significant (p-value = 0.129 > 0.05).

Table 7.4 Independent samples t-test statistics of corporate governance score on manufacturing and services sector

Mean CGR for services group ($N = 61$)	Mean CGR for manufacturing group ($N = 121$)	Mean difference	t-value	Significance level
74.01	70.98	3.03	1.52	0.129

7.3 Impact of Corporate Governance Score on Short-Term Abnormal Returns

If the corporate governance structure is effective, the managers are less likely to pursue those mergers and acquisitions which result in shareholders' wealth reduction. This leads to the first hypothesis

There is positive relationship between corporate governance score and shareholders' wealth due to announcements of mergers and acquisitions.

Table 7.5 summarizes the results of short-term event study of the respondent companies. The relevant data contained in the Table shows that respondent companies earn 1.35 % average abnormal returns on the announcement day; the returns are significant. Precision-weighted CAAR is 1.29 % and median abnormal return is 0.96 %. It is evident from the Table that highest CAAR (2.77 %) is observed during 5 days window (−5, +5); almost 60 % respondent companies earn positive abnormal returns. Moreover, the returns are significant.

Figure 7.1 exhibits the average abnormal returns of the respondent companies during event window (–20, 20). It is obvious from the graph that share prices jump up to 1 % on the announcement day. Figure 7.2 displays the cumulative average abnormal returns of the respondent companies during event window (−20, 20). It is evident from the graph that share prices start rising 5 days before event (−5), shoot up to almost 5 % on day 3, and start falling (afterwards).

Table 7.6 presents the quartile-wise CAAR of the respondent companies. The respondent companies have been classified, using quartiles based on their corporate governance score, into four governance portfolios. It is evident from the Table that average abnormal return on the announcement day for the respondent companies is 1.35 %, while the companies in upper quartile (Q_4) have positive average abnormal return of 6.21 % which is significantly (p-value = $0 < 0.01$) higher than the

Table 7.5 Summary statistics of event study abnormal returns to the respondent companies

Event window	(0, 0)	(−1, + 1)	(−2, + 2)	(−5, + 5)
CAAR (%)	1.35	1.78	2.35	2.77
PWCAAR (%)	1.29	1.59	1.95	2.27
Median (%)	0.96	1.27	1.67	2.48
Positive (%)	66.2	59.3	64	59.3
CDA t	5.105[b]	3.882[b]	3.974[b]	3.152[b]
CSS t	4.831[b]	4.072[b]	4.463[b]	3.896[b]
SCS Z	4.767[b]	3.606[b]	3.814[b]	3.384[b]
GSign Z	5.778[b]	3.878[b]	5.193[b]	3.878[b]
Rank Z	5.703[b]	3.972[b]	3.973[b]	3.296[b]
Jackknife Z	5.046[b]	3.624[b]	3.740[b]	3.217[b]

[a], [b]Denote significance at 5 and 1 % respectively

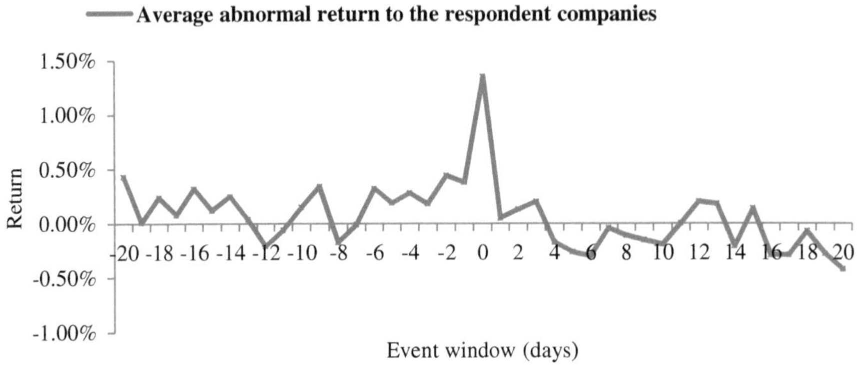

Fig. 7.1 Average abnormal returns to the respondent companies over event window (−20, +20)

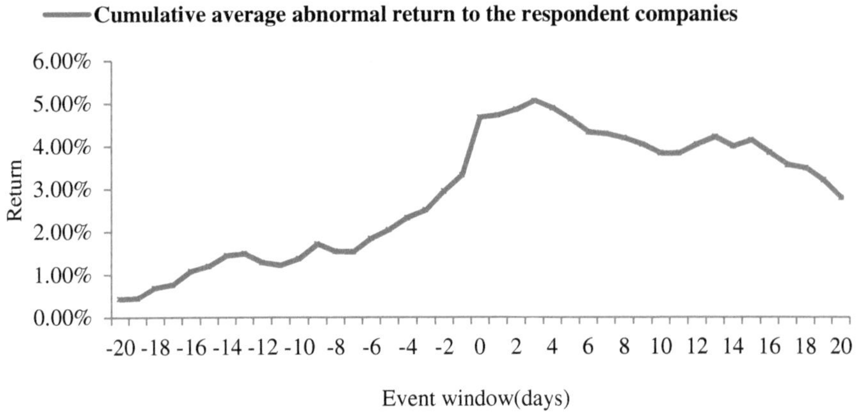

Fig. 7.2 Cumulative average abnormal returns to the shareholders of respondent companies over event window (−20, +20)

Table 7.6 Cumulative average abnormal returns to the shareholders of respondent companies

Quartile corporate governance ranking	(0, 0) (%)	(−1, + 1) (%)	(−2, + 2) (%)	(−5, + 5) (%)
Upper quartile (Q_4)	6.21	5.06	5.47	5.35
Q_3	1.78	2.25	2.38	3.15
Q_2	−1.85	0.66	1.17	1.91
Lower quartile (Q_1)	−0.69	−0.80	0.43	0.64
Mean	1.35	1.78	2.35	2.77

Table 7.7 Independent samples t-test for difference of mean CAR [Upper quartile (Q_4), Lower quartile (Q_1)]

	Mean CAR (Q_4) (%)	Mean CAR (Q_1) (%)	Mean difference (%)	*t*-value	Significance value
(0, 0)	6.21	−0.69	6.91	4.99[b]	0.000
(−1, + 1)	5.06	−0.80	5.86	3.67[b]	0.000
(−2, + 2)	5.47	0.43	5.04	2.52[b]	0.013
(−5, + 5)	5.35	0.64	11.9	2.59[a]	0.011

[a, b]Denote significance at 5 and 1 % respectively

abnormal return of companies in lower quartile (Q_1). Companies in the lower quartile (Q_1) have negative average abnormal return (−0.69 %).

Table 7.7 depicts that a significant mean difference of 5.9 % (p-value $= 0 < 0.01$), 5 % (p-value $= 0 < 0.01$), and 11.9 % (p-value $= 0.011 < 0.05$) respectively, between CAAR of companies in upper quartile (Q_4) and lower quartile (Q_1) has also been observed for event window of 3 days (−1, 1), 5 days (−2, 2), and 11 days (−5, 5).

On the basis of empirical results, it is reasonable to conclude that there is a positive association between corporate governance score and shareholders' wealth due to announcements of mergers and acquisitions. Companies with better corporate governance create higher shareholders wealth in short-term. It is reasonable to conclude that the stock market responds positive to the acquisitions by better-governed companies.

7.4 Impact of Corporate Governance Score on Post-M&A Performance

If better corporate governance is related to better firm performance, better-governed firms should perform better than not so well governed firms. This section conducts a cross-section comparison of the performance of firms with corporate governance score in upper quartiles (Q_4) with the firms in lower quartiles (Q_1).

7.4.1 Impact of Corporate Governance Score on Post-M&A Financial Performance

Financial performance has been measured in terms of the important profitability ratios which measure how efficiently financial resources are deployed by the management. The study tests the following hypotheses to measure the impact of corporate governance on financial performance.

Firms with better overall corporate governance have better financial performance, i.e., the financial performance of the companies with higher corporate governance score is higher than the financial performance of the companies with lower corporate governance score.

The financial performance has been judged on the basis of profitability ratios related to investments, namely, capital employed and equity funds. Accordingly, the following two ratios have been computed for 5 years (t + 1, t + 2, t + 3, t + 4, t + 5) subsequent to mergers and acquisitions:

- ROCE (return on capital employed) and
- ROE (return on equity funds).

Return on the basis of sales has been computed in terms of net profit margin (NPM). Actual economic gains from assets are captured by operating cash flows. The change in acquisition-related performance of the acquirer is examined by comparing operating performance before and after the acquisition. For this purpose, operating cash flow profit ratio (OCFR) based on sales has also been calculated.

Table 7.8 depicts the results of post-M&A ratios of the respondent companies. It is evident from the relevant data that mean return on the capital employed of the respondent companies 1 year post-M&A is 21.1 % while the companies in upper quartile (Q_4) have an mean return of 26.2 % which is significantly higher than the mean ROCE of companies in lower quartile (Q_1). Companies in the lower quartile (Q_1) have mean ROCE of 21.1 %. Mean return on capital employed of companies in upper quartile (Q_4) is 33.1, 28.3, 30.9, and 28.2 for 2 years, 3 years, 4 years, and 5 years, respectively. Mean return on capital employed of companies in lower quartile (Q_1) is 21.5, 15.6, 17.7, and 17.4 for 2 years, 3 years, 4 years, and 5 years, respectively.

Mean ROE of the respondent companies one year post-M&A has been observed to be 17.4 % whereas the ROE for the upper quartile companies (Q_4) is 26.2 % but in the lower quartile (Q_1) ROE is 15.1 %. Mean return on equity funds of companies in upper quartile (Q_4) is 23.9, 18.6, 18.8, and 20.4 for 2 years, 3 years, 4 years, and 5 years, respectively. Mean ROE of respondent companies in lower quartile (Q_1) is 10.4, 12.1, 11.2, and 11.4 for 2 years, 3 years, 4 years, and 5 years, respectively.

The relevant data contained in Table 7.8 reveals that mean net profit margin (NPM) of the respondent companies 1 year post-M&A is 11.8 % while the companies in upper quartile (Q_4) have a mean NPM of 17.2 % which is significantly higher than the mean NPM of companies in lower quartile (Q_1). Companies in the lower quartile (Q_1) have mean NPM of 8.4 %. Mean NPM of companies in upper quartile (Q_4) is 16.3, 13.1, 16.8, and 13.5 for 2 years, 3 years, 4 years, and 5 years, respectively. Mean NPM of companies in lower quartile (Q_1) is 9.2, 8.4, 7.6, and 8.6 for 2 years, 3 years, 4 years, and 5 years, respectively.

Table 7.8 Corporate governance ranking and financial performance post-M&A of the respondent companies, Quartile-wise

Quartile corporate governance ranking	ROCE	ROE	NPM	OCFR
A: One year post-M&A (t + 1) N = 188				
Upper quartile (Q_4)	26.2	24.5	17.2	19.1
Q_3	24.8	17.2	11.4	15.8
Q_2	18.1	13.5	10.1	14.7
Lower quartile (Q_1)	15.1	14.4	8.4	12.2
Mean	21.1	17.4	11.8	15.5
B: Two years post-M&A (t + 2) N = 180				
Upper quartile (Q_4)	33.1	23.9	16.3	25.9
Q_3	27.2	16.3	13.2	20.4
Q_2	25.9	13.8	10.1	20.2
Lower quartile (Q_1)	21.5	10.4	9.2	11.7
Mean	24.6	16.1	12.2	19.5
C: Three years post-M&A (t + 3) N = 176				
Upper quartile (Q_4)	28.3	18.6	13.1	25.7
Q_3	22.9	17.5	12.9	20.2
Q_2	19.6	16.4	9.7	19.8
Lower quartile (Q_1)	15.6	12.1	8.4	11.2
Mean	21.6	16.1	11.4	19.2
D: Four years post-M&A (t + 4) N = 156				
Upper quartile (Q_4)	30.9	18.8	16.8	20.5
Q_3	31.9	16.1	11.1	16.1
Q_2	21.2	14.2	10.7	14.5
Lower quartile (Q_1)	17.7	11.2	7.6	9.7
Mean	23.7	15.1	11.6	15.2
E: Five years post-M&A (t + 5) N = 148				
Upper quartile (Q_4)	28.2	20.4	13.5	22.6
Q_3	24.4	14.9	12.9	14.6
Q_2	20.4	12.1	9.2	13.6
Lower quartile (Q_1)	17.4	11.4	8.6	10.3
Mean	22.5	14.7	11.1	15.2

Mean OCFR of the respondent companies is 15.5, 19.5, 19.2, 15.2, and 15.2 for 1 year, 2 years, 3 years, 4 years, and 5 years, respectively. Mean OCFR of companies in upper quartile (Q_4) is 19.1, 25.9, 25.7, 20.5, and 22.6 for 1 year, 2 years, 3 years, 4 years, and 5 years respectively. Mean ROE of respondent companies in lower quartile (Q_1) is 12.2, 11.7, 11.2, 9.7 and 10.3 for years, 1 year, 2 year, 3 years, 4 years, and 5 years, respectively.

To test the hypothesis H1, i.e., the financial performance of the companies with higher corporate governance score is higher than the financial performance of the

Table 7.9 Independent sample t-test statistic for profitability ratios [Upper quartile (Q_4), Lower quartile (Q_1)]

Year Post-M&A	Mean ratio (Q_4)	Mean ratio (Q_1)	Mean difference (%)	*t*-value	Significance value
A: ROCE					
t + 1	26.2 % (*N* = 47)	15.1 % (*N* = 47)	11.1	5.50[b]	0.000
t + 2	33.1 % (*N* = 45)	17.8 % (*N* = 45)	15.3	6.67[b]	0.000
t + 3	28.3 % (*N* = 43)	15.6 % (*N* = 43)	12.7	5.06[b]	0.000
t + 4	30.9 % (*N* = 39)	17.7 % (*N* = 39)	13.2	2.63[b]	0.010
t + 5	28.2 % (*N* = 37)	17.4 % (*N* = 37)	10.9	4.16[b]	0.000
B: ROE					
t + 1	24.5 % (*N* = 47)	14.4 % (*N* = 47)	10.1	4.14[b]	0.000
t + 2	23.9 % (*N* = 45)	10.4 % (*N* = 45)	13.5	3.30[b]	0.001
t + 3	18.6 % (*N* = 43)	12.1 % (*N* = 43)	6.46	3.02[b]	0.003
t + 4	18.8 % (*N* = 39)	11.2 % (*N* = 39)	7.6	3.0[b]	0.004
t + 5	20.4 % (*N* = 37)	11.4 % (*N* = 37)	8.95	5.6[b]	0.000

[a, b]Denote significance at 5 and 1 % respectively

companies with lower corporate governance score. We have conducted t-test for the difference of mean for ROCE, ROE and NPM and OCFR for upper quartile (Q_4) and lower quartile (Q_1).

Table 7.9 reveals the results of profitability ratios (ROCE and ROE) and Table 7.10 tabulates the results of performance ratios (NPM and OCFR). It is evident from relevant data that companies in upper quartile (Q_4) have 11.1, 15.3, 12.7, 13.2, and 10.9 % higher ROCE 1 year post-M&A, 2 years post-M&A, 3 years post M&A, 4 years post-M&A, and 5 years post-M&A, respectively; moreover, the difference is statistically significant at 1 %.

Panel B of Table 7.9 depicts that the companies with higher corporate governance score earn better return on equity funds. The higher returns are in the range of 10.1–13.5 % as is evident from the difference in ROE of companies in upper quartiles (Q_4) and lower quartile (Q_1). The difference is statistically significant at 1 % (p-value = 0 < 0.01) and (p-value = 0.001 < 0.01) 1 year and 2 years post-M&A respectively.

Such findings lead to conclusion that the null hypothesis of no difference between the profitability of companies with different corporate governance score is

Table 7.10 Independent sample t-test statistic for performance ratios [Upper quartile (Q_4), Lower quartile (Q_1)]

Year Post-M&A	Mean ratio (Q_4)	Mean ratio (Q_1)	Mean difference (%)	*t*-value	Significance value
A: NPM					
t + 1	17.2 % ($N = 47$)	8.4 % ($N = 47$)	8.8	5.73[b]	0.000
t + 2	16.3 % ($N = 45$)	9.2 % ($N = 45$)	7.1	3.49[b]	0.001
t + 3	13.1 % ($N = 44$)	8.38 % ($N = 44$)	4.7	4.35[b]	0.00
t + 4	16.8 % ($N = 39$)	7.6 % ($N = 39$)	9.2	2.1[a]	0.040
t + 5	13.5 % ($N = 37$)	8.6 % ($N = 37$)	4.8	2.5[a]	0.015
B: OCFR					
t + 1	19.1 % ($N = 47$)	12.2 % ($N = 47$)	6.95	2.84[b]	0.005
t + 2	25.9 % ($N = 45$)	11.7 % ($N = 45$)	14.2	3.49[b]	0.001
t + 3	25.7 % (44)	11.2 % (44)	14.5	5.79[b]	0.000
t + 4	20.5 % ($N = 39$)	9.7 % ($N = 39$)	10.8	3.67[b]	0.000
t + 5	22.6 % ($N = 37$)	10.3 % ($N = 37$)	12.5	3.21[b]	0.002

[a, b]Denote significance at 5 and 1 % respectively

rejected. It may be, therefore, concluded that *companies with better overall corporate governance have better profitable ratios.*

Table 7.10 illustrates the results of t-test for the difference of mean for performance ratios. It is evident from relevant data that companies in upper quartile(Q_4) have 8.8, 7.1, 4.7, 9.2, and 4.8 % higher NPM 1 year post M&A, 2 years post-M&A, 3 years post M&A, 4 years post-M&A, and 5 years post-M&A, respectively; moreover, the difference is statistically significant.

Panel B of Table 7.10 depicts that the companies with higher corporate governance score earn better operating cash flow ratios. The higher returns are in the range of 6.95–14.5 % as is evident from the difference in OCFR of companies in upper quartile (Q_4) and lower quartile (Q_1). The difference is statistically significant at 1 % (p-value = 0.005 < 0.01), (p-value = 0.001 < 0.01), (p-value = 0 < 0.01), (p-value = 0 < 0.01), and (p-value = 0.002 < 0.01) 1 year, 2 years, 3 years, 4 years, and 5 years post-M&A, respectively.

Such findings lead to conclusion that the null hypothesis of no difference between the performances of companies with different corporate governance score is rejected. It may be, therefore, concluded that *companies with better overall corporate governance have better performance ratios.*

7.4.2 Impact of Corporate Governance Score on Post-M&A Valuation

To test the relationship between corporate governance score and financial valuation, price to book ratio (PB) and price-earnings ratio (PE) have been computed. It is hypothesized that firms with better overall corporate governance have higher firm value, i.e., the financial valuation of the companies with higher corporate governance score is higher than the financial valuation of the companies with lower corporate governance score.

Table 7.11 illustrates mean and the quartile-wise PB and PE ratio for the four governance profile respondent companies. The relevant data contained in the

Table 7.11 Corporate governance ranking and firm valuation post-M&A of respondent companies, quartile-wise

Quartile corporate governance ranking	PB	PE
A: One year post-M&A (t + 1) N = 188		
Upper quartile (Q_4)	10.3	26.21
Q_3	3.9	19.35
Q_2	2.84	14.78
Lower quartile (Q_1)	1.87	11.16
Mean	4.71	17.84
B: Two years post-M&A (t + 2) N = 180		
Upper quartile (Q_4)	8.35	28.67
Q_3	2.19	19.05
Q_2	1.69	13.36
Lower quartile (Q_1)	1.32	11.80
Mean	3.39	18.22
C: Three years post-M&A (t + 3) N = 176		
Upper quartile (Q_4)	8.52	25.07
Q_3	2.89	14.85
Q_2	2.06	12.29
Lower quartile (Q_1)	1.46	11.03
Mean	3.7	15.76
D: Four years post-M&A (t + 4) N = 156		
Upper quartile (Q_4)	8.98	26.15
Q_3	3.75	16.52
Q_2	2.23	11.44
Lower quartile (Q_1)	1.66	7.08
Mean	4.26	15.29
E: Five years post-M&A (t + 5) N = 148		
Upper quartile (Q_4)	6.63	31.87
Q_3	2.03	18.85
Q_2	0.96	12.09
Lower quartile (Q_1)	0.43	7.37
Mean	2.51	17.54

Table depicts that mean PB ratio of the respondent companies 1 year post-M&A is 4.71 % while the companies in upper quartile (Q_4) have mean PB ratio of 10.3 % which is significantly higher than the mean PB ratio of companies in lower quartile (Q_1). Companies in the lower quartile (Q_1) have mean PB ratio of 1.87 %. Mean PB ratio of companies in upper quartile (Q_4) is 8.35, 8.52, 8.98, and 6.63 for 2 years, 3 years, 4 years, and 5 years, respectively. Mean PB ratio of companies in lower quartile (Q_1) is 1.32, 1.46, 1.66, and 0.43 for 2 years, 3 years, 4 years, and 5 years, respectively.

Mean PE ratio of the respondent companies 1 year post-M&A has been observed to be 17.84 % whereas the PE ratio for the companies in upper quartile (Q_4) is 26.21 % but in the lower quartile (Q_1) PE ratio is 11.16 %. Mean PE ratio of companies in upper quartile (Q_4) is 28.67, 25.07, 26.15, and 31.87 for 2 years, 3 years, 4 years, and 5 years, respectively. Mean PE ratio of respondent companies in lower quartile (Q_1) is 11.8, 11.03, 7.08 and 7.37 for 2 years, 3 years, 4 years, and 5 years, respectively.

Table 7.12 presents the results of the independent t-test to compare the mean post-M&A PB and PE ratios of sample companies in upper quartile (Q_4) and lower quartile (Q_1). It is evident from relevant data that companies in upper quartile (Q_4) have 8.38, 7.03, 7.06, 7.31, and 6.2 % higher PB ratio 1 year post-M&A, 2 years post-M&A, 3 years post M&A, 4 years post-M&A, and 5 years post-M&A, respectively; moreover, the difference is statistically significant.

Panel B of Table 7.12 depicts that the companies with higher corporate governance score are valued more by market as revealed by their PE ratios. The higher valuations are in the range of 14.04–24.4 % as evident from the difference in PE ratios of companies in upper quartile (Q_4) and lower quartile (Q_1). The difference is statistically significant at 1 % (p-value $= 0<0.01$), (p-value $= 0.001 < 0.01$),

Table 7.12 Independent sample t-test statistic for valuation ratios [Upper quartile (Q_4), Lower quartile (Q_1)]

Year Post-M&A	Mean ratio (Q_4)	Mean ratio (Q_1)	Mean difference	t-value	Significance value
A: PB					
t + 1	10.25 ($N = 47$)	1.87 ($N = 47$)	8.38	8.57[b]	0.000
t + 2	8.35 ($N = 45$)	1.32 ($N = 45$)	7.03	6.75[b]	0.000
t + 3	8.52 ($N = 43$)	1.46 ($N = 43$)	7.06	7.95[b]	0.000
t + 4	8.97 ($N = 39$)	1.66 ($N = 39$)	7.31	8.61[b]	0.000
t + 5	6.63 ($N = 37$)	0.43 ($N = 37$)	6.2	6.25[b]	0.000
B: PE					
t + 1	26.21 ($N = 47$)	11.16 ($N = 47$)	15.05	5.57[b]	0.000
t + 2	28.67 ($N = 45$)	11.80 ($N = 45$)	16.87	3.55[b]	0.001
t + 3	25.07 ($N = 43$)	11.03 ($N = 43$)	14.04	2.96[b]	0.004
t + 4	26.15 ($N = 39$)	7.08 ($N = 39$)	19.04	2.96[b]	0.007
t + 5	31.87 ($N = 37$)	7.37 ($N = 37$)	24.4	3.5[b]	0.001

[a], [b]Denote significance at 5 % and 1 % respectively

(p-value = 0.004 < 0.01), (p-value = 007 < 0.01), and (p-value = 0.001 < 0.01) 1 year, 2 years, 3 years, 4 years, and 5 years post-M&A, respectively. These results indicate that the companies with better corporate governance score are valued higher than the companies with lower corporate governance score.

7.5 Concluding Observations

The present chapter examines the impact of corporate governance practices of the acquirers on short-term abnormal returns and long-term financial performance.

The results are revealing. The empirical findings show that companies with high corporate governance score have positive abnormal returns in the short-term, better financial performance and higher valuations post-M&A, while companies with lower corporate governance score have lower financial performance and lower valuations post-M&A. The results are consistent with La Porta et al. (2002) that firms with better corporate governance enjoy higher valuation.

These findings have important implications. For investors, the findings imply that, as far as agency costs are concerned, investments in companies with better corporate governance score are more profitable. For corporate managers, the results imply that the management should be aware of the need for efficient corporate governance structure and mechanism to control agency problems. Better governance and disclosure practices increase investor confidence which, in turn, have positive influence on valuation. Companies with good governance are likely to be valued higher. For policy makers, the findings that firm performance is significantly influenced by effective corporate governance could serve to justify regulatory measures and actions towards enforcing healthy corporate governance regime and initiatives to encourage corporates to adopt and adhere to these measures.

References

Botosan, C. (1997). Disclosure level and the cost of equity capital. *Accounting Review, 72*(3), 323–349.

La Porta, R., Lopaz-de-Silanes, F., Schleifer, A., & Vishny, R. (2000). Investor protection and corporate governance. *Journal of Financial Economics, 58*(2), 3–27.

Lang, M., & Lundholm, R. (1999). Corporate disclosure policy and analysts behavior. *Accounting Review, 71*(4), 467–493.

Chapter 8
Summary and Conclusions

Abstract The objective of this chapter is to provide a brief summary of the research findings contained in this book. The findings are related to the assessment of short-term and long-term performance of the acquirers who have adopted the strategy of M&A during the chosen time span of the study. Based on the findings of the study, certain recommendations have been made for investors, corporate managers, and policy makers.

Keywords Financial performance · Abnormal returns · Corporate governance · Return on equity · Corporate governance index · Acquisitions

8.1 Introduction

Performance of mergers and acquisitions is like puzzles in finance that researchers have been trying to solve. The present study is also an effort in the same direction. It has been conducted to capture management's views, market reaction, financial and operating performance, pertaining to mergers and acquisitions in the Indian context.

This chapter presents a summary of major findings, recommendations, and contributions of the study. The study attempts to evaluate the impact of mergers and acquisitions on the returns in short-term as well as long-term. For the purpose, well-established research techniques, namely, event study methodology and two experimental designs viz. 'before- and-after design' and 'after-only design' have been used. The ratio analysis, a well-accepted tool to measure the financial performance, has been employed to analyze the data. Statistical tools such as paired *t*-test and independent *t*-test are also used for testing various hypotheses and drawing inferences. Besides these techniques, two surveys have also been conducted for top-level Indian corporate managers of the organizations that adopted the strategy of M&A during the chosen time span of the study. The surveys aim to gauge the managerial views about the corporate governance practices and the motives of mergers and acquisitions. The findings of the surveys have been corroborated with the secondary data analysis.

N. Rani et al., *Mergers and Acquisitions*, India Studies in Business and Economics, DOI 10.1007/978-981-10-2203-6_8

The rest of the chapter is divided into five sections. Section 8.2 presents the major empirical findings, summarized objective-wise. Based on the findings of the study, certain recommendations have been made in Sect. 8.3. This section is divided into two Sects. 8.3.1 and 8.3.2 providing a set of recommendations for investors and corporate managers respectively. Major contributions of the study have been reported in Sect. 8.4. The chapter concludes with Sect. 8.5.

8.2 Major Findings of the Research

The major findings have been summarized objective-wise in the following subsections.

8.2.1 Findings Related to Short-term Abnormal Returns of M&A

Objective 1: To measure the effect of the announcement of mergers and acquisitions on stock returns of acquiring firms by

1.1 Ascertaining the magnitude and the direction of the abnormal returns for the entire sample.

- Market starts reacting prior to the announcement. The moment the announcement information becomes public, investors start reacting and the stock price jumps high, providing positive abnormal returns to the investors. This reaction clearly indicates that investors perceive synergies in mergers and acquisitions and they appear to be beneficial for them. "EARLIER HE SELLS, MORE HE GAINS" is the major finding of short-term abnormal returns.

1.2 Conducting analysis of the abnormal returns for subsamples on the basis of:

(i) Domestic and cross-border M&A.
(ii) Method of payment (cash, stock).
(iii) Form of target firm acquired (listed, unlisted).
(iv) Status of target firm (remains wholly owned subsidiary, absorbed with the operations of the acquirer).
(v) Stake of acquisitions (partial/majority control, complete control).
(vi) Origin of target firm (developed market, emerging market).

- Cross-border as well as domestic acquisitions have created value for shareholders of the acquiring company on the announcement. The results indicate that value creation is higher for cross-border acquisitions vis-a-vis domestic acquisitions.
- The acquisitions, financed with cash, experience higher returns than the acquisitions financed with stock. This could be a signal in favor of "asymmetric information hypothesis and free cash flow hypothesis". "ISSUANCE OF STOCK IS NOT GOOD NEWS" as per the findings.
- The acquirers of unlisted target firms experience higher returns than the acquirers of listed target firms.
- The acquirer earns when target remains as a wholly owned subsidiary (WOS). In contrast, the acquirer shareholder loses when the target firm is absorbed with the operations of the acquiring firm.
- The acquisitions of targets from non-US developed market outperform the return from the acquisition of US targets.

8.2.2 Findings Related to Management Views on Motives for M&A

Objective 2: To gain insight into managerial views about motives and sources of synergies of M&A.

- Survey findings reveal that the primary motive of mergers in India during the period of study has been to take advantage of synergies.
- Operating economies, increased market share and financial economies (lower risk leading to lower cost of capital) have been indicated in order of importance as the desired synergies to be gained through corporate mergers and acquisitions in India

8.2.3 Findings Related to Financial Performance of M&A

Objective 3: To measure the magnitude and the direction of change in the financial performance of the acquiring firms post-M&A.

- M&A appear to have been financially beneficial for the acquiring companies. The findings suggest that profitability of acquiring firms has improved during post-M&A phase.
- Better management of liquidity position during the post-M&A period has also been observed.
- M&A has no impact on the leverage of acquiring firms before and after M&A.

- Operating profit margin based on sales have improved post-M&A. The significantly higher post-M&A operating margin indicates that the acquirers appear to have generated higher operating profit per unit net sales, post-M&A.
- The better operating margin seems to be due to the lower costs as a result of economies of scale. Negative *t*-values identified by paired samples *t*-test on expense ratios also corroborate this finding.
- The efficiency of utilization of assets does not appear to have improved as revealed by total assets turnover ratio post-M&A.

8.2.4 Findings Related to Corporate Governance Score

Objective 4: To gain insight into corporate governance practices of acquirers by developing a corporate governance index.

- Practice of corporate governance has progressed in a big way in Indian companies as revealed by their average score. There are several companies which made proactive initiatives in introducing good governance norms and standards even before these became mandatory.
- Companies in the lower quartiles are those complying with the minimum mandatory standards of corporate governance.
- Companies in service sector vis-à-vis manufacturing sector have better corporate governance score. It implies that companies in service sector are more conscious for their corporate governance practices and put their corporate governance structures in place.
- Mean corporate governance score has improved over time.

8.2.5 Findings Related to Impact of Corporate Governance Score

Objective 5: To ascertain the impact of corporate governance on stock returns due to the announcement of mergers and acquisitions and financial performance.

- There is a positive association between corporate governance score and shareholders' wealth due to announcements of mergers and acquisitions. Companies with better corporate governance create higher shareholders' wealth in short-term.
- Companies having higher corporate governance score show better financial performance on the basis of all measures of rate of return.

- Companies with higher corporate governance score show better valuations.
- Companies with higher rank of corporate governance index are good performers (manifested in their better profitability ratios). Their post-M&A better financial performance and valuation shows that well-governed companies bring positive synergies from their M&A activities which is recognized by market, as evidenced by higher valuation ratios

8.3 Recommendations from the Study

Based on the concluding observations and notable findings of the research, the following recommendations are made for the investors and the corporate managers.

8.3.1 Recommendations for Investors

Based on the notable findings and the concluding observations of the present research study, it has been noticed that an investor can gain substantial returns, if he/she makes the right moves when acquirers' decisions on M&A are announced. The following recommendations/guidelines have been made for the investors.

- **"EARLIER HE SELLS MORE HE GAINS" and "ISSUANCE OF STOCK IS NOT GOOD NEWS"** are the major recommendations.
- The results show that positive abnormal returns can be earned during the pre-announcement window due to the information about the board meeting as well as agenda item communicated to the exchange. An investor can gain substantial returns, if he/she purchases the share on the day the news of board meeting (announcing the deal) comes to the market and sells them one day after the announcement
- An investor can also earn substantial returns if the shares of the acquiring company are purchased two days prior to the announcement day and sold two days after the announcement day.
- The announcement of cross-border acquisitions provides much higher returns vis-a-vis domestic acquisitions. In addition, the cumulative abnormal returns in the case of cross-border acquisitions are relatively more while they are temporary in the case of domestic acquisitions.
- The announcement of complete acquisitions of target firm as a wholly owned subsidiary provides much higher returns than that for partial/majority control acquisitions. In addition, the cumulative abnormal returns in the case of

complete acquisitions are relatively more permanent while they are temporary in the case of partial/majority control acquisitions.
- The announcement of acquisitions, financed with cash payment, provides substantial returns.
- As far as agency costs are concerned, investments in companies with better corporate governance score are more profitable.

8.3.2 Recommendations for Corporate Managers

The findings of this study have certain implications for the corporate managers and policy makers as well. They have been presented as follows.

- The findings and examples we present here indicate that managers can consider cross-border as well as domestic acquisitions as an option to strengthen their competitiveness since the effects of these announcements appear to be a good indicator of longer term success. The study suggests that the Indian managers could adopt mergers and acquisitions as effective strategy for corporate growth.
- The findings also have a message for the managers about stock versus cash as the mode. Issuance of shares is not as good as payment in cash as shown in market reaction to acquisitions financed with stocks.
- Third, implication for management is that the shareholders of acquiring firms earn substantial return when the target firm is acquired as a subsidiary. The management may acquire the target firm as a subsidiary and may absorb it with its own operations later on. The advantages of acquiring complete control of a firm arise from assets owned and capacity to acquire complimentary assets.
- For corporate managers, the results imply that the management should be aware of the need for efficient corporate governance structure and mechanism to control information asymmetry. Better governance and disclosure practices increase investor confidence which, in turn, has positive influence on valuation. Companies with good governance are likely to be valued more.

8.3.3 Recommendations for Policy Makers

- The findings that firm performance is significantly influenced by effective corporate governance could serve to justify regulatory measures and efforts for better corporate governance.

8.4 Contribution of the Study

The contributions made by the study are as follows:

- The study contributes to the literature on performance of mergers and acquisitions in short-term as well as long-term.
- The research includes a detailed study of corporate governance practices of acquires. It adds to the limited literature on corporate governance practices of acquiring firms by developing a corporate governance index. This study uses a well-established method to develop comprehensive corporate governance index of acquirers. The results establish an association between corporate governance and performance of acquiring firms. Moreover, it uses well established and comprehensive approaches to analyze the long-term financial performance of acquirers in order to corroborate the findings from the primary data.
- The findings of this study have certain implications for the shareholders/ investors, stakeholders, corporate managers, and policy makers as well. The findings that firm performance is significantly influenced by effective corporate governance could serve to justify regulatory measures and initiatives to encourage corporates to adopt and adhere to these measures.
- On a methodological level, the present study has demonstrated use of the seven major significance tests to check the robustness of average abnormal returns and cumulative average abnormal returns. The use of seven main test statistics for assessing significance levels of average abnormal return and cumulative average abnormal return has proved to be useful, since these test statistics take into account effects of event-induced variance and offer, therefore, an alternative evaluation of significance.

8.5 Concluding Observations

The positive returns observed on announcement and during pre-event window are in sync with the expectations of the Indian managers to realize synergies. Perhaps, this may be due to the reason that companies acquire another company for strategic reasons so as to exploit economies of scale and scope, and leverage available resources and capabilities, thus creating more scope for value creation. Mergers and acquisitions provide an opportunity to the acquiring company to combine and judiciously utilize intangible resources of both the companies on a broader scale. It seems Indian companies have managed to develop their acquisition capabilities over time. The market responds positively if the acquisition is considered value-adding to the existing product portfolio of the acquiring company. Indian firms use cross-border acquisitions for strategic assets-seeking in order to facilitate organizational transformation of the firms. Moreover, access to developed markets for products, resources, and capabilities enable Indian firms to leapfrog to the global league and, thus, create greater value than what could be achieved by acquiring a domestic firm.

Further, better governance and disclosure practices increase investor confidence which, in turn, has positive influence on valuation. Companies with good governance are likely to be valued more. The management should be aware of the need for efficient corporate governance structure and mechanism to control information asymmetry.

References

Rani, N., Yadav, S. S., & Jain, P. K. (2013a). The impact of domestic acquisitions on acquirer shareholders' wealth in India. *Global Journal of Flexible Management System, 13*(4), 179–193.

Rani, N., Yadav, S. S., & Jain, P. K. (2013b). Du Pont analysis of post M&A operating performance of Indian acquiring firms. *International Journal of Economics and Finance, 5*(8), 65–73.

Rani, N., Yadav, S. S., & Jain, P. K. (2014). Impact of corporate governance score on abnormal returns and financial performance of mergers and acquisitions. *Decision, 41*(4), 371–398.

Appendix A
Respondent Companies in Survey

Sr. No.	Company name
1	20 Microns Ltd.
2	3I Infotech Ltd.
3	A B B Ltd.
4	A C C Ltd.
5	Aban Offshore Ltd.
6	Abbott India Ltd.
7	Accentia Technologies Ltd.
8	Aditya Birla Nuvo Ltd.
9	Aftek Ltd.
10	Alchemist Ltd.
11	Alembic Ltd.
12	Allsec Technologies Ltd.
13	Alok Industries Ltd.
14	Anant Raj Industries Ltd.
15	Ansal Properties & Infrastructure Ltd.
16	Apollo Tyres Ltd.
17	Asahi India Glass Ltd.
18	Ashok Leyland Ltd.
19	Asian Paints Ltd.
20	Associated Alcohols
21	Aurionpro Solutions Ltd.
22	Aurobindo Pharma Ltd.
23	Axis-I T & T Ltd.
24	Bajaj Electricals Ltd.
25	Bajaj Hindusthan Ltd.
26	Ballarpur Industries Ltd.
27	Balrampur Chini Mills Ltd.
28	Batliboi Ltd.

(continued)

N. Rani et al., *Mergers and Acquisitions*, India Studies
in Business and Economics, DOI 10.1007/978-981-10-2203-6

(continued)

Sr. No.	Company name
29	Bayer Cropscience Ltd.
30	Bharat Forge Ltd.
31	Bharat Heavy Electricals Ltd.
32	Bharti Airtel Ltd.
33	Bhuwalka Steel Industries Ltd.
34	Bilcare Ltd.
35	Biocon Ltd.
36	Bliss Gvs Pharma Ltd.
37	Bombay Rayon Fashions Ltd.
38	Brigade Enterprises Ltd.
39	Cable Corpn. Of India Ltd.
40	Cadila Healthcare Ltd.
41	California Software Co Ltd.
42	Ceat Ltd.
43	Chowgule Steamships Ltd.
44	Ciba India Ltd. [Merged]
45	Clariant Chemicals (India) Ltd.
46	Colgate-Palmolive (India) Ltd.
47	Control Print Ltd.
48	Core Education & Technologies Ltd.
49	Coromandel International Ltd.
50	Cranes Software Intl. Ltd.
51	Crisil Ltd.
52	Crompton Greaves Ltd.
53	Cyber Media (India) Ltd.
54	D C M Shriram Consolidated Ltd.
55	Dabur India Ltd.
56	Datamatics Global Services Ltd.
57	Deepak Fertilisers & Petrochemicals Corpn. Ltd.
58	Dolphin Offshore Enterprises (India) Ltd.
59	Dr. Reddy'S Laboratories Ltd.
60	E I D-Parry (India) Ltd.
61	EdServ Softsystems Ltd.
62	Educomp Solutions Ltd.
63	Elder Pharmaceuticals Ltd.
64	Escorts Ltd.
65	Essar Steel Ltd.
66	Essel Propack Ltd.
67	Exide Industries Ltd.
68	Firstsource Solutions Ltd.

(continued)

(continued)

Sr. No.	Company name
69	Forbes & Co. Ltd.
70	Fortis Healthcare Ltd.
71	Fulford (India) Ltd.
72	Future Retail Ltd.
73	G T L Ltd.
74	Gateway Distriparks Ltd.
75	Geometric Ltd.
76	Gitanjali Gems Ltd.
77	Glaxosmithkline Pharmaceuticals Ltd.
78	Glenmark Pharmaceuticals Ltd.
79	Glodyne Technoserve Ltd.
80	Godrej Consumer Products Ltd.
81	Grasim Industries Ltd.
82	Great Eastern Shipping Co. Ltd.
83	Greaves Cotton Ltd.
84	Greenply Industries Ltd.
85	GV Films Ltd.
86	H C L Technologies Ltd.
87	Havells India Ltd.
88	Hercules Hoists Ltd.
89	Hexaware Technologies Ltd.
90	Hindalco Industries Ltd.
91	Hinduja Ventures Ltd.
92	Hindustan Unilever Ltd.
93	Hitech Plast Ltd.
94	HOV Services Ltd
95	I T C Ltd.
96	Idream Film Infrastructure Co. Ltd.
97	Indian Hotels Co. Ltd.
98	Infosys Ltd.
99	J C T Ltd.
100	J S W Ispat Steel Ltd.
101	J S W Steel Ltd.
102	Jaiprakash Associates Ltd.
103	Jindal Drilling & Inds. Ltd.
104	Jindal Poly Films Ltd.
105	Jubilant Life Sciences Ltd.
106	Jyothy Laboratories Ltd.
107	K S B Pumps Ltd.
108	Kale Consultants Ltd.

(continued)

(continued)

Sr. No.	Company name
109	Kamat Hotels (India) Ltd.
110	Kohinoor Broadcasting Corpn. Ltd.
111	Larsen & Toubro Ltd.
112	Lupin Ltd.
113	Maharashtra Seamless Ltd.
114	Mahindra & Mahindra Ltd.
115	Mahindra Forgings Ltd.
116	Mahindra Ugine Steel Co. Ltd.
117	Manugraph India Ltd.
118	Marico Ltd.
119	Marksans Pharma Ltd.
120	Maruti Suzuki India Ltd.
121	Mastek Ltd.
122	Maxwell Industries Ltd.
123	Moser Baer India Ltd.
124	Motherson Sumi Systems Ltd.
125	N I I T Technologies Ltd.
126	Navneet Publications (India) Ltd.
127	Oil & Natural Gas Corpn. Ltd.
128	Omaxe Ltd.
129	Opto Circuits(India)Ltd.
130	Paramount Communications Ltd.
131	Patel Integrated Logistics Ltd.
132	Patni Computer Systems Ltd.
133	Pfizer Ltd.
134	Pidilite Industries Ltd.
135	Pioneer Embroideries Ltd.
136	Piramal Healthcare Ltd.
137	Plethico Pharmaceuticals Ltd.
138	Polaris Software Lab Ltd.
139	Premier Energy & Infrastructure Ltd.
140	Pricol Ltd.
141	Prime Focus Ltd.
142	Punj Lloyd Ltd.
143	Punjab Chemicals & Crop Protection Ltd.
144	R P G Cables Ltd.
145	R Systems International Ltd.
146	Rajesh Exports Ltd.
147	Rallis India Ltd.
148	Ranbaxy Laboratories Ltd.

(continued)

(continued)

Sr. No.	Company name
149	Reliance Communications Ltd.
150	Reliance Industries Ltd.
151	Rolta India Ltd.
152	Ruchi Soya Inds. Ltd.
153	Ruttonsha Intl Rectifier Ltd.
154	Saksoft Ltd.
155	Shilpa Medicare Ltd.
156	Shree Renuka Sugars Ltd.
157	Siel Ltd.
158	Siemens Ltd.
159	Silverline Technologies Ltd.
160	Spentex Industries Ltd.
161	SQL Star International Ltd.
162	Standard Industries Ltd.
163	Sterlite Industries (India) Ltd.
164	Sun Pharmaceutical Inds. Ltd.
165	Sundram Fasteners Ltd.
166	Supreme Industries Ltd.
167	Suzlon Energy Ltd.
168	Tata Chemicals Ltd.
169	Tata Communications Ltd.
170	Tata Consultancy Services Ltd.
171	Tata Global Beverage Ltd.
172	Tata Motors Ltd.
173	Tata Power Co. Ltd.
174	Tata Steel Ltd.
175	Technocraft Industries(India)
176	Thermax Ltd.
177	Thomas Cook (India) Ltd.
178	Tilaknagar Industries Ltd.
179	Tips Industries Ltd.
180	Tricom India Ltd.
181	Triton Corp Ltd.
182	United Phosphorus Ltd.
183	V I P Industries Ltd.
184	Videocon Industries Ltd.
185	Voltas Ltd.
186	Wanbury Ltd.
187	West Coast Paper Mills Ltd.
188	Wipro Ltd.
189	Wockhardt Ltd.

Appendix B
Sample Companies in Event Study (Cross-Border Complete Acquisitions)

N. Rani et al., *Mergers and Acquisitions*, India Studies
in Business and Economics, DOI 10.1007/978-981-10-2203-6

Sr. No.	BSE code	Acquirer name	Target name	Announcement date	Target type	Payment method	Country
1	500024	Assam Co. Ltd.	Duncan Macneill Natural Resources Ltd.	14-Jun-06	Unlisted	Cash	Germany
2	500092	CRISIL Ltd.	EconoMatters Ltd.	17-Dec-03	Unlisted	Cash	UK
	500092	CRISIL Ltd.	Coalition Development Ltd.	1-Jun-12	Unlisted	Cash	UK
3	500093	Crompton Greaves Ltd.	Microsol Holdings Ltd.	28-May-07	Unlisted	Cash	Ireland
4	500093	Crompton Greaves Ltd.	Societe Nouvelle De Maintenance Transformateurs/Sonomatra	2-Jun-08	Unlisted	Cash	France
5	500093	Crompton Greaves Ltd.	M S E Power Systems Inc.	15-Sep-08	Unlisted	Cash	USA
6	500124	Dr. Reddy's Laboratories Ltd.	Trigenesis Therapeutics In	6-May-04	Unlisted	Cash	USA
7	500124	Dr. Reddy's Laboratories Ltd.	Betapharm Arzneimittel GmbH	6-Mar-06	Unlisted	Cash	Germany
8	500135	Essel Propack Ltd.	Arista Tubes	5-Aug-04	Unlisted	Cash	UK
9	500135	Essel Propack Ltd.	Telcon Packaging	12-Apr-05	Unlisted	Cash	UK
10	500160	G T L Ltd.	Genesis Consultancy Ltd.	17-Oct-06	Unlisted	Cash	UK
11	500160	G T L Ltd.	Ada Cellworks Sdn. Bhd.	15-Nov-07	Unlisted	Cash	Malaysia
12	500171	G H C L Ltd.	ROSEBYS	31-Jul-06	Unlisted	Cash	UK
13	500171	G H C L Ltd.	BEST MANUFACTURING	12-Feb-07	Unlisted	Cash	USA
14	500184	Himadri Chemicals & Inds. Ltd.	Team Paramount Ltd.	26-Sep-06	Unlisted	Cash	HongKong
15	500189	Hinduja Ventures Ltd.	Source One Communications Inc.	1-Oct-04	Unlisted	Cash	USA
16	500189	Hinduja Ventures Ltd.	AFFINA	9-Jan-07	Unlisted	Cash	USA
17	500209	Infosys Technologies Ltd.	Expert Information Services Pty Ltd.	18-Dec-03	Unlisted	Cash	Australia
18	500209	Infosys Technologies Ltd.	Mainstream Computing Pty Ltd.	1-Apr-08	Unlisted	Cash	Australia
19	500209	Infosys Technologies Ltd.	McCamish Systems LLC	12-Nov-09	Priv.	UNKNOWN	United States
20	500209	Infosys Ltd.	Lodestone Management	10-Sep-12	Priv.	CASHO	Switzerland

(continued)

(continued)

Sr. No.	BSE code	Acquirer name	Target name	Announcement date	Target type	Payment method	Country
21	500209	Infosys Ltd.	Panaya Inc.	16-Feb-15	Priv.	CASHO	United States
22	500219	Jain Irrigation Systems Ltd.	Chapin Watermatics	3-May-06	Unlisted	Cash	USA
23	500219	Jain Irrigation Systems Ltd.	Aquarius Brands In	15-Feb-07	Listed	Cash	USA
24	500227	Jindal Poly Films Ltd.	Rexor	23-Sep-03	Unlisted	Cash	France
25	500241	Kirloskar Brothers Ltd.	SyncroFlo Inc.	5-Mar-14	Priv.	Cash	United States
26	500257	Lupin Ltd.	Hormosan Pharma Gmbh	30-Jul-08	Unlisted	Cash	Germany
27	500257	Lupin Ltd.	Laboratorios Grin SA de CV	27-Mar-14	Priv.	Cash	Mexico
28	500257	Lupin Ltd.	GAVIS Pharms LLC,Novel Labs	23-Jul-15	Priv.	Cash	USA
29	500302	Piramal Healthcare Ltd.	Avecia Pharmaceuticals	27-Oct-05	Unlisted	Cash	UK
30	500302	Piramal Healthcare Ltd.	Minrad International Inc.	22-Dec-08	Unlisted	Cash	USA
31	500303	Aditya Birla Nuvo Ltd.	Minacs Worldwide Inc.	26-Jun-06	Public	CASHO	Canada
32	500303	Aditya Birla Nuvo Ltd.	Compass BPO Ltd.	10-Mar-10	Priv.	Cash	UK
33	500304	N I I T Ltd.	Element K	27-Jul-06	Unlisted	Cash	USA
34	500308	Nirma Ltd.	Searles Valley Minerals Co	27-Nov-07	Unlisted	Cash	USA
35	500325	Reliance Industries Ltd.	Trevira GmbH	24-Jun-04	Unlisted	Cash	Germany
36	500331	Pidilite Industries Ltd.	Pulvitec do Brasil Industria	4-Jul-07	Unlisted	Cash	Brazil
37	500339	Rain Commodities Ltd.	RCUSA	3-Mar-06	Listed	Cash	USA
38	500359	Ranbaxy Laboratories	RPG Aventis	13-Dec-03	Unlisted	Cash	France
39	500359	Ranbaxy Laboratories	Mundogen Farma SA	18-Jul-06	Unlisted	Cash	Spain
40	500359	Ranbaxy Laboratories	Terapia SA	28-Mar-06	Unlisted	Cash	Romania
41	500359	Ranbaxy Laboratories	Be-Tabs Pharmaceuticals Ltd.	8-May-07	Unlisted	Cash	South Africa
42	500366	Rolta India Ltd.	Piocon Technologies Inc.	29-Dec-08	Unlisted	Cash	USA

(continued)

(continued)

Sr. No.	BSE code	Acquirer name	Target name	Announcement date	Target type	Payment method	Country
43	500366	Rolta India Ltd.	WhittmanHart Consulting	29-Jul-08	Unlisted	Cash	USA
44	500376	Satyam Computer Services Ltd.	Bridge Strategy Group	21-Jan-08	Unlisted	Cash	USA
45	500403	Sundram Fasteners Ltd.	Peiner Unformtechnik Gmbh,	10-Nov-05	Unlisted	Cash	Germany
46	500403	Sundram Fasteners Ltd.	P U T Grundstucks Gmbh	2-Aug-07	Unlisted	Cash	Germany
47	500420	Torrent Pharmaceuticals Ltd.	Heumann Pharma GmbH & Co	27-Jun-05	Unlisted	Cash	Germany
48	500440	Hindalco Industries Ltd.	Straits (Nifty) Pty. Ltd.	25-Jan-03	Unlisted	Cash	Australia
49	500440	Hindalco Industries Ltd.	Novelis Inc.	12-Feb-07	Listed	Cash	USA
50	500464	Ucal Fuel Systems Ltd.	AMTEC Precision Products, Inc, (AMTEC)	2-Apr-05	Unlisted	Cash	USA
51	500470	Tata Steel Ltd.	NatSteel Ltd.	16-Aug-04	Unlisted	Cash	Singapore
52	500470	Tata Steel Ltd.	Corus Group PLC	17-Oct-06	Listed	Cash	UK
53	500483	Tata Communications Ltd.	Tyco Global Network	1-Nov-04	Listed	Cash	USA
54	500483	Tata Communications Ltd.	Teleglobe Intl Hldg Ltd.	25-Jul-05	Listed	Cash	Bermuda
55	500493	Bharat Forge Ltd.	Carl Dan Peddinghus Gmbh	22-Nov-03	Unlisted	Cash	Germany
56	500493	Bharat Forge Ltd.	CDP Aluminiumtechnik GmbH & Co	11-Dec-04	Unlisted	Cash	Germany
57	500493	Bharat Forge Ltd.	Federal Forge Inc.	29-Jun-05	Unlisted	Cash	USA
58	500493	Bharat Forge Ltd.	Imatra Kilsta AB	22-Sep-05	Unlisted	Cash	Sweden
59	500510	Larsen & Toubro Ltd.	Thalest Ltd.	4-Apr-12	Priv.	CASHO	United Kingdom
60	500520	Mahindra & Mahindra Ltd.	Tractorul UTB SA	16-Sep-05	Govt	Cash	Romania
61	500520	Mahindra & Mahindra Ltd.	G R Grafica Ricerca Design S R L	8-Jan-08	Unlisted	Cash	Itlay
62	500550	Siemens Ltd.	Morgan Construction Company	2-Jan-08	Unlisted	Cash	USA

(continued)

(continued)

Sr. No.	BSE code	Acquirer name	Target name	Announcement date	Target type	Payment method	Country
63	500570	Tata Motors Ltd.	Daewoo Commercial Vehicle Co	5-Nov-03	Unlisted	Cash	South Korea
64	500570	Tata Motors Ltd.	Hispano Carrocera SA	25-Feb-05	Listed	Cash, call option	Spain
65	500570	Tata Motors Ltd.	Cedis Mechanical Engg. Gmbh	12-Jan-06	Unlisted	Cash	Germany
66	500570	Tata Motors Ltd.	Jaguar Cars Ltd.	26-Mar-08	Unlisted	Cash	UK
	500570	Tata Motors Ltd.	Land Rover	26-Mar-08	Unlisted	Cash	UK
67	500770	Tata Chemicals Ltd.	General Chemical Indl. Products Inc.	31-Jan-08	Unlisted	Cash	USA
68	500770	Tata Chemicals Ltd.	Cheshire Salt Holdings Ltd.	20-Dec-10	Priv.	Cash	United Kingdom
69	500800	Tata Tea Ltd.	Good Earth Teas	13-Oct-05	Unlisted	Cash	USA
70	500800	Tata Tea Ltd.	JEMCA	2-May-06	Unlisted	Cash	UK
71	500820	Asian Paints Ltd.	Taubmans, Fiji	11-Sep-03	Unlisted	Cash	Fiji
72	500850	Indian Hotels Co. Ltd.	Campton Place Hotel,CA	3-Apr-07	Unlisted	Cash	USA
73	500875	I T C Ltd.	Technico Pty Ltd.	17-Aug-07	Unlisted	Cash	Australia
74	500377	Apollo Tyres Ltd.	Dunlop Tyres International Ltd.	30-Jan-06	Unlisted	Cash	South Africa
75	500900	Sterlite Industries (India) Ltd.	Asarco L L C	2-Jun-08	Unlisted	Cash	USA
76	502742	Sintex Industries Ltd.	Nief Plastics SA	30-Oct-07	Unlisted	Cash	France
77	502742	Sintex Industries Ltd.	Nero Plastics	3-Dec-07	Unlisted	Cash	USA
78	503806	S R F Ltd.	Thai Baroda Inds. Ltd.	27-May-08	Unlisted	Cash	Thailand
79	503806	S R F Ltd.	Industex Holdings (Pty) Ltd. (IH)	15-Jul-08	Unlisted	Cash	South Africa
80	504067	Zensar Technologies Ltd.	PSI Holding Group Inc.	22-Nov-10	Priv.	CASHO	United States

(continued)

(continued)

Sr. No.	BSE code	Acquirer name	Target name	Announcement date	Target type	Payment method	Country
81	505200	Eicher Motors Ltd.	Design Intent Engineering Inc.	30-Jun-05	Unlisted	Cash	USA
82	505200	Eicher Motors Ltd.	Hoff & Associates	25-Apr-07	Unlisted	Cash	USA
83	505255	G M M Pfaudler Ltd.	Mavag A G	24-Dec-07	Unlisted	Cash	Switzerland
84	505324	Manugraph India Ltd.	Dauphin Graphic Machines Inc.	7-Nov-06	Unlisted	Cash	USA
85	505854	TRF Ltd.	HR Intl Crushing & Screening	22-Mar-10	Priv.	CASHO	United Kingdom
86	506618	Punjab Chemicals & Crop Protection Ltd.	Pevobel N.V. and Gevobel N.V	27-Aug-07	Unlisted	Cash	Netherland
87	507315	Sakthi Sugars Ltd.	INTERMET Europe GmbH & Co	30-Apr-07	Unlisted	Cash	Germany
88	507315	Sakthi Sugars Ltd.	Arvika Gjuteri AB	22-Feb-08	Unlisted	Cash	Sweden
89	507315	Sakthi Sugars Ltd.	Sakthi Auto Mauritius Ltd.	31-Mar-11	Priv.	Cash	Mauritius
90	507685	Wipro Ltd.	NewLogic Technologies AG	19-Dec-05	Unlisted	Cash	Austria
91	507685	Wipro Ltd.	cMango Inc.	20-Feb-06	Unlisted	Cash	USA
92	507685	Wipro Ltd.	Quantech Global Services Ltd.	15-May-06	Unlisted	Cash	USA
93	507685	Wipro Ltd.	Hydrauto Group AB	28-Sep-06	Unlisted	Cash	Sweden
94	507685	Wipro Ltd.	OKI Techno Centre Singapore Pte Ltd.	28-Sep-07	Unlisted	Cash	Singapore
95	507685	Wipro Ltd.	Opus Capital Markets	2-Dec-13	Priv.	CASHO	United States
96	508976	Spanco Ltd.	Great IT Pte Ltd.	5-Feb-08	Unlisted	Cash	Singapore
97	509472	Cravatex Ltd.	BB(UK) Ltd.	10-Mar-11	Priv.	Cash	United Kingdom
98	509480	Berger Paints India Ltd.	Bolix SA	29-Apr-08	Unlisted	Cash	Poland
99	509550	Gammon India Ltd.	Sofinter SpA	10-Sep-08	Priv.	CASHO	Italy
100	511389	Videocon Industries Ltd.	Encana Brasil Petroleo Limitada (EBPL)	13-Sep-07	Unlisted	Cash	Brasil

(continued)

(continued)

Sr. No.	BSE code	Acquirer name	Target name	Announcement date	Target type	Payment method	Country
101	511658	Nettlinx Ltd.	Nettlinx Inc.	28-Jan-06	Unlisted	Cash	USA
102	511658	Nettlinx Ltd.	Host Department, L L C	3-Sep-07	Unlisted	Cash	USA
103	511658	Nettlinx Ltd.	Anchor Systems Pty. Ltd.	14-May-08	Unlisted	Cash	Australia
104	512070	United Phosphorus Ltd.	AG Value, Inc.	5-Nov-04	Unlisted	Cash	USA
105	512070	United Phosphorus Ltd.	REPOSO S.A.I.C	31-Oct-05	Unlisted	Cash	Argentina
106	512070	United Phosphorus Ltd.	Advanta Netherlands Holdings B V	14-Feb-06	Unlisted	Cash	Netherland
107	512070	United Phosphorus Ltd.	Cropserve	9-Aug-06	Unlisted	Cash	South Africa
108	512070	United Phosphorus Ltd.	Evofarms Group of Cos	18-Feb-08	Unlisted	Cash	Colombia
109	512093	Cranes Software Intl. Ltd.	Engineering Mechanics Research Corporation (EMRC)	23-May-05	Unlisted	Cash	USA
110	512093	Cranes Software Intl. Ltd.	Analytix Systems Pvt. Ltd.	27-Jul-06	Unlisted	Cash, ESOP	USA
111	512093	Cranes Software Intl. Ltd.	Engineering Technology Associates In	7-Jan-08	Unlisted	Cash	USA
112	512093	Cranes Software Intl. Ltd.	Cubeware GmbH	24-Jul-08	Unlisted	Cash, stock	Germany
113	512579	Gujarat N R E Coke Ltd.	Gujarat N R E Resources NL	31-Aug-07	Listed	Stock	Australia
114	514043	Himatsingka Seide Ltd.	DWI Holdings Inc.	19-Oct-07	Unlisted	Cash	USA
115	517195	O R G Informatics Ltd.	D G I T Solutions Pte. Ltd.	3-Jan-07	Unlisted	Cash	Singapore
116	517334	Motherson Sumi Systems Ltd.	Empire Rubber	15-May-07	Unlisted	Cash	Australia
117	517344	Mindteck (India) Ltd.	ISS Consultants Inc.	3-Apr-06	Unlisted	Cash	USA
118	517344	Mindteck (India) Ltd.	Primetech Solutions Inc.	2-Apr-08	Unlisted	Stock	USA
119	517354	Havells India Ltd.	Greek Electrical Company	4-Oct-05	Unlisted	Cash	Greece
120	517354	Havells India Ltd.	SLI Sylvania	13-Mar-07	Unlisted	Cash	Netherland

(continued)

(continued)

Sr. No.	BSE code	Acquirer name	Target name	Announcement date	Target type	Payment method	Country
121	517518	Lloyd Electric & Engineering Ltd.	Luvata Czech S R O	14-May-08	Unlisted	Cash	Czech Republic
122	520077	Amtek Auto Ltd.	Ketlon Ltd.	7-Nov-07	Unlisted	Cash	UK
123	520086	Sical Logistics Ltd.	Bergen Offshore Logistics Pte	27-Sep-06	Unlisted	Cash	Singapore
124	521082	Spentex Industries Ltd.	Tashkent To'yetpa Tekstil LLC	27-Jul-06	Govt.	Cash	Uzbekistan
125	521082	Spentex Industries Ltd.	Schoeller Litvinov ks	3-Jul-07	Unlisted	Cash	Czech Republic
126	522004	Batliboi Ltd.	Quickmill Inc.	26-Mar-07	Unlisted	Cash	Canada
127	522295	Control Print Ltd.	Liberty Chemicals(Pvt) Ltd.	8-Apr-11	Priv.	Cash	Sri Lanka
128	523204	Aban Offshore Ltd.	Rowan Texas	5-Sep-05	Unlisted	Cash	USA
129	523204	Aban Offshore Ltd.	West Africa Drilling N.V	4-Feb-06	Unlisted	Cash	Netherland
130	523283	Superhouse Leathers Ltd.	Linea De Seguridad SL	20-Sep-12	Priv.	Cash	Spain
131	523704	Mastek Ltd.	Systems Task Group Intl Ltd.	10-Mar-08	Unlisted	Cash, future cash earn	USA
132	523820	Neo Corp Intl. Ltd.	Europlast Ltd.	26-Jun-08	Unlisted	Cash	UK
133	524404	Marksans Pharma Ltd.	Hale Group	31-Dec-07	Unlisted	Cash	UK
134	524404	Marksans Pharma Ltd.	Relonchem Ltd.	28-Aug-08	Unlisted	Cash	UK
135	524404	Marksans Pharma Ltd.	Time-Cap Labs Inc.	30-Jun-15	Priv.	Cash	United States
136	524715	Sun Pharmaceutical Industries Ltd.	Chattem Chemicals Inc.	27-Nov-08	Unlisted	Cash	USA
137	524794	Matrix Laboratories Ltd.	Docpharma NV,	19-Jun-05	Listed	Cash	Belgium
138	524804	Aurobindo Pharma Ltd.	Milpharm Ltd.	10-Feb-06	Unlisted	Cash	UK
139	524804	Aurobindo Pharma Ltd.	Pharmacin International B.V.	29-Dec-06	Unlisted	Cash	Netherland
140	524804	Aurobindo Pharma Ltd.	TAD Italy IP	24-Mar-08	Unlisted	Cash	Itlay

(continued)

(continued)

Sr. No.	BSE code	Acquirer name	Target name	Announcement date	Target type	Payment method	Country
141	526137	Shetron Ltd.	Shetron Sobemi Europe N.V.	14-Nov-07	Unlisted	Cash	Belgium
142	526299	MphasiS BFL Ltd.	Princeton Consulting Ltd.	14-Feb-05	Priv.	CASHO	United Kingdom
143	526407	Ritesh Industries Ltd.	Catalina Bay Inc.	27-Jun-07	Unlisted	Cash	USA
144	526433	A S M Technologies Ltd.	Enterprise Software Resources (ESR)	29-Nov-07	Unlisted	Cash	USA
145	526797	Greenply Industries Ltd.	GIL Intercontinental Pte Ltd.	28-Jul-06	Priv.	Cash	Singapore
146	526853	Bilcare Ltd.	ProClinical Inc.	15-Jul-05	Unlisted	Cash	USA
147	526853	Bilcare Ltd.	DHP Ltd.	19-Sep-06	Unlisted	Cash	UK
148	526853	Bilcare Ltd.	Singular ID Pte Ltd.	4-Jan-08	Priv.	Cash	Singapore
149	530007	JK Tyres & Industries Ltd.	Compania Hulera Tornel SA	11-Apr-08	Priv.	CASHO	Mexico
150	530019	Jubilant Organosys Ltd.	Target Research Associates Inc.	5-Oct-05	Unlisted	Cash	USA
151	530019	Jubilant Organosys Ltd.	Hollisterstier Laboratories L L C	25-Apr-07	Unlisted	Cash	USA
152	530549	Shilpa Medicare Ltd.	Loba Feinchemie	31-Mar-08	Unlisted	Cash	Austria
153	530555	Paramount Communications Ltd.	AEI Cables Ltd.	4-Sep-07	Listed	Cash	UK
154	530703	Info-Drive Software Ltd.	Bhari Information Technologies SDN BHD (BITECH)	13-Sep-07	Unlisted	Cash	Malaysia
155	531131	Mascon Global Ltd.	ebusinessware Inc.	15-May-08	Unlisted	Cash	USA
156	531500	Rajesh Exports Ltd.	Valcambi Gold Refineries Hldg	2-Jul-15	Private	CASHO	Switzerland
157	531642	Marico Ltd.	Enaleni Pharmaceuticals Consumer Division (Pty) Ltd.	31-Oct-07	Unlisted	Cash	USA
158	531675	Tricom India Ltd.	Tricom Document Management Inc.	23-Jul-04	Priv.	Cash	United States
159	531816	Panoramic Universal Ltd.	Future Travels	24-Dec-07	Unlisted	Cash	USA

(continued)

(continued)

Sr. No.	BSE code	Acquirer name	Target name	Announcement date	Target type	Payment method	Country
160	531816	IT Hospitality Inc.	Holiday Inn Hotel,Hudson,Ohio	31-Oct-05	Priv.	Cash	United States
161	531847	Asian Star Co Ltd.	Inter Gems DMCC	28-Apr-08	Unlisted	Cash	Dubai
162	531897	Accentia Technologies Ltd.	GSR Systems Inc.	2-Jul-07	Unlisted	Cash, stock	USA
	531897	Accentia Technologies Ltd.	GSR Physicians Billing Service	2-Jul-07	Unlisted	Cash, stock	USA
163	532129	Hexaware Technologies Ltd.	Focus Frame Inc.	7-Nov-06	Unlisted	Cash	USA
164	532133	IFGL Refractories Ltd.	Monocon Intl Refractories Ltd.	5-Aug-05	Listed	Cash	UK
164	532249	SQL Star International Ltd.	TalentFuse Inc.	17-Apr-07	Priv.	Cash	United States
165	532254	Polaris Software Lab Ltd.	Seec Inc.	30-Sep-08	Unlisted	Cash	USA
166	532268	Kale Consultants Ltd.	Zero Octa UK Ltd.	7-Aug-07	Unlisted	Cash	UK
167	532281	H C L Technologies Ltd.	Capital Stream Inc.	20-Feb-08	Unlisted	Cash	USA
168	532281	H C L Technologies Ltd.	Control Point Solutions, Inc.	25-Aug-08	Unlisted	Cash	USA
169	532282	Amtek India Ltd.	Sigma Cast Group Ltd.	7-Feb-05	Unlisted	Cash	UK
170	532283	Kaashyap Technologies Ltd.	Logistics Solutions Inc.	4-Jul-07	Unlisted	Cash	USA
171	532296	Glenmark Pharmaceuticals Ltd.	Laboratorios Klinger	2-Apr-04	Unlisted	Cash	Brazil
172	532300	Wockhardt Ltd.	C P Pharmaceuticals Ltd.	8-Jul-03	Unlisted	Cash	UK
173	532300	Wockhardt Ltd.	Pinewood Laboratories Ltd.	3-Oct-06	Unlisted	Cash	Ireland
174	532300	Wockhardt Ltd.	Negma Lerads SAS	3-May-07	Unlisted	Cash	France
175	532301	Tata Coffee Ltd.	Eight'O Clock Coffee Holdings Inc.	25-Jun-06	Unlisted	Cash	USA
176	532311	Amex Information Technologies	Siacom	22-Dec-03	Unlisted	Stock	UK

(continued)

(continued)

Sr. No.	BSE code	Acquirer name	Target name	Announcement date	Target type	Payment method	Country
177	532312	Geometric Ltd.	TekSoft Inc.	4-Jan-05	Unlisted	Cash	USA
178	532318	Gemini Communication Ltd.	Point Red Tech	14-Jun-06	Unlisted	Cash	USA
179	532321	Cadila Healthcare Ltd.	Quimica e Farmaceutica Nikkho do Brasil Ltd.	25-Jun-07	Unlisted	Cash	Brazil
180	532321	Cadila Healthcare Ltd.	Laboratories Combix	30-May-08	Unlisted	Cash	Spain
181	532321	Cadila Healthcare Ltd.	Etna Biotech Srl	11-Nov-08	Unlisted	Cash	Itlay
182	532321	Cadila Healthcare Ltd.	Nippon Universal Pharm	20-Apr-07	Unlisted	Cash	Japan
183	532322	Elder Pharmaceuticals Ltd.	Max Healthcare Ltd.	1-Jul-13	Priv.	Cash less	United Kingdom
184	532341	Logix Microsystems Ltd.	Prize Corp-ReckonUp Prod Line	2-Aug-07	Unlisted	Cash	USA
185	532347	Helios & Matheson Information Technology Ltd.	Maruthi Info Tech Inc.	31-Aug-04	Unlisted	Cash	USA
186	532347	Helios & Matheson Information Technology Ltd.	vMoksha Technologies Inc USA	12-Apr-05	Unlisted	Cash	USA
187	532348	Subex Ltd.	Alcatel's Fraud Management Group	28-Jul-04	Unlisted	Cash	France
188	532348	Subex Ltd.	Azure Solutions Ltd.	25-Apr-06	Unlisted	Cash, stock	UK
189	532348	Subex Ltd.	Syndesis Ltd.	18-Jan-07	Unlisted	Cash	Canada
190	532368	L G S Global Ltd.	Lanco Global Systems Inc.	14-Dec-05	Unlisted	Stock	USA
191	532372	Virinchi Technologies Ltd.	KSoft Systems Inc.	27-Aug-05	Priv.	Cash, preferential shares	United States

(continued)

(continued)

Sr. No.	BSE code	Acquirer name	Target name	Announcement date	Target type	Payment method	Country
192	532386	California Software Co. Ltd.	International Innovations Inc.	13-Nov-07	Unlisted	Cash	USA
193	532391	Opto Circuits (India) Ltd.	Eurocor GmbH	20-Oct-05	Unlisted	Cash	Germany
194	532391	Opto Circuits (India) Ltd.	Criticare Systems Inc.	25-Feb-08	Listed	Cash	USA
195	532391	Opto Circuits(India)Ltd.	Cardiac Science	2-Dec-10	Listed	Cash	USA
196	532395	I T & T Ltd.	Axis Inc.	19-Dec-03	Unlisted	Cash	USA
197	532400	K P I T Cummins Infosystems Ltd.	Panex Consulting Inc.	25-Aug-03	Unlisted	Cash, ESOP	USA
198	532407	Moschip Semiconductor Technology Ltd.	Verasity Technologies Inc.	20-Mar-03	Listed	Stock	USA
199	532411	Visesh Infotecnics Ltd.	Opentech Thai Network	7-Nov-03	Priv.	Cash	Thailand
200	532424	Godrej Consumer Products Ltd.	Godrej Global Mid East F Z E	1-Oct-07	Unlisted	Cash	Sharjah
201	532424	Godrej Consumer Products Ltd.	Argencos SA	3-Jun-10	Priv.	Cash	Argentina
202	532432	United Spirits Ltd.	Whyte & Mackay Group Plc.	16-May-07	Unlisted	Cash	UK
203	532440	M P S Ltd.	Interactive Composition Corpn.	6-Mar-06	Unlisted	Cash	USA
204	532466	Oracle Financial Services Software Ltd.	SuperSolutions Corp	16-Dec-03	Unlisted	Cash	USA
205	532479	I S M T Ltd.	Structo Hydraulics A B	5-Jun-07	Unlisted	Cash	Sweden
206	532517	Patni Computer Systems Ltd.	ZAiQ Technologies Inc.	29-Jun-06	Unlisted	Cash	USA

(continued)

(continued)

Sr. No.	BSE code	Acquirer name	Target name	Announcement date	Target type	Payment method	Country
207	532517	Patni Computer Systems Ltd.	Cymbal Corp	12-Oct-04	Priv.	Cash	United States
208	532517	Patni Computer Systems Ltd.	Taratec Development Corp	23-Jul-07	Priv.	CASHO	United States
209	532521	Four Soft Ltd.	Comex Frontier Ltd.	27-May-05	Unlisted	Cash	Singapore
210	532521	Four Soft Ltd.	Transaxiom Holding A/S	20-Dec-06	Unlisted	Cash, stock	Denmark
212	532526	Dishman Pharma & Chem Ltd.	CARBOGEN AMCIS AG	22-Aug-06	Unlisted	Cash	Switzerland
213	532526	Dishman Pharma & Chem Ltd.	Solvay Pharmaceuticals-Fine	8-Jul-07	Unlisted	Cash	Netherland
214	532526	Dishman Pharma & Chem Ltd.	Synprotec Ltd.	20-Apr-05	Priv.	Cash	United Kingdom
215	532531	Strides Arcolab Ltd.	Haw Par Healthcare	1-Sep-06	Unlisted	Cash	Singapore
216	532531	Strides Arcolab Ltd.	Diaspa S P A	6-Aug-07	Unlisted	Cash	Itlay
217	532531	Strides Arcolab Ltd.	Drug Houses of Australia(Asia)	1-Sep-06	Sub.	CASHO	Singapore
218	532540	Tata Consultancy Services Ltd.	Finl Network Svcs Pty Ltd.	20-Oct-05	Unlisted	Cash	Australia
219	532541	N I I T Technologies Ltd.	Room Solutions Ltd.	8-May-06	Unlisted	Cash	UK
220	532541	N I I T Technologies Ltd.	Softec Gmbh	28-Feb-08	Listed	Cash	Germany
221	532607	Ontrack Systems Ltd.	Intellisys Technology LLC	17-May-06	Unlisted	Stock	USA
222	532607	Ontrack Systems Ltd.	I Q Technologies LLC	1-Aug-08	Unlisted	Cash	USA
223	532628	3I Infotech Ltd.	Regulus Group L L C	29-Apr-08	Unlisted	Cash	USA
224	532643	Shree Ganesh Forgings Ltd.	Hertecant NV (OutoKumpu group)	9-Apr-07	Unlisted	Cash	Belgium

(continued)

(continued)

Sr. No.	BSE code	Acquirer name	Target name	Announcement date	Target type	Payment method	Country
225	532663	Sasken Communication	Botnia Hightech Oy	26-Jul-06	Priv.	CASHO	Finland
226	532667	Suzlon Energy Ltd.	Eve Holding NV	17-Mar-06	Priv.	CASHO	Belgium
227	532668	AurionPro Solutions Ltd.	SENA Systems Inc, USA	4-Mar-08	Unlisted	Stock	USA
228	532672	Glodyne Technoserve Ltd.	Links Group International Inc.	29-Mar-07	Unlisted	Cash	USA
229	532672	Glodyne Technoserve Ltd.	Front Office Technologies Inc.	31-Oct-07	Unlisted	Cash	USA
230	532694	Bartronics India Ltd.	Proximities Inc.	29-Jan-08	Unlisted	Cash	USA
231	532715	Gitanjali Gems Ltd.	Rogers Ltd. Inc.	20-Nov-07	Unlisted	Cash	USA
232	532715	Gitanjali Gems Ltd.	Crown aim Ltd.	5-Dec-11	Priv.	Cash	Hongkong
233	532715	Gitanjali Gems Ltd.	Japan Jewel K K	5-Mar-12	Priv.	Cash	Japan
234	532735	R Systems International Ltd.	Sento Europe	28-Dec-07	Unlisted	Cash	France
235	532735	R Systems International Ltd.	Computaris International Ltd.	13-Dec-10	Priv.	CASHO	United Kingdom
236	532735	R Systems International Ltd.	WebConverse, Inc.	24-Aug-06	Unlisted	Cash	USA
237	532735	R Systems International Ltd.	IBIZCS Group Pte. Limited, Singapore	1-May-15	Priv.	Cash	Singapore
238	532748	Prime Focus Ltd.	Post Logic Studios	28-Nov-07	Unlisted	Cash	USA
		Prime Focus Ltd.	Frantic Films Corp-Visual	28-Nov-07	Unlisted	Cash	USA
239	532749	Allcargo Global Logistics Ltd.	FCL Marine Agencies, Rotterdam	18-Dec-13	Unlisted	Cash	Netherlands
240	532749	Allcargo Global Logistics Ltd.	Econocaribe Consolidators Inc.	27-Sep-13	Priv.	Cash	United States

(continued)

(continued)

Sr. No.	BSE code	Acquirer name	Target name	Announcement date	Target type	Payment method	Country
241	532749	Allcargo Global Logistics Ltd.	China Consolidation Services Shipping Ltd. and Ningbo Star Express Shipping Co. Ltd.	25-Oct-10	Unlisted	Cash	Singapore
242	532761	Hov Services Ltd.	Lason Inc.	26-Feb-07	Sub.	Cash	United States
243	532761	HOV Services Ltd.	SOURCECORP Inc.	14-Mar-11	Sub.	Stock	United States
244	532783	LT Foods Ltd.	Kusha Inc.	24-Dec-07	Priv.	cash	United States
245	532791	Pyramid Saimira Theatre Ltd.	FunAsia	30-Oct-07	Priv.	Cash	United States
246	532801	Cambridge Tech Ent Ltd	Comcreation Inc.	28-May-07	Priv.	CASHO	United States
247	532801	Cambridge Tech Ent Ltd	Reilly & Associates Inc.	19-Jul-07	Priv.	Cash	United States
248	532808	Pearl Global Industries Limited	FX Imports Ltd.	6-Dec-07	Priv.	Cash	United Kingdom
249	532832	Indiabulls Real Estate Ltd.	Dev Property Development PLC	28-Feb-08	Listed	Stock	UK
250	532834	Camlin Fine Chemicals Ltd.	Borregaard Italia	16-Dec-10	Unlisted	Cash	Italy
251	532835	ICRA Ltd.	Sapphire International Inc.	20-Mar-09	Sub.	Cash	United States
252	532856	Time Technoplast Ltd.	Gulf Powerbeat WLL	27-Dec-07	Priv.	Cash	Bahrain
253	532866	Quintegra Solutions Ltd.	PA Corp	3-Dec-07	Priv.	CASHO	United States
254	532927	eClerx Invesments Ltd.	Agilyst Inc.	12-Apr-12	Priv.	CASHO	United States
255	532927	eClerx Services Ltd.	CLX Europe SpA	31-Mar-15	Priv.	Cash	Italy
256	532967	Kiri Holding Singapore Pvt Ltd.	DyStar Textilfarben GmbH	4-Feb-10	Sub.	Cash	Germany

(continued)

(continued)

Sr. No.	BSE code	Acquirer name	Target name	Announcement date	Target type	Payment method	Country
257	590041	Kavveri Telecom Products Ltd.	DCI Digital Communications Ltd.	25-Apr-07	Unlisted	Cash	Canada
258	590041	Kavveri Telecom Products Ltd.	Spotwave Wireless Inc.	17-Jan-08	Unlisted	Cash	Canada
259	590051	Saksoft Ltd.	Acuma Group Ltd.	3-Oct-06	Priv.	CASHO	United Kingdom
260	590051	Saksoft Inc.	Electronic Data Professionals	1-Jan-13	Priv.	Cash	United States

Appendix C
Sample Companies in Event Study (Cross-Border Partial/Majority Control Acquisitions)

N. Rani et al., *Mergers and Acquisitions*, India Studies
in Business and Economics, DOI 10.1007/978-981-10-2203-6

Sr. No.	BSE code	Acquirer name	Target name	Announcement Date	Stake acquired	Target type	Payment method	Country
1	500024	Assam Co(India)Ltd.	Austin Exploration Ltd.	15-May-06	51	Unlisted	Cash	Australia
2	500096	Dabur India Ltd.	African Consumer Care Ltd.	24-Jul-04	90	Unlisted	Cash	Nigeria
3	500102	Ballarpur Industries Ltd.	Sabah Forest Industries (SFI) Sdn Bhd,	5-Jun-06	97.8	Unlisted	Cash	Malaysia
4	500135	Essel Propack Ltd.	Medical Engineering & Design	5-Sep-08	74	Unlisted	Cash	USA
5	500171	G H C L Ltd.	S. C. Bega Upsom S.A	7-Dec-05	65	Unlisted	Cash	Romania
6	500179	HCL Infosystems Ltd.	NTS Group	8-Jul-10	60	Priv.	cash	Utd Arab Em
7	500189	Hinduja Ventures Ltd.	Customer Contact Centre (c3)	30-Oct-03	51	Unlisted	Cash	Philippines
8	500219	Jain Irrigation Systems Ltd.	Thomas Machines SA	20-Nov-06	69.75	Unlisted	Cash	Switzerland
9	500219	Jain Irrigation Systems Ltd.	Cascade Specialties Inc.	3-Mar-08	51	Unlisted	Cash	USA
10	500257	Lupin Ltd.	Pharma Dynamics	18-Sep-08	60	Unlisted	Cash	South Africa
11	500257	Lupin Ltd.	Multicare Pharm Philippines	26-Mar-09	51	Priv.	Cash	Philippines
12	500331	Pidilite Industries Ltd.	Chemson Asia Pte Ltd.	27-Jan-05	75	Unlisted	Cash	Singapore
13	500331	Pidilite Industries Ltd.	Bamco(Thailand)Co Ltd.	1-Mar-06	75	Unlisted	Cash	Thailand
14	500425	Ambuja Cements Ltd.	Dang Cement Industries Pvt Ltd.	6-Jun-11	85	Priv.	Cash	Nepal
15	500470	Tata Steel Ltd.	Millennium Steel PCL	15-Dec-05	62.89	Listed	Cash	Thailand
16	500520	Mahindra & Mahindra Ltd.	Bristlecone Inc.	9-Feb-04	51	Listed	Cash	USA
17	500520	Mahindra & Mahindra Ltd.	Stokes Forgings Ltd.	4-Jan-06	98.76	Unlisted	Cash	UK
18	500520	Mahindra & Mahindra Ltd.	JECO Holding AG	28-Sep-06	67.9	Unlisted	Cash	Germany
19	500520	Mahindra & Mahindra Ltd.	Schoeneweiss & Co GmbH	22-Dec-06	90.47	Unlisted	Cash	Germany
20	500570	Tata Motors Ltd.	Miljobil Grenland AS	14-Oct-08	50.3	Unlisted	Cash	UK

(continued)

(continued)

Sr. No.	BSE code	Acquirer name	Target name	Announcement Date	Stake acquired	Target type	Payment method	Country
21	500770	Tata Chemicals Ltd.	Brunner Mond Group Ltd.	24-Nov-05	63.7	Listed	Cash	UK
22	500800	Tata Global Beverage Ltd. (formerly Tata Tea)	Suntyco Holding Limited	26-Mar-09	51	Priv.	Cash	Cyprus
23	500900	Sterlite Industries (India) Ltd.	Konkola Copper Mines pl	20-Aug-04	51	Unlisted	Cash	Zambia
24	502742	Sintex Industries Ltd.	Wausaukee Composites Inc.	1-Jun-07	81	Unlisted	Cash	USA
25	502742	Sintex Industries Ltd.	GEIGER technik GmbH	31-Jul-08	90	Unlisted	Cash	Germany
26	505854	T R F Ltd.	York Transport Equipment (Asia) Pte Ltd.	23-Jul-07	51	Unlisted	Cash	Singapore
27	506480	IDL Industries Limited	Gulf Oil Yantai Co Ltd.	21-Apr-05	51	Unlisted	Cash	China
28	513375	Carborundum Universal Ltd	OAO Volzhsky Abrasive Works	7-Sep-07	84	Listed	Cash	Russia
29	514043	Himatsingka Seide Ltd.	Giuseppe Bellora SpA	29-Jan-07	70	Unlisted	Cash	Itlay
30	514043	Himatsingka Seide Ltd.	Divatex Home Fashions Inc.	3-Jul-07	80	Unlisted	Cash	USA
31	514162	Welspun India Ltd.	CHT Holdings Ltd.	3-Jul-06	85	Unlisted	Cash	UK
32	514162	Welspun India Ltd.	Sorema - Tapates e Cortinas de Banho, SA	19-Dec-07	76	Unlisted	Cash	Portugal
33	517140	Moser Baer India Ltd.	Koninklijke Philips Electronics NV	6-Feb-07	81	Unlisted	Cash	Netherland
34	520077	Amtek Auto Ltd.	GWK Group Ltd.	16-Mar-04	85	Unlisted	Cash	UK
35	520077	Amtek Auto Ltd.	Zelter GmbH	5-Jul-05	70	Unlisted	Cash	Germany
36	521070	Alok Industries Ltd.	Mileta A S	26-Sep-06	60	Unlisted	Cash	Czech Republic
37	522004	Batliboi Ltd.	AESA Air Engineering SA	20-Jun-07	70	Unlisted	Cash	France
38	523236	Shrenuj & Company Ltd.	Simon Golub & Sons Inc.	8-May-07	84.6	Unlisted	Cash	USA

(continued)

(continued)

Sr. No.	BSE code	Acquirer name	Target name	Announcement Date	Stake acquired	Target type	Payment method	Country
39	523704	Mastek Ltd.	Vector Insurance Services LLC	16-Jul-07	90	Unlisted	Cash	USA
40	524404	Marksans Pharma Ltd.	Nova Pharmaceuticals Australasia Pty. Ltd.	2-Mar-06	60	Unlisted	Cash	Australia
41	524715	Sun Pharmaceutical Industries Ltd.	Caraco Pharmaceutical Laboratories Ltd.	3-Feb-04	60	Listed	Cash	USA
42	524715	Sun Pharmaceutical Industries Ltd.	Taro Pharmaceutical	21-May-07	51	Listed	Cash	Israel
43	524735	Hikal Ltd.	Marsing & Co Ltd. A/S	6-Sep-04	50.1	Priv.	Cash	Denmark
44	524816	Natco Pharma Ltd.	Nicks Drugs	31-Jan-06	65	Priv.	Cash	United States
45	526015	Kemrock Industries & Exports Ltd.	Top Glass Spa.	11-Feb-08	51	Unlisted	Cash	Itlay
46	526109	Pricol Ltd.	Melling do Brasil Componentes	12-Dec-14	99.99	Priv.	Cash	Brazil
47	526881	Financial Technologies (India) Ltd.	IC X Platform (Pty.) Ltd.	10-Apr-08	90	Unlisted	Cash	South Africa
48	530019	Jubilant Organosys Ltd.	Trinity Laboratories, Inc.	1-Jul-05		Unlisted	Cash	USA
49	530079	Faze Three Ltd.	Pana Textil Gmbh	13-Nov-07	76	Unlisted	Cash	Germany
50	530239	Suven Pharmaceuticals	Synthon Chiragenics Corp	20-May-03	51	Unlisted	Cash	USA
51	530703	Info-Drive Software Ltd.	Technoprism Inc.	25-Aug-08	51	Unlisted	Cash	USA
52	530707	Aftek Infosys Ltd.	V-Soft Inc.	29-Aug-05	51	Unlisted	Cash	USA
53	531642	Marico Ltd.	Sundari LLC	26-Feb-03	70.5	Unlisted	Cash	USA
54	531897	Accentia Technologies Ltd.	Oak Technologies Inc.	1-Apr-08	51	Unlisted	Cash	USA

(continued)

(continued)

Sr. No.	BSE code	Acquirer name	Target name	Announcement Date	Stake acquired	Target type	Payment method	Country
55	532221	Sonata Software Ltd.	TUI InfoTec GmbH	27-Sep-06	51	Listed	Cash	Germany
56	532281	H C L Technologies Ltd.	Aalayance Inc.	17-Dec-04	51	Unlisted	Cash	USA
57	532296	Glenmark Pharmaceuticals Ltd.	Medicamenta A.S	26-Mar-07	90	Unlisted	Cash	Czech Republic
58	532296	Glenmark Pharmaceuticals Ltd.	Servycal SA	26-Oct-05	51	Sub.	Cash	Argentina
59	532341	Logix Microsystems Ltd.	AOA Izmo LLC USA	5-Jan-08	51	Priv.	Stock, cash	United States
60	532347	Helios & Matheson Information Technology Ltd.	The A Consulting Team Inc., NY	3-Apr-06	51	Listed	Cash	USA
61	532386	California Software Co. Ltd.	CODEX Co. Ltd.	28-Jul-06	66	Unlisted	Cash	Japan
62	532408	Megasoft Ltd.	Boston Communications Group Inc.	11-Jul-07	51	Listed	Cash	USA
63	532424	Godrej Consumer Products Ltd.	Darling Group Holdings	1-Jun-11	51	Priv.	Cash	Nigeria
64	532424	Godrej Consumer Products Ltd.	Frika Hair (Pty) Ltd.	6-Jan-15	60	Priv.	Cash	South Africa
65	532466	Oracle Financial Services Software Ltd.	Castek Software Inc.	19-Aug-05	51	Unlisted	Cash	Canada
66	532523	Biocon Ltd.	AxiCorp GmbH	11-Feb-08	70	Unlisted	Cash	Germany
67	532526	Dishman Pharma & Chem Ltd.	I03S Ltd. (IO3S)	19-Dec-05	51	Listed	Cash, option	Switzerland
68	532531	Strides Arcolab Ltd.	Biopharma	1-Jun-05	60	Unlisted	Cash	Venezuela
69	532540	Tata Consultancy Services Ltd.	TKS-Teknosoft SA	31-Oct-06	75	Unlisted	Cash	Switzerland
70	532605	JBM Auto Ltd.	ThyssenKrupp JBM Pvt Ltd.	17-Apr-09	73.89	Priv.	Cash	UK
71	532656	Facor Alloys Ltd.	Dillenburg Bergen NH Realty BV	5-Mar-13	51	Priv.	CASHO	Netherlands

(continued)

(continued)

Sr. No.	BSE code	Acquirer name	Target name	Announcement Date	Stake acquired	Target type	Payment method	Country
72	532668	AurionPro Solutions Ltd.	E2E Infotech Ltd.	25-Apr-07	51	Sub.	Stock	United Kingdom
73	532678	Bombay Rayon Fashions Ltd.	DPJ Clothing Ltd.	23-Feb-07	70	Unlisted	Cash	UK
74	532696	Educomp Solutions Ltd.	Savicca Inc.	18-Sep-07	70.05	Unlisted	Cash	Canada
75	532696	Educomp Solutions Ltd.	Learning.com	20-May-08	51	Unlisted	Cash	USA
76	532715	Gitanjali Gems Ltd.	Tri-Star Worldwide Inc.	14-Feb-07	70	Priv.	Cash	United States
77	532715	Gitanjali Gems Ltd.	Giantti Italia S.R.L.	28-Dec-10	90	Priv.	Cash	Itlay
78	532715	Gitanjali Gems Ltd.	Diamlink Inc. (Diamlink) New York	13-Jul-09	51	Priv.	Cash	USA
79	532739	Plethico Pharmaceuticals Ltd.	Natrol Inc.	19-Nov-07	51	Listed	Cash	USA
80	532790	Tanla Solutions Ltd.	Openbit Oy	5-Jun-08	85	Priv.	CASHO	Finland
81	532804	Technocraft Industries(India)	Swift Engineering Inc.	15-Apr-13	59	Priv.	Cash	Canada
82	532808	Pearl Global Industries Limited	Simple Approach Ltd.	14-Jan-08	78	Unlisted	Cash	Hongkong
83	532875	Allied Digital Services Ltd.	EnPointe Global Services Llc	9-July-08	80.5	Listed	Cash, stock	USA
84	532887	Sujana Towers Ltd.	Telesuprecon Ltd.	18-Jun-08	51	Priv.	Cash	Mauritius
85	533022	20 Microns Ltd.	20 Microns SDN BHD	17-Mar-09	99.9	Priv.	Cash	Malaysia
86	533412	Aanjaneya Lifecare Ltd.	Eros Pharmachem Pte Ltd.	12-Mar-12	90	Priv.	Cash	Singapore
87	533482	Readymade Steel India Ltd.	KH Foges Pte Ltd.	28-Mar-12	90	Priv.	Cash	Singapore

Appendix D
Sample Companies in Event Study (Domestic Complete Acquisitions)

N. Rani et al., *Mergers and Acquisitions*, India Studies
in Business and Economics, DOI 10.1007/978-981-10-2203-6

Sr. No.	BSE code	Acquirer name	Target name	Announcement date	Target type	Payment method
1	500002	A B B Ltd.	Raman Boards Ltd.	21-Dec-06	Unlisted	Cash
2	500003	Aegis Logistics Ltd.	Konkan Storage Systems (Kochi) Pvt. Ltd.	26-Mar-07	Unlisted	Cash
3	500009	Ambalal Sarabhai Enterprises Ltd.	Suvik Hi-Tek Pvt Ltd.	17-Sep-08	Unlisted	Cash
4	500024	Assam Co(India)Ltd.	Duncan Macneill Power	18-Dec-10	Priv.	OTHER
5	500032	Bajaj Hindusthan Ltd.	Parashar Sugars Pvt Ltd.	8-Jun-05	Priv.	Cash
6	500067	Blue Star Ltd.	Naseer Electricals Pvt. Ltd.	5-Dec-07	Unlisted	Cash
7	500086	Exide Industries Ltd.	Caldyne Automatics Ltd.	20-Jul-07	Unlisted	Cash
8	500092	Crisil Ltd.	Irevna Research Services Ltd.	20-Oct-04	Unlisted	Cash
9	500096	Dabur India Ltd.	Balsara Home Products Limited	28-Jan-05	Listed	Cash
	500096	Dabur India Ltd.	Besta Cosmetics Ltd.	28-Jan-05	Listed	Cash
10	500103	Bharat Heavy Electricals Ltd.	Bharat Heavy Plate and Vessels Ltd.	12-May-08	Public Sector Undertaking	Cash
11	500125	E I D-Parry (India) Ltd.	Parry Nutraceuticals Ltd.	19-Jul-06	Unlisted	Cash
12	500135	Essel Propack Ltd.	Packaging India Pvt. Ltd.	30-Aug-06	Unlisted	Cash
13	500179	H C L Infosystems Ltd.	Natural Technologies Pvt Ltd. (NTPL)	5-May-08	Unlisted	Cash
14	500193	Hotel Leelaventure Ltd.	Kovalam Hotels Ltd.	22-Jul-05	unlisted	Cash
15	500239	KG Denim Ltd.	Trigger Apparels Ltd.	30-Jan-06	Priv.	Cash
16	500241	Kirloskar Brothers Ltd.	ABAN Constructions Pvt Ltd.	29-Sep-06	Unlisted	Cash
17	500241	Kirloskar Brothers Ltd.	Gondwana Engineers Ltd.	10-Sep-07	Unlisted	Cash
18	500250	LG Balkrishnan & Bros Ltd.	Apten Forgings Pvt Ltd.	3-Jul-03	Priv.	cash
19	500250	LG Balakrishnan & Bros Ltd.	LGB Textiles Ltd.	20-Nov-04	Priv.	cash
20	500257	Lupin Ltd.	Lupin Herbal Pvt	13-Aug-04	Unlisted	Cash

(continued)

(continued)

Sr. No.	BSE code	Acquirer name	Target name	Announcement date	Target type	Payment method
21	500257	Lupin Ltd.	Rubamin Laboratories Ltd.	27-09-07	Unlisted	Cash
22	500300	Grasim Industries Ltd.	Harish Cement Ltd.	7-Sep-06	Unlisted	Cash
23	500302	Piramal Healthcare Ltd.	Health Line Pvt. Ltd.	22-Jan-08	Unlisted	Cash
24	500303	Aditya Birla Nuvo Ltd.	TransWorks Information Services Pvt	21-Jun-03	Unlisted	Cash
25	500329	Pentamedia Graphics Ltd.	Intelivision Ltd.	25-Aug-03	Unlisted	Stock
26	500339	Rain Commodities Ltd.	Rain Calcining Ltd.	20-Mar-07	Public	SHARES
27	500350	Rajasthan Spinning & Weaving	Mordi Textiles & Processors	21-Mar-05	Priv.	SHARES
28	500354	Rajshree Sugars & Chemicals Ltd.	Trident Sugars Ltd.	21-Apr-06	Listed	Cash
29	500368	Ruchi Soya Inds. Ltd.	Aneja Solvex Ltd.	7-Jan-04	Unlisted	Cash
30	500400	Tata Power Co. Ltd.	Duncans North Hydro Power Company Ltd.	16-Dec-03	Unlisted	Cash
31	500413	Thomas Cook (India) Ltd.	Travel Corporation (India) Ltd.	1-Dec-06	Unlisted	Cash
32	500470	Tata Steel Ltd.	Rawmet Ferrous Inds. Pvt. Ltd.	16-Jan-07	Unlisted	Cash
33	500470	Tata Steel Ltd.	Indian Steel & Wire Products Ltd.	23-Dec-03	Unlisted	Cash
34	500483	Tata Communications Ltd.	DishnetDSL Ltd-Broadband Bus	19-Mar-03	Unlisted	Cash
35	500483	Tata Communications Ltd.	Direct Internet Ltd.	8-May-06	Unlisted	Cash
	500483	Tata Communications Ltd.	Primus Telecommunications India Ltd. (PTIL)	8-May-06	Unlisted	Cash
	500483	Tata Communications Ltd.	Tata Power Broadband Co Ltd.	5-Sep-06	Unlisted	Cash
	500510	Larsen & Toubro Ltd.	Spectrum Infotech Pvt. Ltd.	3-Feb-06	Unlisted	Cash
38	500520	Mahindra & Mahindra Ltd.	Plexion Technologies (India) Ltd. (Plexion)	12-Dec-05	Unlisted	Cash

(continued)

(continued)

Sr. No.	BSE code	Acquirer name	Target name	Announcement date	Target type	Payment method
39	500550	Siemens Ltd.	Siemens Building Technologies Pvt. Ltd.	20-Feb-03	Unlisted	Cash
40	500550	Siemens Ltd.	Siemens Public Communication Networks Pvt. Ltd.	15-Feb-05	Unlisted	Cash
41	500645	Deepak Fertilisers & Petrochemicals Corpn. Ltd.	Smartchem Technologies Ltd.	24-Oct-03	Listed	Cash
42	500730	Nocil Ltd.	Sushripada Plastics Pvt. Ltd.	22-Feb-07	Unlisted	Cash
43	500780	Zuari Industries Ltd.	Anil Kumar M N Developers Pvt	26-Dec-07	Priv.	OTHER
44	501425	Bombay Burmah Trdg. Corpn. Ltd.	Electromags Automotive Products Pvt. Ltd.	15-Dec-06	Unlisted	Cash
45	501833	Chowgule Steamships Ltd.	Dockyard Pvt Ltd.	17-Oct-06	Unlisted	Cash
46	502937	Kesoram Industries Ltd.	Assam Cotton Mills Ltd.	16-Sep-06	Unlisted	Cash
47	503015	Modern India Ltd.	Modern India Realty & Infrastructures Ltd.	2-Jul-07	Unlisted	Cash
48	503100	Phoenix Mills Ltd.	Big Apple Real Estate Pvt. Ltd.	1-Apr-08	Private	Cash
49	503205	Shree Ram Mills Ltd.	Raghuveer Urban Infrastructure	18-Mar-09	Priv.	OTHER
50	503205	Shree Ram Urban Infrastructure	Shree Ram Realinfra Ventures	26-Mar-10	Sub.	OTHER
51	503699	Geodesic Ltd.	Picopeta Simputers Pvt. Ltd.	24-Nov-05	Unlisted	Cash
52	504067	Zensar Technologies Ltd.	OBT Global Pvt Ltd.	13-Dec-05	Priv.	Cash
53	505872	WPIL Ltd.	Mody Industries(FC)Pvt Ltd.	28-Mar-13	Priv.	cash
54	506142	Vyapar Industries Ltd.	Escoteric Reality Pvt Ltd.	7-Jul-08	Priv.	cash
55	506186	Galaxy Entertainment Corpn. Ltd.	Ceezee Foods Private Ltd.	7-May-04	Unlisted	Cash
56	506197	Bliss G V S Pharma Ltd.	G V S Laboratories Pvt. Ltd.	15-Feb-07	Unlisted	Cash

(continued)

(continued)

Sr. No.	BSE code	Acquirer name	Target name	Announcement date	Target type	Payment method
57	506390	Clariant Chemicals (India) Ltd.	Chemtreat Composites India Pvt. Ltd.	14-Feb-06	Unlisted	Cash
58	506390	Clariant Chemicals (India) Ltd.	Plastichemix Industries	16-Dec-13	Priv.	Cash
59	506559	Siemens Healthcare Diagnostics Ltd.	Dade Behring Diagnostics India Pvt. Ltd.	31-Jul-07	Unlisted	Cash
60	506618	Punjab Chemicals & Crop Protection Ltd.	IA & IC Chem Pvt Ltd.	27-Feb-06	Priv.	Cash
61	507205	Tilaknagar Industries Ltd.	Punjab Expo Breveries Pvt Ltd.	4-Oct-11	Priv.	Cash
62	507685	Wipro Ltd.	Citi Technology Services	23-Dec-08	Unlisted	Cash
63	507856	Uniproducts(India)Ltd.	HP Pelzer India Pvt Ltd.	27-Jan-03	Private	Cash
64	508869	Apollo Hospitals Enterprise Ltd.	Samudra Healthcare Enterprises Ltd.	4-Nov-05	Unlisted	Cash
65	508869	Apollo Hospitals Enterprise Ltd.	Nova Specialty Surgery Pvt Ltd.	6-Jan-15	Sub.	CASHO
66	509557	Garware-Wall Ropes Ltd.	Garware Envi Svcs Pvt Ltd.	9-Apr-08	Priv.	Cash
67	511525	PAN India Corp Ltd.	Shalani Dhoop Pvt Ltd.	21-Nov-08	Priv.	Cash
68	511658	Nettlinx Ltd.	Nettlinx Realty Pvt Ltd.	27-Oct-06	Unlisted	Cash
69	512070	United Phosphorus Ltd.	S W A L Corporation Ltd.	29-Jun-05	Unlisted	Cash
70	512093	Cranes Software Intl. Ltd.	Tilak Autotech Pvt. Ltd.	19-Jun-07	Unlisted	Cash
71	512233	Jaybharat Textiles & Real Estate Ltd.	Real Time Properties Ltd.	2-Mar-07	Unlisted	Cash
72	512267	Media Matrix Worldwide Ltd.	Proximus Knowledge & Techn Services Pvt. Ltd.	22-Oct-07	Unlisted	Cash
73	512529	Sequent Scientific Ltd.	Elixir Chemicals Pvt. Ltd.	20-Apr-06	Unlisted	Cash
74	513121	Oricon Enterprises Ltd.	U S L Auto Services Ltd.	3-May-06	Unlisted	Cash

(continued)

(continued)

Sr. No.	BSE code	Acquirer name	Target name	Announcement date	Target type	Payment method
75	513333	Bhuwalka Steel Industries Ltd.	Benaka Sponge Iron Pvt Ltd.	26-Feb-08	Priv.	CASHO
76	513349	Ajmera Realty & Infra India Ltd.	Jolly Brothers Pvt. Ltd.	31-Oct-06	Unlisted	Cash
77	513414	Sujana Metal Products Ltd.	Glade steels, Sree Ganga Steels	30-May-08	Unlisted	Cash
78	513536	Lesha Energy Resources Ltd.	Gorlas Oil & Gas Pvt Ltd.	19-Mar-09	Priv.	SHARES
79	513583	S B & T International Ltd.	Mimansa Jewellery Pvt. Ltd.	13-Oct-05	Unlisted	Preferential issues
80	514043	Himatsingka Seide Ltd.	A B C Trading Pvt. Ltd.	28-Jan-03	Unlisted	Cash
81	514300	Pioneer Embroideries Ltd.	Mas Embroideries Pvt. Ltd.	3-Apr-06	Unlisted	Cash
82	515055	Anant Raj Industries Ltd.	Jubilant Software Service	3-Sep-10	Priv.	Cash
83	515055	Anant Raj Industries Ltd.	Aakarshak Realators Pvt Ltd.	13-Oct-10	Priv.	Cash
84	516022	Star Paper Mills Ltd.	Pallmall Edusystems & Medicare Services Pvt. Ltd.	6-Sep-07	Unlisted	Cash
85	517035	Ruttonsha Intl Rectifier Ltd.	Orient Semiconductors Pvt Ltd.	19-Jan-08	Priv.	P Shares
86	517546	Alfa Transformers Ltd.	PHOENIX SURGICARE PVT LTD.	11-Nov-08	Unlisted	Cash
87	517973	DMC International Ltd.	Vsoft Services Pvt Ltd.	16-Mar-10	Priv.	SHARES+Cash
88	518091	Anjani Portland Cement Ltd.	Hitech Print Systems Ltd.	4-Aug-07	Priv.	Cash
89	519602	Kellton Tech Solutions Ltd.	Skan Dbydx Software Pvt Ltd.	27-Dec-12	Priv.	Cash
90	521194	SIL Investments Ltd.	Sutlej Textiles & Industries	22-Aug-05	Sub.	Shares
91	522207	Rasandik Engineering Inds. India Ltd.	Rasandik Auto Components Pvt. Ltd.	30-Jul-06	Unlisted	Cash
92	522261	Dolphin Offshore Enterprises (India) Ltd.	Procyon Offshore Services Ltd.	27-Jun-06	Unlisted	Cash
93	523277	GV Films Ltd.	Thangam Theatre	15-May-06	Priv.	Cash

(continued)

(continued)

Sr. No.	BSE code	Acquirer name	Target name	Announcement date	Target type	Payment method
94	523323	Kovai Medical Center & Hospital Ltd.	Idhayam Hospitals Erode Ltd.	21-Mar-07	Unlisted	Cash
95	523387	Triton Corp Ltd.	Maple Esolutions Ltd.	26-Dec-06	Unlisted	Cash
96	523574	Future Retail Ltd.	Officedge India Pvt Ltd.	16-Jan-07	Priv.	Cash
97	523628	Poddar Developers Ltd.	Gopi Resorts Pvt. Ltd.	21-Feb-07	Unlisted	Cash
98	523704	Mastek Ltd.	Keystone Solutions Pvt Ltd.	5-Sep-09	Priv.	Cash
99	524388	Crazy Infotech Ltd.	Animantz Creative Animators Pvt. Ltd.	8-Sep-08	Unlisted	Cash, preferential shares
100	524510	Rathi Graphic Technologies Ltd.	Rathi Rajasthan Steel Mills Ltd.	24-Sep-07	Unlisted	Cash
101	524669	Hester Biosciences Ltd.	Gujarat Agrofarm Ltd.	20-Nov-14	Priv.	Cash
102	524715	Sun Pharmaceutical Inds Ltd.	Ranbaxy Laboratories Ltd.	7-Apr-14	Public	SHARES
103	526025	Globus Power Generation Ltd.	Globus Solar Power Pvt Ltd.	15-Sep-15	Priv.	Cash
104	526217	Hi-Tech Plast Containers Ltd.	Plastic & Precision Machinefabrik Ltd.	10-Mar-03	Priv.	Cash
105	526409	Kalpena Industries Ltd.	Bavaria Associates Pvt. Ltd.	3-Dec-07	Unlisted	Cash
106	526409	Kalpena Industries Ltd.	Kalpana Plastics Pvt Ltd.	23-Mar-05	Private	Stock
107	526610	Vans Information Ltd.	Inhouse Creations Pvt Ltd.	27-Jan-06	Priv.	Combination (Shares, PS, Cash)
108	526723	RDB Industries Ltd.	RDB Realty & Infrastructure	8-Apr-09	Public	Cash
109	526829	Confidence Petroleum India Ltd.	Agwan Coach Pvt. Ltd.	13-Mar-08	Unlisted	Cash
110	526871	Intec Capital Ltd.	Amulet Technologies Pvt Ltd.	12-Mar-12	Priv.	Cash
111	526917	CHD Developers Ltd.	Delight Spirits Pvt Ltd.	1-Oct-13	Priv.	Cash
112	530049	JJ Exporters Ltd.	Pooja Creations Ltd.	14-Jun-05	Unlisted	Stock

(continued)

(continued)

Sr. No.	BSE code	Acquirer name	Target name	Announcement date	Target type	Payment method
113	530091	Zyden Gentec Ltd.	Sree Venkateshwara Medichem	8-Aug-05	Priv.	Cash
114	530139	Kreon Finnancial Services Ltd.	Krios Media Venture Pvt Ltd.	26-Dec-12	Priv.	Cash
115	530407	Epic Energy Ltd.	Sathian Sun Power Systems	16-Jul-08	Priv.	OTHER
116	530773	I V R C L Infrastructures & Projects Ltd.	Alkor Petroo Ltd.	12-Nov-07	Unlisted	Cash
117	530977	Shri Keshav Cements & Infra Ltd.	Katwa Construction Co. Ltd.	16-Aug-07	Unlisted	Cash
118	531241	Linc Pen & Plastics Ltd.	Shree Writing Aids Pvt Ltd.	7-Apr-08	Priv.	Stock
119	531269	K L G Systel Ltd.	First Power Utilities Distribution Ltd.	23-Feb-04	Unlisted	Cash
120	531366	Kohinoor Broadcasting Corpn. Ltd.	Tagore Theatres Ltd.	7-Jan-08	Unlisted	Cash
121	531404	Zicom Electronic Security Systems Ltd.	Zicom Global Security Pvt Ltd.	2-Jul-07	Unlisted	Stock
122	531508	Eveready Industries (India) Ltd.	BPL Soft Energy Systems Ltd.	19-Sep-05	Unlisted	Cash
123	531544	Vertex Spinning Ltd.	Green Cottage & Resorts Ltd.	12-Dec-06	Unlisted	Cash
124	531590	Bilpower Ltd.	Tarapur Transformers Pvt. Ltd.	29-Nov-06	Unlisted	Cash
125	531615	Era E-Zone India Ltd.	Era Buildwell(India)Ltd.	27-Mar-09	Priv.	Cash
126	531816	Panoramic Universal Ltd.	Rishi Garden Resort Pvt Ltd.	26-Mar-08	Priv.	OTHER
127	531897	Accentia Technologies Ltd.	Asscent Infoserve Pvt Ltd.	26-Mar-07	Priv.	Convertibles
128	531898	Sanguine Media Ltd.	Godavari Ads Pvt. Ltd.	12-Sep-06	Unlisted	Cash, stock
129	531898	Sanguine Media Ltd.	Rohinie Media	24-Nov-06	Priv.	Cash
130	532175	Infotech Enterprises Ltd.	Tele Atlas India Pvt. Ltd.	24-Mar-05	Unlisted	Cash, stock
131	532175	Infotech Enterprises Ltd.	T T M (India) Pvt. Ltd.	8-Sep-08	Unlisted	Cash

(continued)

(continued)

Sr. No.	BSE code	Acquirer name	Target name	Announcement date	Target type	Payment method
132	532184	Ciba India Ltd.	Diamond Dye Chem	18-Aug-03	Unlisted	Cash
133	532219	Energy Development Co Ltd.	Dhanashree Power Projects Ltd.	20-May-09	Priv.	Cash
134	532254	Polaris Software Lab Ltd.	SFL Properties Pvt Ltd.	2-Dec-10	Priv.	Cash
135	532268	Kale Consultants Ltd.	Cognosys Software Private Limited/Kale Etravel Technologies Ltd.	23-Oct-03	Unlisted	Cash
136	532287	Entegra Ltd.	PSC Engineers Pvt Ltd.	19-Dec-07	Unlisted	Cash
137	532300	Wockhardt Ltd.	Dumex India Pvt. Ltd.	30-Jun-06	Unlisted	Cash
137	532307	Melstar Info Tech Ltd.	Melstar Fashions Pvt Ltd.	28-Mar-06	Priv.	Stock
137	532307	Melstar Info Tech Ltd.	iDV Tech Solutions Pvt Ltd.	23-Dec-15	Private	Cash
137	532355	Telephoto Entertainments Ltd.	AGS Properties Development	3-Mar-06	Unlisted	Cash
137	532375	Tips Industries Limited	Tips Films Ltd.	23-Nov-05	Sub.	OTHER
137	532385	Aztecsoft Ltd.	Disha Technologies (India) Ltd.	20-Sep-04	Unlisted	Cash, stock
137	532386	California Software Co Ltd.	Webspectrum Software Ltd.	22-Dec-04	Priv.	Cash
137	532391	Opto Circuits (India) Ltd.	M/s Altron Industries (Pvt) Ltd.	17-Jan-06	Unlisted	Cash
138	532391	Opto Circuits (India) Ltd.	Devon Innovations Pvt. Ltd.	24-Apr-07	Unlisted	Cash
	532391	Opto Circuits (India) Ltd.	Ormed Medical Technology Ltd.	24-Apr-07	Unlisted	Cash
139	532391	Opto Circuits(India)Ltd.	NS Remedies Pvt Ltd.	5-Apr-10	Priv.	CASHO
140	532400	K P I T Cummins Infosystems Ltd.	CG-Smith Software Pvt Ltd.	6-Mar-06	Unlisted	Cash
141	532414	IKF Software.com Ltd.	Netwatch Digital Solutions Pvt Ltd,	30-Jun-08	Unlisted	Cash
142	532424	Godrej Consumer Products Ltd.	Naturesse Consumer Care Prod	3-Dec-10	Priv.	Cash
143	532440	M P S Ltd.	Charon Tech Pvt Ltd.	8-Jun-05	Unlisted	Cash

(continued)

(continued)

Sr. No.	BSE code	Acquirer name	Target name	Announcement date	Target type	Payment method
144	532466	Oracle Financial Services Software Ltd.	I-Flex Processing Services Ltd.	12-Apr-06	Unlisted	Cash
145	532497	Radico Khaitan Ltd.	M/s Anab-e-Shahi Wines & Distilleries Pvt Ltd.	5-Apr-04	Priv.	Cash
146	532531	Strides Arcolab Ltd.	Grandix Pharmaceuticals Ltd.	10-Apr-07	Priv.	UNKNOWN
147	532532	Jaypee Fertilizers & Indus Ltd.	Duncans Fertiliser Industries	17-Jun-10	Unlisted	Cash
148	532540	Tata Consultancy Services Ltd.	T C S E-Serve Ltd.	8-Oct-08	Unlisted	Cash
149	532612	Indoco Remedies Ltd.	La Nova Chem (India) Pvt. Ltd.	4-Jul-07	Unlisted	Cash
150	532612	Indoco Remedies Ltd.	Shree Herbal Technologies Ltd.	29-Jan-08	Unlisted	Cash
151	532617	Jet Airways (India) Ltd.	Jet Lite (India) Ltd.	12-Apr-07	Unlisted	Cash
152	532628	3I Infotech Ltd.	G 4 Software Technologies (I) Ltd.	5-Sep-06	Unlisted	Cash
153	532633	Allsec Technologies Ltd.	B2K Corp Pvt Ltd.	12-Dec-05	Priv.	Cash
154	532644	JK Cement Ltd.	Jaykaycem Ltd.	29-Jul-06	Priv.	Cash
155	532670	Shree Renuka Sugars Ltd.	Godavari Biofuel Pvt. Ltd.	23-Jul-08	Unlisted	Cash
		Shree Renuka Sugars Ltd.	Ratnaprabha Sugars Ltd.	23-Jul-08	Unlisted	Cash
156	532682	A B G Shipyard Ltd.	Vipul Shipyard	24-May-07	Unlisted	Cash
157	532689	PVR Ltd.	DT Cinemas	9-Jun-15	Unlisted	Cash
158	532699	Royal Orchid Hotels Ltd.	Hotel Royal Orchid Central	12-Nov-07	Priv.	Cash
159	532705	Jagran Prakashan Ltd.	Suvi Info Management Pvt Ltd.	2-Apr-12	Priv.	Cash
160	532706	Inox Leisure Ltd.	Calcutta Cine Private Limited	24-Jun-06	Priv.	Stock
161	532706	Inox Leisure Ltd.	Satyam Cineplexes Ltd.	31-Jul-14	Unlisted	Cash
162	532706	Inox Leisure Ltd.	Multiplex Cinema Theatre(3)	1-Sep-15	Priv.	Cash
163	532708	G V K Power & Infrastructure Ltd.	G V K Aviation Pvt. Ltd.	21-Jun-07	Unlisted	Cash

(continued)

(continued)

Sr. No.	BSE code	Acquirer name	Target name	Announcement date	Target type	Payment method
164	532708	G V K Power & Infrastructure Ltd.	G V K Energy Ltd.	9-May-08	Unlisted	Cash
165	532708	GVK Power & Infrastructure Ltd.	GVK Infratech Pvt Ltd.	6-Jul-07	Priv.	Cash
166	532715	Gitanjali Gems Ltd.	Eureka Finstock Pvt. Ltd.	10-Jun-08	Unlisted	Cash
		Gitanjali Gems Ltd.	Decent Securities & Finance Pvt. Ltd.	10-Jun-08	Unlisted	Cash
167	532715	Gitanjali Gems Ltd.	Desire Lifestyle Pvt Ltd.	25-Jul-06	Priv.	Cash
168	532715	Gitanjali Gems Ltd.	Brightest Circle Jewellery Pvt	7-Jan-08	Priv.	Cash
169	532715	Gitanjali Gems Ltd.	Renaissance Retail Venture Pvt	10-Mar-08	Priv.	Cash
170	532715	Gitanjali Gems Ltd.	B Vijay Ret Ventures Pvt Ltd.	24-Jul-08	Priv.	Cash
171	532715	Gitanjali Gems Ltd.	Nascent	12-Dec-12	Priv.	Cash
172	532715	Gitanjali Gems Ltd.	Alliance Jewelleries Pvt	6-Oct-09	Priv.	Cash
173	532715	Gitanjali Gems Ltd.	N & J Finstocks Pvt Ltd.	17-Mar-11	Priv.	Cash
174	532727	Adhunik Metaliks Ltd.	Orissa Manganese & Minerals	9-Apr-07	Unlisted	Cash
175	532749	Allcargo Global Logistics Ltd.	Hindustan Cargo Ltd.	2-Jan-07	Unlisted	Cash
176	532749	Allcargo Global Logistics Ltd.	MHTC Logistics Private Limited	25-Feb-11	Unlisted	Cash
177	532777	Info Edge (India) Ltd.	MakeSense Technologies Pvt Ltd.	1-Mar-13	Priv.	Cash
178	532786	Great Offshore Ltd.	KEI-RSOS Maritime	2-Sep-08	Unlisted	Cash
		Great Offshore Ltd.	Rajamahendri Shipping & Oilfield Services Ltd.	2-Sep-08	Unlisted	Cash
179	532830	Astral Poly Technik Ltd.	Astral Biochem Pvt. Ltd.	22-Sep-08	Unlisted	cash
180	532868	DLF Cyber City Developers Ltd.	Caraf Builders & Constructions	16-Dec-09	Priv.	Stock
181	532876	Everonn Systems India Ltd.	Toppers Tutorial Pvt Ltd.	11-Feb-08	Priv.	Cash

(continued)

(continued)

Sr. No.	BSE code	Acquirer name	Target name	Announcement date	Target type	Payment method
182	532880	Omaxe Ltd.	Golden Peak Township Pvt. Ltd.	14-Oct-08	Unlisted	cash
183	532880	Omaxe Ltd.	Oasis Township Pvt Ltd.	27-Apr-09	Priv.	Cash
184	532926	Jyothy Laboratories Ltd.	Snoways	10-Mar-09	Priv.	Cash
185	532926	Jyothy Laboratories Ltd.	Diamond Fabcare Private Ltd.	22-Mar-11	Priv.	Cash
186	532929	Brigade Enterprises Ltd.	Brooke Bond REs Pvt Ltd.	23-Mar-15	Sub./Pvt	Cash
187	533055	EdServ Softsystems Ltd.	SmartLearn Telcomp Pvt Ltd.	2-Mar-10	Priv.	Cash
188	533160	DB Realty Ltd.	L&T Bombay Developers Pvt Ltd.	15-Sep-10	Priv.	Cash
189	533168	Rossell India Ltd.	Namsang Tea Estate	20-Apr-12	Priv.	Cash
190	533168	Rossell India Ltd.	Kharikatia Tea Estate	7-Dec-12	Priv.	Cash
191	533260	Career Point Infra Ltd.	Coupler Enterprises Pvt Ltd.	10-Jul-13	Priv.	Cash
192	533309	Dalmia Bharat Ltd.	Adhunik Cement Ltd.	28-Sep-12	Sub.	UNKNOWN
193	533317	Omkar Speciality Chemicals Ltd.	Lasa Laboratory Pvt Ltd.	7-Apr-12	Unlisted	Cash
193	590001	Chettinad Cement Corpn. Ltd.	Valliammai Limes Pvt. Ltd.	17-Jan-06	Unlisted	Cash
		Chettinad Cement Corpn. Ltd.	Alagappa Cements Pvt. Ltd.	17-Jan-06	Unlisted	Cash
194	590034	Sharon Bio-Medicine Ltd.	Stonewood Cem-Fab (India) Pvt. Ltd.	19-Oct-07	Unlisted	cash
195	590051	Saksoft Ltd.	Synetairos Technologies Ltd.	2-Jul-11	Unlisted	Cash

Appendix E
Sample Companies in Event Study (Domestic Partial/ Majority Control Acquisitions)

N. Rani et al., *Mergers and Acquisitions*, India Studies in Business and Economics, DOI 10.1007/978-981-10-2203-6

Sr. No	BSE code	Acquirer name	Target name	Announcement date	Stake acquired	Target type	Payment method
1	500003	Aegis Logistics Ltd.	Sealord Containers Ltd.	3-Mar-06	75	Listed	Cash
2	500032	Bajaj Hindusthan Ltd.	Pratappur Sugar and Industries Lt	30-Aug-05	55	Listed	Cash
3	500084	CESC Ltd.	Dhariwal Infrastructure Ltd.	28-Aug-09	51	Sub.	UNKNOWN
4	500086	Exide Industries Ltd.	Leadage Alloys India Ltd.	18-Jun-08	51	Unlisted	Cash
5	500093	Crompton Greaves Ltd.	Malanpur Captive Power Ltd.	2-Jun-06	59	Unlisted	Cash
6	500096	Dabur India Ltd.	Fem Care Pharma Ltd.	21-Nov-08	67.33	Listed	Cash
7	500125	E I D-Parry (India) Ltd.	East India Sugars Pvt Ltd.	29-Mar-04	95	Unlisted	Cash
8	500125	E I D-Parry (India) Ltd.	Phytoremedies Biolabs Pvt. Ltd.	14-Feb-08	51	Unlisted	Cash
9	500201	India Glycols Ltd.	Shakumbari Sugar & Allied Inds	16-Dec-07	96.56	Unlisted	Cash
10	500233	Kajaria Ceramics Ltd.	Soriso Ceramic Pvt Ltd.	25-Feb-11	51	Priv.	CASHO
11	500251	Trent Ltd.	Landmark Commercial Pvt. Ltd.	30-Aug-05	70	Unlisted	Cash
12	500325	Reliance Industries Ltd.	Network 18 Media & Investments	29-May-14	71.29	Public	CASHO
13	500338	Prism Cement Ltd.	Small Tiles Pvt Ltd.	22-Nov-11	50	Priv.	OTHER
14	500350	Rajasthan Spinning & Weaving	Jaipur Polyspin Ltd.	10-Nov-04	59.32	Public	CASHO
15	500370	Salora International Ltd.	Jadoonet Ltd.	6-Mar-03	98.3	Unlisted	Stock
16	500400	Tata Power Co. Ltd.	Industrial Energy Pvt Ltd.	26-Feb-07	70	Unlisted	Stock
17	500405	Supreme Petrochem Ltd.	SHIN HO Petrochmicals(India)	20-Mar-06	55	Listed	Cash
18	500410	Associated Cement Cos Ltd.	IDCOL Cement Ltd.	22-Dec-03	86.79	Unlisted	Cash
19	500425	Ambuja Cements Ltd.	Dirk India Pvt Ltd.	14-Sep-11	60	Sub.	CASHO
20	500444	West Coast Paper Mills Ltd.	Rama Newsprint & Papers Ltd.	11-Sep-03	57.57	Listed	Stock
21	500550	Siemens Ltd.	Imetrex Technologies Ltd.	23-Apr-07	77	Unlisted	Cash

(continued)

(continued)

Sr. No	BSE code	Acquirer name	Target name	Announcement date	Stake acquired	Target type	Payment method
22	500575	Voltas Ltd.	Rohini Industrial Electricals (P) Ltd.	12-Aug-08	51	Unlisted	Cash
23	500780	Zuari Industries Ltd.	Zuari Investments Ltd.	31-Mar-09	50	J.V.	Cash
24	500830	Colgate-Palmolive (India) Ltd.	C C Health Care Products Pvt. Ltd.	3-Apr-08	75	Unlisted	Cash
25	500875	I T C Ltd.	Classic Infrastructure & Dvlp	7-Dec-15	87.06	Private	CASHO
26	505368	Revathi Equipment	Semac Pvt Ltd.	8-May-08	70	Private	Cash
27	506197	Bliss Gvs Pharma Ltd.	Kremoint Pharma Pvt Ltd.	28-Jun-12	70	Priv.	Cash
28	506248	Amines & Plasticizers Ltd.	Aditya Internet Services Ltd.	16-May-06	51	Unlisted	Cash
29	506395	Coromandel International Ltd.	Ficom Organics Ltd.	16-Mar-06	51	Listed	Cash
30	506520	Jayshree Chemicals Ltd.	East Coast Powers Ltd.	3-Apr-08	92.31	Unlisted	Cash
31	506618	Punjab Chemicals & Pharmaceuticals Ltd.	Alpha Drug India Ltd.	24-Feb-03	51	Listed	Cash
32	506618	Punjab Chemicals & Crop Protection Ltd.	Parul Chemicals Ltd.	29-Aug-08	70	Priv.	Cash
33	507526	Associated Alcohols	Vedant Energy Pvt Ltd.	16-Apr-13	57.45	Priv.	OTHER
34	507598	K L R F Ltd.	Eltex Super Castings Ltd.	2-Dec-05	64.53	Unlisted	Cash
35	512296	Bhagyanagar India Ltd.	Solar Dynamics Pvt Ltd.	5-Jun-12	74	Priv.	Cash
36	512493	Garnet International Ltd.	Sukartik Clothing Pvt Ltd.	13-Sep-10	51	Priv.	Cash
37	512634	Savera Industries Ltd.	Elkhill Agrotech Pvt. Ltd.	28-Apr-06	85	Private	Cash
38	513519	Pitti Laminations Ltd.	Fitti Castings Pvt Ltd.	29-Jun-12	51	Priv.	Cash
39	517530	Surana Telecom & Power Ltd.	Yellow Renewable Energy(P)Ltd.	5-Oct-11	60	Priv.	Cash

(continued)

(continued)

Sr. No	BSE code	Acquirer name	Target name	Announcement date	Stake acquired	Target type	Payment method
40	519457	Virat Crane Industries Ltd.	Durga Dairy Ltd.	13-Nov-06	51	Priv.	Cash
41	519532	Asian Tea & Exports Ltd.	Indong Tea Company Pvt Ltd.	17-Sep-14	63.37	Priv.	Cash
42	520151	Shreyas Shipping & Logistics Ltd.	Haytrans (India) Ltd.	5-Sep-07	51	Unlisted	Cash
43	521153	Pantaloon Industries Ltd.	Indus-League Clothing Ltd.	26-Feb-05	68.29	Unlisted	Cash
44	521180	Super Spinning Mills Ltd.	Elgi Building Products Ltd.	30-Mar-11	58.32	Priv.	Cash
45	522059	Champagne Indage Ltd.	Seabuckthorn Indage Ltd.	17-Jan-07	52.63	Unlisted	Cash
46	523160	Morganite Crucible (India) Ltd.	Diamond Crucible Co. Pvt. Ltd.	3-Apr-06	51	Private	Cash
47	523574	Pantaloon Retail(India) Ltd.	CIG Infrastructure Pvt Ltd.	28-Apr-06	51	Priv.	Cash
48	526217	Hitech Plast Ltd.	Mipak Polymers Ltd.	31-May-06	60	Unlisted	Cash
49	526668	Kamat Hotels (India) Ltd.	Concept Hospitality Ltd.	5-Dec-07	60	Unlisted	Cash
50	526707	Alchemist Ltd.	Valiant Healthcare Ltd.	26-May-05	60	Priv.	CASHO
51	530149	KSL & Industries Ltd.	Reward Mercantile Co Pvt Ltd.	11-Jul-05	75	Priv.	Cash
52	530323	Era Infra Engg. Ltd.	Era E-Zone India Ltd.	3-Apr-06	51	Listed	Cash
53	530461	Saboo Sodium Chloro Ltd.	Fortress Hotels & Resorts Pvt. Ltd.	27-Sep-07	75	Unlisted	Cash
54	530627	Vipul Dye-Chem Ltd.	Shree Ambika Naturals Pvt Ltd.	31-Mar-11	56	Priv.	Cash
55	530773	I V R C L Infrastructures & Projects Ltd.	Hindustan Dorr-Oliver Ltd.	27-Apr-05	70	Listed	Cash

(continued)

(continued)

Sr. No	BSE code	Acquirer name	Target name	Announcement date	Stake acquired	Target type	Payment method
56	531269	K L G Systel Ltd.	Atlantis Lab Pvt. Ltd.	27-Aug-07	51	Unlisted	Cash
57	531349	Panacea Biotec Ltd.	Umkal Medical Institute Pvt. Ltd.	4-Jul-08	75.2	Unlisted	Cash
58	531374	Saag R R Infra Ltd.	Techni Bharathi Ltd.	13-Feb-07	60	Unlisted	Cash
59	531794	Seshachal Technologies Ltd.	Labcal Biometric Technologies	4-Dec-07	98.57	Priv.	SHARES
60	531816	Panoramic Universal Ltd.	Sri Vatsa Hotels Pvt Ltd.	20-Oct-08	51	Unlisted	Cash
61	531816	Panoramic Universal Ltd.	Hi-Flyers Travel Svcs Pvt Ltd.	12-Nov-07	51	Priv.	OTHER
62	531897	Accentia Technologies Ltd.	Iridium Technologies (India) Pvt. Ltd.	8-Mar-06	51	Unlisted	Stock
63	532051	Numeric Power Systems Ltd.	Amex Alloys Pvt Ltd.	6-Dec-10	92	Priv.	Cash
64	532081	K Sera Sera Productions Ltd.	Lemon Entertainment Ltd.	4-Dec-06	80	Unlisted	Stock
65	532100	Indo-City Infotech Ltd.	T A C Technosoft Pvt. Ltd.	2-Feb-05	51	Unlisted	Cash
66	532175	Infotech Enterprises Ltd.	Geospatial Integrated Solution Pvt. Ltd.	15-May-07	74	Unlisted	Cash
67	532219	Energy Development Co Ltd.	Ayyappa Hydro Power Ltd.	30-Oct-06	60	Priv.	Cash
68	532299	Television Eighteen India Ltd.	Infomedia 18 Ltd.	12-Dec-07	51	Listed	Cash
69	532318	Gemini Communication Ltd.	Veeras Infotek Pvt. Ltd.	16-Jun-08	51	Unlisted	Cash
70	532338	Valuemart Info Technologies Ltd.	Tejas Infoscripts Pvt. Ltd.	29-Aug-05	74	Unlisted	Cash

(continued)

(continued)

Sr. No	BSE code	Acquirer name	Target name	Announcement date	Stake acquired	Target type	Payment method
71	532338	Valuemart Info Technologies Ltd.	Datatalk Services (India) Pvt. Ltd.	28-Nov-07	74	Unlisted	Cash
72	532338	Valuemart Info Tech Ltd.	HVO Technologies Ltd.	14-Oct-05	51	Priv.	Cash
73	532345	Gati Ltd.	Kausar India Ltd.	27-Aug-07	52.96	Listed	Cash
74	532357	Mukta Arts Ltd.	Coruscant Tec Pvt. Ltd.	19-Sep-08	51	Unlisted	Cash
75	532357	Mukta Arts Ltd.	Red Carpet Films Pvt Ltd.	29-Oct-07	50.01	Priv.	OTHER
76	532374	Sterlite Technologies Ltd.	Sterlite Infrastructure Pvt. Ltd.	1-Oct-07	58.7	Unlisted	Cash
77	532386	California Software Co. Ltd.	Ina Tech Infosolutions Pvt. Ltd.	14-Sep-06	51	Unlisted	Cash
78	532386	California Software Co. Ltd.	Aspire Communications Pvt. Ltd.	22-May-07	58.76	Unlisted	Cash
79	532399	Reliance Mediaworks Ltd.	Synergy Communications Pvt Ltd.	7-Sep-06	51	Unlisted	Cash
80	532413	Cerebra Integrated Tech Ltd.	Geeta Monitors Pvt Ltd.	13-Jun-11	51	Priv.	Cash
81	532440	M P S Ltd.	Frank Brothers & Co. (Publishers) Ltd.	21-Aug-07	80	Unlisted	Cash
82	532454	Bharti Televentures Ltd.	Hexacom India Limited	7-May-04	67.5	Unlisted	optionally convertible redeemable debentures
83	532466	Oracle Financial Services Software Ltd.	Flexcel International Pvt. Ltd.	4-Apr-08	60	Unlisted	Cash
84	532475	Aptech Ltd.	Synergetics Information Technology Services (India) Pvt. Ltd.	12-Oct-06	70	Unlisted	Cash

(continued)

(continued)

Sr. No	BSE code	Acquirer name	Target name	Announcement date	Stake acquired	Target type	Payment method
85	532493	Astra Microwave Products Ltd.	Komoline Electronics Pvt Ltd.	26-Jul-06	70	Unlisted	Cash
86	532494	Micro Technologies (India) Ltd.	Databyte Svcs & Sys Pvt Ltd.	31-Jan-05	50	Unlisted	Cash
87	532531	Strides Arcolab Ltd.	Medgene Pharm Pvt Ltd.	6-May-05	90	Priv.	Cash
88	532626	Pondy Oxides & Chemicals Ltd.	Lohia Metals Ltd.	16-Jun-08	51	Priv.	Cash
89	532628	3I Infotech Ltd.	KNM Services Pvt Ltd.	29-May-07	60	Unlisted	Cash
90	532628	3i Infotech Ltd.	FinEng Solutions Pvt Ltd.	11-Jun-08	51	Priv.	Cash
91	532629	Mcnally Bharat Engg. Co. Ltd.	Sayaji Iron & Engineering Co. Ltd.	16-May-08	68.28	Listed	Cash
92	532640	Cyber Media India Ltd.	CVP-CyberMedia LLC	4-Apr-08	50	Unlisted	Cash
93	532647	Provogue (India) Ltd.	Sporting & Outdoor Ad-Agency Pvt. Ltd.	23-Jan-08	51	Unlisted	Cash
94	532670	Shree Renuka Sugars Ltd.	K B K Chem-Engineering Pvt. Ltd.	27-Jul-07	51	Unlisted	Cash
95	532670	Shree Renuka Sugars Ltd.	Gokak Sugars Ltd.	23-Oct-08	80	Unlisted	Cash
96	532683	AIA Engineering Ltd.	DCPL Foundries Pvt Ltd.	14-Dec-10	70	Priv.	CASHO
97	532689	PVR Ltd.	Zea Maize Pvt Ltd.	21-Aug-15	70	Priv.	CASHO
98	532696	Educomp Solutions Ltd.	Authorgen Technologies Pvt. Ltd.	17-Aug-07	51	Unlisted	Cash
99	532696	Educomp Solutions Ltd.	ThreeBrix E-Svcs Pvt Ltd.	10-Apr-07	76	Unlisted	Cash
100	532696	Educomp Solutions Ltd.	A-Plus Education Solutions Pvt Ltd.	24-Jul-08	70	Priv.	Cash
101	532696	Educomp Solutions Ltd.	EuroKids International Ltd.	10-Sep-08	50	Priv.	Cash

(continued)

(continued)

Sr. No	BSE code	Acquirer name	Target name	Announcement date	Stake acquired	Target type	Payment method
102	532699	Royal Orchid Hotels Ltd.	Maruti Comforts & Inn Pvt Ltd.	3-Apr-06	51	Priv.	Cash
103	532699	Royal Orchid Hotels Ltd.	Cosmos Premises Ltd.	2-Apr-08	50	Priv.	Cash
104	532715	Gitanjali Gems Ltd.	Salasar Retail Ltd.	16-Dec-09	76	Priv.	Cash
105	532715	Gitanjali Gems Ltd.	MobileNXT Teleservices Pvt. Ltd.	1-Jul-09	70	Priv.	Cash
106	532725	Solar Industries India Ltd.	Navbharat Coalfields Ltd.	12-Nov-07	74	Unlisted	Cash
107	532787	Ess Dee Aluminium Ltd.	India Foils Ltd.	19-Nov-08	90	Listed	Cash
108	532791	Pyramid Saimira Theatre Ltd.	Dimples Cine Advg Pvt Ltd.	28-Nov-07	51	Priv.	Cash
109	532804	Technocraft Industries (India)	Shreyan Infra & Power LLP	27-Mar-14	90	Priv.	Cash
110	532832	Indiabulls Real Estate Ltd.	Piramyd Retail Ltd.	8-Dec-07	63.92	Listed	CASHO
111	532834	Camlin Fine Chemicals Ltd.	Sangam Laboratories Pvt Ltd.	25-Feb-08	60	Unlisted	Cash
112	532848	Delta Corp Ltd.	Advani Pleasure Cruise Co	19-Jan-10	50.99	Sub.	OTHER
113	532865	Meghmani Organics Ltd.	Latasha Exports Ltd.	1-Aug-08	51	Priv.	Cash
114	532875	Allied Digital Services Ltd.	Digicomp Complete Solutions	11-Apr-08	51.05	Priv.	Cash
115	532920	Empee Distilleries Ltd.	EDL Properties Pvt Ltd.	6-Aug-08	75	Priv.	Cash
116	532931	Burnpur Cement Ltd.	Burnpur Natural Resources	8-Aug-08	60	Priv.	Cash
117	532945	Shriram EPC Ltd.	Blackstone Group Technologies	28-Aug-08	55	Priv.	Cash

(continued)

(continued)

Sr. No	BSE code	Acquirer name	Target name	Announcement date	Stake acquired	Target type	Payment method
118	532946	Bang Overseas Ltd.	A S Raiment Pvt Ltd.	4-Jul-12	99.99	Priv.	Cash
119	533271	Ashoka Buildcon Ltd.	Viva Infrastructure Pvt Ltd.	2-Apr-12	50	Priv.	Cash
120	533282	Gravita India Ltd.	KM Udyog Ltd.	4-Apr-11	60	Priv.	Cash
121	533282	Gravita India Ltd.	Metal Inc.	12-Jul-11	80	Priv.	Cash
122	533309	Dalmia Bharat Ltd.	Bokaro Jaypee Cement Ltd.	25-Mar-14	74	Unlisted	CASHO
123	534742	Zuari Agro Chemicals Ltd.	Zuari Rotem Speciality	11-Dec-15	50.00	Private	CASHO
124	590051	Saksoft Ltd.	Threesixty Logica Testing Svcs Pvt Ltd.	1-Jan-15	51	Priv.	Cash
125	590120	Provestment Services Ltd.	Saab Travel & Tours Pvt Ltd.	10-Jan-13	86.03	Priv.	OTHER

Appendix F
Sample Companies in Event Study (Target Firms Totally Absorbed With the Acquirers' Operations)

	BSE code	Acquirer name	Target name	Announcement date	Target type	Payment method
1	500003	Aegis Logistics Ltd.	Tapi Finvest India Pvt Ltd.	2-Sep-08	Priv.	Stock
2	500013	Ansal Properties & Infrastructure Ltd.	Ansal Township & Projects Ltd.	15-Apr-06	Unlisted	Stock
3	500032	Bajaj Hindusthan Sugar & Industries	Phenil Food Pvt. Ltd.	20-Sep-08	Unlisted	Stock
4	500038	Balrampur Chini Mills Ltd.	Khalilabad Sugar Mills Ltd.	26-Sep-13	Priv.	SHARES
5	500039	Banco Products (India)Ltd.	Ganga Investments Pvt Ltd.	1-Sep-08	Priv.	SHARES
6	500041	Bannari Amman Sugars Ltd.	Maheswara Sugar Ltd.	27-Jun-07	Unlisted	Cash
7	500066	Blow Plast Ltd.	VIP Industries Ltd.	9-Mar-06	Listed	SHARES
8	500084	C E S C Ltd.	Pathik Foods Pvt. Ltd.	17-Apr-07	Unlisted	Stock
9	500085	Chambal Fertilizers Ltd.	India Steamship Co. Ltd.	16-Sep-04	Listed	Stock
10	500097	Dalmia Cement (Bharat)Ltd.	Eswar Cements Pvt Ltd.	17-Sep-08	Priv.	stock
11	500165	Kansai Nerolac Paints Ltd.	Polycoat Powders Ltd.	24-Jan-06	Unlisted	Stock

(continued)

N. Rani et al., *Mergers and Acquisitions*, India Studies in Business and Economics, DOI 10.1007/978-981-10-2203-6

(continued)

	BSE code	Acquirer name	Target name	Announcement date	Target type	Payment method
12	500219	Jain Irrigation Systems Ltd.	Terra Agro Technologies Ltd.	31-May-05	Unlisted	Stock
13	500219	Jain Irrigation Systems Ltd.	Orient Vegetexpo Ltd.	4-Sep-06	Listed	Stock
13	500219	Jain Irrigation Systems Ltd.	Eurisko Agro Ltd.	4-Sep-06	Unlisted	Stock
14	500228	Jindal Vijayanagar Steel Ltd.	Jindal Iron Steel Co. Ltd.	21-Oct-03	Listed	Cash
	500228	Jindal Vijayanagar Steel Ltd.	Euro Coke & Energy Pvt. Ltd.	9-May-05	Unlisted	Stock
	500228	Jindal Vijayanagar Steel Ltd.	J S W Power Ltd.	9-May-05	Unlisted	Stock
	500228	Jindal Vijayanagar Steel Ltd.	Euro Ikon Iron Steel Pvt. Ltd.	9-May-05	Unlisted	Stock
15	500279	Mirc Electronics Ltd.	Onida Savak Ltd.	6-Apr-05	Listed	Stock
16	500279	Mirc Electronics Ltd.	Guviso Holdings Pvt Ltd.	25-Jul-08	Priv.	Stock
17	500302	Piramal Healthcare Ltd.	Canere Actives & Fine Chemicals Pvt. Ltd.	28-Jan-04	Unlisted	Stock
18	500329	Pentamedia Graphics Ltd.	Pentasoft Technologies Ltd.	15-Oct-08	Listed	Stock
19	500413	Thomas Cook (India) Ltd.	L K P Forex Ltd.	30-Jun-06	Unlisted	Stock
20	500510	Larsen & Toubro Ltd.	Datar Switchgear Ltd.	25-Aug-05	Listed	Cash
21	500660	Glaxosmithkline Pharmaceuticals Ltd.	Burroughs Wellcome (India) Ltd.	17-Mar-04	Listed	Stock
22	500680	Pfizer Ltd.	Pharmacia Healthcare Ltd.	13-Jul-04	Listed	Stock
23	500770	Tata Chemicals Ltd.	Hind Lever Chemicals Ltd.	22-Jan-03	Listed	Stock
24	500945	Value Industries Ltd.	Ranjangaon Industries Pvt. Ltd.	2-Apr-07	Unlisted	Cash

(continued)

(continued)

	BSE code	Acquirer name	Target name	Announcement date	Target type	Payment method
25	502445	Rohit Pulp & Paper Mills Ltd.	Marathon Realty Ltd.	30-Mar-07	Priv.	Stock
26	502465	Speciality Paper Ltd.	Reliable Paper (India) Ltd.	5-Jul-07	Unlisted	Cash
	502465	Speciality Paper Ltd.	Opel Paper Mill Ltd.	5-Jul-07	Unlisted	Cash
	502465	Speciality Paper Ltd.	Prime Industries	5-Jul-07	Unlisted	Cash
27	503031	Morarjee Realties Ltd.	Dawn Mills Co. Ltd.	5-May-06	Listed	Stock
28	503722	Banswara Syntex Ltd.	Banswara Textile Mills Ltd.	10-Dec-04	Listed	Stock
29	503837	Shree Rajasthan Syntex Ltd.	Shree Rajasthan Texchem Ltd.	31-Jul-06	Listed	Stock
30	504028	G E E Ltd.	Ferroseal India Pvt. Ltd.	30-Jan-08	Unlisted	Cash
	504028	G E E Ltd.	Filarc Engineers Pvt. Ltd.	30-Jan-08	Unlisted	Cash
	504028	G E E Ltd.	Sagar Merchandise Pvt. Ltd.	30-Jan-08	Unlisted	Cash
31	504092	Indokem Ltd.	Sovereign Trading Enterprises Ltd.	24-Dec-07	Unlisted	Stock
32	504212	Universal Cables Ltd.	Optic Fibre Goa Ltd.	24-Jan-06	Unlisted	Stock
33	504614	Sarda Energy & Mineral Ltd.	Raipur Gases Pvt. Ltd.	29-Sep-06	Unlisted	Stock
	504614	Sarda Energy & Mineral Ltd.	Chhattisgarh Electricity Co. Ltd.	29-Sep-06	Unlisted	Stock
34	505400	Texmaco Ltd.	Evershine Merchants Pvt. Ltd.	14-Aug-07	Unlisted	Stock
35	506172	Sampada Chemicals Ltd.	Debonair Publications Ltd.	14-Jan-05	Sub.	OTHER
36	506186	Galaxy Entertainment Corpn. Ltd.	Pan India Restaurants Ltd.	27-Oct-06	Unlisted	Stock
37	506401	Deepak Nitrite	Aryan Pesticides	5-Jun-03	Listed	Stock
38	506618	Punjab Chemicals & Crop Protection Ltd.	Alpha Drug India Ltd.	12-May-05	Listed	Stock

(continued)

(continued)

	BSE code	Acquirer name	Target name	Announcement date	Target type	Payment method
39	506985	Twilight Litaka Pharma Ltd.	Care Unipac Pvt. Ltd.	19-Sep-05	Unlisted	Cash
40	507794	Khaitan Chem & Fertilizers Ltd.	Mahadeo Fertilizers Ltd.	13-Apr-06	Public	Stock
41	507796	Jhaveri Flexo India Ltd.	Jhaveri Flexi Laminate Pvt. Ltd.	21-Jan-06	Unlisted	Cash
42	507880	V I P Industries Ltd.	Blow Plast Ltd.	9-Mar-06	Listed	Stock
44	508996	Satra Properties India Ltd.	OM Housing Co Pvt Ltd.	24-Nov-06	Priv.	Stock
45	509930	Supreme Industries Ltd.	Siltap Chemicals Ltd.	7-Feb-03	Listed	Stock
46	511664	BGIL Films & Technologies Ltd.	Kriti Communications Pvt Ltd.	18-May-09	Priv.	Stock
47	511672	Scan Steels Ltd.	Scan Steels Ltd.	12-Jul-10	Priv.	Stock
48	511760	Kosian Industries Ltd.	Ideal Systems	11-Mar-05	Priv.	Stock/PF
49	512087	Parijat Trading Ltd.	Multilayer Films Pvt Ltd.	19-Mar-10	Priv.	Stock
50	512179	Sunteck Realty Ltd.	Satguru Corporate Services Pvt	25-Jan-07	Priv.	Stock
51	512185	I O L Netcom Ltd.	Exatt Technologies Pvt. Ltd.	14-Apr-07	Unlisted	Stock
52	512529	Visistha Trade & Finance Ltd.	PI Drugs & Pharmaceuticals Ltd.	11-Sep-03	Priv.	Stock
53	512587	Zodiac-Jrd-Mkj Ltd.	M K J Jewellery Pvt. Ltd.	6-Feb-08	Unlisted	Stock
54	513121	Oricon Enterprises Ltd.	Scientific Vaccum Coating Pvt. Ltd.	23-May-05	Unlisted	Stock
55	513349	Ajmera Realty & Infra India Ltd.	Anik Development Corpn. Pvt. Ltd.	22-Jan-07	Unlisted	Cash
56	513446	Monnet Ispat & Energy Ltd.	Mounteverest Trading & Invest	16-Mar-10	Public	SHARES
57	514034	J B F Industries Ltd.	Microsynth Fabrics (India) Ltd.	28-Mar-08	Unlisted	Stock
66	514036	Loyal Textile Mills Ltd.	Shri Chintamani Textile Mills	17-Sep-10	Priv.	Stock
67	514128	Konark Synthetic Ltd.	Konark Silk Mills Pvt Ltd.	30-Jul-07	Priv.	SHARES
68	514162	Welspun India Ltd.	Glofame Cotspin Industries Ltd.	1-Nov-04	Unlisted	Stock
69	515018	Regency Ceramics Ltd.	Regma Ceramics Ltd.	2-Apr-07	Unlisted	Cash

(continued)

(continued)

	BSE code	Acquirer name	Target name	Announcement date	Target type	Payment method
70	515055	Anant Raj Inds. Ltd.	Jasmine Promoters Pvt. Ltd.	18-Jan-07	Unlisted	Cash
	515055	Anant Raj Inds. Ltd.	Parkland Promoters Pvt. Ltd.	18-Jan-07	Unlisted	Cash
	515055	Anant Raj Inds. Ltd.	Mayur Buildtech Pvt. Ltd.	18-Jan-07	Unlisted	Cash
	515055	Anant Raj Inds. Ltd.	Greenwood Promoters Pvt. Ltd.	18-Jan-07	Unlisted	Cash
	515055	Anant Raj Inds. Ltd.	Rockfield Buildtech Pvt. Ltd.	18-Jan-07	Unlisted	Cash
	515055	Anant Raj Inds. Ltd.	Anant Raj Exports Pvt. Ltd.	18-Jan-07	Unlisted	Cash
	515055	Anant Raj Inds. Ltd.	Sunrise Buildtech Pvt. Ltd.	18-Jan-07	Unlisted	Cash
	515055	Anant Raj Inds. Ltd.	Northland Estates Pvt. Ltd.	18-Jan-07	Unlisted	Cash
	515055	Anant Raj Inds. Ltd.	Springdales Estates Pvt. Ltd.	18-Jan-07	Unlisted	Cash
	515055	Anant Raj Inds. Ltd.	Anant Raj Agencies Pvt. Ltd.	18-Jan-07	Unlisted	Cash
	515055	Anant Raj Inds. Ltd.	West Land Buildtech Pvt. Ltd.	18-Jan-07	Unlisted	Cash
	515055	Anant Raj Inds. Ltd.	Victor Promoters Pvt. Ltd.	18-Jan-07	Unlisted	Cash
	515055	Anant Raj Inds. Ltd.	Jasmine Promoters Pvt. Ltd.	18-Jan-07	Unlisted	Cash
	515055	Anant Raj Inds. Ltd.	Parkland Promoters Pvt. Ltd.	18-Jan-07	Unlisted	Cash
	515055	Anant Raj Inds. Ltd.	Mayur Buildtech Pvt. Ltd.	18-Jan-07	Unlisted	Cash
	515055	Anant Raj Inds. Ltd.	Greenwood Promoters Pvt. Ltd.	18-Jan-07	Unlisted	Cash
	515055	Anant Raj Inds. Ltd.	Rockfield Buildtech Pvt. Ltd.	18-Jan-07	Unlisted	Cash
71	516076	Ador Technopak Ltd.	J B Advani & Co Pvt Ltd.	5-May-04	Priv.	Cash
72	517059	Salzer Electronics Ltd.	Salzer Cables Ltd.	29-Aug-08	Unlisted	Cash
73	517496	Ricoh India Ltd.	Gestetner (India) Ltd.	24-Aug-04	Unlisted	Stock
74	517556	SSI Ltd.	P V P Ventures Pvt. Ltd.	9-Jan-08	Unlisted	Cash
75	517556	PVP Ventures Pvt Ltd.	Malaxmi Energy Ventures(India)	16-Jun-08	Priv.	Cash

(continued)

(continued)

	BSE code	Acquirer name	Target name	Announcement date	Target type	Payment method
76	517565	Ashco Niulab Inds. Ltd.	Niulab Equipment Co. Pvt. Ltd.	20-Nov-07	Unlisted	Cash
77	517973	DMC Vaults Ltd.	Swen Television Ltd.	17-Jan-06	Priv.	Shares
78	518111	Swastik Roofing Ltd.	New Sahyadri Industries Ltd.	14-Mar-05	Priv.	Shares
79	519003	Anil Modi Oil Industries Ltd.	J P Management Systems Pvt Ltd.	17-Aug-05	Priv.	Shares
80	519383	Madhya Pradesh Glychem	Anik Industries Pvt. Ltd.	7-Oct-05	Unlisted	Stock
81	519475	Chordia Food Products Ltd.	Agri Food Park India Ltd.	8-Mar-06	Unlisted	Cash
82	520021	Omax Autos Ltd.	Indital Tintoria Ltd.	15-Mar-03	Unlisted	Stock
83	521046	Vanasthali Textile Inds. Ltd.	Regal Weavers Pvt. Ltd.	14-Mar-05	Unlisted	Cash
84	521123	Pearl Global Ltd.	Pearl Styles Ltd.	7-Feb-06	Unlisted	Cash
85	522004	Batliboi Ltd.	Batliboi SPM Pvt Ltd.	17-Oct-06	Sub.	Shares
86	522285	Jayaswal Neco Inds. Ltd.	Inertia Iron & Iron & Steel Inds. Pvt. Ltd.	19-Nov-08	Unlisted	Stock
87	523254	Casil Health Products Ltd.	Diacon and Hospicon, Biosulin Intern	18-Nov-04	Unlisted	share
88	523277	G V Films Ltd.	One World Media Network Infotainment Ltd.	17-Feb-04	Listed	Cash
89	523315	Purity Flexpack Ltd.	Vaikunth Packaging Ltd.	Confusion	Unlisted	Stock
90	523371	Siel Ltd.	Mawana sugarLtd.	11-Jan-07	Unlisted	Cash
91	523385	Nilkamal Ltd.	Nilkamal Crates & Bins Pvt. Ltd.	21-Apr-07	Unlisted	Stock
92	523385	Nilkamal Ltd.	Stackwell Marketing Services Pvt. Ltd.	21-Apr-07	Unlisted	Stock
93	523606	Sika Interplant Systems Ltd.	Spaceciti Projects Pvt. Ltd.	13-Jun-06	Unlisted	Stock
94	523724	Vijay Shanthi Builders Ltd.	High End Homes Pvt Ltd.	21-Dec-09	Priv.	Stock
95	523736	Dhunseri tea & Inds. Ltd.	Tezpore tea Co. Ltd.	28-Sep-07	Listed	Stock
96	523736	Dhunseri tea & Inds. Ltd.	Uni Stock Pvt. Ltd.	31-Mar-08	Unlisted	Stock
97	523890	D S Kulkarni Developers Ltd.	Oyster Promoters & Developers Pvt. Ltd.	9-Oct-07	Unlisted	Stock

(continued)

(continued)

	BSE code	Acquirer name	Target name	Announcement date	Target type	Payment method
98	524226	Gujarat Ambuja Exports Ltd.	Jupiter Biotech Ltd.	25-Jul-03	Listed	Cash
99	524310	V B C Industries Ltd.	Bharat Alloys & Energy Ltd.	19-Jul-06	Listed	Stock
100	524370	Bodal Chemicals Ltd.	Milestone Organics Ltd.	14-Aug-07	Listed	SHARES
101	524689	Parenteral Drugs (India) Ltd.	P F L Holdings Pvt. Ltd.	5-Aug-08	Unlisted	Cash
101	524689	Parenteral Drugs (India) Ltd.	Goa Holdings (India) Pvt. Ltd.	5-Aug-08	Unlisted	Cash
102	524715	Sun Pharmaceutical Inds. Ltd.	Phlox Pharmaceuticals Ltd.	8-Feb-05	Unlisted	Stock
103	524742	Caplin Point Laboratories Ltd.	Malind Laboratories Pvt Ltd.	7-May-08	Priv.	Stock
104	524794	Matrix Laboratories Ltd.	Vera Laboratories Ltd.	30-Mar-04	Listed	Stock
104	524794	Matrix Laboratories Ltd.	Medikon Laboratories Ltd.	30-Mar-04	Listed	Stock
104	524794	Matrix Laboratories Ltd.	Fine Drugs & Chemicals Ltd.	30-Mar-04	Listed	Stock
105	524820	Panama Petrochem Ltd.	Mobil Petrochem Pvt. Ltd.	31-Aug-07	Unlisted	Stock
106	526109	Pricol Ltd.	Xenos Automotive Limited	24-Jan-14	Unlisted	Stock
107	526117	Shervani Industrial Syndicate	Tara Snacks & Foods Pvt Ltd.	20-Feb-06	Priv.	Cash
108	526263	Mold-Tek Technologies Ltd.	Teck-Men Tools Pvt. Ltd.	10-Jan-07	Unlisted	Cash
109	526299	Mphasis Ltd.	E D S Electronic Data Systems India Pvt. Ltd.	26-Jul-06	Unlisted	Stock
110	526371	National Mineral Development	Sponge Iron(India)	13-Oct-06	Govt./ Unlisted	Cash
111	526538	Maximaa Systems Ltd.	Good Living Shelters Pvt. Ltd.	3-Mar-08	Unlisted	Stock
	526538	Maximaa Systems Ltd.	Meera'S Land Developers Pvt. Ltd.	3-Mar-08	Unlisted	Stock
	526538	Maximaa Systems Ltd.	Meera'S Real Estate Developers Pvt. Ltd.	3-Mar-08	Unlisted	Stock
	526538	Maximaa Systems Ltd.	Mapara Furniture Pvt. Ltd.	3-Mar-08	Unlisted	Stock

(continued)

(continued)

	BSE code	Acquirer name	Target name	Announcement date	Target type	Payment method
112	526668	Kamat Hotels (India) Ltd.	Himco (India) Ltd.	10-May-05	Unlisted	Stock
113	526707	Alchemist Ltd.	Kaiser Hospital Ltd.	31-Aug-06	Unlisted	Cash
114	526829	Confidence Petroleum India Ltd.	Khara Gas Equipments Pvt. Ltd.	13-Jun-07	Unlisted	Stock
	526829	Confidence Petroleum India Ltd.	Maharashtra Cylinders Pvt. Ltd.	13-Jun-07	Unlisted	Stock
	526829	Confidence Petroleum India Ltd.	Hans Gas Appliances Pvt. Ltd.	13-Jun-07	Unlisted	Stock
115	530163	Kerala Ayurveda Ltd.	Katra Healthcare Pvt. Ltd.	28-Apr-05	Unlisted	Stock
116	530239	Suven Life Sciences Ltd.	Asian Clinical Trails Pvt. Ltd.	6-Mar-06	Unlisted	Stock
117	530377	Nila Infrastructure Ltd.	Pearl Stock Holdings Pvt Ltd.	25-Sep-09	Priv.	Stock
118	530433	Shiva Fertilizers Ltd.	Parvati Fertilizers Pvt. Ltd.	21-Mar-06	Unlisted	Cash
119	530435	Media Video Ltd.	Kool Auto Pvt. Ltd.	23-Dec-05	Unlisted	Stock
	530435	Media Video Ltd.	Shri Venkateshwara Electronics Pvt. Ltd.	23-Dec-05	Unlisted	Stock
	530435	Media Video Ltd.	Paradox Motors Pvt. Ltd.	23-Dec-05	Unlisted	Stock
	530435	Media Video Ltd.	Beech Tree Buildcon Pvt. Ltd.	23-Dec-05	Unlisted	Stock
	530435	Media Video Ltd.	Valerian Property Developers Pvt. Ltd.	23-Dec-05	Unlisted	Stock
	530435	Media Video Ltd.	Acacia Buildwell Pvt. Ltd.	23-Dec-05	Unlisted	Stock
120	530549	Shilpa Medicare Ltd.	Shilpa Organics Pvt Ltd.	29-Aug-05	Private	Stcok
121	530611	Sturdy Industries Ltd.	Swati Storwel Pvt Ltd/ and M/s. Nu-line Industries Pvt Ltd.	1-Oct-07	Priv.	Stock
122	530619	Asian CERC Information Technology	Regius Infotech Pvt. Ltd.	22-Jan-08	Unlisted	Stock

(continued)

(continued)

	BSE code	Acquirer name	Target name	Announcement date	Target type	Payment method
123	530707	Aftek Ltd.	Elven Micro Circuits Pvt. Ltd.	11-Dec-06	Unlisted	Stock
	530707	Aftek Ltd.	Elven Micro Circuits Pvt. Ltd. (EMPL)	11-Dec-06	Unlisted	Stock
	530707	Aftek Ltd.	C2Silicon Software Solutions Pvt. Ltd.	11-Dec-06	Unlisted	Stock
124	530723	Nucleus Securities Ltd.	Nucleus Netsoft & GIS(India)	11-Jul-05	Priv.	Stock
125	530871	Chembond Chemicals Ltd.	Shree Mahalasa Electronics Pvt. Ltd.	16-Jan-08	Unlisted	Stock
126	530889	Alka India Ltd.	Janice Textiles Ltd.	28-Mar-04	Listed	Cash
127	531153	Diligent Industries Ltd.	Adithya Agro Allied Oils Ltd.	11-Jan-13	Priv.	Stock
128	531175	B L S Infotech Ltd.	Bossom Exim Pvt. Ltd.	20-Feb-06	Unlisted	Stock
	531175	B L S Infotech Ltd.	Business Point Ltd.	20-Feb-06	Unlisted	Stock
	531175	B L S Infotech Ltd.	DKS Homes Pvt Ltd.	20-Feb-06	Unlisted	Stock
129	531429	Advent Computer Services Ltd.	Itheories Business Factory (India) Pvt. Ltd.	13-Jun-05	Unlisted	Stock
130	531486	Filmcity Media Ltd.	Wellness Communication Pvt Ltd.	15-Nov-06	Priv.	Stock
131	531645	Southern Ispat & Energy Ltd.	Kerala Sponge Iron Ltd.	16-Jan-08	Unlisted	Stock
132	531651	National General Industries	Modi Metal Udyog Pvt Ltd.	28-Aug-08	Priv.	Stock
133	531716	Rids Securities Ltd.	Tricom Agrochem Ltd.	19-Sep-08	Priv.	Stock
134	531972	Trident Tools Ltd.	Quickcut Engineering Co	16-Dec-11	Priv.	Stock
135	532039	Sunline Technologies Ltd.	Zenotech Laboratories Pvt Ltd.	20-Nov-03	Priv.	Stock
136	532161	Baffin Engineering Projects	Uniworld Telecom Ltd.	24-Jan-05	Sub.	Stock
137	532196	NCL Seccolor Ltd.	Alltek Coating Products Ltd.	3-Dec-03	Priv.	Stock
138	532321	Cadila Healthcare Ltd.	German Remedies Ltd.	15-Jan-03	Listed	Stock

(continued)

(continued)

	BSE code	Acquirer name	Target name	Announcement date	Target type	Payment method
139	532342	I T People (India) Ltd.	Orient Information Technology Ltd. (OITL)	27-Nov-07	Unlisted	Stock
	532342	I T People (India) Ltd.	Marketplace Technologies Pvt Ltd.	27-Nov-07	Unlisted	Stock
140	532395	I T & T Ltd.	Axis Computers India Pvt Ltd.	29-Apr-04	Unlisted	Stock
141	532408	Megasoft Ltd.	Visualsoft Technologies Ltd.	1-Oct-06	Listed	Stock
142	532411	Visesh Infotecnics Ltd.	M P S Techno Soft Ltd.	22-Sep-04	Unlisted	Stock
143	532414	IKF Technologies Ltd.	Visual Vistas	30-Dec-05	Priv.	Stcok
144	532486	Pokarna Ltd.	Pokarna Engineered Stone Ltd.	16-Sep-08	Unlisted	Stock
145	532531	Strides Arcolab Ltd.	Shasun Phamaceutical	30-Sep-14	Listed	stock
146	532548	Century Plyboards (India) Ltd.	Sharon Wood Inds. Pvt. Ltd.	3-Jun-07	Unlisted	Stock
	532548	Century Plyboards (India) Ltd.	Sharon Veneers Pvt. Ltd.	3-Jun-07	Unlisted	Stock
	532548	Century Plyboards (India) Ltd.	Century Panels Pvt. Ltd.	3-Jun-07	Unlisted	Stock
147	532727	Adhunik Metaliks Ltd.	Sri M P Ispat & Power Pvt. Ltd.	29-Jul-08	Unlisted	Stock
	532727	Adhunik Metaliks Ltd.	Vedvyas Ispat Ltd.	29-Jul-08	Unlisted	Stock
	532727	Adhunik Metaliks Ltd.	Zion Iron & Steel Ltd.	29-Jul-08	Unlisted	Stock
148	532747	Deccan Aviation Ltd.	Kingfisher Airlines Ltd.	20-Dec-07	Priv.	SHARES
149	532748	Prime Focus Ltd.	Reliance MediaWorks-Film & Med	2-Jul-14	Sub.	Stock, Preferntial allotment
150	532761	HOV Services Ltd.	SOURCECORP Inc.	14-Mar-11	Sub.	Stock
151	532815	S M S Pharmaceuticals Ltd.	Plant Organics Ltd.	30-Jul-08	Unlisted	Stock
152	532819	Mindtree Ltd.	Aztecsoft Ltd.	29-Sep-08	Listed	Stock

(continued)

(continued)

	BSE code	Acquirer name	Target name	Announcement date	Target type	Payment method
153	532821	Indus Fila Ltd.	Tulip Apparels Pvt. Ltd.	12-Mar-08	Unlisted	Stock
154	532822	Idea Cellular Ltd.	Spice Communications Ltd.	25-Jun-08	Listed	Stock
155	532966	Titagarh Wagons Ltd.	Titagarh Steels Ltd.	30-Mar-09	Public	SHARES
156	532981	Anu's Laboratories Ltd.	Nitya Laboratories Ltd.	10-Mar-10	Priv.	Stock
157	533100	Premier Energy	Valagam Power Projects Ltd.	28-Jun-10	Priv.	Stock
158	533166	Sundaram Multi Pap Ltd.	Vidarbha Paper Products Mills Ltd.	11-May-07	Unlisted	Stock
	533166	Sundaram Multi Pap Ltd.	Sihora Paper Products Mills Ltd.	11-May-07	Unlisted	Stock
159	590022	Eastern Silk Inds. Ltd.	Sstella Silks Ltd.	19-Jul-04	Unlisted	Cash
	590022	Eastern Silk Inds. Ltd.	Eastern Jingying Ltd.	19-Jul-04	Unlisted	Cash
159	590037	Steel Exchange India Ltd.	Vizag Profiles Ltd.	31-Oct-06	Unlisted	Stock
160	502207	Alembic Glass Industries Ltd.	Shreno Ltd.	6-Jan-06	Priv.	Stock

Index

N. Rani et al., *Mergers and Acquisitions*, India Studies in Business and Economics, DOI 10.1007/978-981-10-2203-6